1914 EUROPE

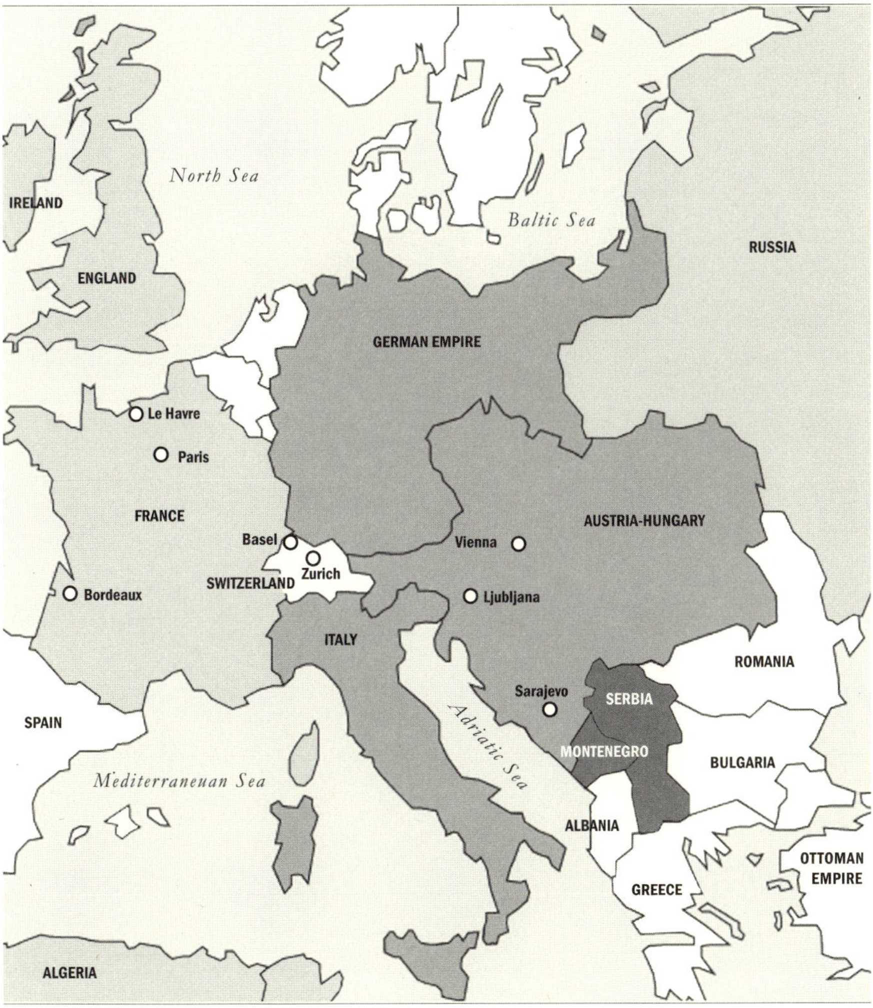
North Sea
IRELAND
ENGLAND
Baltic Sea
RUSSIA
GERMAN EMPIRE
Le Havre
Paris
FRANCE
AUSTRIA-HUNGARY
Basel
Vienna
Zurich
SWITZERLAND
Bordeaux
Ljubljana
ITALY
ROMANIA
Sarajevo
SERBIA
SPAIN
Adriatic Sea
MONTENEGRO
BULGARIA
Mediterraneuan Sea
ALBANIA
OTTOMAN
EMPIRE
GREECE
ALGERIA

EAST
OF THE
EAST
SIDE

EAST OF THE EAST SIDE

A TRUE STORY

CHRISTY
LESKOVAR

COVER DESIGN BY James Powers, Pasco, Washington
BOOK DESIGN, MAP ENHANCEMENT BY Arrow Graphics, Missoula, Montana
TYPESET IN Stempel Garamond and Trajan
PRINTED BY Friesens, Altona, Manitoba

Photographs not credited are from the Leskovar and Lozar families' collections

24   23   22   21   1   2   3   4

ISBN 978-1-59152-285-0

LIBRARY OF CONGRESS CONTROL NUMBER 2020921714

For more information or to order extra copies of this book
call Farcountry Press toll free at (800) 821-3874.

sweetgrassbooks
an imprint of Farcountry Press

PRODUCED BY Sweetgrass Books
PO Box 5630, Helena, MT 59604; (800) 821-3874;
www.sweetgrassbooks.com

Sweetgrass Books is not responsible for the content of the author/publisher's work.

PRODUCED IN THE UNITED STATES OF AMERICA. PRINTED IN CANADA.

*For Mom and in memory of Dad
and my grandparents*

Contents

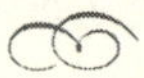

MAPS

TONY LESKOVAR FAMILY TREE

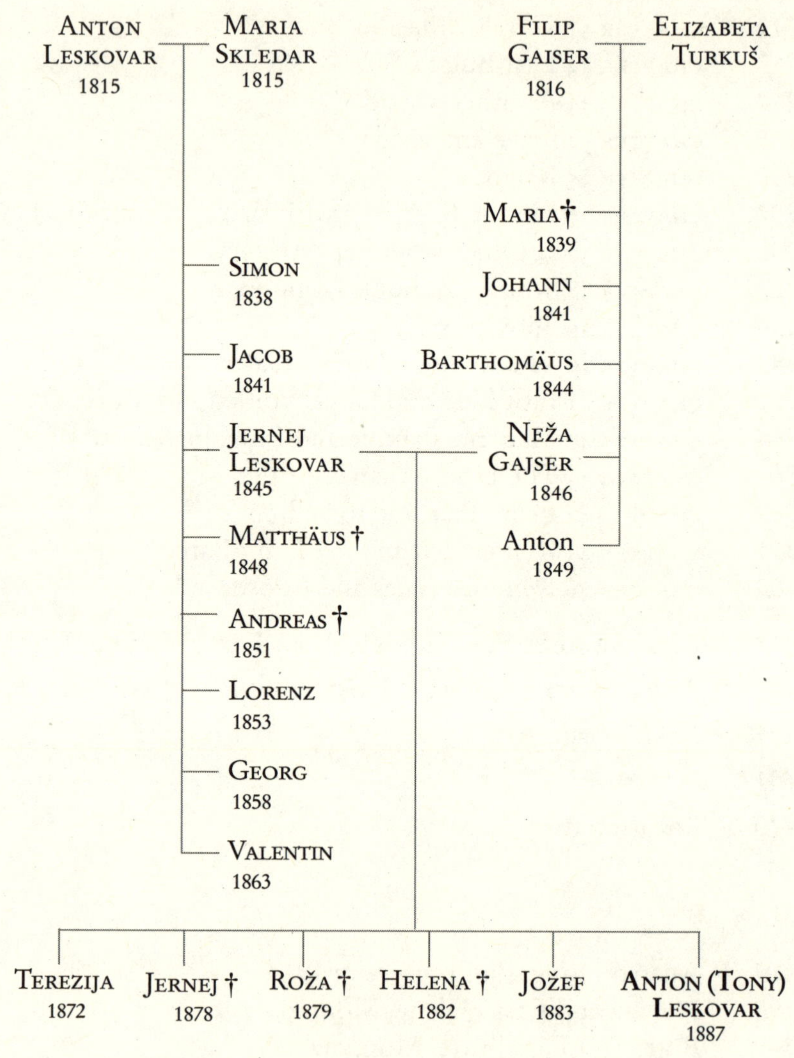

† DIED AS CHILDREN

ANNIE LOZAR
FAMILY TREE

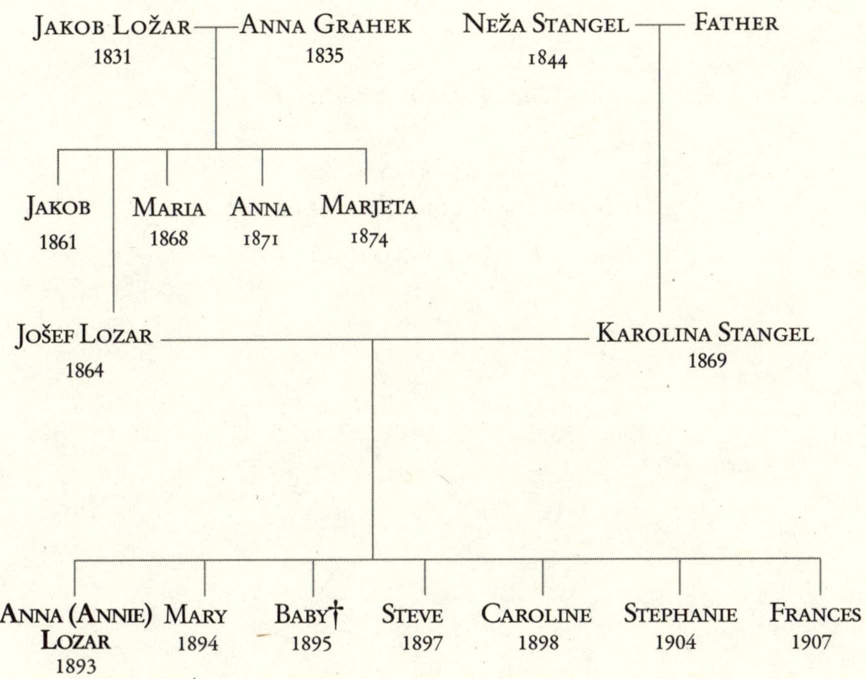

PRONUNCIATION

Jernej *(jer-nee)*
Neža *(nay-ja)*
Gajser *(geyser)*
Stangel *(stang-gul)*

There are more detailed family trees on the website www.christyleskovar.com.
Spellings used are those found in the church books. Years are year born.

Also by Christy Leskovar

One Night in a Bad Inn

Finding the Bad Inn
Discovering My Family's Hidden Past

Dear Reader,

I have endeavored to find the facts, to tell the truth of this story, though ascertaining exactly what happened was at times slippery, difficult to pin down. I tried to confirm all I was told. Much of what you are about to read was told to me firsthand, some secondhand, much in letters, a diary, and audio recordings. Anything quoted is from a source; those sources are listed in the endnotes. The historical backdrop is the fruit of exhaustive research. I did this to make sense of what I was told and to provide perspective and depth and context to the story.

—Christy Leskovar

"... the West—a great country, gentlemen. The place for a young fellow of spirit to pick up a fortune, simply pick it up, it's lying round loose here..."

—*The Gilded Age: A Tale of Today*
by Mark Twain and Charles Dudley Warner

" ... how could the dead archduke in his sarcophagus affect my life?"

— *The World of Yesterday*
by Stefan Zweig

PART ONE

TONY

1

Ptujska gora

To our way of thinking, he was only a boy when he left the family farm for good.

The year was 1903. This Slovenian peasant boy leaves the family farm in the alpine foothills of Austria, goes off to the big city to study music, achieves his dream of becoming a concert bassoonist, and travels across Europe performing for kings and queens.

By 1914, he has grown to be a tall, dashing, handsome man. He is having the time of his life performing with the opera in Paris. It is everything he could have dreamed of and more. Then, overnight, his world is shattered. Shock waves emanating from Sarajevo and Vienna and St. Petersburg and Berlin reach Paris and upend his life forever.

France and Austria are at war. Through no fault of his own, he is an enemy of the state.

He was my grandfather, Anton Leskovar.

He certainly wasn't the first Anton Leskovar. His grandfather was Anton Leskovar. His great-grandfather was Anton Leskovar. For generations, his forebears lived in the same house on the same farm at Stogovci 8 (sto-go-vee-chee), near the village called Ptujska gora (push-ka-gora), in the Duchy of Styria, then part of Austria, now Slovenia, a land populated by Slovenians going back to the seventh century. We won't go back quite that far. We will leap ahead to Grandpa's grandpa's time, the Anton Leskovar born in 1815. His father was a farmer, his father's father was a farmer, and he grew up to be a farmer on that same farm near Ptujska gora. The Anton Leskovar born in 1815 married a young woman from a farm down the road. Her name was Maria Skledar. They had eight sons. None did they name Anton. The last son, Valentin, was born when

Maria was forty-seven years old. Then she died. Anton married again. His second wife was also named Maria. They had a son named Anton who died when only seven months old.

Our story involves the third son, Jernej (jer-nee). When Jernej was twenty-five years old, he married a young woman from a farm down the road. That was in 1871. Her name was Neža Gajser (nay-ja geyser). Jernej and Neža are my great-grandparents. They married in the beautiful Catholic church high atop the hill at Ptujska gora, as did their parents before them and their grandparents and great-grandparents and so on.

Both witnesses to the marriage of Jernej and Neža were illiterate farmers. The church book tells us that.

Even though Jernej wasn't the eldest child nor even the eldest son, he and Neža settled on the family farm at Stogovci 8. I'm told his two elder brothers might have come to this country in the 1860s, leaving Jernej to inherit the farm.

You might say Jernej and Neža were raising children the minute they married in that Jernej still had young brothers at home, the youngest of whom was eight. I was going to name all those brothers here, but I was afraid it might be confusing. You needn't worry about keeping track of all these names. The only one you need to remember is the next Anton Leskovar, called Tony. He was my grandfather.

My grandfather Anton Leskovar was Jernej and Neža's youngest child. He would not grow up to run the family farm at Stogovci 8, and he would not marry a young woman from a farm down the road.

He was born at home with help from the same midwife who delivered his sister fifteen years earlier, though she wasn't a certified midwife back then. The day after Anton was born, the midwife swaddled him, and she and Anton's godfather took him to the Catholic church high atop the hill at Ptujska gora. It was the custom for godparents to bring one yard of fabric and a candle to the baptism. It was also the custom to give the first person they met a piece of bread; this was to ensure that the child would never suffer hunger. I wonder, did they not pass anyone along the way or did they forget the bread? Anton was probably born late in the day, which was why he was baptized the next day. Babies were taken in haste to the church to be baptized, infant mortality being a real danger. Jernej and Neža's first child, Terezija (ter-ez-ee-a), was baptized the day she was born. Their second child, also named Jernej, was baptized the day after he was born and lived only eleven more days. I found no record of the death of their third child, Roža, but since Grandpa never mentioned this sister, I suspect she also died young. Their fourth child, Helena, lived only one day. What a heartbreak for Neža and Jernej, losing three children in a row. Of six children, only three grew to adulthood: the eldest Terezija, born October 7, 1872; Jožef, born March 9, 1883; and my grandfather Anton, born May 17, 1887.

Anton's mother was forty years old when he was born.

The new baby, Anton, was called Tony, possibly because there was already an Anton in the house, his grandfather. It is spelled Tone in Slovenian but pronounced pretty much the same as in English. I debated whether to call him Anton or Tony as I tell you his story. I like Anton better, it sounds so continental, but he was always called Tony, so I'll call him Tony. Tony Leskovar.

Tony was only six when his father, Jernej, died in 1893. This meant Tony's seventy-seven-year-old grandfather was the only man in the house. He may have been strong and fit, since he lived to be ninety-four; even so, farm work takes tremendous endurance and strength. They lived in the foothills of the Alps with four distinct seasons and plenty of snow and cold in winter.

Two years after their father died, Tony's sister, Terezija, married Janez Gajser (no relation to Neža). The farm was Terezija's dowry with the agreement that her mother and grandfather could live there, and she and her husband would take care of them through old age. This was quite common among the Slovenians, if not the norm, and sometimes put in writing in a marriage contract, which was registered at the parish church.

Terezija and Janez (ya-ness) had eleven children; eight lived to adulthood.

Their farm sat on a hill overlooking breathtakingly beautiful land—verdant green hills sloping down to forests, a charming story-book setting masking the rigorous, never-ending work of planting and harvesting and caring for the animals, all to feed the family. Even the uncultivated land looked perfectly groomed, as if God sent His angels down every night to comb the grass. Such was the case throughout the Austrian duchies populated by Slovenians.

Tony said the house was two hundred years old when he was born and that a beam in the main room had a date carved in it. The first

Leskovar farm.

two numbers were 14. He said there were many Leskovars around but no relations.

Their farmhouse, typical of the region, did not have an open fireplace or open hearth in the main room of the house, as was the case in other parts of the world in the nineteenth century. The fire was in the oven in the black kitchen, which was just inside the main door and was closed off to the rest of the house. The oven was made of chamotte bricks and built into the wall, similar to a pizza oven, and was heated by burning wood. My great-grandmother Neža and my great-aunt Terezija cooked the food in the oven, there was no cook top. This same wood-burning fire that heated the oven for cooking also heated a large clay block on the other side of the wall in the main room. This large clay block, about six feet high, four feet long, two feet deep, in the corner of the main room was called a *lončena peč* in Slovenian, a *kachelofen* in German. There is no English word for it, because as far as I can tell, it does not exist in the English-speaking world. It was covered with ceramic tile, and there was a bench around it. It radiated heat from the wood fire inside, lit from the black kitchen, thereby heating the main room. In the cold winter months, the children liked to climb on top, where it was toasty warm, or sidle up to it on the bench. Since the fire was closed off from the rest of the house, there was no soot where the family slept and ate and bathed.

The main room was about twelve by twelve feet. The family ate and bathed in that room. The grown-ups and babies slept there. The floor was dirt, actually packed clay, hard enough that it was swept and kept tidy, no doubt swept daily. No matter how simple the home was, the typical Slovenian housewife kept the house neat and tidy and clean. The entire farm was neat and tidy, no junk lying about. Neatness, tidiness, a love of beauty and order seem to be inherent in the Slovenian DNA.

A crucifix hung prominently on the wall flanked by statues of the Blessed Mother Mary and St. Joseph on tiny shelves in the corners of the room.

On the other side of the black kitchen was a smaller room where the older children slept. There was no oven, no heat, on that side. The door to that room squeaked on purpose to alert the parents should a teenager attempt to sneak out at night. The house was white-washed stucco inside and out with a thatched roof. The thatch was made from the bottom of the stalks of wheat grown on the farm. Everything was used, nothing wasted. Boxes full of flowers adorned the windows in the warm months. The windows were covered by closing the outside shutters.

Their barn was next to the house. The pigs were kept there, pork being the main meat the family ate. Pigs have large litters and are easy to feed, they eat anything. The cow gave milk and pulled the plow. The family raised chickens for eggs. In winter when the snow was deep, Tony might have used stilts to walk from the house to the barn. The house and barn were next to each other, but they had to go outside to walk from one to the other. Nary a smell came from the barn. It was kept so clean, you wouldn't know there were animals inside.

There was no electricity on the farm. They used oil lamps. Before that, they used candles.

They grew grapes and made their own wine.

Every year on St. Martin's Day, which is on the eleventh day of the eleventh month, at 11:11am the family gathered, the fermented juice of the grapes was blessed and declared wine, which the family imbibed merrily.

Every Palm Sunday, the family took a bouquet of branches to Mass at the Catholic church high atop the hill at Ptujska gora. The priest

Catholic church the Leskovars attended in Ptujska gora.
Now called the Basilica of the Virgin of Mercy.
Si-Žiga. Wiki Commons.

blessed the branches. They put one blessed branch in their home for blessings on the family, one in the fields for a good harvest, one in the barn for blessings on the livestock, and they used one to light the fire in the oven in the black kitchen. The following Saturday, Holy Saturday, they took a basket of food to the church to have it blessed. This was food for Easter dinner, usually bread, ham, eggs, horseradish, sausages, and walnut potica. Potica is rolled, similar to strudel, but denser. It is made with a yeast dough, sort of a cross between cake and bread.

Tony's family made their own sausages and hung them in the attic. They raised bees for honey.

They grew corn and dried it on the corn drying rack, which was under a roof and raised up off the ground to allow good air circulation. They ground the dried corn into cornmeal.

Tony and his brother Jožef foraged for berries in the forest. Their farm consisted of three noncontiguous parcels. There were forests on two of the parcels. They had several acres of walnut trees. Theirs was a good-sized farm, ten hectares (twenty-five acres). They had almost everything they needed to eat and stay warm right there on the farm, but it was a tremendous amount of work. There were, of course, things they bought or traded for, such as salt and shoes. Cobblers traveled from farm to farm in winter repairing and making shoes. In the summer, farmers hired cobblers to help work the fields.

Apple, pear, and plum trees grew near the house. With the plums, they made Slivovitz, plum brandy, a Slovenian staple; one whiff can raise the dead and flatten the living.

In late summer or early fall, they harvested pumpkins, lots of pumpkins. Everybody, young and old, helped pull out the seeds. They toasted the seeds and pressed them to draw out the oil. Pumpkin oil is black. They used it for salad, not cooking. They didn't eat the pumpkin flesh, and instead, broke up the pumpkin carcasses and used them as mulch.

With apples from their trees they made apple cider and apple cider vinegar. Salad dressing was pumpkin oil and apple cider vinegar.

They had a second, smaller house on the farm, about one hundred meters down the hill from the family home, near the creek and forest. The wine cellar was there, built into the side of the hill to keep the wine at the perfect temperature year round. It also served as the root cellar, there being no refrigeration, no icebox. In Tony's memory, no one lived there. Later, a tailor lived there.

As for transportation, they used their wagon or sled, both pulled by horses. They drew water from two wells: one by the house, one by the barn. They turned the wheel that pulled up the bucket of water affixed to a rope. Next to the well by the barn was a wooden trough in which they poured water for the animals to drink.

They rendered fat from the goose and used the goose grease to heal burns and cuts. They applied it to the animal where the harness for the plow rubbed the hide. They made chamomile tea. In the fenced vegetable garden next to the house, they grew lettuce, tomatoes, onions, peas, beans. Herbs grew around the perimeter. They hung herbs to dry in the attic with the sausages.

Tony's first language was Slovenian, the language his family spoke at home. He also knew German, the language of Austria.

In November of 1893, Tony started school in Ptujska gora. He walked. It was about a mile away. He was six years old. School started around the end of the harvest. Most children attended school for only a few years. To say that a successful man of Tony's time and place dropped out of school in fourth or fifth grade might sound romantic, but it isn't really accurate. Unless he was part of the small minority of children who went on to *Gymnasium*, he was done with school. Very few children went on to *Gymnasium*, which was a combination of middle school and high school, after which the students attended university. Girls and boys attended separate *Gymnasiums*. The curriculum was rigorous: Latin, Greek, several modern languages, geometry, physics. Don't be confused by the name; sports were not part of school. The Austrian novelist Stefan Zweig observed about his time at *Gymnasium*: "One can make up later for neglecting to exercise the muscles, but the mind can be trained only in those crucial years of development to rise to its full powers of comprehension, and only someone who has learnt to spread his intellectual wings early will be able to form an idea of the world as a whole later."

Tony's life changed forever when he was around ten years old. Somebody gave him a harmonica, and he learned to play it. He was hooked. He was not destined for *Gymnasium*, though I doubt many Slovenian peasant boys at that time were, regardless of how bright. No matter. Tony had another school in mind.

Once Tony learned to read and write and do simple math, he was big enough to work more on the farm. There was always a tremendous amount of work—chopping wood, plowing the land, harvesting the grapes, harvesting the wheat, grinding the corn, feeding the animals, making the wine, making the cider, pressing the dried seeds to make pumpkin oil, harvesting the honey. It never ended.

They hired help during the harvest. Tony was taught to work harder than the help, to be the pacesetter, a work ethic he never forgot.

While Ptujska gora was the closest village, with the church, the school, and a store for those things they didn't grow on the farm, the largest town near the Leskovar farm was the old medieval town of Ptuj (peh-tu-ee). It went back to Roman times—the Romans built a settlement there because it was a perfect spot to easily cross the River Drava. Much later, Ptuj was vital to the line of defense against the Ottoman Turks. However, when the Habsburgs first ruled that area back in 1511, the emperor couldn't afford to fortify the town, so he sold it to the archbishop of Salzburg. The archbishop fortified Ptuj with walls and towers. The Habsburg emperor bought it back a few decades later, in 1555. After attacks from the Ottoman Turks subsided, the town's fortifications weren't needed and fell into decay. In the nineteenth century a rich widow bought the castle and restored it.

Ptuj is known for the celebration of Mesopust. People dress in Kurent masks, which symbolize chasing away winter and evil spirits and celebrating the coming of spring. It goes back to pagan times and was adapted to the Catholic pre-Lenten celebration of Carnival.

The Slovenians were a Slavic people who adopted the western religion, Roman Catholicism, and the culture that goes with it. They were ethnic Slavs with a western religion, ethnically eastern, culturally western. A crossroads in many ways.

Tony and his family worked six days a week. On Sundays, they walked to the beautiful Church of the Virgin Mary at Ptujska gora for Mass, about a mile away. The church sits atop a hill like a beacon seen from miles around. Actually, beacon does not begin to describe what a beautiful sight it is. Back in the late fourteenth century, a baron and his wife had a daughter who was born blind. One night, the girl saw a light far off. She told her father. He proceeded to build a church on the spot. It was to be one of the largest churches in Austria at that time, second only to St. Stephen's Cathedral in Vienna. As Tony told the story, three other barons helped him build it, and they all went broke doing so, but in the end, they built a beautiful church, said to be the most beautiful Gothic church in Slovenian lands. The church became a spiritual and physical refuge during attacks by the Turks. The people built bonfires around it to warn of the invaders. Fire was a help in the right place and a peril in the wrong place. A statue of St. Florian was erected next to the steps leading to the square in front of the church. Florian is the patron saint of firefighters.

Wolves were a menace, a threat to the family's larder, that is, the pigs and chickens. If a wolf killed a pig, the family could be in desperate straits. To defend against this, they would tie a pig to the wagon, Tony would stand in the back with a rifle while someone else drove the wagon, the pig squealed as it was pulled by the wagon, the wolf heard it and came out of the forest, and Tony shot it.

2

LJUBLJANA

Now Tony is sixteen years old. It is 1903. He was the youngest in the family and the first to leave home. There had to have been a pang in his mother's heart when she said goodbye to him, her youngest child, as he left to make his way in the world. Rather than my telling you what happened next, we can hear directly from Tony. My uncle recorded him.

"Where did you go when you left home?"

"Ljubljana."

"Ljubljana? What did you do there?"

"I went to the school of music."

"Did your parents send you to school there?"

"No, I was on my own." He paid his tuition and earned his keep by working in a cooperative store earning eighty-five dinars a month. He lived in the back of the store.

"You just went on your own to study music? Why?"

"Because I liked it."

"You liked music."

"Yeah."

"When you were a little boy did you like it?"

"Yes, in the church."

"Did you play any instrument at home?"

"Harmonica."

"How old were you when you played the harmonica?"

"I would say around ten or eleven."

"What do you remember most about going to that school? Did you study all day?"

"No, no, no I worked on the side. I had most afternoon and evening classes. During the day I usually had study of instrument. In the evening it was usually harmony and history and stuff like that."

"Wasn't it expensive?"

"No, no. It was not expensive. It was a state school of music. It wasn't private, no. It was state. Oh, I remember it was some fifty cents for special instruction on instrument. For one hour. That was just instrument. Wasn't a lot of money."

"Where did you sleep?"

"I room and board outside," meaning not at the school.

"Did somebody do your washing? Did you do your own washing?"

"No."

"You sent your clothes to the laundry?"

"Oh, yes."

America gave the world Jefferson and Madison. The English gave us Shakespeare and Dickens. The French gave us cuisine nonpareil. The Italians gave us Leonardo and Michelangelo. And as for the Austrians, they gave us Mozart and Haydn and Strauss and Schubert; these

Part of the Austro-Hungarian Empire in 1914
(Ministry for Culture and Heritage), updated 14-Aug-2014.
Map produced by Geographx with research assistance from
Damien Fenton and Caroline Lord. Additions by the author.

were Austria's cultural luminaries. When an opera diva died, the flags were lowered to half staff in Vienna. Austria was an empire in love with music, and it was in this vessel, this cradle, that Tony Leskovar became a concert musician. The city in which he studied, Ljubljana (lu-blee-ah-nah), was one of the Austro-Hungarian Empire's remarkable centers of music. There in Ljubljana the young Gustav Mahler conducted his first full-scale opera, Verdi's *Il Trovatore*.

Back in the eighteenth century, reacting to the bloody French Revolution, fearing that it could spread, the Austrian government censored books and plays, spied on her own subjects. By the time Tony was born in 1887, all that was gone. With liberty, a stable political situation, and very little restriction on commerce, people were free to innovate, and they did.

When Tony began his studies at the music conservatory, the Austro-Hungarian Empire was experiencing terrific economic growth; it was "one of the fastest-growing economies in Europe." Cambridge professor Christopher Clark wrote that at this time in Austria: "Free markets and competition across the empire's vast customs union stimulated technical progress and the introduction of new products." The fruits of this could be seen in her principal Slovenian city, Ljubljana.

The city was still recovering from the massive earthquake that struck on Easter Sunday 1895. New buildings were being built in the

Ljubljana.
SLOVENIAN STATE ARCHIVES, AS-1085/88 4/22

Ljubljana.
SLOVENIAN STATE ARCHIVES, AS-1085/88 2/9 2/15

style of Art Nouveau, also called the Secessionist movement. The city was beautiful before the earthquake, and the new city was becoming even more beautiful. Ljubljana means "the beloved one," a lyrical name for a beautiful city.

The medieval castle overlooking the city had been home to the dukes of Carniola, the Austrian duchy of which Ljubljana was the largest city. When Tony lived in Ljubljana the tower was used as a fire watch; the watchman fired a cannon if he spotted a fire. The cannons were also fired to herald special events.

Two years before Tony arrived, the Jubilee Bridge was erected to mark the fortieth anniversary of the reign of Emperor Franz Josef (now called the Dragon Bridge). Indeed, Ljubljana was a city full of promise, a city transforming before his eyes into an architectural jewel. The first department store was built the year Tony arrived. It was hailed an Art Nouveau palace. Construction of the city's most fashionable hotel, the Grand Hotel Union, began that year. Around the corner from it, the beautiful Baroque Franciscan Church of the Annunciation dominated the city's main square and still does. It was built in the seventeenth century and survived the earthquake, though the frescos were damaged. Two years into Tony's studies, the statue of the Slovenian poet Prešeren was erected in the main square, across from the church. That tells us something about the Slovenians—the hero given the distinction of a statue in the main square was not a general, not an emperor, not a duke, but a poet.

Ljubljana was a modern city in every way. This peasant boy, Tony, who heretofore got where he was going on his own two feet or on horse-back or horse-drawn wagon, could now hop on an electric streetcar.

"How long did you stay in Ljubljana?"

"Until 1908, then I joined a military band and orchestra, yes." He was twenty-one.

Young men in Austria were conscripted to serve three years in the army. This was universal conscription, no draft lottery—everybody, well, almost. The government found conscripting all young men to be too expensive, so loopholes were devised to allow men to get out of it. Many who did serve, didn't have to serve all three years. It was as if the Austrians thought, we need a big standing army, not sure why we need it, we think we do, but not really.

"Did you join it [the military band] because you had to be a soldier anyway?"

"Yes. I could join when I wanted to go. I was accepted right away because I had a recommendation, I mean a certificate of music."

"What did you play in the band in the army?"

"Bassoon. And the clarinet."

"Why did you pick those instruments?"

"Because I liked it. The deep tone, I always admire. I didn't have much use for violin, for string instruments, but for woodwind, yes."

"What did you do in the army?"

"Music. I did train for military purpose one week, and I don't think it was that long. After first year, we did sharpshooting outside."

"How did they train?"

"March, left, right. Drilling. I was just shoved into some company. Three years in the army—1908, 1909, 1910. Nineteen-eleven I got out. I was through with service. Every year supposed to go back for two weeks or three weeks, I don't know how to say that. You renew your training, your army. I asked for exemption one year. It was second year. Then the third year I didn't go for ten days, they give you notice to come to the service. Military service. They sent me from Ljubljana to Graz. I came to Graz, he didn't know anything about it, we got no room for you, you go back where you come from. So I went back, report to the lieutenant and captain, we have no room for you. You live here in this town? I say, yeah. You just stay in your room, you come in. [The army paid his rent.] I was playing with a band and orchestra. I didn't even have to exercise for military purposes. They want me in the worst way to stay in. You know, you could stay, better pay. Well, no, I couldn't see it in military. Oh, it was good place. It was German [speaking] regiment, it wasn't Slovenian."

Tony also served as an interpreter for negotiations between the German-speaking Austrian officers and Slovenian farmers when the army wanted to use a farmer's land for maneuvers. This was to pay for the damage, to rent the land temporarily.

The year Tony joined the army, 1908, ethnic Germans rioted in Ptuj during a meeting of the St. Cyril and Methodius Society. Slovenians struck back in Ljubljana by breaking the windows of German-speaking shops. The army shot at the demonstrators. Two people were killed. Who was stoking the fires of resentment? Did this start with the uprising in 1848? The fuse of revolution was lit all

Ljubljana.
SLOVENIAN STATE ARCHIVES

over Europe in 1848. Revolutionaries forced the Austrian army out of Vienna. How humiliating. The chancellor fled the country. Emperor Ferdinand abdicated. And yet, the Habsburgs still ruled, as they had for centuries. Eighteen-year-old Franz Josef ascended the throne. The people demanded democracy and a constitution, and they got it. Austria became a constitutional monarchy. The dual monarchy of Austria-Hungary was established. Slovenian became the language of instruction in Slovenian grade schools. Though my grandfather Tony Leskovar was an Austrian subject, he considered himself Slovenian.

WHEN THE ARMY discharged Tony in 1911, he returned to the lovely Ljubljana, where he was engaged by the Slovenian Philharmonic Orchestra under the direction of Vaclav Talich, who was Czech, "a big gentle fellow," Tony said, a violinist who studied in Prague. Tony never said he was hired by an orchestra; he said he was engaged by the orchestra. As a bassoonist, Tony was in demand. It is considered one of the most difficult woodwind instruments. It has two reeds. Tony was the sole bassoonist in the orchestra. Many of the musicians had been in military bands, but very few had a certificate of music from a music conservatory, as did Tony. Though the orchestra had a gorgeous concert hall in which to perform, they also performed for dances, carnivals, and at the Grand Union restaurant.

The Slovenian Philharmonic began in 1908. It was organized on a subscription basis; 718 people contributed 800 krone (crowns). My source, which is a Slovenian book translated into English, says subscribers contributed 800 krone per month. I wonder if that should be per year. If per year, that comes to around 16,000 krone per musician. A provincial mayor earned 12,000 krone per year at that time.

The first year of the orchestra, they gave one hundred and ninety performances.

Not only was the beautiful city around him transforming into something even more wonderful, so was our young Tony. Now in his twenties, the barber gave him a chic modern haircut. He bought a dapper suit of clothes. He grew a dashing *au courant* mustache. He looked the part of the elegant, continental musician, and that he was. He acquired a taste for cognac, not any cognac, the best cognac, Hennessy. As the fictional Slovenian Baron von Trotta told his son, "Tell him we only drink Hennessy."

Yes, Tony Leskovar was born not in a country, but an empire. He carried the confidence of one born into an empire, an empire in love with music. The novelist Stefan Zweig recalled, as a young boy, meeting the great Johannes Brahms. He said he walked around in a daze afterward, so dazzled was he at meeting one of his heroes. Classical musicians were adored, revered as the pop stars and athletes of today. Tony must have been conscious of this. How could he not be? Could such attention go to the head of a handsome young man such as Tony? Quite possibly. He definitely appreciated the finer things in life. I imagine him sitting at the Hram, one of the most elegant restaurants in Ljubljana, now sipping his Hennessy cognac, now drawing thoughtfully on his cigarette, all the while discussing Mr. Talich's conducting style with a fellow musician. Always the continental man, he was, with his Hennessy taste and deliberate manner. Tony was never in haste.

The Austro-Hungarian Empire was a polyglot of ethnic Germans, Slovenians, Czechs, Croats, and more. The makeup of the orchestra reflected this. At its inception, most of the members were Czech, a few were Slovenian, a few were ethnic Germans. Back in 1909, before Tony joined the philharmonic, during a performance in Tivoli Park in Ljubljana, a few troublemakers, or drunks, started yelling catcalls or worse at the German and Italian musicians. They responded by walking out. Talich was away when this happened. For whatever reason, the fill-in conductor was blamed for the bad behavior of the audience. Once Talich returned, all was well again.

During the 1911–1912 season, Tony was one of thirty-four musicians in the orchestra. They gave concerts every other Sunday from October to March. Food and drink were no longer served. Talich wanted the people to be able to hear the music.

I wonder if the high standards the Viennese held for musicians cascaded to concertgoers in Ljubljana. The Viennese were a tough crowd. They knew the music. One incorrect note, they caught it and remarked upon it, one might say obsessed over it. Every musician had to give his best in every performance; the honor of the city, the honor of the Austrian people, was at stake. This applied as equally to a small band as a full orchestra.

In 1912, Talich left the orchestra and a new conductor, Peter Tepley from Trieste, took over. The orchestra shrank a little. Tony was now

*Neža Leskovar (Tony's mother), Tony, Janez and Terezija and their baby
Pavlina (Tony's sister and brother-in-law). Sept 15, 1913.*
Joh.Winkler Photogr. Atelier

one of twenty-eight musicians. It seems Talich was the glue essential to
keeping the orchestra together, because once he left, it didn't last long.

On October 1, 1913, the philharmonic performed at the train
station in Ljubljana and promptly disbanded. Tony and several of
the musicians formed their own orchestra and toured Dalmatia and
Bosnia-Herzegovina. They performed in Sarajevo. Tony performed
with the opera in Zagreb, then called the Agram Opera, Agram being
the German name for Zagreb.

This single act—the disbanding of the orchestra—would have un-
foreseeable and far-reaching consequences for Tony. If the orchestra
had not disbanded that October day, would my grandfather have ever
left his homeland? It's impossible to know.

"Did you write to your mother? Did she come visit?"

"I visit home," he said.

"When was the last time you went home?"

"1913. That was the last visit. Last time I saw my mother and my
sister was 1913. I was there before. 1913 was the last time."

Tony had his music credentials. He was free to go where he wanted,
when he wanted. He took full advantage.

"Then I played in Switzerland, Zurich," he said.

"Was that a big orchestra?"

"Oh yes, yes."

"What was the name of the orchestra?"

"Zurich Philharmonic. Opera and symphony. They combined, they used the same orchestra for opera as they play in the symphony."

"Did you wear a uniform?"

"No, just tuxedo."

He performed one season with the Zurich Opera, and then he went to the place Richard Wagner called "the heart of modern civilization."

3

AN AUSTRIAN IN PARIS

AFTER A CENTURY OF TURMOIL, what with the French Revolution that began in 1789 and the bloody Reign of Terror, the First Republic, the Napoleonic wars, the First Empire, the Second Republic, and the Second Empire, at long last, the Third Republic seemed to have stuck and, with it, stability and a time of relative calm in France. This had been the case for the past forty-five years when Tony Leskovar arrived in Paris. With that calm came innovation and prosperity.

One of the innovations made by the director of the Paris Opera was to bring in touring orchestras. I always had the impression that when Tony performed in Paris, he was touring with an orchestra, but after hearing him on those recordings, I realize that was not the case. He was engaged by the orchestra in Paris. Tony was living there. He wasn't just passing through.

Wagner had firmly pushed Verdi aside in terms of popularity with Parisian audiences. One-fourth of the performances of the Paris Opera were works by Wagner.

The opera performed through the summer; they didn't take several weeks off back then. I found a program for the August 31, 1910, performance of Berlioz's *Faust* at the Théâtre National de l'Opera, as it was then called.

Now it is 1914 and Tony is performing there.

No doubt Tony had heard about the musical sensation that occurred the year before he arrived. It was the first performance of Stravinsky's ballet *The Rite of Spring*. It begins with a gentle, melodic bassoon solo interrupted by screeching violins. It is a very complex piece of music; bizarre is more like it. I use the term "music" lightly to describe it. I'd call it sound effects, something appropriate to the scary part of an

Le Palais Garnier, the Paris opera house, 1890.
Brown University, digital file 1161805834

Alfred Hitchcock movie. It was avant-garde for the avant-garde. The Ballet Russe was to dance to it. Their "dance" amounted to stomping, since there is nothing rhythmic about the piece. The dancers did not like it. The audience did not like it. First they booed, then they rioted. The dancers kept stomping, the musicians kept playing, the audience kept rioting. The police came. All calmed down, the lights were lowered, the music continued, the stomping continued. More rioting. Imagine well-dressed Parisians punching each other over artistic differences. Couldn't they simply have walked out if they didn't like the performance? The same thing happened during an avant-garde concert in Vienna. Audience members yelled at the orchestra, threw their programs at the musicians, then started punching each other. This was a time when intellectual differences between students at the University of Vienna often exploded into fistfights.

When Tony traveled to Zurich and Paris and worked in those grand cities, he did so with no impediment. Passports had been required in earlier times, but with the advent of the railroad, which greatly facilitated travel, such requirements fell off. Imagine all the functionaries the government would have had to hire to keep track of all those travelers. Too much bother. Too expensive. France did away with passports in 1861. People could travel about as they pleased, could work anywhere. Unless they were independently wealthy, they had to work to eat. The practice of the government giving money to the unemployed did not exist.

Ah, the life of a young, handsome twenty-seven-year-old man with a facility for language, performing with the opera, and in Paris no less. In the restaurants, Tony enjoyed delicious meals for a pittance. Should he wander over to the Left Bank, *Le Quartier Latin*, he saw students sporting berets. Should he stroll through the Tuileries, or ascend Montmartre to Sacre Coeur, he saw artists sitting at their easels, wearing broad-brimmed hats and black velvet jackets. In the parks, he might see a nanny sporting a Breton bonnet with her charges. Each profession and station in life had its own form of dress, a well-known code, if you will, as if all were part of an impressionist tableau and wanted to look their parts.

And of course, there were the ever fashionable upper-class Parisians, wearing whatever was *au courant*, and knowing how to wear it well.

Ladies attended the opera wearing ball gowns. The men wore tuxedos.

The immense and glorious department store Galeries Lafayette had recently opened, a palace of commerce.

The Eiffel Tower was now a radio tower.

With no obvious provocation, Tony might see a young couple burst into dance anywhere, anytime.

In a nod to the nineteenth century, policemen still wore sheathed swords by their sides. In a nod to the twentieth century, horse-drawn buses had vanished; people rode around Paris in electric streetcars. The automobile industry was booming.

Despite the occasional artistic or intellectual brawl, it was indeed a golden age, the Gilded Age, *La Belle Epoque*. Europe was "full of confidence in the present and the future."

Tony surely frequented Café de la Paix, a favorite of his fellow countrymen across from the opera house. How ironic, Café of Peace. His lodgings were nearby in this neighborhood of wide boulevards built by Napoleon III, the thinking behind the design being that the wider the street the more difficult for the rabble to erect barricades, as they had done decades earlier during revolution after revolution.

"How was living in France?"

"Good," Tony said. "Plenty of food. Good living, I would say. There was enough money to live."

"What did you think of Paris?"

"Good. Big city. More foreigners than natives in Paris at that time. Even before, they always say more foreigners in Paris than Frenchmen."

There was the sense that everything was getting better, as if the world were in a cosmic springtime of promise and possibility. It was a golden age in the arts and sciences. What a time to be young, independent, and successful, and living in Paris.

4

WHERE IS SARAJEVO?

ON A LOVELY AFTERNOON at the end of June 1914, the wealthy American writer Edith Wharton attends a garden party at the home of a friend in Auteuil, one of Paris' most fashionable neighborhoods, near the Bois de Boulogne. She sits down at one of the tea tables and joins the conversation. She overhears someone say, "Haven't you heard? The Archduke Ferdinand assassinated . . . at Sarajevo."

"Where is Sarajevo?"

Of course, Tony knew. He had performed there. It was in Bosnia, then part of Austria-Hungary, but to those at the party, just a name with no further import. Another royal dead. Sad. Talk went on about the new play.

But Archduke Franz Ferdinand wasn't just another European royal who met an unfortunate untimely end. He was the Austrian crown prince, a Habsburg, the next in line to the throne of the immutable, imperturbable, massive Austro-Hungarian Empire.

He was fifty years old. His beautiful wife, Sophie, was also murdered. She was forty-six. They had been married almost fourteen years, a royal couple who married for love. Their three young children, Sophie, Max, and Ernst, were orphaned in an instant.

You can be sure there was much chatter about the assassination among Tony's fellow countrymen at the Café de la Paix. Archduke Franz Ferdinand, which one is he? The dour one, never smiled, didn't seem to enjoy performances, next in line to Emperor Franz Josef. There's still Archduke Karl, seems a fine fellow, charming young man. He'd make a wonderful emperor, almost as good as the old man.

I wonder if Archduke Franz Ferdinand didn't smile during performances in Vienna because he was shy, forced into a role he didn't choose but was born into, or was it because he resented having to be in Vienna. He had married for love, to the disapproval of the royal family. His wife, Sophie, was an aristocrat, a countess, a noblewoman, but not noble enough. Franz Ferdinand resented how the love of his life was shunned by official Vienna. Now they were both officially dead.

The Austrian painter Paul Cohen-Portheim happened to be in Paris when the archduke was shot. While at a fete in a Parisian ballroom, he asked an Austrian count, "What happens now?"

"Why should anything happen?" replied the count.

After all, such unfortunate things do happen. Why only the year before, the king of Greece was shot in the back by a lone Socialist alcoholic vagabond. President McKinley was shot and killed by a lone anarchist in 1901. Austrian Emperor Franz Josef's own wife, the beautiful Empress Elisabeth, known affectionately as Sisi, was stabbed and killed by a lone anarchist in Geneva in 1898. And there was that unfortunate business in Mexico. And now, how sad, it was the heir to the Austrian throne and his wife who were shot and killed.

Kaiser Wilhelm of Germany sent condolences to Emperor Franz Josef.

The Serbian prime minister sent condolences and denounced the assassins and cancelled the St. Vitus Day celebrations.

King George of England ordered seven days of mourning.

Czar Nicholas of Russia ordered twelve days of mourning.

The *Neue Freie Presse* in Vienna wrote, "The political consequences of this act are being greatly exaggerated."

The great controversy in Vienna was about the funeral arrangements. I mean really, Sophie, she wasn't all that royal, how could she have the same funereal honors as her husband, she couldn't. But her husband was heir to the throne. What was a royal funeral planner to do?

The *New York Tribune* of July 5 reported that the new heir to the Austrian throne, Archduke Karl, "hates luxury . . . cares little for soldiering . . . but much for music." He would certainly smile during performances.

Three weeks after the assassination, in mid-July 1914, the sophisticated bankers at Morgan, Grenfell in London were impatient to proceed with their loan to Bosnia. The Austrian banker Felix Somary urged caution because of the political situation. What political situation? The London bankers saw no additional risk. Felix Somary was a prescient soul. As soon as he heard that the archduke was shot, he feared it meant war. His opinion was not widely shared. He was what we call a Jeremiah—he could see what others could not see. The sentiment of those around him was: since nothing had happened yet, nothing would happen. No great European power had gone to war in Europe in the last thirty-seven years, almost two generations. Austria had not waged a war of aggression in I don't know how long. The idea was preposterous. All seemed quiet, business as usual. To Felix, it was an ominous quiet, the calm before the storm, the catastrophe, Armageddon. He converted all assets under his management to gold held in Switzerland and Norway, both neutral countries that would assuredly remain neutral, at least he hoped so, and he did it just in time.

A young German woman named Edith Stein was working on her doctorate in philosophy that summer of 1914: "Our placid student life was blown to bits by the Serbian assassination of royalty. July was dominated by the question: will war break out in Europe. Everything seemed to indicate that a terrible storm was brewing. But we found it inconceivable that it would really come to that. No one growing up during or since the war can possibly imagine the security in which we assumed ourselves to be living before 1914. Our life was built on an indestructible foundation of peace, stability of ownership of property, and on the permanence of circumstances to which we were accustomed." Austrian novelist Stefan Zweig and American novelist John Dos Passos wrote much the same about the idyllic security of life before the First World War. Tony no doubt felt the same. Why wouldn't he. He was on top of the world.

Meanwhile, the Austrians captured and interrogated the assassins. This time the assassin was no lone anarchist, no alcoholic vagabond, no lone gunman. The man who shot the archduke and his wife was part of a group of assassins, Bosnian Serbs, members of the Serbian terrorist group the Black Hand. They hatched their murderous plot in the coffeehouses of Belgrade, the capital of Serbia. Now came the real shock. The assassins said their guns and bombs were provided by the head of Serbian intelligence, Colonel Dimitrijevic.

Serbia. A foreign power. This was different. This was a matter of national honor. This could mean war. But still, it would just amount to a little spat between Austria and Serbia, would it not? They might knock each other around a bit, after a few weeks it would be over.

Nothing to worry about. All in Vienna could return to their favorite coffeehouses.

Whether this would be an isolated campfire or a conflagration that burned down the entire forest, the cities, and everything else for miles depended on the actions of leaders and diplomats outside of Austria and Serbia.

I must note here, Emperor Franz Josef was eighty-four years old. He died two years after these events.

Archduke Franz Ferdinand and his wife were killed on June 28, 1914. Now that Austria believed that Serbia was complicit in the assassination, Serbia must be brought to heel, at least so said Army Chief of Staff General Baron Franz Conrad von Hötzendorf. He'd been angling for war with Serbia for some time.

On July 23, Austria sent a list of demands to Serbia and gave her forty-eight hours to respond.

During earlier saber rattling, there had been a strong, persuasive voice for restraint and peace within the empire, a man who had the old emperor's ear, but that voice was gone; he was the archduke. He was dead. A year and a half earlier Archduke Franz Ferdinand wrote a vehement letter opposing General Conrad when Conrad tried to push the emperor into war with Serbia. General Conrad was upset with Serbia for stirring up trouble in the Balkans. Conrad wanted to go to war against Serbia now to prevent trouble later. Archduke Franz Ferdinand said this idea of a preventive war against Serbia was absurd, and even worse, it would provoke Russia. He said, "If we march on Serbia, Russia will march on us." He said such a war would be lunacy. It would spell disaster for both Austria and Russia, and the ensuing chaos would foment revolution that would topple the monarchies in both countries. He said it is the "duty of government to preserve peace." He believed restraint was sensible, not weak, that it was wisdom to avoid war, not weakness.

The terrorists killed the one person in the best position to restrain Austria from going to war against Serbia. Did they know this? They killed the archduke because he supported reforms giving more autonomy to those in Slavic lands. This was at cross purposes with those who sought unification of southern Slavic lands, which meant breaking away part of Austria-Hungary and uniting it with Serbia. If Austro-Hungarian Slavs were happy, it would be that much harder to stoke the flames of revolution and secession. To stoke revolution, the people must be made unhappy first.

An earlier crown prince of Austria, Rudolf, who was long deceased by this time, had been at odds with Kaiser Wilhelm of Germany. The historian Frederic Morton speculated that had Rudolf lived, he might have turned Austria away from Germany and toward France. Rudolf had also been good friends with Edward, Prince of Wales. They used to go to the horse races together in Vienna.

Rudolf had worried that King Milan of Serbia's servility toward Austria might provoke resentment among the Serbs.

The diplomats, the generals, the leaders of these European lands came of age during the nineteenth century. What did a nineteenth-century gentleman do to defend his honor? He dueled. Now we had a duel at the national level, possibly on an epic level. Austria threw down the gauntlet, which came in the form of ultimatums to Serbia, and she enlisted a second, the mighty Germany. Unless Serbia acquiesced to all demands, it would be pistols at dawn, except with cannons. (The ultimatum didn't say that per se, but it was understood.) Serbia enlisted Russia as a second, and since Russia was an ally of France, that meant France came along too.

Once Austria sent those ultimatums to Serbia, everything changed. She had pulled the trigger on a gun she hoped wasn't loaded.

Anti-war protestors took to the streets of Paris.

The answer from Serbia was unsatisfactory. On July 28, Austria declared war on Serbia.

On hearing this, the American ambassador to France, Myron Herrick, said he was "seized with the darkest of forebodings." He dashed off a cable to Secretary of State William Jennings Bryan in Washington. "CONFIDENTIAL—To be communicated to the President. Situation in Europe is regarded here as the gravest in history. . . . Civilization is threatened by demoralization which would follow a general conflagration . . . There is a faith and reliance in our high ideals. . . . I believe expression from our nation would have weight in this crisis. . . . I believe that a strong plea for delay and moderation from the President of the United States would meet with respect and approval of Europe."

No answer from Bryan. Not a word from President Wilson.

Secretary of State Bryan sent a telegram to the ambassador in London asking: "Is there in your opinion any likelihood that the good offices of the United States if offered under Article 3 of the Hague Convention would be acceptable or serve any high purpose in the present crisis?"

Article 3 of the Hague Convention, signed in 1907, said a belligerent nation who violates the rules set forth by the Convention shall be liable to pay compensation and shall be responsible for all acts of the belligerent nation's armed forces. There was supposed to be another convention in 1914, a gathering of the nations of the world to outlaw war. How ironic. It didn't happen. It was preempted by war.

One month before the archduke was shot, President Wilson's most trusted advisor, Colonel House, toured Europe. He told the president that he saw "militarism run stark mad." He said only someone from outside of Europe can calm the waters, or else there will be "an awful cataclysm."

When Ambassador Herrick sent that cable, Mrs. Wilson was on her deathbed. She died the next week. Ambassador Herrick never knew whether Secretary of State Bryan showed the grieving president his cable. Even if Mrs. Wilson had not been dying, Wilson himself had said, "It would be an irony of fate if my administration had to deal chiefly with foreign affairs."

We weren't a military superpower in 1914, but we were an economic superpower. The Europeans would need American capital and American goods to fight this war. Woodrow Wilson knew well the ravages of war. He was a young boy living in Augusta, Georgia, during the Civil War. Could he have convinced the great European powers to stand down and not go to war? Would Old World leaders have listened to the leader of a New World upstart, albeit a rich behemoth?

In Berlin, the bureau chief for *The Times* of London prepared to go home to England. He said goodbye to his friend the Austrian banker Felix Somary in such a way as to intimate he'd never be back. He told Felix, "The [German] Foreign Ministry are behaving as if they intend to repudiate our treaties." When Felix told the German diplomat Arthur Zimmerman this, Zimmerman scoffed that this was nonsense and that the man was an "alarmist" and the kaiser's brother had just returned from England and King George assured him that England had no interest in joining this war.

Did the kaiser's brother and King George know that the secret German war plan, the Schliffen Plan, dictated that the German army invade neutral Belgium, so as to avoid France's well-fortified frontier, in violation of the treaty guaranteeing Belgian neutrality, a treaty to which both Britain and Prussia, now part of Germany, were signatories?

In Vienna, General Conrad was certain that Russia would not come in on the side of Serbia. Austria would quickly and decisively smash the troublesome Serbia, dust herself off, bask in a glorious victory, and life would go on as before. He was sure of it.

On July 30, two days after Austria declared war on Serbia, a French journalist in Berlin wrote, "Germany does not desire war." That is quite a different view from the London *Times* man and from the Austrian banker Felix Somary, who said Berlin "was intoxicated by war fever." I suppose it depended on whom you talked to. I wonder how well the French journalist spoke German, or did he depend on French-speaking sources.

Felix Somary made it home to Vienna just in time; he caught the last train before Germany sealed the borders. He found the mood in Vienna to be quite the opposite of what he had just seen in Berlin. "The irrepressible Viennese gaiety had disappeared," he said. They knew what war would bring. The mood in the city was one of "resignation without hope."

Russia refused to stay out of a war between Austria-Hungary and her fellow Slavic country Serbia. For that reason, on August 1, Germany declared war on Russia. France refused to remain neutral. The French government ordered mobilization of the army. There was no draft lottery, it was conscription of all young men. As soon as the notices could be printed, gendarmes began posting the mobilization order throughout cities, towns, and villages. Church bells rang heralding the mobilization order.

The railroad depot for northbound trains out of Paris was set to close at six o'clock. Germans, Russians, and Dutch massed at the approaches to the Brussels express, desperate to get home. Soldiers with bayonets blocked them. The barriers came down and people rushed onto the train, baggage and all. No porters were to be found. Only a skeletal crew was working, only old men, too old for war.

Spontaneous processions broke out with people carrying the French flag, *Le Bleu, Blanc, Rouge*, and singing the *La Marseillaise*. They wanted to be part of something bigger than themselves.

The American writer Edith Wharton was traveling through Poitiers

Crowds at the Gare d'Est in Paris as French soldiers mobilize, August 2, 1914.
WIKI COMMONS, NATIONAL LIBRARY OF FRANCE

on her way back to Paris. During the night in her hotel room, she could hear the people on the street singing *La Marseillaise.* "What nonsense! It can't be war," she said.

Tony heard the same singing in Paris.

"Thrilling Scenes in Paris with Cries 'On to Berlin,'" reported an American newspaper.

By August 2, mobilization notices had been posted throughout Paris. Germany declared war on France the next day.

Notice anybody missing in all that? Austria-Hungary. Thus far, the only country Austria-Hungary had declared war on was Serbia. It would take her a week to declare war on Russia. She never declared war on France. France declared war on Austria-Hungary. Lunacy.

Don't feel bad if you find this confusing. It was to the people

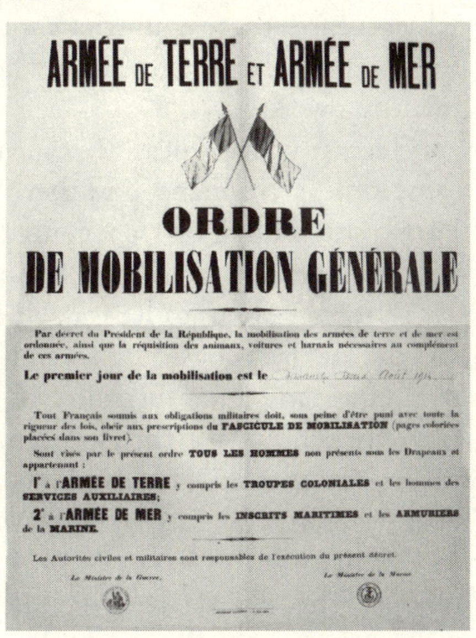

French mobilization poster.
CREATIVE COMMONS

French soldiers guarding the subway entrance in Paris.
LIBRARY OF CONGRESS LC-B2-3208-14

involved too. It was very confusing because it was hard to understand why on earth these countries should be enemies. Overnight, for some reason unintelligible to those who would do the fighting and suffering, they were.

Germany was going to war against France, Austria was on the same side as Germany, and there was Tony Leskovar, an Austrian in Paris. This made him the enemy.

On August 4, President Wilson declared American neutrality.

Why was agrarian Russia, albeit in the process of industrializing, so confident about going to war against the vastly more industrialized Germany and Austria? Did the Russians not notice how badly this worked out for the agrarian South against the industrial North in the American Civil War? Though Russia was industrializing her economy, her railroad system was nowhere near as advanced as those in Germany and Austria. In 1914, the railroad was vital to mobilizing troops. This cannot be overstated. And Germany was the greatest military power in the world. Were the Russians out of their minds? Previous saber rattling hadn't come to blows, why now? What was different this time?

As a bit of background, the Ottoman Turks had ruled Serbia as well as Bosnia and Herzegovina for centuries. In 1875, Christian peasants in Herzegovina revolted against their Muslim overlords. It started as a tax revolt and quickly spread to Bosnia. In 1876, the Serbs joined the rebellion, and the Serbo-Turkish War ensued. In 1877, the Russians jumped in to support their fellow Slavs, the Serbs, and the Russo-Turkish War ensued. In 1878, a peace conference of the great European powers granted Serbia her independence from the Ottoman Empire and asked neighboring Austria-Hungary to rule Bosnia and Herzegovina. Thirty years later, in 1908, Austria-Hungary fully annexed Bosnia and Herzegovina. It sounds like a fine point to me, but this enraged some Serbs. How dare Austria-Hungary rule over Serbs in Bosnia, even though they had effectively done so since 1878, and before that, the Ottoman Turks had ruled over them for centuries. Why, you might ask, should the Serbs be upset about this and why now? Serbs didn't only live in Serbia. There were lots of Serbs in Bosnia. There were also a lot of people who were not Serbs in Bosnia. Nevertheless, in 1908, the Serbs were up in arms, literally, ready to wage war against the mighty Austro-Hungarian Empire over what had actually been settled decades earlier. Russia mobilized her army in support of Serbia. Germany told Russia, stop or we'll come in on the side of Austria. It worked. The Russians and Serbs backed down. No war. That was in 1908.

In January of 1913, Austrian army chief General Conrad told Emperor Franz Josef that the Serbs were making incursions into Albania. The emperor sent troops to the borders with Serbia and Russia, the Russians sent troops to their side of the border, they stared each other down but that was it, just a few troop movements, nothing came to blows.

Now in 1914, we had Germany again telling the Russians the same thing, stop your mobilization or we will come in on the side of Austria, but this time it didn't work. Nobody backed down. Russia was the first domino, and once one domino fell, they kept falling, and all went to war. What had changed during the intervening years? Why were the Russians so cocksure about going to war against Austria-Hungary and Germany? Did they figure Germany couldn't fight two fronts—against France and Russia at the same time?

One very big thing was different this time—Austria fired on Belgrade. That had not happened before. And yet, why did the

Russians get involved? Were the Russians acting blindly out of fealty for their fellow Slavs, the Serbs? Or was there something more, something that gave them more confidence?

Could the reason be, at least in part, *L'Affaire Redl*? What I am about to tell you could be described as a cross between John LeCarre and Graham Greene, except it actually happened.

In April of 1913, German intelligence tipped off Austrian intelligence of some funny business with the mail. They had discovered money being sent in a suspicious manner, presumably money for secrets, government secrets—evidence of espionage. A letter stuffed with six thousand kronen and addressed to "Herr Nizetas" would be waiting at the Fleischmarkt Square post office in Vienna. The police kept the investigation tightly guarded on a strict need-to-know basis. They set up a trap to unmask the spy.

Two plainclothes policemen installed a buzzer in the post office and told the mail clerk to furtively press the button when "Herr Nizetas" arrived to collect the letter. The policemen hid in the room where the buzzer would ring and waited. Days went by, weeks went by, and no "Herr Nizetas" arrived to collect his mail, which now numbered three kronen-stuffed letters, letters that had been carefully opened and resealed by the police. Then at long last, on May 24, 1913, the mail clerk pressed the button. The buzzer sounded in the room, but no policemen appeared. The mail clerk pressed the button again. No police. He made small talk with "Herr Nizetas" to delay him until the police arrived. He pressed the button again and again. No policemen came, because there were no policemen in the room to hear the buzzer. One had gone out for a cup of coffee and the other was in the restroom. The mail clerk kept pressing the button, and once they got back to the room and heard the buzzer, they raced to the post office.

He just left, said the mail clerk.

They ran outside just in time to see a cab drive off. They dashed back inside to question the mail clerk.

What did he look like?

It's hard to say, his hat was pulled down, and he didn't look up.

They had the license number of a cab that might have carried off the traitor, but how to find that cab in all of busy Vienna. That part of the old city is full of narrow helter-skelter streets, a great place to disappear. As the policemen were pondering their options, miracle of miracles, the cab came back. The policemen waved him down. He said he had taken the man to the Café Kaiserhof.

And then another stroke of luck. The cabbie said, The man dropped the sheath of the knife he used to open his mail. Here it is.

And he gave it to the police.

The policemen took it and rushed off to the Café Kaiserhof. They dashed inside and asked the waiter, Who came into the café in the last few minutes?

No one, said the waiter.

The policemen went back outside and questioned the cabbies.

Yes, said one of the cabbies, I saw a man with his hat pulled down get out of one cab and immediately get into another. I heard him say Hotel Klomser.

Another lucky break. I don't know about you, but this is beginning to stretch credulity, but we'll stay with it. Much of real life falls under the category of too outlandish for fiction. I've read about this in several sources. The details vary but the essential elements are the same. This one seems the most plausible. We'll keep going with it.

Off raced the policemen to the Hotel Klomser. They asked the concierge, Who entered the hotel in the last few minutes?

Lots of people, said the concierge, and he started to list them: Herr this, Frau that, and on and on, and Colonel Redl, a regular guest, such a gentleman.

Colonel Redl?

Colonel Redl had until recently been the head of Austrian counter-intelligence. As you can imagine, this threw the two policemen back on their heels. Should we consult him about the case, he might be of help, one suggested. No. Absolutely not. The policemen had been strictly ordered not to discuss the case with anyone.

They handed the knife sheath to the concierge and asked him, When Colonel Redl comes down for dinner, would you be so kind as to ask him if this is his?

It would be my pleasure, replied the concierge. Here I imagine a slight bow and click of the heels.

The policemen found discreet places from where to watch. I imagine one seated behind a large potted palm.

When the dapper Colonel Redl came down to the lobby for dinner, the concierge asked, I beg your pardon, Herr Colonel, could this be yours?

Why yes, thank you, he said, and held out his hand to take the knife sheath, thought better of it, pulled it back, but it was too late.

Now came the big guns, including Army Chief of Staff General Baron Franz Conrad von Hötzendorf, to question Colonel Redl. They questioned him for one day, just one day, obtained a signed statement, and left him alone with a loaded pistol.

The newspaper reported that Colonel Redl had shot himself, so sad, such a brilliant officer, overwrought by overwork, the stress became too much . . .

It was only a matter of time before the truth came out. How that happened is another remarkable story. A Viennese locksmith was supposed to be playing in a soccer game but was called away by the police to unlock an apartment, which turned out to be Colonel Redl's lair. This spy had secrets. The Russians knew it and had been blackmailing Redl and paying him beyond his wildest dreams, which supported a very lavish and very debauched lifestyle, the sordid evidence of which was in abundance behind that locked apartment door. Later, the locksmith received a scolding from his soccer coach for missing the big game. You wouldn't believe what I was called away for, the locksmith told his coach. And he told him.

The coach was a newspaper reporter.

When Archduke Franz Ferdinand learned what happened, he was furious. How on earth could they be sure they learned everything from Redl after only one day of questioning him. How could they possibly be sure they knew all he had sold to the Russians. How could they allow Redl to kill himself? From his Catholic point of view, it was appalling and wrong. From his government point of view, it was foolish and reckless. General Conrad's response was dismissive. It didn't amount to much, he said. How could he know that?

It turned out Redl had been in the pay of the Russians for thirteen years. He sold Austria's troop mobilization plans, secret army codes, border fortification details, names of spies, their entire intelligence network, and Austria's battle plan should they go to war against Serbia, and he had given false information to the Austrian military about Russia's battle strength. I've yet to figure out when the Austrians learned all this—was it from Redl or during the war or not until after the war.

Around the same time Colonel Redl was unmasked, General Conrad was told that several of his son's friends, including his son's mistress, were selling Austrian military secrets to the Italians who were passing them on to the Russians. Just when you think you've peeled the whole onion on this, there's more. It's like Russian nesting dolls, you look inside, there's another, now another, now another. As for our story, we'll stop here.

Colonel Redl was apprehended in May of 1913. Archduke Franz Ferdinand was assassinated on June 28, 1914. Austria declared war on Serbia on July 28, 1914. Assuming the Austrians knew all that Redl had sold to the Russians, one year was not a lot of time for the Austrians to rework their war plans, mobilization schedules, and so on. Remember, it took them thirty years to fully annex Bosnia. They were never in haste. Old bureaucracies can be slow and cumbersome and resistant to change. So sad they weren't slow about going to war.

From Russia's point of view, all those secrets that the Russians bought from Redl now had an unknown, but possibly fast approaching, expiration date. If Russia were to remain at an advantage because of what she had bought from Redl, she couldn't dawdle. It was only a matter of time before Austria would undo the damage.

Kaiser Wilhelm of Germany had been confident that the Russians would back down, just as they had in 1908. Did he know about *L'Affaire Redl*? Were the Austrians too embarrassed to tell him that their highest ranking intelligence officer had been a spy for the Russians for thirteen years? Did Emperor Franz Josef know? Had the Austrians changed their war plans? Did the Russians assume they had not?

GERMAN DOCTORAL STUDENT Edith Stein wrote, "One thing was certain. It would differ totally from all previous wars. The destruction would be so terrible that it could not possibly last long. It would be all over in a few months . . . I have no private life anymore . . . All my energy must be devoted to this great happening. Only when the war is over, if I'm alive then, will I be permitted to think of my private affairs once more."

She told her mother, "I'm not afraid. But it is entirely possible that the Russians will cross the border in a few days."

"Then we'll take a broomstick and beat them back," her mother said.

"World war. World ruin," wrote the Viennese writer Arthur Schnitzler.

"The lamps are going out all over Europe; we shall not see them again in our lifetime," said British Foreign Minister Sir Edward Grey.

"The [German] Chancellor expects that a war, whatever its outcome, will result in the uprooting of everything that exists. . . . Doom greater than human power hanging over Europe and our own people," wrote Kurt Reizler, who was secretary and confidant to the German chancellor.

Edith Wharton, still in Paris, wrote, "France was paralyzed with horror" at the prospect of war.

As with rigor mortis, the paralysis didn't last. It took only sixteen days to put the entire country of France on a war footing.

So where does this leave us? To briefly recap: Imagine you are a concert musician at the dawn of the twentieth century. You are Slovenian but you are from Austria. Musicians are idolized. In Vienna, the flags are lowered to half mast when an opera star dies. Now this young musician, Tony Leskovar, who has already performed with great orchestras in Austria-Hungary and Switzerland, is performing with the opera in Paris, the City of Lights, the center of music and culture and all things wonderful. He has arrived. Handsome, accomplished, enjoying the profession he was born to do, plenty of money to live on, he is on top of the world, and what happens—a terrorist, a Serb in Sarajevo murders the archduke. Archduke who? The grumpy one. Never smiled during the performances. Oh, that one. Nothing to cause concern. Another in a long line of assassinations. There was the beautiful empress Elisabeth, stabbed by a mad man in Geneva; President McKinley shot by an anarchist while shaking hands in Buffalo; the list goes on. At a garden party of American expatriates in Paris, upon hearing the news, someone asks, where is Sarajevo? The talk in Vienna is over the funeral. The archduke's wife was also murdered. She was from the aristocracy but not quite up to the aristocracy of the Habsburgs, the ruling family. She couldn't possibly receive the same pomp as the archduke, yet she was his wife. Such a dilemma for a royal funeral planner. The moneyed prepare to quit Paris for Deauville and Trouville on the sea, fleeing the oppressive summer heat in a world before air conditioning. If only all the diplomats and generals across Europe had vacated their capitals to relax away from the heat and left well enough alone. If only all could have continued as it had been.

If only.

5

∽

BEHIND ENEMY LINES

RESTAURANTS ACROSS PARIS STARTED TO CLOSE, hotels started to close, shops started to close. The men who ran them are leaving, they are soldiers now, preparing to fight the Germans.

Why isn't Monsieur Leskovar going with them?

The army requisitioned personal cars and buses for the war effort. Train service was in disarray as the country switched to a war footing. Civilian travel was severely limited.

Myron Herrick, the American ambassador to France, had been appointed by President Taft. When the Democrat Wilson defeated the Republican incumbent Taft in the 1912 election, Wilson offered this plum ambassadorship to his campaign manager, who dithered and dithered and dithered and eventually turned it down. Wilson then offered it to a man named Sharp, who agreed to take it, but had not arrived. Ambassador Herrick and his wife had been packing and readying to leave once Mr. Sharp arrived, which they expected to be soon. This is why, a year and a half after Woodrow Wilson took office, Ambassador Herrick, who was appointed by Taft, was still at his post as the American ambassador in Paris.

Edith Wharton went to her bank in Paris. She couldn't get her money. She cabled her banker in New York. "Impossible," he said.

American tourists in Paris were perplexed. War was breaking out in Europe. They wanted to go home as soon as possible. *We aren't at war, why can't we get our money? We have hotel bills to pay. How can we pay them if the bank won't give us our money?* Frantic, they went to the American embassy. Ambassador Herrick pleaded with the French bankers. No luck. He appealed to the French government. No luck. The answer: "We are at war. No money can be taken out of the country."

41

The same was true for Tony. Any money he had in the bank was frozen. He couldn't get it. That's probably why later in life he kept so much cash in his wallet.

Ambassador Herrick worked out a deal with the French, which quite honestly I didn't understand so can't explain. The result was—Americans could pay their hotel bills, buy a steamship ticket home, and leave. At the same time, the American government dispatched the armored cruiser the *Tennessee* with a load of gold to help stranded Americans settle their bills so they could leave Europe, six million dollars in gold. The French government deposited that amount in French francs with the firm J.P. Morgan.

This was in response to numerous newspaper stories about Americans stranded in Europe and what was Wilson going to do about it.

Tony's brother, Joe, who was now living in Aurora, Illinois, urged him to come to America and sent him a steamship ticket. Tony sent the ticket back. He'd wait it out. Performing with the opera in Paris was not a gig he'd easily give up. *The war won't last long*, people said. *Six weeks, it can't last any longer than that,* they said. *One big battle and that will turn the tide to France, and it will be over.* The Austro-Prussian war lasted seven weeks back in the 1860s. The Franco-Prussian War lasted ten months in the 1870s. Tony would wait it out in Paris.

But Paris was fast being emptied of young men, men Tony's age, men of military age. What was a young Slovenian-Austrian man to do, one who had already served in the Austrian army? What was he doing in Paris? The French police would want to know.

More hotels, restaurants, and shops across Paris closed. The men who ran them, gone to war. French families were losing their husbands, fathers, sons, and livelihoods.

The Austrian painter Paul Cohen-Portheim continued with his planned trip to London. Surely, Britain wouldn't be involved in this war. He was wrong. Once the German army invaded neutral Belgium, Britain declared war on Germany and Austria-Hungary. Now in London, he couldn't get his money either. He ended up in a British internment camp. He said the worst of it was never being alone, never having a quiet moment to himself. It was enough to drive a person crazy, and did. It came to be known as the barbed-wire disease.

The Germans waited several months before they started interning

British citizens stuck in Germany. They must have thought the war would be over so fast, why bother. No one could have imagined how long it would drag on.

Some sixty thousand civilians from France's newfound enemy nations would be detained in France over the course of the war. This included naturalized French citizens who originally hailed from Germany or Austria-Hungary or the Ottoman Empire. Most were like my grandfather Tony, innocent people living their lives but stranded in the wrong place at the wrong time, and assumed to be sympathetic to their homeland. This made them enemy aliens. Information about how this played out in France is sketchy. People such as Tony were detained, questioned, and many were held in internment camps. As for those deemed not a threat, I haven't been able to find out if the French authorities deported them or simply let them go. As for when the French started to do this, that I wasn't able to find out either. By June of 1915, the Germans had rounded up 48,513 enemy civilians. By November of 1915, the British had rounded up 32,440 Germans, Austrians, and Hungarian civilians and held them in internment camps. These unfortunate people were stranded in a country they didn't know was their enemy until their leaders decided to declare war on each other, which was unthinkable until it happened.

All over Europe, on both sides of the war, enemy aliens were being interned for the crime of being in the wrong place at the wrong time.

And there was Tony Leskovar, a young Slovenian-Austrian in Paris.

The French police begin demanding that all foreigners show their passports. Nervous Americans scurry to the embassy. The United States doesn't require passports. France didn't require them before the war. Only Russia and Turkey required passports before the war. Ambassador Herrick orders his staff to prepare makeshift certificates for anyone they can be reasonably sure is an American. This mollifies the French police.

Since the United States was neutral, Ambassador Herrick agreed to represent the interests of Germans and Austro-Hungarians who were stuck in Paris when the war started.

Was Tony questioned by the police? I imagine he was. A Slovenian accent, a Serbian accent, they sounded alike to a French policeman. As long as his friends at the Café de la Paix and his fellow musicians didn't give him away, how would the French police know he wasn't

Serbian. Let us remember that France entered the war ostensibly to help the Serbs.

Tony and friendly foreigners and old men were left to perform in the orchestra for the opera, but no Wagner. Wagner was out, no more Wagner, not for a very, very long time.

IN ONLY A FEW WEEKS, the German army plowed across Belgium and into eastern France and were so close to Paris that the government decided to evacuate to Bordeaux. Most of the diplomatic delegations readied to evacuate with the French government. American Ambassador Herrick was one of few who chose to remain in Paris. The King of Spain ordered his ambassador to do whatever the American ambassador did with regard to evacuating or remaining in Paris. The Spanish ambassador tried to convince Ambassador Herrick to flee Paris. When the King of Spain found out, he replaced him.

French President Poincaré thanked Ambassador Herrick for his decision to remain in Paris. He said the French cabinet believed that the Germans would be in Paris in a few days and intended to lay waste to every piece of the city until the French capitulated and surrendered unconditionally. "This would never be done," said Poincare. "It is better that the capital be laid in ashes than that France surrender."

Ambassador Herrick set to work to do what he could to preserve the city's vast artistic treasures. I have no idea how he was going to do that short of convincing the Germans not to destroy the city.

A rumor started that Paris was to be declared an open city. This meant it would not be defended by French troops, and then, hopefully, the German troops would not bombard and destroy it. When French General Joseph Gallieni, who was sixty-five years old and had just been pulled out of retirement to defend Paris, heard the rumor, he asked the minister of war if this were true. No, it wasn't. Even if it meant all the beautiful treasures of Paris were destroyed, even if the city were flattened, burned to the ground, the city must be defended. Gallieni was aghast. The minister of war told him, "You will defend Paris to the last ditch."

On September 2, 1914, the French government and most of the diplomatic community fled Paris by train and went to Bordeaux. Why Bordeaux? It is the French city farthest from Germany.

General Gallieni posted hours of departing trains, free trains, in hopes that civilians would leave the city. Many left. Tony stayed.

The Germans were now shelling Paris. One bomb narrowly missed Ambassador Herrick.

In desperation General Gallieni made the bold decision to strip Paris of all troops. He enlisted every taxi driver in Paris to drive all those soldiers to the front, and with the biggest army he could muster, he attacked the Germans at the Marne. It worked. After five days, the Germans pulled back. Paris was saved, for now. (This was the Battle of the Marne, September 6 to 12, 1914.)

Refugees from eastern France and Belgium straggled into Paris, their homes having been destroyed by the advancing German army. The Belgians were from Flanders and didn't speak French. No one had anticipated such a flood of refugees. It was a mess. Charities sprang up to help.

Meanwhile in Vienna, the Viennese were waiting in line for flour and bread. Before long, they were waiting in line for milk, potatoes, sugar, oil, coffee, eggs, soap, just about everything. Wealthy city dwellers bartered with farmers for food. People swore never to speak French or watch Shakespeare.

Weeks passed. Months passed. Where was Tony? He was still in Paris. Even if he passed himself off as a Serb, who was left to attend the opera? How could the opera pay him?

"Weren't you making good money in France?"

"There was cut down to half pay which was three hundred francs," Tony said. "Regular pay was six hundred francs per month. They pay by the month, not by the week."

Half pay became no pay. Tony smoked cigarettes to kill his appetite, to stave off hunger.

Edith Wharton opened her apartment for concerts to provide work for out-of-work musicians who "were starving." This was in January 1915.

Survival became everyone's new profession, including Tony's.

His situation became untenable. To the rescue, an opera singer. A woman.

6

SWITZERLAND TO NEW YORK

"DID YOU SEE MANY AMERICANS in Paris?"

"I saw more Americans in Switzerland," Tony said, "because that was a neutral country."

The day after Germany declared war on Russia, Switzerland mobilized her army and militia to guard the border and train stations. Switzerland was a neutral country, but how could the Swiss be sure their neutrality would be honored? Belgium's wasn't, as the world discovered two days later when the German army invaded neutral Belgium. Switzerland had a standing army, and reserves, and the militia. All men age seventeen to fifty were eligible to serve in the militia and were expected to keep their rifles at home and at the ready should they be called upon.

Switzerland was not invaded, remained neutral, and became a haven for the displaced, and the displaced were many. A German man married to an English woman—they weren't welcome in Germany, where "God punish England" became a common greeting, nor were they welcome in England. But they could go to Switzerland, a neutral country where German was spoken. The cafes were full of the chatter of armchair generals who knew exactly what the combatants should be doing but weren't.

It was also a place where anyone could complain openly and bitterly about the war, where they couldn't at home.

With people from the warring countries fleeing to Switzerland, it also became a haven for spies and intrigue. One never knew who was listening to whose conversation in the cafes. The porter at your hotel might notice from whom you received mail. The maid who cleaned your room might be collecting the trash for whoever slipped her a few extra francs.

The writer Somerset Maugham was a British spy in Switzerland. His cover was he was the writer Somerset Maugham.

In February of 1915, the British fleet sailed through the Dardanelles and attacked Turkey, the seat of the Ottoman Empire. A month later, they were still fighting. This was not going to end any time soon.

Yes, Serbs kill the Austrian archduke, and in no time, the British attack Turkey.

Tony left Paris around March of 1915. He went to Basel, on the Rhine, just over the French border and near the German border. It is in the German-speaking part of Switzerland; Tony spoke German. If he took the train, he had to go through Mulhouse, which was then part of Germany, and he couldn't do that. Somehow, he made his way to Basel. He never said how.

In the course of conversation with a man in Basel, Tony mentioned that he had performed with the philharmonic in Ljubljana. This man had heard them perform, and was so delighted to meet a musician from the philharmonic that he put Tony up in a hotel.

Tony said, "They got immigration territory for foreigners in Switzerland. It's just a place you can stay as long as you can pay your way. What you call, transcontinental train goes through, in the depot. It's international. You can stay there as long as you want to. Nobody bother you or touch you. Paper, no paper, passport, no passport. He put me up in hotel for two weeks in Basel. Paid every cent, after I told him that I was playing in that orchestra when he was visiting in Austria. He was so surprised."

I thought this was strange, that this man would pay Tony's expenses just because he was a musician in the philharmonic. Then I remembered how revered concert musicians were in Austria back then. Then I remembered what a neighbor from Los Angeles told me about people giving wealthy celebrities free this and free that.

I don't know whether it was in Zurich or Paris or Basel that Tony met the beautiful Swiss opera singer who helped him. She gave him money when he couldn't find work. He would repay her.

Somebody with an unpronounceable name (which I couldn't spell) gave him a ticket to Thessaloniki, Greece. Tony said, "A young fellow come to me say, 'Don't go there. That's the worst part.' He say, 'Better join the French army, far better.' I couldn't stay in Switzerland any more because I didn't have passport. That was fifteen hundred francs. Then I'd be short."

I haven't been able to figure out what was going on in Switzerland that, all of a sudden, he needed a passport. He didn't need a passport to enter the United States.

"Joe send me the ticket to come to the United States," Tony said. Joe was his brother. The first time Joe sent him a ticket, he sent it back. The second time Joe sent him a ticket, he sent it back. He kept this one.

When asked why he left, Tony said Germans were threatening him.

History bumped into him and sent him down a new path.

He had to take the train back to Paris. This was scary. After nine months of war, the French police had no patience for anyone they suspected shouldn't be there. Once in Paris, Tony boarded another train. The journey took around twelve hours. I imagine his heart was in his throat every time a conductor made his rounds. He arrived in Bordeaux around ten o'clock the next morning.

Tony met a man who was in the business of helping people flee Europe. He told Tony about two Americans he helped. "They were turned back from Austria because Austria chased all the foreigners out, you see, because they were American citizens." They went to Paris, and the French police threw them in jail. It didn't matter that we were not in the war; they were foreigners and nobody wanted them. The man told Tony, "They were so frightened and scared." Eventually he got them on a ship home.

Knowing that Tony's situation was even more precarious, he asked, "How did you manage to come across France by yourself?"

"It's a long story," Tony replied.

TONY WAITS THREE DAYS in Bordeaux, three long days avoiding the scrutiny of overwrought French policemen. At last, the day of departure arrives. Tony masses with the crowd of 2,128 passengers eager to board the *Rochambeau* and escape the war. She is a fairly new ship. Before the war, she departed from Le Havre on the English Channel. It is too close to Germany, too close to the war. Bordeaux is safer, the farthest French port from Germany. It is a noisy scene as more than two thousand passengers jostle to board the massive ship, a cacophony of people talking, children crying, workmen shouting, the clang and bang of cargo being loaded. Tony reaches the boarding point. The ship's doctor asks his name. The doctor writes down what he hears through the noise. He writes "Antoine Leskover" on the ship manifest. He asks more questions, writing each answer on the manifest, which is on a form mandated by the United States government. Since this is a French ship leaving from a French port, the doctor is French. Tony speaks enough French to understand the questions.

"How old are you?" the doctor asks.

"Twenty-seven," says Tony.

"Are you married?"

"No."

"Can you read?"

"Yes."

"Can you write?"

"Yes."

"What is your occupation?"

"Musician. I play the bassoon."

He looks Tony over. He writes eyes gray, hair chestnut, five feet eight inches tall (he was more like five feet eleven).

"What is your last permanent address?"

"Paris."

"What is the address of your nearest relative in France?"

"I have no family in France."

"What is your nationality?"

"Servian."

"How much money do you have?"

"One hundred and fifty francs." That was around thirty dollars.

LE ROCHAMBEAU, *the ship on which Tony left Bordeaux in 1915.*
(This is the ship but not at Bordeaux)
Wiki Commons

Tony boards the ship and goes down into steerage. Other passengers near him are from France, Switzerland, Belgium, Russia, Spain.

The *Rochambeau* leaves Bordeaux on May 2, 1915.

Tony was faithful about practicing the bassoon. He was a serious musician, and serious musicians practice regularly. He did this until the day he died. He no doubt did so on board ship. I wonder if other musicians on board heard each other practicing and joined together to perform for their fellow steerage passengers.

About the ship he said, "Two stacks, half freight, half passengers. Steam boat."

"How long did it take to get across?"

"Eleven days. Supposed to be six days or seven days, something like that, but we have to go on account of what you call, submarine, they change the course. They change the course south. 1915. War was declared in 1914. August."

"Were you concerned about being sunk by the submarines?"

"Oh yes."

German U-boat captains were firing on and sinking any enemy ship they found, passenger ships, merchant ships, military ships, all ships. The *Rochambeau* was a French-flagged ship.

"What kind of passengers were on board?"

"Quite a few Americans, yes, yes. Neutral countries people. I think Italian. I know there were quite a few Americans on that boat. For three days we were in the life preservers, yes. In the middle of the ocean, there was something floating on the top of the water. What do you call, caution. Everybody on board put on the life preservers. We thought it was the periscope of the submarine. It was a dead horse, bloated. They were transporting the horses from America to Europe."

"They sunk the ship?"

"Well, it could be sunk the ship or the horse died and they threw it overboard. And then one propeller broke off in the middle of the ocean. That's the reason it take that much longer too. They change the course. That wasn't so easy."

Five days after the *Rochambeau* left Bordeaux and was still at sea, a German U-boat captain fired torpedoes at the British passenger liner *Lusitania* and sank her. That could be why the ship's captain changed course.

Tony had about thirty dollars in French francs in his pocket when he boarded the ship. He thought he'd improve that by gambling, informal gambling. That didn't work out well, he lost, but he wasn't worried. He had forty dollars in a bank in New York. Whether that was thanks to his brother, Joe, or the beautiful Swiss opera singer, I don't know.

"You landed at New York?"

"New York."

"You had to go through Ellis Island?"

"Yes."

"Did you know any English?"

"Yes. I didn't speak, I understand. I spoke German."

The *Rochambeau* docked at Lower Manhattan on May 12, 1915. The first and second class passengers, unless they were ill, disembarked and went on their way into the city. Since Tony traveled in steerage, he had to board the ferry to Ellis Island. Once off the ferry, he went through a quick medical inspection, about six seconds, and kept going with the mass of steerage passengers up the stairs to the great hall.

As he waited, he struck up a conversation with a Jewish Russian tailor. The tailor told Tony that he had been sent back before because he didn't have enough money. He said a person entering the country had to have at least twenty dollars. The tailor said two times before, he didn't have enough and couldn't enter the country and had to take the next ship home. (Immigrants had to purchase round-trip tickets.) He told Tony that this time he had plenty of money—four hundred dollars.

Ellis Island Immigrant Landing Station, February 24, 1905.
A. Coeffler, Library of Congress, Wiki Commons

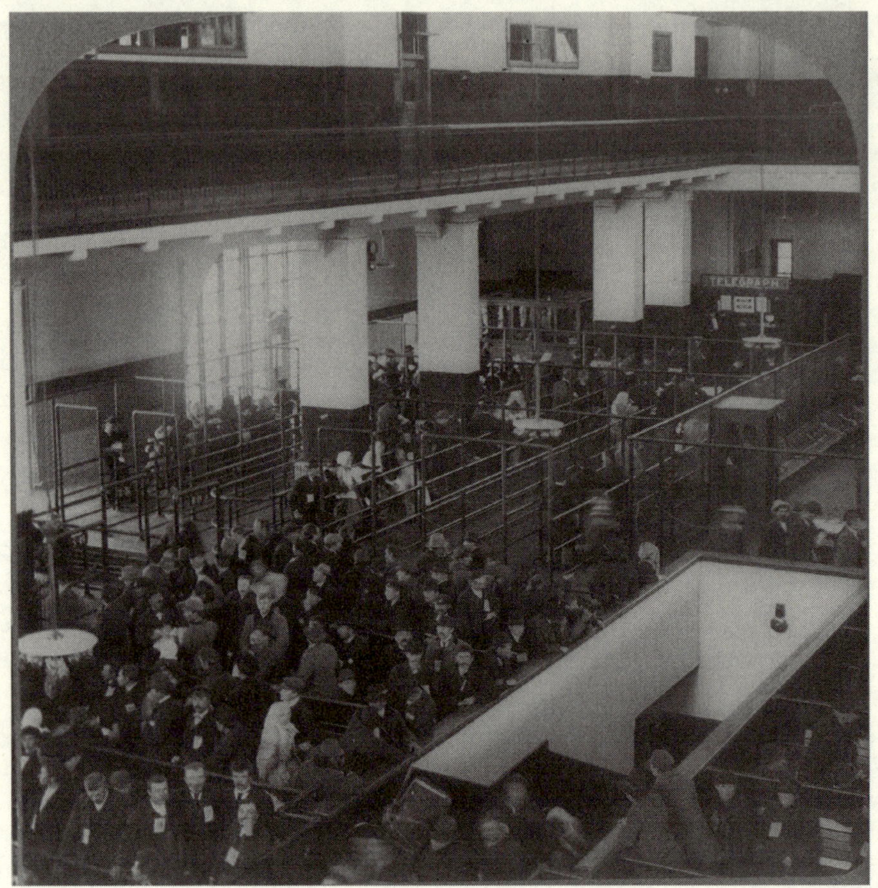

Ellis Island Grand Hall, 1904.
Underwood & Underwood, Library of Congress, Wiki Commons

Tony had five francs in his pocket, about one dollar.

The immigration officer summoned the Russian tailor. The tailor approached the counter. The immigration officer asked him a couple of questions and then asked, "How much money do you have?"

"Four hundred dollars."

"Show it."

He showed him the money. The immigration officer waved him on.

The immigration officer summoned Tony. Tony walked up to the counter. When the immigration officer realized that Tony did not speak English, he summoned a translator.

The immigration officer asked, "How old are you?"

"Twenty-seven."
"Where are you going?"
"New York."
"Who are you going to see?"
"My brother, Jožef Leskovar."
"How much money do you have?"
"Twenty dollars."
Tony held his suitcase in one hand and the bassoon case in the other. As he started to put them down, the immigration officer waved him on.
Welcome to America.

PART TWO

KAROLINA AND JOE

7

Novo mesto

During the second decade of the rule of Emperor Franz Josef, in the far southern reaches of the vast Austro-Hungarian Empire, in the charming alpine foothills of the Duchy of Carniola, near the town of Novo mesto, a baby girl was born. The year was 1869.

The priest opened the huge leather-bound church book, picked up his pen, dipped it in ink, and wrote the particulars of her birth and baptism. He wrote her mother's name, but he left her father's name blank. An earlier Austrian emperor had decreed that, unless the father would attest to paternity, no father's name could be recorded.

As I looked through those nineteenth-century church books, I was shocked to see so many entries for children with no father's name. The priest wrote for many of those: "Mother maid in the house." Lest there be any ambiguity, there was a column for "born in marriage" and "born outside of marriage." It was said that more children were born outside of marriage than in marriage in the alpine villages of Austria back then. Everyone to whom I mentioned this seemed well aware of the situation and offered a variety of explanations, all of which I attribute to conjecture: the man of the house took advantage of the help, he believed it was within his purview to do so; it was the woman's fault, the women seduced the men (and he would know this how?); they were too poor to get married (that doesn't explain it).

The philosophy student and later Carmelite nun Edith Stein wrote about her experience as a nurse in Austria during the First World War. Her classmates at the university had left to join the army. She wanted to do her part, so she volunteered to be a nurse. She was German, but the German army had plenty of nurses and asked if she would be willing to go to Austria and work in a lazaretto, which is a hospital for patients with infectious disease. She said yes. She wanted to help in any way she could.

Many doctors saw having their way with the nurses as a perk of the job, an entitlement. This was so rampant at the time in that part of the world, and so commonly known to be so, that one of the administrators at the university, knowing her father had died, felt obliged to step in and counsel Edith as a father. He advised her not to become a nurse at a lazaretto, lest it ruin her reputation. She appreciated his concern but was undaunted and undeterred. When one of the doctors did make inappropriate advances, she told him that such behavior would not be tolerated, and he was to speak to her as a lady or not speak to her at all. She never had a problem again.

As for the maid in our story, her name was Neža Stangel (stang-gul), but so as not to confuse her with the Neža in Part One of this book, I'll call her by the English equivalent, which is Agnes. Being with child meant Agnes could no longer work as a maid in the house. She went home to live with her mother. Her father had already passed away.

It was on All Saints Day, November 1, 1869, that Agnes gave birth to her baby, a daughter she named Karolina, which means little Karla. The priest baptized her the next day. He wrote in the church book that her godparents were a farmer and a peasant girl.

That baby was my great-grandmother Karolina Stangel.

Though the priest did not write her father's name in the church book, since he was prohibited by law from doing so, her mother, Agnes, said who he was. She, or someone she told, told Karolina, and Karolina told her daughters, who told my dad, who wrote it down and told me.

She said her father's name was Baron Carl von Belin. (She pronounced it Bay-lin. Whether Carl was spelled with a K or a C, I don't know.)

It is odd that Karolina's father's name was passed down in my family, but not her mother's name. I learned her mother's name from the church book.

Who was this Baron Carl von Belin? Was he really a baron? I was skeptical.

When I asked a Viennese archivist about him, he said he'd heard this many times and seemed to disregard the story out of hand.

I dug for clues.

"I know nothing about this man," came the response when I asked the archivist in Novo mesto about Karolina's father. Her hometown seemed the logical place to start, but her mother could have worked anywhere as a maid in the house. It was an oft-repeated story—the man of the house and the maid, the lord of the manor and the maid, and a baby. Were these stories handed down precisely as first told, or was it more like the telephone game where along the way family members subconsciously inserted their own imaginations and jumped to conclusions. Who was the baby's father? Was he assumed to be the man of the house, or was he the man of the house? Was he a son? An uncle? A visitor? Another servant? Was the liaison consensual mutual attraction or something awful? Was it a case of the master of the house feeling neglected and a naive young maid gives a sympathetic ear and one thing leads to another? Was it an older, predatory man taking advantage of hero worship from a young woman?

A couple named Franz and Maria Stangel, who lived in Novo mesto, had a baby girl they named Maria. She was a year older than Karolina. Maria was baptized by Monsignor Anton Belin. Could he have been a relative of Carl—a brother, an uncle, a cousin?

Our Stangels lived at Rakovnik 5, in Smihel, a tiny hamlet outside Novo mesto, in the Duchy of Carniola (today the Dolenjska region of Slovenia), a place that looked like it was plucked from a fairy tale. Though this was a Slovenian area of Austria, Stangel is a German surname, originally from Bavaria. Karolina's grandmother was a Zimmerman, which is also German. There was a landlocked island of ethnic Germans in that part of Carniola called Gottschee. Karolina's grandfather Georg Stangel was born in 1803 in the same house in Smihel where Karolina was born. Sometime before Georg Stangel was born, his ancestors no doubt drifted over to Novo mesto from the German enclave of Gottschee, meaning they were either ethnic German or a mix of German and Slovenian. Karolina always called her hometown by its Slovenian name, Novo mesto, never by its German name, Rudolfswerth. If they were ethnic Germans, they were Slovenized ethnic Germans.

As I searched for the elusive Baron von Belin, I discovered that Belin is not a German surname, nor is it a Slovenian surname. Grandma said we had "a drop of French" from a soldier in Napoleon's army. And there I found it. Belin is a French name.

Just to be thorough here, the first opera written in Slovenian, in the eighteenth century, was called *Belin*, after the Slavic god; however, I found no evidence of Belin being used as a Slovenian surname.

But how would Agnes Stangel, a Slovenian-Austrian peasant girl, meet a French nobleman?

First I must mention that Austria of the nineteenth century was much larger than the country we know as Austria today, considerably larger. The Austria of Karolina's time evolved from the Holy Roman Empire and had been governed by the House of Habsburg for centuries. The Austro-Hungarian Empire extended from way past Prague in the north, all the way south to Croatia, encompassing under her mantle ethnic Croats, Czechs (Bohemians), Germans, Hungarians, Italians, Magyars, Poles, Slovaks, and more, including my ancestors, who were Slovenian. It was the polyglot of polyglots. Though German was the language of Austria, the people of each of those ethnic groups spoke their own language and many people spoke several languages. The Slovenians spoke Slovenian and German. In the Duchy of Carniola where Karolina lived, towns had an official German name and a Slovenian name. During most of the nineteenth century, when the parish priest wrote the details of a baby's birth and baptism in the church book, he wrote in German using the Gothic alphabet. By the time Karolina was born in 1869, some priests in Carniola wrote those details in Slovenian, which uses the Latin alphabet, a sign the Old World was changing.

Centuries earlier, the Duchy of Carniola had been heavily fortified to protect against repeated attacks from the south by the Ottoman Turks. Long after the Turks tired of harassing Austria, Napoleon decided he needed to take over that part of the world, and for a time, the Duchy of Carniola, where Karolina's story begins, was under French rule. French troops occupied Carniola beginning in 1797. French rule under Napoleon was formalized in 1809.

We might say it was once again ruled by the French in that Charlemagne, King of the Franks, conquered the area centuries earlier, and it became part of the Holy Roman Empire, not to be confused with ancient Rome, but I digress, which is easy to do when diving into European history.

Under Napoleon, the Slovenian language was taught in school, and Slovenian was used as the official language. I wonder if the French motivation for doing this was more to break ties with German-speaking Austria than a nod to Slovenian nationalism.

It is interesting that the Slovenians kept their language, as did my Welsh kin, but my Irish kin of the same generation did not. My Irish grandfather spoke English and only a smattering of Gaelic. My Slovenian grandfather spoke Slovenian, it was his first language. Even my Slovenian grandma who was born in the United States grew up speaking Slovenian. The Slovenians and the ruling family of Austria shared the same religion, Roman Catholicism. The British and Irish did not share the same religion. The Irish suffered persecution because of that. Part of the persecution was the British stamping out their language, Gaelic. The previously pagan Slovenians embraced Catholicism in the seventh and eighth centuries.

We return now to the nineteenth century and our drop of French. Once Napoleon was dealt with for the second time, this time decisively at Waterloo in

1815, the French "intermezzo" was over, and the Duchy of Carniola returned to Austrian rule. Many a French soldier remained in Carniola, and why not, it was a lovely place, or they had fallen in love with charming Slovenian girls and had already married. Some settled in the duchy's principal city, Ljubljana (Laibach in German). At least one of those Frenchmen was named Belin. His son Anton Belin was born in Ljubljana in 1804. Anton grew up to become a Catholic priest. The bishop sent him to Novo mesto, and while there, he baptized Maria Stangel, a year before my great-grandmother Karolina Stangel was born. He wrote the details of her birth in Slovenian, not German.

The name Carl von Belin is German for the French name Charles de Belin. I found a Charles de Belin, a Frenchman living in England around the same time; however, I'm sure he is not our Carl. The name Belin goes back to before Eleanor of Aquitaine. She was born around 1121 at Chateau de Belin, near Bordeaux, in the Aquitaine region of France. Eleanor of Aquitaine had the unique distinction of having been married to the King of France and later the King of England. Several of her sons became kings. A formidable woman indeed.

BELIN WAS CERTAINLY A NOBLE NAME in France. There is a book about the Lords of Belin; however, that does not necessarily mean that all those named Belin were of noble birth. When the French started to assume fixed surnames around 1000AD, some used place names. People who lived around the castle could have assumed Belin as their surname.

As for the Belin who settled in Ljubljana, the nobiliary particle "von" did not necessarily mean of noble birth. The emperor ennobled industrialists, entrepreneurs, military heroes. Such was the case of Baron von Trapp of *Sound of Music* fame. His father was made a baron by the emperor and the title passed down to his son. And in this predominantly Catholic country, we know of famous Jews whose family name was ennobled by the emperor: the economist Ludwig von Mises to name one.

Hearing about Baron Carl von Belin, I always wondered if it were something someone wanted to be true. *Your father lives far away in a castle, dear. He is a baron.* But if a woman in such a situation were to invent a father for her child, why not invent a deceased husband?

Karolina's mother, Agnes, never did marry. She was twenty-five when Karolina was born and died seven years later. Agnes' mother was almost forty-four years old when Agnes was born, which made her seventy-six when Agnes died. She sent Karolina to live with her aunt. I'm told the baron paid Karolina's aunt to take care of her.

Late one night Karolina's aunt woke her up and told her to go to the miller's to get flour. Off went the tiny child in the dead of night without a lantern, through the forest, all alone. Fortunately, it was a clear moonlit night. She arrived at the miller's and woke him up with the order from her aunt. He was aghast. He took her home and gave the aunt a tongue lashing for sending a small child out in the dead of night, what with wolves and other perils lurking in the dark. This makes me wonder if the aunt were off her head to do such a thing.

Karolina's name was entered in the book of "Children in Need of Care." The neighbor Franc Jakse became her guardian.

Children were required to attend grade school for four, five, or six years; I found all those numbers in various sources. This began in the eighteenth century by order of Empress Maria Theresa. Apparently this did not apply to a little girl living in the outskirts of Novo mesto, or else she had inept teachers, for Karolina did not learn to write. This was not unusual.

When she turned twelve, it was time for her to go to work.

8

VIENNA

THE YEAR WAS 1881. The train did not yet go to Novo mesto. Karolina had to travel by horse-drawn coach or wagon to board the train. She was twelve years old. She had probably never left her village before this. She had never seen a locomotive, a massive machine, moving mysteriously under its own terrific power, not by oxen, not by horses. The prospect of boarding this enormous mechanized beast had to be terrifying or exciting. From all I know about Karolina, it was exciting, very exciting.

There she sat on the train, a scarf tied snugly under her little chin, a small satchel in hand containing a change of clothes and a nightgown. I imagine her eyes full of wonderment, looking out the window as mountains and farms and villages swept by, hearing the rhythmic clack, clack, clack of the mechanism turning the wheels as the train zipped along. Hours pass. Now the train pulls into an enormous train station and stops. This is her destination. Her journey had been one not only of miles but a giant leap across time.

Little peasant girl Karolina Stangel stepped off that train and walked out of the station into the Imperial City of Vienna. Vienna was not merely the capital of a country, Vienna was the capital of an empire, the vast Austro-Hungarian Empire. Anyone entering the city sensed her grandeur. I can't imagine what was going through this little girl's mind, this child from a tiny hamlet in the alpine foothills, seeing these beautiful, massive stone buildings and churches and statues, people wearing magnificent clothes, riding in magnificent carriages, and women wearing enormous, elegant hats.

Vienna was the picture of a beautiful woman in her prime.

And one in love with music. The Viennese were a people who loved music, who enjoyed good wine and good food, the good life. The Austrians,

63

the Viennese, so loved music that it was in their speech, a softer more lyrical German rather than the gruff, guttural-sounding language spoken to the north in Germany. As one Austrian man said to me, "Ah, the Viennese, they sing when they speak."

Coffeehouses abounded where a Viennese could sip a *mokka* (a slow espresso) while reading newspapers from across the world and discussing those events with his or her friends. Good conversation was a favorite pastime. As for the local paper, there was the theater to read about and the goings-on in Parliament and business. If a Viennese was not discussing the opera, someone within earshot was.

"Making music, dancing, the theater, conversation, proper and urbane deportment, these were cultivated here as particular arts," wrote the Viennese author Stefan Zweig, who was born around the time Karolina arrived.

When I think of Vienna, which I've been fortunate to visit, in my mind's eye I see swirling couples dancing the Viennese waltz. Music and Vienna are inseparable.

Street scene early 1900s, Vienna.
"Dancing over the edge: Vienna 1914," Bethany Bell, BBC News

Coffeehouse, early 1900s, Vienna.
"Dancing over the edge: Vienna 1914," Bethany Bell, BBC News

The well-dressed Viennese promenaded and attended operettas, the plots of which often playfully depicted a clandestine romantic liaison between a servant girl and the man of the house.

Paintings of Viennese homes of this period indicate that the Viennese favored happy colors.

It was a time of political change. Trade unions were legalized. Laws insuring workers against accident and sickness were enacted. Sunday became a day off, except for kitchen maids. Everybody still had to eat.

The railroad was expanding rapidly. Infant mortality was dropping.

Karolina, this impressionable young girl with no parents around, was living in a city where prostitutes were omnipresent on the streets. A prostitute had to obtain a license from the police, who in turn gave her a certificate documenting her profession. She set her own prices. She underwent a medical exam twice a week. Should a man refuse to pay, that was too bad. The law would do nothing for her. Should she steal a man's money or pocket watch, he would be too embarrassed to go to the police. Though her profession was officially acknowledged, it was officially frowned upon.

Specialists in venereal disease advertised openly.

For a young girl to ride a bicycle was a scandal.

How do I know that Karolina arrived with a scarf tied under her chin? Because she was too poor to afford a hat. Women in all of the western world in the nineteenth century wore hats or head scarves when outside. They wouldn't be seen in public without something covering their heads. Some Viennese women still wore veils of sheer silk covering their faces. Men wore hats too, but removed them once inside. Apart from a few proscribed exceptions, one being train stations, it was not proper for a man to wear a hat inside. A lady did not have to remove her hat or scarf inside. A Viennese gentleman always doffed his hat to a lady.

In this predominantly Catholic country, Jews, Muslims, and Protestants now practiced their faiths freely. On the streets of Vienna, Karolina might have seen a Coptic priest, a Muslim wearing a red fez, or a Carpathian peasant wearing a white fur hat.

Austrian military men were much in evidence, though with more of a dashing than policing demeanor. No matter how aristocratic those army officers looked, they might not have begun life that way. The Austrian army of the late nineteenth century was a meritocracy in which a talented peasant boy from Galicia could rise to become the head of counter-intelligence. Indeed, the army officer corps was replete with self-made men from the provinces. They were an ethnically diverse lot.

A Viennese doctor was trying to cure his patients of depression by giving them cocaine. His name was Sigmund Freud. Though little Karolina took the train all the way to Vienna, he was deathly afraid of it and wouldn't ride on it.

A charming politesse governed social and business interactions. This was not restricted to courtiers and cavaliers. "I lay myself at the gracious lady's feet" was a form of greeting not only to a duchess, but also to the wife of a tradesman. Even one hundred years later, my Austrian boss always prefaced giving me an assignment with "Christy, would you be so kind as to . . ." Profuse graciousness was in their DNA.

Couple this with the new technology—the telephone. By 1876, telephones were in use across the world though not yet widely. Only three towns in Austria had the telephone in 1883, while seventy-five towns in Britain had it. But the Austrians were catching up, especially after the first International Electrical Exhibition in Vienna in 1883, which spurred interest and use. At the beginning, phone calls were restricted to a few minutes. Frederic Morton, in his book *A Nervous Splendor*, gave us half an interchange between two fraulein operators:

The party whom I have the honor to serve at this end of the wire, University Professor Dr. Dr. Alois Zechner, would like to convey to you and your party a hand kiss for the courtesy of awaiting completion of this connection. Fraulein Operator, if it is still convenient for his Excellency the Privy Councillor Baron von Wieck to entertain the connection, Herr Professor Dr. Dr. would be only too deeply pleased . . .

All this before Herr Doctor Doctor and the baron began their pro forma greetings, eating up even more of the allotted minutes before they began the purpose of the call, and I'm guessing that it takes longer to say all that in German than in English.

Perhaps the Austrians were slower to adopt the telephone because they thought, like the American Clarence Day (the protagonist of the book *Life with Father*), that "messenger boys were quite enough of a nuisance, suddenly appearing at the door and expecting an answer. But they came only a few times a year, and a telephone might ring every week."

This reminds me of a story Mark Twain told of an altercation that put him in the hands of the Austrian police (he lived in Vienna in 1898). After telling them a whopper, that he "belonged to the same family as the Prince of Wales" (he meant the human race), the police profusely apologized, begged forgiveness (I picture obsequious bowing), and promised to hang the offending officer.

Lethal dueling was still practiced with swords or pistols. Honor was a deadly serious matter. According to Mark Twain, this was in stark contrast to dueling in France, where it was more symbolic than lethal, in other words, saner. He said in France the wounded duelist might have to circle the scratch with a pen in order to find it to show the doctor. Twain was horrified at dueling as practiced in Vienna. They shot to kill.

From Epiphany, the twelfth day of Christmas commemorating when the Three Wise Men arrived, until the penance of Lent began on Ash Wednesday, it was *Fasching* in Vienna, elsewhere called Mardi Gras or Carnival, which comes from the Latin *carne vale*, meaning "bye bye meat." Fasching was the season for balls, masquerade balls, a time of "strenuous merrymaking." Physicians had their own ball, policemen had their own ball, as did chimney sweeps, bakers, pharmacists, lawyers, confectioners, coffee brewers, and the list goes on. Even the inmates of the lunatics' asylum had their own ball. At the bankers' ball; a woman might arrive dressed as an elegant receipt. A lawyer might arrive at his ball as a dapper deposition. I suppose Karolina attended a servants' ball, perhaps she went dressed as a spoon. The revelers waltzed until the wee hours, such merriment, who can't be happy within earshot of a waltz, especially a Strauss waltz. Then as dawn approached, they went out for a bit of goulash. But once Ash Wednesday arrived, no balls, no waltzing, no goulash. To Mass they went, ashes on the forehead, and no more revelry and no more meat until Easter.

One notable absent from the waltzing was the Waltz King himself. Johann Strauss did not dance.

Fasching was ruined, absolutely ruined, in 1889 when an emotional earthquake struck the city, indeed, all of the Empire: the beloved Crown Prince Rudolf was dead—by suicide. Vienna descended into mourning. He was with his mistress who was also dead. For some insane reason the two of them agreed to this. Officially, he was alone.

Age was respected, youth was suspect. Gray emerging along the temples was a sign of dignity. Young marriages were frowned upon by the Viennese bourgeoisie, or I should say, the prospect of a young groom, for no father "would have entrusted his daughter to a young man of twenty-two."

Worry abounded when Gustav Mahler was appointed director of the Imperial Opera. He was only thirty-eight years old.

Where other European powers aggressively colonized faraway lands, Austria only dabbled in colonizing. She assumed the Nicobar Islands a century earlier, thinking the Danes had left, but kept the islands only five years. Mexico requested an emperor in 1864, thinking that would stabilize the country. The Habsburgs provided one. That did not end well. He was assassinated.

Over the centuries, the contiguous borders of Austria grew and shrank. The Kingdom of Lombardy became part of Austria for a time. Tired of being harassed by the Venetians, the people of Trieste knocked at the door and asked to become part of the empire (1382). The emperor welcomed them. This gave Austria another route to the sea. Trieste was an open city where the Italians spoke Italian, the Slovenians spoke Slovenian, and the Croatians spoke Croatian. Yes, the Austrians were happy to stay home, drink coffee, discuss world events, eat Sachertorte, and waltz to Strauss. The Germans, the British, the Belgians, the Dutch, the French could go colonize faraway lands, if that's what they wanted to do. The Austrians would read about these foreign adventures in the newspapers, while not taking part, and discuss them with friends in the comfort of their coffeehouses.

Any Viennese might catch sight of Emperor Franz Josef as he traveled the same route at the same time every day from his imperial residence in the Hofburg to Schonbrunn Palace. Even though a deranged Hungarian tailor attacked him with a knife in 1853, the emperor moved about the city without a security detail, accompanied only by his adjutant, no entourage, no armed soldiers protecting him, so confident was he in his city, his country, his subjects.

Karolina thought Emperor Franz Josef was wonderful, absolutely wonderful. She wasn't alone. There persisted in Austria a "deep-seated veneration" for Emperor Franz Josef. The Habsburgs had ruled Austria since 1273, while over the centuries in France, the House of Capet came and went, and the House of Valois, the House of Lancaster, the Bourbons, Bonaparte, the House of Orleans. In England, the Plantagenets came and went, and the House of Lancaster, the House of York, the Tudors, the Stuarts, Cromwell, and on and on. In Austria, it was the House of Habsburg; they ruled for centuries, as permanent and immutable as the Alps, the royal glue that held the disparate, multi-lingual empire together. Even when there was no direct male heir back in the eighteenth century, the emperor decreed that his eldest daughter could rule, and she did, and the Habsburg bloodline continued. As sure as the sun rose and set, a Habsburg ruled Austria.

"It was simply assumed that the Habsburg Empire had a divinely ordained role to fulfill," wrote the historian William Johnston.

Why would it ever change?

Early in his reign, Emperor Franz Josef married his first cousin Elisabeth, said to be one of the most beautiful women in Europe. It was love at first sight on his part. Even when she was in her fifties, she was still the beauty of Europe.

The city had been surrounded by massive stone walls, ramparts, to protect against attack. The Ottoman Turks launched many attacks on Austria over the centuries. The last time they laid siege to Vienna was in 1683. The Turks were at the gates, no one could get in or out, the people were starving, the Turks were tunneling under the city walls; all was desperate until on September 11, 1683, King John of Poland arrived, "a date that ought to be among the most famous in all of history," wrote Hilaire Belloc in 1938. In battle the next day, the Poles, the Austrians, and the Germans together stopped the Ottoman Turks and threw them back, never to attack Vienna again. That was a long time ago by the time the young Franz Josef ascended the throne. He concluded that the threat from the Turks was no more; the walls surrounding the city were no longer needed. He ordered the walls torn down, and the stones dumped into the old moat. He sold much of the land and used that money to build the Ringstrasse, the grand boulevard encircling Vienna today. On that grand boulevard, he built the opera house, and the Rathaus (townhall), and the Parliament, and the university, and the art museum. The Danish architect of the Parliament hoped that the classical lines of the building "would produce with irresistible force an edifying and idealizing effect on the representatives of the people." The Parliament faced the royal family's residence, the Hofburg, which means "court fortress." The two were positioned this way to be a constant reminder to each of the other.

Only two years before Karolina was born, Austria became a constitutional monarchy, the dual monarchy of Austria-Hungary was established, and freedom of religion was granted.

Indeed, Vienna was entering the modern age; she was a city full of promise—happy, hopeful, grand, swelling to further greatness. This was the new Vienna; her walls gone, she was now a city quite literally looking out to the world, and much of the world was coming to her. This building boom was still going on in 1881. There was work for craftsmen. Business opportunities abounded. People from all parts of the empire were flocking to Vienna amid all this growth and excitement. One of them was twelve-year-old Karolina Stangel. She went to Vienna to work as a kitchen maid.

Being a kitchen maid was probably as good an arrangement as could be expected for a little girl in Karolina's situation. I'm told she worked for a wealthy family in Vienna, though I don't know their name. I wondered how grand a house this could have been, where she worked and lived. It wasn't only the owners of grand estates who employed servants. The bourgeoisie employed servants as well. I wondered how common it was to have more than a cook in the kitchen. Since Karolina was a kitchen maid, that meant there was more than a cook, she was part of the cook's staff, or she was the cook's staff. Not able to find such records for Vienna, I searched census records here in the United States, looking at the homes of moneyed men to see how many live-in servants they employed. I looked up the homes of several wealthy Americans who will come into our story later. One of them employed a Chinese cook. I found this to be the case for other wealthy families, just one cook in the kitchen. I went up a notch in my search as far as wealth, way, way up, and I found a household that employed more than one cook in the kitchen—the house of Morgan—J.P. Morgan. He employed two cooks. Though wildly rich, he lived in a townhouse on Madison Avenue, not the grand mansion one might expect. John

D. Rockefeller did live in a mansion. He also employed two cooks, one Irish, one American, as well as an Irish butler and several Irish maids. The closest I found geographically were households in Britain. Lord Lothian, who would assist Lloyd George at the Paris Peace Conference in 1919, employed a cook, a kitchen maid, and a scullery maid. Based on this anecdotal bit of research, and in other countries to boot, I suspect that this was no bourgeoisie home, but a sizable home, where our little Karolina was sent to work. The cook was her cousin.

Her duties probably included getting up early, before everybody else, to light the fire for the stove, and put on the kettle, and lay breakfast for the other servants. There was a tradition of hunting in Austria. They ate what they hunted—pheasant, ducks, geese. Fowl came to the kitchen feathers and all. It fell to the kitchen maid to pluck it, and to peel and cut the vegetables, and to scrub the kitchen, all the menial tasks necessary to feed a household in the nineteenth century. Her tools were knives and whisks and spoons, nothing automated. If the master or mistress of the house wanted orange juice, it fell to her to juice the oranges. The midday meal was the family's main meal.

The formal afternoon snack consisted of coffee and cake or pastries. Legend has it that after the siege of Vienna in 1683, as the retreating Turks fled, they dropped a few things. The Austrians collected what they dropped and found bags full of coffee berries. Soon coffeehouses became a fixture of Viennese life. My Slovenian grandma made coffee the Turkish way: boiling the coffee grounds in water.

A popular beverage Karolina might have prepared was Viennese hot chocolate, which was made with cream and egg yolks, a drinkable chocolate custard.

She learned to be an excellent cook.

But she didn't only work in the kitchen. One of the daughters of the family was crippled and confined to a wheelchair, and she was an artist. When she saw the cheerful, pretty, tiny kitchen maid, she asked that Karolina sit for her. Day after day, the girl had Karolina dress up in a variety of folk costumes, and she painted her portrait. She had Karolina's hair done up to suit the costume. One day the girl had Karolina dress as a Tyrolean peasant girl, wearing a blue pinafore and white blouse, her long hair tied in braids. Decades later when Karolina saw a tin of Swiss Miss hot chocolate, she said that girl looked exactly like one of the paintings.

So this Viennese family hires a kitchen maid from the hinterlands of the empire, from back of beyond as the Irish would say, but they do not cotton to her working in the kitchen all the time and waiting on them. Now if I were writing fiction, I might hint that something else was behind the family's being so good to Karolina, this gentle treatment, sitting to have her portrait painted much of the day rather than work serving them, perhaps a familial connection of which she had no knowledge, they didn't want other people to know, but they didn't want to have a relative wait on them.

But I am not writing fiction.

Since she learned to be an excellent cook while working for this family, we know that she did work in the kitchen. She didn't sit to have her portrait painted all day every day. Though the job of kitchen maid was the lowliest in the household, the job of cook was close to the top. If a kitchen maid could graduate to cook, and a good one, and apparently those were the only kind tolerated in Vienna, that would stand her in good stead for steady employment for the rest of her life.

That was all Karolina would one day tell her daughters about her years in Vienna—all she had to do was sit and have her portrait painted. She made it sound like a lark. No complaints about how hard the work was. No complaints about humble living quarters, which were no doubt nicer than the farmhouse near Novo mesto. No resentment toward her employer. No complaints about all that cooking and cleaning for the family. No complaints about anything. That tells us something about her. Actually, it tells us a lot about her. I guess I mention this because I read the opposite in a British cook's memoir, lots of complaining even though she didn't know how to cook and the family still kept her on and suffered through her ineptness.

I searched for firsthand accounts of maids in Austria in the nineteenth century, but I couldn't find any. Then it occurred to me, in that time period, they were probably all like Karolina, illiterate. They didn't know how to write. I did read memoirs of maids in early twentieth-century England, though the cultures were different and the time frame was later, when more labor-saving household tools were available. An Englishwoman named Edith Sellers, bemoaning the dearth of good cooks in England, wrote in 1895: "Most English women have just about as much idea of cooking as they have of flying." The solution she proposed: hire foreign cooks, in particular, those trained in Vienna. She said Viennese households held high standards for their kitchen staffs. No doubt Karolina received excellent training.

Those coveted cooks in Vienna were not necessarily native Viennese. Many were from other parts of the empire: Czechs from Bohemia, Poles from Silesia, Ruthenians from Galicia, Slovenians, like Karolina, from Carniola or Styria or Carinthia. Vienna became a melting pot of great recipes.

The only personal account I found about domestic help in Vienna around this time was from Mark Twain. His family employed two maids, a cook, and another part time maid. He thought their cook was a marvel. Any food that passed through her hands came out scrumptious. One of the maids, whom he also adored, he called Wuthering Heights. She was energetic, good-natured, efficient, and bossy. Karolina was energetic and good-natured, lively and cheerful. As for bossy, not at first, she was a young girl when she went into service, but as she grew into adulthood, based on what her future son-in-law told me, she became if not bossy, definitely take charge. You can't be a passive person and do what Karolina was about to do.

Yes, Karolina was anything but timid. Timid people don't wake up one day and say, I think I'll board an ocean liner, which I've never seen, and cross the ocean, which I've never seen, and go to America, where I'll be on my own and don't speak the language.

I will add fearless to her list of attributes.

The "Book of Children in Need of Care" in Novo mesto says that Karolina's guardian sent her money in 1891. Her guardian was the neighbor Franc Jakse. By this time she had worked in Vienna for ten years. She was twenty-one years old.

Franc Jakse's brother bought the Stangel's house after Karolina's grandmother died. Could the money have been split between Karolina (as far as I know she was her mother's only child) and her aunt and two uncles? But that was in 1888. The money was sent to Karolina in 1891. Why wait three years if the money was from the sale of the house?

Did the money come from a benefactor, and if so, whom?

One family member told me the money came from her father via her father's brother. Did the brother give the money to Mr. Jakse to give to Karolina?

Another family member told me the baron's brother gave Karolina the money under the condition that she relinquish any claim to his estate. The latter part cannot be true. Under the law, Karolina had no father. She had no claim on his estate.

I heard this from other families in that part of the world with similar situations: a child born out of wedlock, the father does not openly acknowledge the child but feels responsible and furtively channels money for support of the child through an intermediary. If the money Karolina received before she left for America came from her father, it was her dowry.

I never found Karolina on a passenger list, so I don't know between which ports she traveled. She agreed to help a woman with young children on the voyage. She could have been listed under their surname. As I perused those old lists from before Ellis Island opened in 1892, I was surprised to see how many people were traveling without baggage. I assume that meant checked baggage. All they brought was what they could carry, possibly just a change of clothes, one to wear, one to wash, and a nightshirt or nightgown.

Karolina traveled in steerage. She said the crossing was rough and many passengers became horribly seasick, but she didn't. One of the few things she brought with her was a bottle of Slivovitz, that powerful Slovenian plum brandy. One of the first class waiters befriended her, and they worked out a trade. She'd give him a shot of Slivovitz, and he'd smuggle down food for her from the first class dining room.

Of all places in these United States—New York, Chicago, Pittsburgh, Cleveland—why on earth did Karolina decide to go to Calumet, Michigan? I thought where my Welsh great-grandparents homesteaded in eastern Montana was back of beyond, but at least it was on the road to somewhere. Calumet was way, way, way back of back of beyond, on the way to no-where, out on the long narrow Keweenaw Peninsula, keep going and you fall into Lake Superior, a place that seemed an afterthought of God, a lonely finger sticking into Lake Superior pointing at Canada. At least the railroad went there. Calumet did have one very big thing going for it—copper. A community of Slovenians was growing in Calumet along with the mining.

And it was in Calumet that Karolina met Joe.

9

ČRNOMELJ

My great-grandfather Jožef Lozar was born on April 30, 1864, at Rožanec 9, in or near Črnomelj (Chur-nome-lee), in the Duchy of Carniola, about twenty miles south of where Karolina was born. He was baptized the next day.

Long, long ago, even before the Romans lived in these parts, who else but the Celts arrived, a Celtic tribe called the Carni; hence, the place came to be called Carniola, which comes from the Latin, because people writing history that survived back then wrote in Latin. The Celts, not letting the grass grow under their feet, moved on, or some marauding band pushed most of them out. Not all of them left. Some stayed. Much later, in the sixth century, a Slavic people called the Slovenians were on the move, moving west, and when they arrived in this part of the world (present-day Slovenia) they, liking the lay of the land, stayed there. After all, it was the sunny side of the Alps, lovely and fertile. The soil was rich for agriculture. It also turned out to be good for mining. Why not stay? So they did, and they are still there. They mixed with the vestiges of peoples who settled there long before them—the Illyrians, the Celts, the Romans. In the eighth century the Slovenians joined with neighboring Slavs and chose a Frankish merchant to be their king; he called himself King Samo. After King Samo died, the Avars came in and took over until Charlemagne, King of the Franks, defeated them. The area became part of the Holy Roman Empire, ruled by Charlemagne, and centuries later, ruled by the House of Habsburg. The Holy Roman Empire became known as Austria. In 1867, the Austro-Hungarian Empire came to be. An early emperor made Carniola a duchy, the Duchy of Carniola. The nobles spoke German and called it Krain. These southern duchies were particularly valuable to Austria in that they provided a buffer against the Ottoman Turks.

Črnomelj is in the southernmost part of Carniola, an area the Slovenians call Bela Krajina (kra-nee-a). It was a market town as far back as the
1200s. It was surrounded by stone walls and a dry moat to protect against
invasion. The drawbridge opened to the town square. By the time Jožef
was born, the walls were gone.

Though I never saw Jožef's house nor a picture of it, a typical farm in
Bela Krajina consisted of a house, a barn, and a shed all connected to each
other around an inner courtyard. When the door to the courtyard was
closed, the whole place was walled off. You might say, each farm was its
own fortress. It was the custom in Bela Krajina to divide the family farm
between all the children, making these farms tinier and tinier with each
generation to the point that providing for a family off the land became
difficult, if not impossible.

Jožef was the son of Jakob and Anna Lozar, nee Grahek. He had an
older brother named Jakob and three younger sisters—Maria, Anna, and
Marjeta. They were all born at home in the same house where their father
was born. Their tiny farm consisted of only half a hectare (1.2 acres) to
raise livestock and grow food for a family of seven. They were so dirt poor
they hardly had dirt. Dividing it would mean even less.

When Henry David Thoreau wrote, "The mass of men lead lives of quiet
desperation," he could have been talking about the Lozars. Jožef wasn't
content with such a life. He had dreams, and at that time "all dreamed of
America . . . it had leaped with such an ease to modern greatness."

One of the many peoples believed to have inhabited that part of the
world before the Slovenians were the Veneti, who were traveling merchants.
It would seem that long, long ago an ancestor of Jožef's was a Veneti, for
being a merchant was in his blood.

He was only a teenager, not even old enough to do his compulsory
military service, when he left.

Ship manifests in the nineteenth century can't be counted on for precise
spellings of names. The passenger saying his name and the person writing it
down might not have spoken the same language. The point of the passenger
manifest was to list everybody on board; the point was not to help future
generations find their ancestors. Many people didn't know how to spell.
Precise spelling on the manifest wasn't necessary. My great-grandfather
Jožef Lozar may have been the Josef Loser who sailed out of Antwerp in
the fall of 1880, aboard the *Zeeland* bound for New York, in which case

he was sixteen years old. Passenger lists from before Ellis Island opened (twelve years later) tell us little, but 1880 was around the time he arrived and his age is about right. The manifest said this man was German. The passenger manifest that listed my Welsh great-grandmother and her siblings said they were English, which obviously they were not. They were Welsh. Jožef spoke German. It was not unusual for people from Austria to be listed as German.

When the Austrian writer Stefan Zweig visited New York, he observed "how many possibilities this young country held for everyone willing to work." Joe was certainly willing to work. And Joe learned to read and write.

Armed with drive and pluck and a suitcase, Joe earned his keep as a peddler. He made his way across the country selling clothes out of a suitcase.

10

❧

CALUMET

WHEN MY GREAT-GRANDPA JOE LOZAR arrived on these shores, the Calumet and Hecla Mining Company produced half the copper in the United States. Many Slovenians were immigrating to Calumet, Michigan, to work in the mines. Joe joined them, though not to mine. He mined the miners. If only he'd have stuck to that plan.

The town of Calumet, originally called Red Jacket, today called Laurium, sits on the Keweenaw Peninsula, which extends from Michigan's Upper Peninsula. It is a puzzle as to why it is not part of Wisconsin, since that is the only state it actually borders. Did Wisconsin not want it? Did Michigan grab it when Wisconsin wasn't looking? As Michigan was in the throes of leaving territory status to become a state back in the 1830s, Michigan and Ohio bickered over their common border, which is nowhere near the Upper Peninsula. The piece of land they were fighting over included Toledo. Ohio had been a state for a long time and therefore had power in Congress to block Michigan's statehood until it got its way. Ohio got Toledo. As a consolation prize, Michigan got the Upper Peninsula. As for where Wisconsin was in all this, it was a case of the quick and the hungry. Michigan got to the statehood table first. It would be another ten years or so for Wisconsin. I've heard it said: Michigan and Ohio got in a fight and Wisconsin lost. It might have seemed a poor consolation prize for Michigan, losing Toledo, an important port on Lake Erie, to get the Upper Peninsula, a worthless piece of wilderness. But then copper and iron ore were discovered there in the 1840s. Copper was even discovered way up on the Keweenaw Peninsula, so Congress bought it from the Chippewa Indians. Even so, the copper just sat there in the ground, unmolested. Getting there to extract it was no easy feat. An attempt in 1844 almost proved fatal, what with navigating the rough seas of Lake Superior in the days before the railroad, not to mention the harsh winter. It didn't help when Horace Greeley, who was an enthusiastic investor in mining, visited the area and said it was a horrible place full of mosquitos, not a place to throw your money away on mining ventures. But in 1864, a man named Edwin Hulbert, who happened to be a surveyor and civil engineer, was out searching for a wandering pig and spotted ore he knew to be copper. He followed it. It went on and on and on for thirty-five miles.

A mining boom began, the Calumet and Hecla Mining Company was born, and with it came the railroad.

As it is with immigrants, one goes, writes to the folks back home, tells them to come, more arrive, and soon they have an enclave of fellow countrymen in a new land. This was the case with the Slovenians. They settled in Calumet, which is between Houghton and Mohawk. Of the Slovenians who immigrated to the United States prior to 1900, quite a number of them spent time in Calumet before settling elsewhere. It was a Slovenian Ellis Island before there was an Ellis Island.

Soon after Joe arrived, the Slovenians formed their first lodge, which they called St. Joseph's. A few years later, they imported a Slovenian priest. With his guidance, they built their church, which they called St. Joseph's. The Calumet and Hecla Mining Company donated the land and some of the money.

Karolina worked as a hired girl for Mary Puhec. Mary had immigrated about six years earlier and met her husband in Calumet. They'd been married about three years when Karolina arrived. Mary's husband was from the same part of the Old Country as Joe. Is that why Joe went to Calumet? Was he living in Mary Puhec's boardinghouse when Karolina went to work there? Is that how they met? I never heard how they met, just that they met in Calumet.

Then Karolina learned of a new, better opportunity, and she was ready to jump at it, no matter how far back of beyond it was.

11

Last Chance

There they were, four men, wandering through the new Montana Territory in search of gold, not somebody else's gold, their own find, their own strike. They would be known as the Four Georgians. The year was 1864. They had all but given up. They were exhausted and discouraged. Then they decided, we'll go out one more time, one more prospecting trip, it's our last chance. And they went. And they found gold. There it was, a fortune lying about, waiting for them to pick it up. They called the place—Last Chance Gulch.

Mining was the hot opportunity in the nineteenth century. The industrial age needed metals as fodder, and who doesn't want gold. The possible payoffs were enormous. The western territories, fast turning into states, were rich in precious metals, there for the taking if you could get to them, which wasn't easy. The Montana gold rush started when it was still part of the Idaho Territory. Before that, there was the California gold rush, the Colorado gold rush, silver at the Comstock in Nevada, and now gold in Montana. Many a young man "caught the fever of speculation." It was a fever that could burn a man up.

News of gold in Last Chance Gulch drew more miners, and a mining camp started to form. Miners get thirsty, they'd need a saloon; a saloon opened. Miners need supplies; a merchant opened a store. The miners wanted news from the outside world; a man started a newspaper. Those horses and mules would need to be shod; a blacksmith opened up shop. The mining camp was fast becoming a town. The miners voted and named it Helena.

All who live in Helena today can drop down on their knees and thank Almighty God that the miners did not pick one of the other names bandied about for the town, which included Pumpkinville and Crabtown, after John Crab (one of the Four Georgians). I'm going to take a wild guess that those who suggested such names were not sober.

I find it remarkable how fast things happened back then. One day you have a broad, desolate mountain valley, prairie with nothing but pronghorn antelope and deer and a gold-laden creek running through it, nary a soul for miles except the occasional trapper and nomadic Indians wandering through. Only two years after those four men discovered gold, a town has sprung up, a hospital has opened, and Helena has not one but three newspapers.

Miners knew, where there is gold on the surface, there is gold underground. The transition to hard-rock mining began.

By 1870, stagecoaches were hauling half a million dollars in gold out of Helena every month. That would be around nine million dollars today.

It turned out to be one of the richest gold districts in the country. Finding gold was relatively easy in those parts. Finding a rich strike, a big, wide vein—that was not easy. Luck certainly entered into it. Some of those prospectors were very lucky. Gold and silver mining camps popped up all around—Marysville, Diamond City, Lump Gulch. Some mining camps grew into bigger towns, towns that endured, while others faded into obscurity or dissolved into ghost towns after the mines played out. Helena seemed to be well watered, so to speak, for it grew and endured. It was well watered with cash. Helena was fast becoming the banking center of Montana.

Before those four men discovered gold in Last Chance Gulch, prospectors had discovered gold in many places in what came to be known as Montana, and lots of it. The West drew intrepid young men from the East and from foreign lands seeking fortune and adventure. Many of those young men had fled the Rebellion, as it was called in the north, also called the War for Southern Independence. One of the biggest gold strikes was at Alder Gulch in 1863. The miners named the town that grew up there Varina, after Jefferson Davis' wife. A Union-minded judge said, nothing doing, and changed the name to Virginia City. It became the second territorial capital of the new Montana Territory. In the next election, after ballots were burned up, thrown out, and determined fraudulent, Helena wrested the title of territorial capital away from Virginia City. That was in 1875.

One intrepid young man seeking fortune and adventure in the West was Sam Hauser. He was born in Kentucky in 1833, worked as a civil engineer for a railroad in Missouri, and when he was twenty-nine, traveled up the Missouri into the Idaho Territory (which still included Montana) to Fort Benton. He prospected for gold, found some, went to Virginia City, started a bank, then to Argenta, started a mining company, then to the next best new place for gold, which was Helena, where he started the first national bank in the Montana Territory. The bank traded in gold dust. Imagine walking up to the bank teller to deposit your bag of gold dust. Sam Hauser pursued many other business interests, including railroads and cattle, and became successful and rich. The rapidity at which Sam Hauser amassed his fortune is astonishing, and he wasn't the only one. It was said some fifty millionaires lived in Helena, more per capita than any other city in the country. Sam Hauser built a magnificent mansion at 720 Madison Avenue to be his home. In 1888, he built an equally stupendous mansion across the street at 725 Madison as a wedding gift for his stepdaughter. You can drive by those two magnificent homes today in Helena's mansion district.

President Grover Cleveland appointed Sam Hauser territorial governor of Montana in 1885. Hauser resigned after only sixteen months; apparently

Residence of Samuel Hauser, 720 Madison Avenue, Helena, built in 1885.
Montana Historical Society 954-069

Power Block, Helena, Montana, 1899.
Collection of Kennon Baird

political office was too much of a distraction from his more pressing and lucrative business ventures. However, his interest in politics and in the success of the Democrat Party did not abate. I found a letter a Thiel detective wrote to him in 1891 for services rendered to spy on senate Republicans.

Sam Hauser was the driving force behind building a silver-lead smelter a few miles east of Helena. He formed the Helena and Livingston Smelting & Reduction Company to do it. The list of stockholders read like a Helena Who's Who. Montana was the biggest silver producer in the country at that time; expanding local smelting capacity made sense. The site Hauser chose to build the smelter was Prickly Pear Junction, an old stagecoach way station used by gold prospectors. It was a perfect spot with proximity to the railroad, to water, and to limestone, which was used in the smelting process. Construction of the smelter began in June of 1888. An enterprising Ohio veteran of the War of the Rebellion named Gilman Riggs, along with Henry and Emily Clark, platted a town right next to it. I think Prickly Pear Junction is a charming name, but I'm guessing the town fathers decided that attaching their new town to the capital city would give it prestige. They named the new town East Helena. The smelter started operating in December of 1888. (Yes, it took only six months to build.) By the time smelting began, East Helena already had eight saloons, six boardinghouses, one hotel, two general stores, a meat market, a cobbler, and nine homes.

Montana became a state the next year.

It was a time and place of optimism, of swashbuckling risk takers, an era in which men with pluck were fast to roll the dice on big ventures, big bets, resulting in big wins or huge losses.

Meanwhile, several states away off in Calumet, Michigan, a young Slovenian-Austrian woman late of Vienna, pretty Karolina Stangel, who did not speak English, heard about a job cooking for the men who worked at the smelter in a new town in a new state, and off she went.

Joe Lozar followed her.

12

EAST HELENA

HOW EXCITING. Here were Karolina and Joe, both from an old part of the Old Country, setting up stakes in a brand-new town in a brand-new state in this young country—so many opportunities for someone with drive and initiative and not afraid of hard work. They both fit the bill.

I don't know how Karolina heard about the job in East Helena. The town was just born, it wasn't even a wide spot in the road yet. There was a blacksmith in Helena by the name of Joseph Stangle. He was around the same age as she, and he was born in Austria. A cousin? A coincidence, perhaps.

As I understand it, but couldn't confirm because those company records burned up in a fire, the smelter company built a house to serve as the dining room for the supervisory staff. The cooks who fed them lived in the house. Also, in those early days, the company ran a boardinghouse for the smeltermen, a very large boardinghouse, big enough for fifty men. What was passed down in family lore was that my great-grandmother Karolina went to East Helena to cook for the smeltermen. I'm guessing it was in one of those houses. Having the exalted reputation of a Viennese cook, she may well have cooked for the supervisory staff.

Joe made haste to start his own business. He was in a young town, right out of the womb, growing at a fast clip, in a boom country, a thirsty, hungry one. He leased a saloon and lived in it, and in no time he had enough business to hire help, a fellow named Joe Plut. By June of 1892, he had saved enough money to buy half the saloon and everything in it, which cost him $350. He paid cash for the tiny frame building, only eighteen by thirty-six feet but plenty big enough to sell beer and whiskey and groceries.

*Cathedral of the Sacred Hearts of Jesus and Mary, South Ewing Street,
Helena, where Joe and Karolina were married on August 16, 1892.*
MONTANA HISTORICAL SOCIETY 953-255

Joe and Karolina's wedding portrait, they are seated on the left, August 1892.

Karolina Stangel Lozar, 1892.

He asked Karolina to marry him. They were married August 16, 1892, at the Cathedral of the Sacred Hearts in Helena [later replaced by St. Helena's]. Their marriage license says her father's name was Carl.

Karolina wore her best dress, flowers in her hair, and a corsage. Joe wore what was probably his only suit and a boutonniere. The wedding party went to a photographer's studio to have their picture taken. This appears to be the custom of the Slovenians. I found many wedding portraits among my grandmother's and her sister's collections, pictures of friends' weddings. I found no such pictures for my Irish and Welsh relatives of the same time.

Two months later, Joe made his declaration of intention to become an American citizen.

Joe and Karolina lived in the saloon, in tiny living quarters in the back. The whole place was quite small, only 648 square feet, one story. The space where they kept their bed must have been the size of a closet. The privy was outside.

Joe's tax assessment in 1895 showed he owned only the saloon, no horses, hogs, sheep, or cattle. That would change.

Karolina delivered their first child on July 2, 1893. She was born at home in the saloon. Joe fetched a professional midwife (there were at least three in Helena at the time) or a neighbor to help with the delivery. They named the baby Anna. Anna Lozar. She was my grandmother. Yes, you have that right, my grandmother was born in a bar. She was baptized thirteen days later at the Cathedral of the Sacred Hearts in Helena.

The next year Joe renounced "all allegiance and fidelity" to Emperor Franz Josef and became an American citizen. This automatically made his wife, Karolina, an American citizen. It was a sweet mercy that Karolina did not have to renounce all allegiance to Franz Josef. Joe's citizenship was granted by the First Judicial District of the State of Montana. At that time, any court of record could grant citizenship, though the requirement to have resided in the country for at least five years had been dictated by Congress. Right after Joe became a citizen, he vouched for his cousin Peter Lozar, who also became a citizen that day.

Mining in the West during the second half of the nineteenth century was akin to the internet boom of the late twentieth century. Everybody wanted to get in on it. Mining concerns were the hot stocks, the exciting up-and-coming businesses, and as such attracted considerable eastern and foreign investment. It started with gold, then silver, then copper. A few men became wildly rich mining in Montana. Merchants and saloon owners, such as Joe, made comfortable livings mining the miners and smeltermen. Lawyers made good livings litigating the mines.

As I mentioned earlier, the smelter in East Helena was built during the silver boom of the 1880s. Silver mining received a further boost, as if it needed one, when Congress passed, and the president signed, the Sherman Silver Purchase Act of 1890. The Act required that the federal government buy 4.5 million ounces of silver every month. It is no surprise that the output of silver jumped to this amount the very next year, which was a ten percent increase. Sam Hauser and his cohort of investors, who owned the smelter in East Helena, were positioned for a roaring good business, as were the local merchants.

But then (isn't there inevitably a "but then") far, far away, a railroad went under, a railroad so famous you know it from Monopoly—the Reading Railroad, more precisely the Philadelphia and Reading Railroad. Who could have imagined that this stone cast into our nation's economic pond could create ripple upon ripple upon ripple extending all the way across the country to the Prickly Pear Valley of the Rocky Mountains. Alone, it wouldn't have.

In 1833, the Philadelphia and Reading Railroad started hauling anthracite out of Pennsylvania's lucrative coal mines. The company bought other railroads and coal mines and grew to be one of the largest employers in the country. They borrowed a lot to do this. Sixty years later, in February of 1893, the company went bankrupt. This was the third time in thirteen years that the Philadelphia and Reading Railroad had gone bankrupt. No financial panics followed those previous bankruptcies, yet historians seem to think that this particular bankruptcy in 1893 was an important factor in what was to follow. It was to be one element of a financial perfect storm. There were many elements beyond those I'll chronicle here.

In April of 1893, shortly after President Grover Cleveland took office for his second term (his two terms were not consecutive), the value of gold reserves in the U.S. Treasury dropped below one hundred million dollars. This scared people. Congress had mandated that the government maintain at least that amount. People worried that they might not be able to redeem dollars for gold.

On May 4, 1893, a bill of complaint was filed for the appointment of receivers for the National Cordage Company (yes, they made rope, lots of it). It was also one of the biggest employers in the country. This was the first step in bankruptcy.

The New York Stock Exchange crashed the next day.

When these two huge companies failed, this startled bankers who held investments in those companies, or had loaned them money, or had loaned money to businesses to whom the bankrupt companies owed money. All these things, together with the drop in U.S. Treasury gold reserves, sparked the sell-off in the stock market.

On June 27, 1893, the stock market crashed again.

Bankers grew nervous and started calling in loans, which resulted in other businesses going bankrupt. Smaller banks pulled their funds out of larger banks. It was a run on the banks. Banks failed, four thousand of them. As can happen, but doesn't always, a crash (a radical drop in stock prices) begat a panic (a run on the banks).

This, dear reader, was the Panic of 1893.

In August, the Northern Pacific Railroad went bankrupt. The smelter in East Helena shipped and received everything via the Northern Pacific. The smelter processed a lot of ore from the mines around Coeur d'Alene, Idaho, all of which arrived by rail on the Northern Pacific.

In October, the Union Pacific went bankrupt. It also served Montana. Scores of railroads went bankrupt.

Interest rates skyrocketed, up to twenty percent. Money became expensive.

The country was sliding into an economic depression. Some fourteen thousand businesses went under, including thirty steel companies.

Whether both gold and silver should back the dollar was a huge, contentious political issue in the nineteenth century. It was the Gold Bugs versus the Silverites. The Gold Bugs believed in the gold standard, meaning gold should back the dollar. The Silverites believed gold and silver should back the dollar.

The Republican Party Platform of 1892 said: "The American people, from tradition and interest, favor bi-metallism, and the Republican party demands the use of both gold and silver as standard money." The platform also favored "maintenance of the most friendly relations with all foreign powers; entangling alliances with none" and sympathized with the "cause of home rule in Ireland" and protested "the persecution of the Jews in Russia."

The Democrat Party Platform of 1892 denounced the Sherman Silver Purchase Act of 1890 as "cowardly makeshift, fraught with possibilities of danger in the future" and called for its repeal. Even so, the platform called for "the use of both gold and silver as the standard money of the country."

President Grover Cleveland had always been a Gold Bug. He believed in sound money. This could certainly include silver, but the way Congress had written the legislation, pegging the price of silver to gold rather than the market price, threw a huge monkey wrench into the concept of sound money. Though the medicine would be hard, Cleveland believed the patient better take it. His party, the Democrats, held majorities in Congress, but not all in his party agreed with him. Nevertheless, in October of 1893 he pushed through repeal of the Sherman Silver Purchase Act. No more would silver back the dollar, and in one fell swoop, the government pulled the rug right out from under the silver industry. The federal government had puffed and puffed and inflated the silver bubble, and then pulled out its giant pin and popped it. Silver's biggest customer—the U.S. Treasury—quit buying it. There went the silver market. Silver production dropped eighteen percent in one year. Now the silver smelter business was way overbuilt. Though the East Helena smelter also processed lead, it was tough going through the rest of the 1890s, with creditors nipping at the heals of the owners, pushing them toward bankruptcy. Lead production dropped with silver production. The value of lead produced in Montana dropped twenty-four percent from 1893 to 1894.

One way to deal with competition is to buy it. Consolidation was the trend across industries in the nineteenth century in steel, in oil, in mining, in railroads. During flush times in 1890, the company that owned the smelter in East Helena merged with the Montana Smelting Company, which owned the silver smelter in Great Falls, to form the United Smelting and Refining Company. Now in 1899, the East Helena smelter became part of the American Smelting and Refining Company (ASARCo), headquartered in New York. The company was started by a group of industrialists that included two titans of Standard Oil, Henry Rogers and William Rockefeller, and three German immigrants, Adolph Lewisohn, Leonard Lewisohn, and Anton Eilers. Shares of the new company cost one hundred dollars. Mind boggling. In January of 1901, American Smelting and Refining merged with the Guggenheims. Daniel Guggenheim became chairman of the board. The name of the company stayed the same.

One casualty of the Panic of 1893 was Sam Hauser's First National Bank of Helena. It took a tumble after the second stock market crash that year, then limped along for a while as the depression dragged on until it collapsed, made a final gasp, and died. That was in September of 1896. His other business ventures suffered considerably, but he didn't. He still lived in that magnificent mansion at 720 Madison Avenue in Helena.

But out there in East Helena, the scrappy young immigrant speaking broken English, my great-grandpa Joe Lozar, not only survived but thrived.

Apparently he figured a depression was a good time to buy, for buy he did, and buy some more. Joe breathed optimism. It was the Gilded Age. A boom was sure to follow the bust. This depression would be just another storm "certain to end in sunshine." He bought the other half of the saloon for $330 in 1894, then the lot next door for $300, then the lot next to it for $36, right there on Front Street, right across from the Northern Pacific depot, right across from the smelter, where almost all the men in town worked. He paid cash for all of it.

At long last, the American economy crawled out of the pit of the post-Panic depression, stood up, started to walk, then trot, then canter, then gallop to a whopping growth rate of 7.3 percent in 1897. Joe was well fixed to capitalize on that prosperity.

In 1899, Joe built a saloon. It was two stories, built of stone with two-foot-thick walls. One hundred years later, when I began searching for his story, it still stood. Any of you driving past East Helena up until a few years ago could see it from Highway 287—the two-story stone saloon that Joe built, or I should say, hired stonemasons to build. It was nine hundred square feet on each floor, much larger than the original saloon. Joe converted the original saloon into his grocery and dry goods store, where he sold "Staple and Fancy Groceries, Mens' Furnishing Goods, Wines, Liquors, Cigars, Etc." Those thirsty smeltermen were also hungry. Joe built a frame building attached to the stone saloon for the kitchen and storeroom. And, at long last, he built a proper home for Karolina and the children. The house was two stories with five rooms, 1,152 square feet, almost twice the size of that original saloon. Next to the house, he built a warehouse and stable, both under the same roof. Over time, they had seven horses, three cows each with a calf, and two wagons each with a double harness, meaning he always hitched two horses to the wagon. Joe also had a mowing machine and a plow and a hay rake, so he must have used some of the land to grow alfalfa or some other grass for hay for the animals.

He hired a carpenter, an artisan really, to build a beautiful bar out of pine for the saloon. It was fifteen feet long, the kind of bar you see in old Westerns. The carpenter used only wood with no knots. Beveled mirrors adorned the back bar. A brass foot rail ran along the base. Joe placed spittoons at intervals. Behind the bar along the floor was a metal trough. The copper coils that brought the beer from the kegs in the cellar up to the taps ran through this trough, which Joe packed with ice.

Joe and Karolina owned all that property free and clear, no mortgages. The newspaper said Joe spent four thousand dollars building the saloon.

Joe's business license fee for the fourth quarter of 1893 cost sixty dollars, so two hundred and forty dollars a year. I found what Joe paid in the receipt book for the Lewis and Clark County tax collector. An attorney paid four dollars for the quarter, as did a doctor and a dentist. A merchant paid ten dollars. Another merchant paid fifteen. A butcher paid five dollars. Those were in Helena. Three other saloons in East Helena paid the same tax as Joe. That tells us how lucrative the saloon business was—to be able to pay ten times more than a lawyer or doctor. Those thirsty smeltermen drank a lot of beer and whiskey.

A passel of relatives arrived from the Old Country and made their way to East Helena. Joe's sister Anna arrived around the time Joe and Karolina married. I'm sure Joe sent his sister the money for the voyage and train. That was frequently how it worked. One family member came and sent money back for the next family member. Anna helped Karolina cook for the smeltermen, though not for long. She met a countryman who was a miner in Butte, married him, and moved there. Joe's cousin Peter Lozar worked in the smelter until Joe's saloon was built, then he worked as Joe's clerk in the grocery store and sometimes as his bartender in the saloon. Cousin Frank worked as a bartender at Matt Multz's place. Cousin Mathias worked in the smelter. Cousin Matthew

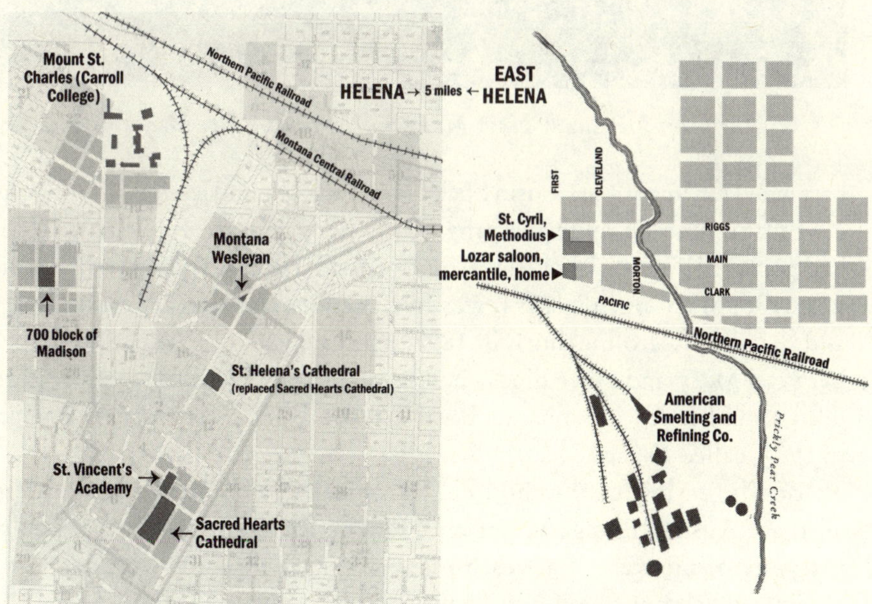

Partial map of Helena, Montana, and East Helena.
Derived from Sanborn map with additional details added.

Annie on Joe Lozar's lap, Mary on Karolina's lap, May 1895.

bartended for Vucovich. Cousin Nick didn't stay long and left for Minneapolis.

By the time East Helena rang in the new century, Karolina and Joe had four little ones: the eldest, Anna, called Annie, my grandma, was six years old; Mary, born in 1894, was five; Stephen, born in 1897, was three; and daughter Caroline, born in 1898, was one year old. Their baby born between Mary and Steve died when only two weeks old. Two more children would follow: Stephanie, born in 1904, called Stephie; and Frances in 1907, called Francie.

Besides caring for the children, Karolina had a house full of boarders, all from Austria-Hungary, ten men ranging in age from twenty-one to forty-six. Some were relatives. Some were married, some were single, all spoke English but one. Eight of the boarders worked at the smelter. I'm guessing the boarders slept on the second floor above the saloon. The stairs were outside in the back.

To help take care of all those boarders and children, Karolina brought a girl named Mary Trebushek over from the Old Country to work for her. Karolina went from being a kitchen maid to hiring one.

IN 1898, THE BOARDERS who worked at the smelter as laborers made $2 a day. Pot pullers and samplers earned $2.50 a day. Carpenters and blacksmiths made $4 a day. They were paid monthly in cash. They worked ten to twelve hours a day and had an hour for lunch. They worked every day, seven days a week.

To put their pay in context, a man living in a boardinghouse paid about a dollar a day for room and board. East Helena housewives paid twenty-two cents for a dozen eggs. A pound of bacon cost seventeen cents, a pound of potatoes cost two pennies, a pound of butter cost two bits (twenty-five cents).

Lozar saloon in East Helena, front and back views.

Ventilation and industrial safety measures were primitive. Smeltermen suffered lead colic and lead rheumatism. They paid $1.50 every month for hospital dues. This was typical for mines, smelters, and railroads, at least in Montana at the time. The Northern Pacific Railroad had a hospital in Missoula. Every railroad worker paid $1 or $1.50 hospital dues each month, depending on his wage level.

Early on, Joe had a falling out with the owner of the brewery from whom he was buying beer. "Whatever the trouble, Papa was so mad at him and decided to not buy his beer," his daughter Stephie told me. Joe looked for a better brewer.

Nicholas Kessler had been well established in the brewery business for some time when this happened. Nicholas was born in 1833 in the Grand Duchy of Luxembourg. He left home for America when he was around twenty-one. He made his way to Bannack in the Idaho Territory right after gold was discovered. He figured it would be easier to make money in beer than in mining. He went to Helena and built his brewery. He married at age forty. Seven years later, after bearing three children, his wife, Louise, died.

While he suffered tragedy in his personal life, his brewery prospered. Soon more and more breweries opened. Competition was becoming fierce.

Delivery wagon at the Kessler Brewing Company, Helena, circa 1904.
MONTANA HISTORICAL SOCIETY 953-066. EDWARD M. REINIG, PHOTOGRAPHER

Streetcar on Main Street, East Helena
COLLECTION OF KENNON BAIRD

Yes, there were lots of thirsty miners and smeltermen, but there was also a lot of beer.

Nicholas needed to expand his market. Joe needed a beer supplier.

Joe told Nicholas Kessler to bring a wagon load of beer to East Helena and give free beer to everyone in town. I'm told that for a time no one would drink anything but Kessler's beer, which was the only beer Joe sold. Joe's daughter Stephie said, "Mr. Kessler never forgot it until years later he was able to repay Papa in the most unique way."

IMMIGRANTS WHO SETTLED IN LARGE CITIES couldn't help but bump into America. Even those who lived in their own ethnic enclave, when at work in a factory, when their children went to school, they encountered immigrants from other countries and native-born Americans. In East Helena, though Karolina and Joe might meet Canadians or Swedes or Irish or Norwegians or Germans, even Welsh people, as well as native-born Americans, the largest ethnic group was their fellow Slovenians. East Helena became known as a Slovenian town, which attracted even more Slovenians. The Lozars could live in a Slovenian bubble. It was Carniola in the Rockies, Slovenia, America, long before there was a country called Slovenia. Joe and Karolina's neighbors were Slovenian, their customers were Slovenian, their boarders were Slovenian. The boarders worked in the smelter with more Slovenians. They bought sausages from a Slovenian butcher. Their children went to school with Slovenian children. There were also many Croatians, Poles, and Bohemians (Czechs), all from Austria-Hungary, living in East Helena.

In 1900, the Lozars' next-door neighbor on one side ran a boarding-house with eleven boarders, all from Austria-Hungary, based on their surnames, probably all Slovenian. On the other side lived a Russian family.

In 1910, the neighbors on both sides were Slovenian. A family of Serbs lived two doors down. A steady influx of Serbs settled in East Helena between 1900 and 1910. The population of East Helena was now twelve hundred. There was one public school and one Catholic school. The town had electric lights and hourly streetcar service to Helena. Two railroads served the town. The smelter processed eight hundred tons of ore a day.

Though Joe and Karolina lived among people with familiar customs and language, the place did not look at all like Carniola. Helena and East Helena lie in an enormous, semi-arid mountain valley. Where the well-watered Slovenian lands of Austria were green, in the heat of summer in Montana the rains taper off and the grasses turn brown. This must have seemed stark.

I wonder why Joe didn't file for a homestead. He grew up on a farm in the Old Country, he knew farming, he could have filed for a homestead and farmed, but he opted not to do that. Instead, he and Karolina built up a business with a saloon and grocery and mercantile and boardinghouse. If he did consider homesteading, perhaps Karolina nixed that idea, she having lived in Vienna all those years. She was a country girl who became a city girl; perhaps she didn't want to go back to secluded country life.

AFTER SEVERAL YEARS IN AMERICA, Karolina still did not speak English, even when her eldest child, Annie, my grandmother, started school. I think it's safe to say that Annie's first language was Slovenian, or a mix of Slovenian and German.

Joe wouldn't stand for his wife not speaking English, nor would he stand for any of his countrymen not speaking English. He took matters into his own hands. In 1899, he started the East Helena Evening School. The purpose of the school was to teach English to foreign-born adults. I wonder if this was when Karolina's name was anglicized to Caroline. Did she anglicize her name? Did Joe insist on it? Did the evening school teacher insist on it? This happened with immigrant children; they went to school and the teacher said, "In America your name is ____." Or could it have been later, when her daughters were teenagers or pre-teens, could one of them have insisted their mother anglicize her name? Young people want to fit in. And truth be told, they were all pretty bossy. However it was decided, from here on, we shall call her Caroline. We always knew her name to be Caroline. It wasn't until I received her baptism record from the old church book at the archives in Ljubljana, Slovenia, that I learned her name was originally Karolina.

Their daughter Stephie told me, "Papa was so proud of being a U.S. citizen that he wouldn't allow us to speak the Austrian language although Mama never did get over her accent. She spoke her language to her friends."

The little town of East Helena had three weekly newspapers: the *East Helena Record*, the *Montana Bimetalist*, and the *Republican*. They became cheerleaders for local commerce. They wanted their community to thrive. They knew how their bread was buttered. The *East Helena Record* of February 10, 1900, wrote, "The best part of this factory [the smelter] is that it not only furnishes employment for hundreds in the works itself, but employs a much greater number in nearby mines, etc. and distributes millions of dollars in wages, directly or indirectly, in Montana. . . . The total number on the payroll exceeds 650. Still, 650 men at work and receiving Montana wages scatter a sum among the Helena merchants which other towns may well envy."

Joe ran ads in the *Slavensko Jedistvo* paper, and he was one of the first to advertise in the *Republican*. His ads ran on the front page, and oh my, did the editor ever know his customers. An article in the November 8, 1899, edition of the *Republican* carried the headline "Our Austrian Residents, Men Who Are Industrious and Mind Their Own Affairs." By Austrian the editor meant citizens of the Austro-Hungarian Empire, which included ethnic Slovenians, Croats, Poles, Bohemians. He said these men are "robust specimens of manhood, inured to hard work. Not given to viciousness . . . always suitably clothed . . . close buyers . . . not disposed to haggle over price . . ." In short, they were a hard-working, frugal, responsible lot, paragons one and all.

As for the women, they are "devoted wives and mothers, hard working and prudent. The home life is pleasant and a spirit of content seems at all times to prevail." Oh, yes, they were "practically perfect in every way," just like Mary Poppins. It's a sweet sentiment, but hard not to laugh at as you get to know my grandma Annie.

What the author did not note, possibly because it was taken for granted, was the homes were kept neat as a pin.

And they were Catholics. Mass was held at the Odd Fellows Hall until they raised enough money to build a church.

There were about twelve hundred people in East Helena at that time. More than a third were children. A large notice on the front page of the *East Helena Record* of April 14, 1899, said that under state law, children age eight to fourteen must attend school for at least twelve weeks every year, six of which must be consecutive.

Immigrants banded together to form ethnic fraternal organizations, which offered sick and death benefits in addition to being social. The Slovenian fraternal societies were Morning Star and St. Cyril and Matod (Methodius). They called them lodges. The women had their lodge, and the men had theirs.

Frank Gorsich trained to be a butcher back in the Old Country. He came to the United States in 1909. After making his way to the West, people told him, *Go to East Helena, lots of Slovenian people there, they'll buy your sausages.* So he went. His Slovenian neighbors loaned him money to buy the equipment he needed to set up shop. He hired a teenage girl, who was also a Slovenian immigrant, to teach him English. He said, "I couldn't afford to pay her, so I married her." He was twenty-three, and she was seventeen. He sold a lot of sausages. "Good fresh meat makes good sausage," he said. "I made good money."

THE ONLY TIME THE SMELTER in East Helena went on strike in the nineteenth century was back in 1891, a little over two years after the smelter opened. This was a wildcat strike, since they had no union. They stayed

Chemistry room at the smelter in East Helena, 1888.
MONTANA HISTORICAL SOCIETY 951-104. EMIL D. KELLER, PHOTOGRAPHER

Men working in the smelter in East Helena.
Picture taken sometime between 1898 and 1920.
Montana Historical Society PAc 80-02.1

Smelter in East Helena. When this picture was taken between 1910 and
1919 it was part the American Smelting and Refining Company.
Montana Historical Society PAc 93-14.3

out for four days. Collectively, they lost more in wages than the owners lost in production. Nothing changed. For the rest of the decade, things were quiet as far as labor issues.

But with the turn of the new century, it was as if a switch had been thrown, a page had been turned. Where labor had been quiet in Montana, it was quiet no more.

There were twenty-four strikes and lockouts across the state in 1901. The next year there were thirty-five.

In 1901, the eight-hour-day law went into effect in Montana for those working in mines and smelters. On April 26, 1901, the plant superintendent at the smelter in East Helena posted notices saying there would be a twelve to twenty percent reduction in wages in all departments as a result of the eight-hour-day law. The smeltermen were paid by the day. The wage cut reflected their hourly pay before the eight-hour-day law. Fewer hours worked meant less pay. If a man worked a ten-hour day for $2, that came to 20 cents an hour. Now with the eight-hour-day law, his 20 cents an hour amounted to $1.60 a day. Upon seeing this, several men quit.

The East Helena smelter was the only smelter in Montana that was not unionized, and it was the only one that cut wages as a result of the eight-hour-day law. The lowest wage in the smelter was $2 a day for laborers. At the smelter in Great Falls, laborers earned $2 to $2.75 a day. The initiation fee to join the union was $1; the monthly dues were 50 cents. At the smelter in Anaconda, owned by the Anaconda Copper Mining Company, the men earned $2.50 to $2.75 a day. (These numbers are for 1898.)

The miners in Butte, the booming, boisterous copper metropolis to the south, had been organized since the 1870s. Just about everybody in Butte was organized, even the chimney sweeps when there were only two of them, at least so said Burton Wheeler, an attorney who arrived in 1905. Whether he meant that literally or as a joke, it illustrates the point.

Dan McDonald, a prominent union organizer from Butte, quickly caught a train to East Helena and met with disgruntled smeltermen. Their leaders met with the plant manager. There was a lot of back and forth over the pay cut. The men insisted that it be lowered to a ten percent cut, even for those previously working a twelve-hour shift. The newspaper accounts differ as to whether the plant manager agreed to that or not, but the big sticking point was not the pay cut. It was the union, the idea of a union. The plant manager insisted that the men sign an agreement saying they would not organize a union. They wouldn't sign. On May 1, the doors to the smelter were shut. A lockout. The smelter employed six hundred men, and nearly all of them lived in East Helena.

With nowhere to take their ore to be processed, mines around the state halted operation, putting miners out of work.

"Business men are blue," said the newspaper. Their customers had no income.

The smelter company fired anyone who joined the union and brought in men from out of state to replace them, derisively known as scabs.

The lockout lasted two weeks. The company agreed to a ten percent wage cut rather than a twenty percent cut for those who had previously worked ten-hour shifts. The men agreed not to form a local of the smelterman's union.

"Merchants feel good in the old town," said the newspaper.

The company announced plans to add two new blast furnaces to the smelter to accommodate more ore expected from outside Montana.

A few renegades formed a union anyway, even though no one working at the smelter could join it and keep his job. The East Helena Mill & Smeltermen No. 126 met every Wednesday evening.

By September the smelter had more ore to process than ever before.

The next spring more men joined the fledgling union local. The company fired anyone who did. The men made no wage or hours demands, they just wanted a union. On April 28, 1902, the men walked out. A wildcat strike.

The union posted pickets to prevent men from going to work.

The company refused to countenance a union and threatened to shut down the smelter for good. They started to draw down the fires.

Five hundred smeltermen were out of work. Men started to leave town to look for work elsewhere. Monthly payroll at the smelter was forty thousand dollars. Now it was gone.

Joe's customers were leaving town to find work. A merchant can't easily do that, pick up and move his saloon or mercantile. Joe and his fellow merchants met to see what they could do to bring about an end to the strike.

If the strike dragged on, it could put two thousand miners out of work, hard rock miners who had no place to take their ore. The East Helena smelter was the only custom smelter around. The people in Red Lodge worried that coal mining at Rocky Fork could be curtailed. That's where East Helena got its coal; the smelter used a lot of coal.

Merchants curtailed their orders.

Representatives of the union and management met over several days. Now Sam Hauser was involved in the negotiations.

The union said, If you will re-hire former employees at current wages, we will not strike for one year.

The plant manager said he would send their proposal to the bosses in New York, and he would recommend that they accept it.

The smelter had been shut down for two weeks. Half the men in East Helena had left town to find work elsewhere. Mines around the state had shut down. The company announced that it would take all the ore it normally processed and send it by rail to other smelters at no additional cost. Mines reopened.

On May 20, the response came back from the bosses in New York: We will speak directly with the employees, not through a union.

A group of smeltermen started collecting signatures of men willing to go back to work.

This dragged on through the rest of May, into June, now into July. On July 7, 1902, this notice was posted at the smelter: "The influence brought to bear upon this company by Ex-Gov. Hauser, as representing the business community of Helena and vicinity, this company [has decided] to make an offer to all former employees to resume work immediately . . . at the old scale of wages for one year."

The newspaper announced: "East Helena Smeltermen May Return to Work if They are Sufficiently Starved" and "To Renounce their Unionism."

That was the deal. They went back to work at the wage scale in effect before the eight-hour-day law and no union.

The year went by, and they kept working. They didn't go on strike. But lots of people across Montana did. In 1903 and 1904, there were strikes all over the state—telephone operators in Butte, painters in Missoula, street laborers in Bozeman, drivers in Yellowstone Park, laundries in Kalispell. Labor was agitated, or was being agitated.

But no strike in East Helena.

Mining the smeltermen was working well for Joe and his family. The saloon, the boardinghouse, the grocery were all thriving. But for Joe, it wasn't enough.

13

∞

GOLD FEVER

"HARD ROCK MINING is characterized by uncertainty, long time horizons, and only rare success," wrote economics professor David Gerard.

Yes, but somebody had to do it.

Joe staked his first claim on a gold mine in July of 1897, a few months after their son Stephen was born. He named it the Atlantic Lode. A lode is an underground hard rock mine. Initially he had one partner, John Pohule, then his cousin Peter Lozar joined them. Each man claimed one-third interest.

A state report said, "Much of the ground in this district [the area of Joe's mine] has hardly been prospected, and there are many very promising claims that only require investment of capital to enrich the investors and add wealth to the communities." It sounds so easy, just investment of capital, that and a lot of hard work.

Yes, indeed, Joe was a young man of spirit, ready to "pick up a fortune, simply pick it up." And why not, look at what Tommy Cruse did, an up-from-the-bootstraps immigrant just like Joe, who discovered the "greatest gold mine in Montana." If Tommy Cruse could do it, why not Joe?

Thomas Cruse staked the Drumlummon mine in May of 1875 at a place he called Marysville, northwest of Helena. It was tough going—mining is always tough going—and it wasn't the first place he tried. He had tried his hand at mining all over the West, but at this spot, the place he named Marysville, his hard work and tenacity paid off. He found his gold bonanza in 1883, and he wasted no time in pocketing his windfall. He sold his mine to an English outfit for an enormous sum and a percentage of future profits. The Drumlummon became the greatest gold mine in a state that was one of the biggest gold producers in the country.

Tommy Cruse then went into ranching and banking. In 1886, at age fifty-two, he got around to getting married. Unfortunately, his young wife died a few days after giving birth.

He weathered the Panic of 1893 just fine, while many Helena bankers did not. As the story goes, when some of those bankers asked him for loans to tide them over during the Panic, he retorted in his thick-as-wool Irish brogue, When I was slaving away on my mine, a mine I knew was good, and I was hungry, I was cold, I needed a grubstake, and you turned me down. So he turned them down, so the story goes.

Yes, if Tommy Cruse could do it, an immigrant prospector who came to these shores from County Cavan, Ireland, with nothing but a willingness to work hard and, as it turned out, a lot of luck, why not Joe. Yes, indeed, why not Joe.

A year after Joe claimed the Atlantic Lode, which was about three miles south of East Helena, he turned his attention nine miles north. It took quite a while to get up there with a wagon and horses and not much of a road. He prospected on foot or horseback once in the general area. I can't help but wonder why he went prospecting in that particular spot. After weeks, perhaps months of prospecting, Joe found his spot. He hired Lucas Papas to dig a discovery shaft. After Lucas finished digging a twelve-foot deep shaft, Joe went down to take a look. "I saw almost four inches of nice looking ore," he said. That nice-looking ore included gold, copper, and silver. "I had my full confidence that it was going to turn out better," he said. And it did.

He named it the Sunrise and staked and claimed it on July 5, 1898. As the law required, he posted the name and description of the mine and staked the four corners with four-foot-high stakes in mounds of dirt or rocks four feet in diameter and at least two feet high. The southeast corner was about half a mile from Prickly Pear Creek and about one mile northeast of the Abe Thomas Ranch. That was as precise as a location could be back in 1898. Joe filed his claim at the courthouse well within the proscribed time, which was ninety days. Joe's partners on the Sunrise lode were Joseph Miljour and J. B. Humphrey. Each claimed one-third.

The same day they staked the Sunrise, Joseph Miljour sold Joe the mine right next to it, the Violet Jane, for twenty-five dollars. The catch was: Joseph Miljour did not own the Violet Jane. It wasn't his to sell. George Reed and Elijah Hicks owned it.

Soon after they claimed the Sunrise, J. B. Humphrey sold his one-third to Joe for twenty-five dollars. Miljour sold his one-third to Joe for one dollar. Perhaps this made it even, since he had bamboozled Joe on the Violet Jane.

The General Mining Act of 1872 mandated that Joe do at least one hundred dollars worth of work on each mine every year. That included the value of his own labor, materials, and others he paid to work the mine.

Year after year, Joe worked on the Sunrise. He hired men to help him. The promise of gold beckoned like a siren. There it was, peeking over the horizon like the morning sun, just waiting for Joe to reach out and grab it, except of course, it was underground. Another few feet of tunnel, and there it would be, the mother lode. It took Tommy Cruse eight long years to discover his gold bonanza in the Drumlummon. With patience and hard work, the same luck could befall Joe, and he was not afraid of hard work, and he was ambitious, and he could match Tommy Cruse in tenacity.

It took several hours to get up to the Sunrise by wagon. It was hilly terrain. Joe must have pitched a tent at the beginning. In time he built a cabin to sleep in and store his tools.

He took his ore to the East Helena smelter for processing. He was earning money from it. I don't have specific information about how much ore Joe mined, or the value of it, but I do have an ore purchase sheet for March, April, and May of 1900, for the ore Hicks and Reed brought to the smelter from the Violet Jane, the mine next to Joe's. Their ore was 35 percent gold, 26 percent silver, and 39 percent lead. The total value of that batch was $84.79.

Joe discovered enough ore to exacerbate his gold fever. In 1903, he turned his sights to the south again, to the same neck of the woods as his first mine, around Mitchell Gulch. He found more gold, silver, and copper and located the Alice and Lorna Doon Lode. He located that one with a partner and then bought out his partner.

Now he was working three mines, not all in the same area. He had a young family. The eldest, Annie, my grandma, was ten years old. He had the saloon and the grocery store to run. How did he find time for all this prospecting? Just getting to those mines was a chore. Any road that went anywhere near his mines wasn't much of a road at all, just dirt. When the road ended, he made do with no road. It had to be slow going by wagon laden with mining tools, pulled by a team of horses or mules. It was cold in the winter, hot in the summer. When the rains came in the spring, it was muddy, awfully muddy. The terrain was hilly; I mean Montana hills, which are big. Prospecting and mining are slow, arduous work requiring the patience of Job. But the promise of riches loomed ever more. There it was, just over the horizon, this next few feet of tunnel, the vein will widen, *we'll be rich, wildly rich.*

Was it the prospect of money that drove him and others like him? Or was it simply the idea of the elusive gold—El Dorado.

As he dug and explored and dug and explored, he discovered that the ore vein in the Sunrise was going in a different direction. It was running north–south rather than east–west. This meant the ore vein Joe was following went under what had been the adjacent mining claim, the Violet Jane. Joe wasn't concerned. The shaft had caved in on the Violet Jane, proving it had been abandoned. Following the law, Joe swung his new lines, showing the new boundaries for the Sunrise and went to the courthouse and amended his claim to reflect the new boundaries. This was on July 30, 1903. He confirmed again that he had found ore bearing gold, silver, and copper. When he described the location, this time he did not say that the Sunrise bounded the Violet Jane, because as far as he could tell, there no longer was such a claim called the Violet Jane.

Indeed, Hicks and Reed had lost interest in working the Violet Jane. They sold the claim to Joe's former partner, Joseph Miljour. This was long after Miljour "sold" the Violet Jane to Joe. Miljour paid Mr. and Mrs. Reed one dollar for their half interest in the Violet Jane. He paid Mr. and Mrs. Hicks one hundred and sixty dollars for their half. Miljour recorded his purchase of the Violet Jane in December of 1903, four months after Joe recorded the new boundaries for the Sunrise. The deed book entry for the Violet Jane said that it bounded the Sunrise Mine on the south.

You may be wondering why I am telling you all this. Trust me, it is important.

The very same day that Miljour bought the rest of the Violet Jane from Mr. and Mrs. Hicks for $160, he turned around and sold the entire mine to another man for $1,000. That Miljour must have been some talker. First he sold the Violet Jane to my great-grandfather when he didn't own it, then he paid $161 for it and turned around and sold it for $1,000. Who would pay $1,000 for an undeveloped mine with a caved-in shaft?

Who indeed.

14

⚭

JOSEPH AND THE WHALE

Henry Neill, that's who.

After he bought the mine from Miljour in a gentleman's agreement, which apparently took place in a cigar store because it is written on Steele & Bahnsen Cigars and Tobacco stationery, Henry Neill deeded one-third of the Violet Jane to his brother, John, and one-third to Joseph Miljour—yes, the very same man from whom he bought the mine for the vastly inflated price of one thousand dollars. This makes no sense to me, but it's all in writing. I saw the cigar store agreement with my own eyes. It also said that any future mining claims Miljour made would be in the name of all three men. Joseph Miljour and Henry Neill signed the cigar store agreement on December 10, 1903.

A few weeks later, on January 18, 1904, John Neill formally bought two-thirds of the Violet Jane from his brother, Henry. He paid Henry ten dollars. Yes, I did say that Henry paid one thousand dollars for it.

Miljour lost no time staking claims around the Violet Jane. He staked claims on nine more mines from January to June 1904, all named Miljour—Miljour No. 1, Miljour No. 2, and so on. The two Neill brothers did none of the mining; they just paid the bills. They were grubstaking Miljour, whom Henry had already paid one thousand dollars. Miljour did the physical work or hired men to do it, at the expense of the Neill brothers. They paid Miljour forty dollars a month. Some invoices said he worked six days in one month, so possibly this was not his only job.

People bought groceries and whatnot on credit. The merchant kept a running tab. This was in the days before credit cards. When Miljour went to the feed store to buy hay or to the butcher to buy bacon, he told the merchant to put it on his employer's account, the Neill brothers. Even though there was nothing strange about this for the times, the brother who handled the bills wrote a note to one merchant saying, "Do not let this man have anything in future except on written order." He wrote much the same to another merchant. By the time Miljour staked the tenth claim, he'd had enough of the Neills or they had had enough of him. I couldn't tell whether they fired Miljour or he quit, possibly over having his bills nitpicked. On June 3, 1904, their business relationship ended. Miljour severed ties with the Neill brothers. He sold them his interest in the mines for the balance of what they owed him, which was one hundred dollars. In other words, they called it even.

The following year, the Neills amended the boundaries of the Violet Jane such that the Violet Jane overlapped Joe's Sunrise Mine by about ten acres.

In May of 1906, the Neill brothers applied for patent for the Violet Jane. This was not necessary for their mining operation, but once they received the patent, they would have full title to the land and could use it for any purpose. It also meant they had to start paying Lewis and Clark County property taxes on it, in addition to the fees required to take the mine to patent.

This is when the trouble started.

Joe found out about it. The Violet Jane jumped (overlapped) his claim, the Sunrise, and he objected. He filed an adverse claim. In other words, he protested the Neills' application for patent for the Violet Jane because they jumped the Sunrise. The Neills wouldn't back down. They refused to alter the boundaries of the Violet Jane. This left only one remedy for Joe. He had to sue them.

When I first heard about this from my dad, all I knew was that my great-grandfather was involved in a big claim jumping lawsuit. I knew none of these particulars. I had not yet waded into Helena history. The first thing I did was get the court records, which is how I learned that his opponents were John and Henry Neill. I didn't know how much they paid for the Violet Jane. With the name Neill, I figured they were a couple of Irish prospectors, upstart immigrants with big dreams, just like Joe. Then one day while reading turn-of-the-century Helena newspapers for a different part of this book, I came across considerable political venom being hurled at a man named John Neill. Could he be the same John Neill?

Yes, he was.

The man whom my great-grandfather decided to sue was no poor immigrant Irish prospector. He was none other than John Selby Martin

Neill—the John Neill who ran the *Helena Independent* newspaper; the John Neill who was the bagman for Copper King William Andrews Clark when Clark bribed his way to the Senate; the John Neill who cooked up the scheme to lure the governor out of the state so the Clark-friendly lieutenant governor would appoint Clark to the Senate after Clark's election chicanery was exposed for all to see; the John Neill for whom Neill Avenue in Helena is named, on which sits the present-day Federal Reserve. Yes, that John S. M. Neill, one of the most powerful politically connected men in the state. A force of nature, he was. This was the man whom my great-grandfather Joe decided to sue, along with John Neill's brother, Henry. No matter how much Joe was in the right, and I believe he was, and he certainly believed he was, he was up against Colossus, Goliath, a Leviathan. Joe was Captain Ahab up against Moby Dick, though Joe was not seeking vengeance, only justice, what he believed was rightfully his.

I will add stubborn to the list of my great-grandfather's traits and a strong sense of justice.

Once I learned this, I was curious to see where John Neill lived. While in Helena, I looked up his address in the city directory and drove over to see it. My jaw dropped. He lived in a huge mansion, seven bedrooms; he paid ten thousand dollars for it in 1904. It was across the street from Sam Hauser's mansion. Then one morning, I woke up with an epiphany—how could the man who ran a newspaper in Helena, Montana, at the turn of the century afford such a house? Ten thousand dollars was an enormous amount of money in 1904. Today the house is worth over a million. Neill said himself in one of his letters, "I never can make a considerable sum of money out of a newspaper in this state." He called himself "a man without means."

Where did he get the money?

John Selby Martin Neill was born March 25, 1860, in St. Paul, Minnesota. His father was a Presbyterian minister. The family lived in Washington, D.C., during the Civil War. In 1869, President Grant appointed Neill's father consul in Dublin, Ireland, and the family moved there. After three years in Dublin, the family returned to Minnesota. I read that Neill attended Delaware College and then studied law at Columbian University (today George Washington University) in Washington, D.C. (I tried but could not confirm that he attended those schools.) As far as I can tell, he never did practice law. On November 7, 1883, he married Margaret Evans, a young woman he met while studying in Delaware. Her father was high up in the Presbyterian Church. The next year John Neill left to seek his fortune in the Montana Territory. His pregnant wife stayed behind until their baby was born, after which she and the baby joined him in Helena.

He borrowed money from his father-in-law, quite a bit actually, and used it to go into the real estate and loans business in Helena. He bought property, including mining claims, and served as a mortgage broker for private loans and for loans with financial institutions. He was the agent for the American Loan and Trust Company. Payment was in gold or equivalent. His office was in the Merchants National Bank building.

Though John Neill bought many properties, early on he rented the homes in which he and his family lived. We know from the census that in 1900 the John Neill household included his wife, his son, his sister, his nephew, and a maid. They lived at 734 East Sixth Avenue. Before that, the family lived at 823 Ninth Avenue.

John Neill worked tirelessly to help Grover Cleveland win the presidency in 1892. He delivered Lewis and Clark County for Cleveland; however, the more populous Silver Bow County, in other words Butte, the copper metropolis to the south, swung the state for Harrison. There were four candidates that year. Besides the Democrat Cleveland (46% of the vote) and the Republican Harrison (43%), Weaver ran as the Populist candidate (8.5%) and Bidwell ran as the Prohibition candidate (2%). Even though John Neill didn't deliver the state, he was Cleveland's man in Montana, and President Cleveland handsomely rewarded him with the plum job of surveyor general and paid him three thousand dollars a year, which was fifty percent more than any other surveyor general in the country was paid.

"No man in the state of Montana exerted a more potent influence in a political way than did . . . John S. M. Neill," wrote contemporary historian Helen Fitzgerald Sanders.

Another contemporary historian said Neill showed "marked power in the manipulation of political agencies," and as for Democrat politics, "he was looked to whenever aggressive action was necessary." He became known as the man who handed out political patronage jobs.

This was a time when newspapers openly worked for the benefit of a particular political party. There were Democrat papers and Republican papers and papers for other political parties. This may not have been the case with all newspapers, but it was not unusual in the nineteenth century. The *Helena Independent* was no different. The *Independent* was "an organ of the Democrat Party," wrote Helen Fitzgerald Sanders. But by 1897, the paper was on shaky financial feet and fell into receivership. To make sure

John Selby Martin Neill.
MONTANA HISTORICAL SOCIETY 944-128.
WILLIAM H TAYLOR, PHOTOGRAPHER

that Republicans didn't scoop it up, John Neill urged his moneyed cronies to keep the paper in Democrat hands with him in charge, and he was successful. Neill convinced mining millionaire Copper King William Andrews Clark to pony up twenty-five thousand dollars to buy the paper. Actually, it was a loan.

William Andrews Clark was a self-made man. He came to Montana with nothing and left with millions. He became one of the richest men in the country. Senator Robert LaFollette called him one of a hundred men who owned America. Why was Clark interested in helping Neill secure Democrat control over the *Independent*? Because being wildly rich and successful wasn't enough for Clark. He wanted to be a U.S. senator. He needed his people in control of a major newspaper.

John Neill became treasurer and manager of the paper. Even though he was not the publisher, A. J. Davidson was, make no mistake, John Neill ran the paper. He would go off on fiery tirades at his editor, complaining of the man's vast shortcomings. Perhaps the editor had some obscure notion of an independent press. John Neill used the paper as a truncheon to wage political warfare. He was by no means unique in this. He and his opponents in the press gave as well as they got. "False charges, vilification, assassination of character, and willful abuse . . . it is second nature for John S.M. Neill to sacrifice others to his gain," wrote his political enemies.

While unraveling this story, one thing led to another led to another. Great-grandpa Joe's lawsuit led me to John Neill, which led me to A. J. Davidson, who was publisher of the *Independent*, which led me to Virginia City, which led me to the Vigilantes, which led me to Wilbur Fisk Sanders, which led me to the Civil War and then back to Helena.

Helena, Montana, between 1905 and 1909
MONTANA HISTORICAL SOCIETY PAc76-56.17, S.J. CULBERTSON PHOTOGRAPHER

In 1863, during what today we call the Civil War, twenty-year-old A. J. Davidson drove an ox team some fifteen hundred miles all the way from Missouri to Alder Gulch in the Idaho Territory, soon to be known as Virginia City. He lived there during the era of the Vigilantes, and he was a top Mason. He became grand master of the Masons and grand commander of the Knights Templar in Helena.

Wilbur Fisk Sanders was the prosecutor in Virginia City at the time. He was also a Mason.

F. Scott Fitzgerald wrote, "There are no second acts in American life." Nothing could be further from the truth. Though he was later called Colonel Sanders, Wilbur Fisk Sanders was a first lieutenant in the Ohio 64th Regiment of the Union Army during the Civil War. He left the army while the war was still raging. A Bozeman paper said he left because he didn't want to enforce the Fugitive Slave Act of 1850. This required people in states that had outlawed slavery to apprehend and return runaway slaves. A person who provided food or shelter to a runaway slave could be punished with six months in prison and a fine of one thousand dollars. Police were required to apprehend and return anyone suspected of being a runaway slave, even with no proof. In other words, the federal government forced people to violate their consciences, forced people to aid and abet a practice they believed to be immoral. General Grant wrote in his memoir about the perniciousness of the Fugitive Slave Act. Grant called it a degradation many in the North could not abide.

Were Sanders a person who could not abide this degradation, he certainly could not state this as a reason for leaving the Union army. It was federal law. His military papers say he asked to be mustered out for business and health reasons. His commanding officer allowed him to be mustered out for health reasons. He then embarked on the long, arduous thousand-mile journey by train, boat, and ox-team all the way to Nowhere, Idaho Territory, also known as Bannack in a place we now call Montana. He arrived in September of 1863. Did I say gold had been discovered? It had.

He traveled with his uncle Sidney Edgerton. President Lincoln had named Edgerton chief justice of the Idaho Territory. He would later become the first territorial governor of Montana.

Parade on Main Street, Helena, Montana, between 1890 and 1910
Montana Historical Society PAc76-56.32

Sanders was a lawyer and became prosecutor in Virginia City.

Huge gold finds were discovered in 1862 and 1863 in the southwest part of modern-day Montana. The towns that sprang up around the mines came to be known as Bannack, Nevada City, and Virginia City. The gold was taken out in stagecoaches, which were repeatedly robbed. Many people were murdered. A man named George Ives was put on trial for murder in December of 1863. Though this was the boondocks of the boondocks, way back of beyond, there was a judge, there was a jury, there were four defense lawyers. Sanders was the prosecutor. Ives was found guilty and executed forthwith. No appeal. Sanders and others were alarmed by the amount of sympathy for Ives and precious little for the victim. They formed a Vigilance Committee.

Sanders' daughter-in-law was the aforementioned historian Helen Fitzgerald Sanders, whose *History of Montana* helped introduce us to John Neill.

Back to Neill's newspaper's publisher, A. J. Davidson. Davidson started out in Helena as a grocer. He went into the harness and saddle business, as well as mining, banking, real estate, and cattle. I find the diversity of interests of these business pioneers in Helena remarkable. Davidson, like Sam Hauser, saw an opportunity and jumped at it. Their business interests poured over into politics to varying degrees. Davidson became a mover and shaker in the Democrat party, and as such, a crony of John Neill. He was elected to the state legislature in 1892. Though sick and bedridden, when it came time to vote for William Andrews Clark for the U.S. Senate, he insisted on being carried on a stretcher to the legislature. No matter what, he was going to vote for Clark even if he died doing it.

A. J. Davidson was also vice-president of Merchants National Bank.

As I mentioned earlier, banks failed one after another throughout the four-year depression that followed the Panic of 1893. Sam Hauser's bank, the First National Bank of Helena, failed in September of 1896. After that, rumors started about Merchants National Bank, rumors that the bank was in trouble, rumors directed at particular depositors. Nervous depositors started withdrawing their money, spurred on by more rumors, which grew into a slow-motion run on the bank to the point that the owners, the Hershfields, had no choice but to close the doors. They posted a sign saying, "Persistent and relentless withdrawals have largely reduced the bank's available resources. Depositors have been withdrawing money since First National [Sam Hauser's bank] closed its doors in September."

Merchants National Bank suspended operations on February 13, 1897.

Who loses in such a situation? Depositors and stockholders. Who wins? Creditors. Two big creditors of the bank were A. J. Davidson and John S. M. Neill. John Neill owed the bank a whopping $74,052— five mortgages plus interest. In addition to that, which was an enormous sum, it seems he owed money to every Tom, Dick, and Harry across the land. A perpetual borrower was he, leveraged to the hilt and then some. He considered bankruptcy. The bank receiver accepted his pleas for delay—which dragged on for two years— and finally in July of 1899, John Neill agreed to hand over all his real estate to the receiver and $1,000 cash. The bank receiver, Mr. Wilson, figured that was the best deal, the only deal, the bank could get out of John Neill, who had no other assets, only an interest in the newspaper, which was heavily mortgaged. Mr. Wilson estimated the real estate to be worth around $15,000. Another source I found estimated it to be $10,000. Either way, that was a huge haircut, around $63,000 in debt wiped away for John Neill. Wasn't he the lucky one.

And somehow, with all that debt hanging over his head, he managed to "buy" the newspaper three months after Merchants Bank failed. He said he bought it, but he didn't. He didn't have two nickels to rub together much less buy a newspaper or anything else. What he did was convince people to loan him money, one of whom was William Andrews Clark. According to what the bank receiver wrote in his letters about him, John Neill had no assets. Somehow he was a Svengali at getting people to loan him money.

Two months later, he borrowed five thousand dollars from William Andrews Clark. He asked Clark to reduce the interest from eight to six percent.

The Clark-Daly feud in the War of the Copper Kings had nothing to do with mining; it was political. Both were copper mining magnates in my hometown of Butte, Montana. William Andrews Clark decided he wanted to become a U.S. senator and Marcus Daly didn't want that. Clark tried in 1890 and lost. He tried again in 1893 and lost. What I am about to describe is the third time, which was in 1899.

Back then, U.S. senators were not elected by the popular vote as they are today. They were elected by each state's legislature, so the battle was over whether a majority of Clark or Daly legislators would be elected.

Daly was not a candidate. He and Clark were both Democrats. He simply did not want Clark elected to the Senate. It was a Democrat internecine battle.

By 1899, Clark had lost interest in running for office. He'd already tried and failed several times. He was consumed with building his sensational palace on Fifth Avenue in New York City. John Neill desperately wanted Clark to run again for the Senate, and he was very persuasive, a force of nature he was. He would not give up until Clark agreed to do it. Sam Hauser and John Neill were allies in this. When Clark agreed to run again, he pulled out all the stops. No matter what the cost, this time he was going to win, by hook or by crook.

John Neill wrote to an associate in Ashville, North Carolina: "You know my feelings in regard to Clark. While he is very selfish . . . still he represents an idea in this state. He is the only man who has sufficient wealth to combat the tyranny of Daly and his crowd, hence I am for him and have always been."

Neill became "a prime mover in the management" of Clark's campaign, a field marshal in Clark's forces in his war against Marcus Daly. And he prevailed. The Montana Legislature elected William Andrews Clark to the Senate. And how was this finally achieved? Bribes.

One might say "money flowed like water down a duck's back, swift and easy. Money was crowned King for the time being, Justice being hog-tied and losing her scales in the shuffle."

According to sworn testimony by several witnesses, John Neill was a bagman for William Andrews Clark in bribing legislators to vote for Clark. I should say he was one of Clark's bagmen. Clark's lawyer John Wellcome also handed out bribes. The going rate for a Democrat was ten thousand dollars; the going rate for a Republican was five thousand. This was in 1899 dollars. It was done clandestinely in a rented room chosen because it had a back entrance, so there wouldn't be a parade of bribe-seeking legislators traipsing through the front door where John Neill and John Wellcome handed out the dirty cash. They would give the legislator a down payment and place the rest of the cash in an envelope that the man initialed. This was all very business-like; they kept receipts. I don't know how many legislators ended up taking the money. All this came out in the investigations, including the disbarment proceeding for John Wellcome, Clark's lawyer, where at least one of those receipts was entered into evidence. Despite the army of lawyers representing John Wellcome, he was disbarred. Great-grandpa Joe no doubt read about it or at least heard about it; all this was reported in newspapers from Los Angeles to New York City.

And now you know part of the reason the Seventeenth Amendment to the United States Constitution was ratified, allowing direct election of senators.

Montana was ridiculed in the national press over the Clark bribery scandal, but this was by no means unique to Montana. A few years before all this, private detective Charlie Siringo, while on a case in Colorado, came across receipts for bribes in elections there. "There were piles of political letters and receipts for votes bought during the past elections. The ruling price of votes was two dollars in cash or one sheep."

One of the attorneys who defended John Wellcome at the disbarment proceeding was Edward C. Day, who happened to be the vice president of John Neill's publishing company, and who happened to be John Neill's lawyer in the claim jumping lawsuit against my dear great-grandpa Joe.

Before the dust could begin to settle on the election bribery scandal, it was time for the state Democrat Central Committee to meet. They met in Butte in June of 1900. The Clark Democrats and the Daly Democrats were still dug in, still in pitched battle. The bribery scandal had only made things worse. When John Neill didn't get his way at the meeting he "raged and tore around like a mad bull" according to the *Kalispell Bee*. The undersheriff was about to throw him out of the place, but Neill's cronies convinced him otherwise. The *Anaconda Standard* of June 21, 1900, a paper controlled by Clark's nemesis Marcus Daly, reported that the chairman of the Democrat state committee refused "to be swayed by hysterical screams and yells of boss bulldozer Neill," and that "Neill jumped on a chair and declared himself chairman. 'Your former chairman is deposed,' yelled Neill." This very lengthy newspaper article had sub-headlines, akin to chapter headings. Two sub-headlines in this article were "Neill Goes Crazy" and "Neill Makes an Ass Out of Himself." I kid you not.

That was one version of events. The *Butte Miner* of June 28, 1900, which was a Clark paper, said Neill and his cronies were just sitting there "peaceably engaged in the transaction of the legitimate business of the committee" when Undersheriff Murphy and ten armed deputies "rushed into the room" and seized them.

According to Neill's paper, or I should say Clark's paper in Helena, the *Independent* of June 21, 1900, Neill was standing on a chair, taking over the committee, when a delegate made a motion that Neill be named chairman "and it was declared carried," then out of the blue, a "posse of deputy sheriffs" swept in, summoned by the dreaded "Dalyites," and a brawl broke out between committee members and deputy sheriffs, all the while John Neill was standing on a chair, the sergeant-at-arms tugging at his coattails as he called roll over the melee, or so we are told by John Neill.

The headlines read:

"Dalyites Fail to Steal Convention."

"Nefarious Attempts to Control and Coerce Democrats comes to an Inglorious End."

"Outrageous Rulings of Stoolpigeon Cockrell Were Not Tolerated by Majority of Members."

Cockrell was chairman of the Democrat State Central Committee.

John Neill couldn't leave it there, oh no. One newspaper story wasn't enough. He re-hashed the whole episode again the next day. The front-page headline of the *Helena Independent* read: "Independent Democracy Will Gain by Being Rid of its Evil Associates, and Rejuvenated and Purged Will Wage the Battle of the People Against Unlawful Financial and Disreputable Political Combinations." This from John Neill, the bagman in the bribery scandal, which had just happened and was fresh in everybody's minds. The front page article began, "Despite the armed interference of Daly thugs and hirelings . . ." and it went on to name the delegates to the national convention followed by a long rambling rant about the evils of Marcus Daly.

And again the next day, a third day, he repeated the exact same front-page story from two days earlier. John Neill was not a man to let anything go. Even after his side prevailed, he wouldn't let it go, he threw verbal punch after verbal punch after verbal punch. His opponent could be dead three days, and he'd keep punching and kicking him. John Neill did not back down, he prevailed, he got his way by hook or by crook; the man was relentless, he bashed his opponents until they were beaten senseless, verbally pounding them again, a pit bull rottweiler.

And this is the man my great-grandfather Joe Lozar decided to sue.

15

How a Man of No Means Bought a Mansion

When the U.S. Senate decided it was having no part of all that election chicanery and voted to deny William Andrews Clark the Senate seat, it was John Neill who cooked up the scheme to lure the governor out of the state and have the Clark-friendly lieutenant governor appoint Clark to the Senate, which is what happened. The Senate still wouldn't accept Clark. You can't say John Neill didn't try.

Neill said it was "a dog's task," all he did to get William Andrews Clark elected. He said he spent a lot of his own money doing it. He said he did everything for the party and it nearly broke him, no man of means am I, said he. He told the Senate committee investigating the bribery allegations, "I presume the senatorial election cost me one thousand dollars." That was in February of 1900, only seven months after his mountain of debt at Merchants National Bank was conveniently wiped away.

Yet, somehow, shortly after he blew all that money, John Neill managed to buy a ten thousand dollar mansion.

Neill said he paid $40,860 for the *Independent* in 1897; that's what he said, but he didn't pay a dime. All of that was debt. He borrowed the money, $25,000 of it from Clark. By 1900, he had paid $16,000 on his IOUs. He, or I should say the paper, still owed Clark $24,860. Assuming he continued to pay the debt at the same rate, it would take another five years to pay what he owed Clark.

It should come as no surprise to learn that the paper was sued for libel during the bribery-soaked Senate campaign. The name calling was ferocious.

The *Independent* called Clark's accuser "a Self-Confessed Criminal." He sued. Clark paid the paper's legal bills. So not only did Clark own at least half the paper, he was also paying the paper's legal bills. Two years later, in August of 1902, Neill sold the paper to Clark for $152,500 cash plus commercial property worth $7,000. Wait a minute, you say, that makes no sense. Didn't Clark hold the mortgage on the paper? Meaning Neill owed Clark almost $25,000 only two years earlier. Why would Clark pay for a newspaper on which he held the note, meaning he already owned it? Clark bought a paper he already owned, and John Neill got the money. Or you might say, Clark bought the paper from himself and gave John Neill the money, a paper that was always bleeding money. William Andrews Clark could do whatever he wanted with his money. This was before the income tax and gift tax.

Yes, John Neill fell into a financial bucket of butter, supplied by one William Andrews Clark. And he used some of that butter to buy his ten thousand dollar mansion. Lucky him.

Right after this, he wrote to his father-in-law in Delaware to tell him about his windfall. He enclosed a check for the interest on the money he had borrowed from him, which he hadn't paid in ten years, not since 1892. The check for the interest was $4,136.25. He asked his father-in-law whether he wanted him to pay the principal as well, which totaled $8,000. I couldn't believe it when I read that letter, and I still can't believe it. That is stunning. I'm thinking of this from his wife's perspective. Her husband borrows money from her father, a lot of money, doesn't pay the interest for ten years, writes to tell her father about how he came into all this money, very proud of himself, pays the interest, and asks his father-in-law, do you want the principal too? He sounds like someone who stepped off the pages of a Sinclair Lewis novel.

He told his father-in-law, "after paying all obligations . . . I will have more than $100,000 left." He said, "I regretted exceedingly to give up the paper." He said he enjoyed being able to "help my friends and punish my enemies, but from a business standpoint, I have made the greatest sale of property ever made in this state."

I should say so.

And he had the gall to ask his elderly father-in-law if he wanted his eight thousand dollars back.

Two years later, John Neill "bought" the paper back from Clark. That sum remains a mystery.

16

∽

Captain Ahab Goes to Court

Why did you do it, Joe? Why did you sue one of the most powerful, politically connected men in the state? Easy for me to wonder, I didn't do all the backbreaking work on the mine and invest a lot of money in it every year for ten years. I also don't know how much ore he was getting out of the mine. Perhaps it was turning a profit and giving him a nice income. Whatever the prospects for the Sunrise Mine, once Joe had this bit in his teeth, he wouldn't let go.

These claim jumping cases were complicated. There was no GPS. Mine boundaries were marked in the wilderness. Jumping a claim could be deliberate or inadvertent. It probably came down to who had the better lawyer or who had the favor of the judge or both.

Joe had at least one previous run-in with the Neills, as far as I know. Joe built a cabin at the Sunrise Mine. He lived with the family in East Helena, but he needed a place to stay while working the mine and to store his tools. Henry Neill said the cabin wasn't entirely on Joe's claim and ordered Joe to move it. That was in April of 1904. Let us recall that the shaft for the Violet Jane was already caved in, not useable. Joe thought it had been abandoned, as would any reasonable person.

Joe hired the firm of Galen & Mettler to represent him in the claim jumping lawsuit. He had used their services before, in particular, Albert Galen back in 1904. Galen had just been elected Montana attorney general. Joe hired him when the federal government charged Joe with mending a fence on public land. The U.S. attorney who brought the charges was also an immigrant; he was Prussian. He charged Joe with the horror of fence mending on September 26, 1904. Bail was set at five hundred dollars. Yes, the U.S. attorney made a federal case of mending a fence out in the Montana wilderness.

Rumor had it that Joe was squatting on the land, but that wasn't so. The court records were clear—he didn't build the fence, he just fixed it. The judge instructed the jury: If you believe that Mr. Lozar intended to file a claim for the land under the Homestead Act and live on it, you must acquit, the verdict must be not guilty.

Joe must have leased the land not knowing that the man who leased it to him did not own it. As for why the fence was there in the first place, all I can guess, and this is just a guess, is that someone claimed the land under the Homestead Act, built the fence, intending to prove up, but didn't and abandoned the land.

Joe could have faced a fine of up to one thousand dollars and a year in prison for the dastardly crime. The judge sentenced Joe to twelve hours in jail and a fine of twenty-five dollars. This would indicate to me that the judge did not take this as seriously as the U.S. attorney.

I wonder who alerted the authorities to the fence mending travesty. A man who testified at the trial owed Joe a lot of money. I don't know if the jury knew that.

The following year the township in which the sinister fence mending took place was withdrawn from settlement or sale by proclamation of President Theodore Roosevelt. The land, which had been somebody's ranch, was in the Elkhorn Forest and could no longer be settled or sold. What was public land would stay public land.

John Neill also had his share of legal troubles in the past, besides his paper being sued for libel over coverage of the election shenanigans. In February of 1906, the editor of the *Helena Independent* printed a story claiming that an "editor doctor" and "former mayor" were owners of a "club saloon" and gambling house. Gambling was illegal. Everyone knew the "editor doctor" was Doc Lanstrum, editor of the rival Republican paper, the *Daily Record*, and that the "former mayor" was former mayor Edwards. The article implied that Swede Sam of Butte sold them his interest in the gambling house.

Lanstrum and Edwards quickly filed a libel suit against the *Independent*. The editor told Neill's lawyer, Edward Day, that a fellow named Sam Goza told him that Swede Sam told him the story. A fellow called Purcell also said Swede Sam told him the story. John Neill's lawyer Edward Day talked to Sam Goza who said he got the story from Con Becker, who heard it from Swede Sam. In other words, Neill's editor heard it from a guy who heard it from a guy who heard it from a guy, and he printed the story without checking it out. Swede Sam denied the whole thing. Lawyer Edward Day wrote to John Neill that it was a "carefully laid trap into which [his editor] has walked unawares. He printed the story without consulting anybody as a result of his rage at the attack of the *Record* on you."

I found all this in a letter Edward Day wrote to John Neill. I think this is hilarious. Here we have two pillars of the community, Neill and Day, conversing about the machinations of some guy from Butte named Swede Sam.

AS FOR MY GREAT-GRANDPA Joe's litigation against the mighty John Selby Martin Neill, he faced off against John Neill and his brother Henry on January 2, 1908. A jury was empaneled in the court of Judge Thomas C. Bach.

Judge Bach was born and raised in New York City. He earned his law degree at Columbia. His first job was in the law office of the man who had been ambassador to Spain. In 1886, President Cleveland appointed Bach to the Supreme Court of the Territory of Montana. Bach's former law partner was Governor Toole. Judge Bach and John Neill had much in common: both had been political appointees of President Cleveland, both were members of the exclusive Montana Club, and both lived in the same lovely neighborhood in Helena, the mansion district. In short, they traveled in the same circles. And there was Joe, the scrappy upstart Catholic immigrant with his heavy accent, serving up beer and whiskey to scrappy, thirsty smeltermen out in East Helena.

Frank Mettler handled Joe's case. He had been an assistant attorney general. His law partner, Albert Galen, was now the Montana attorney general.

Henry Neill testified that when he bought the Violet Jane, he couldn't examine the discovery shaft because it was caved in. Joe said the same thing; it was caved in. Henry said after buying the Violet Jane, he hired a man to dig out the discovery shaft. All in all he invested nineteen hundred dollars in the Violet Jane. I'm guessing that included what he paid for the mine plus improvements. The Neills had shipped three hundred and seventy-five pounds of ore from the Violet Jane to the East Helena smelter. They amended the boundaries of the mine on August 30, 1905. This was two years after Joe moved the boundaries of the Sunrise. They had the Violet Jane surveyed, so it seems they had to know it jumped another claim. Joe said the Violet Jane had been abandoned when he amended his claim on the Sunrise, which everyone agreed was true. Joe's lawyer argued that based on this, under the law, the present Violet Jane did not exist when Joe moved the boundaries of the Sunrise. When Joe recorded the Sunrise at the courthouse, no one objected. The Violet Jane came second, two years later, and jumped Joe's claim on the Sunrise. The argument was, the Sunrise was there first, because that earlier Violet Jane had been abandoned. It didn't exist until the men hired by the Neills started to work it, which was after Joe amended the boundaries of the Sunrise. Joe's shaft for the Sunrise was one hundred and thirty feet deep. There was a twenty-foot drift (tunnel) and a thirty-foot-long crosscut. All of the work Joe had done on the Sunrise amounted to sixteen hundred dollars.

Here's the timetable. Hicks and Reed located the Violet Jane on January 1, 1898. They did not record the claim within the time required by law.

Joe located the Sunrise on June 25, 1898. He recorded the claim a few days later, well within the time required by law. Joe saw that the Sunrise was next to the Violet Jane and so noted this when he recorded his claim.

The law said, to keep a mining claim, the claimant had to put one hundred dollars worth of labor and materials into developing the mine every year. Joe did this on the Sunrise. Somewhere along the line, Reed and Hicks quit working the Violet Jane and the shaft caved in.

As Joe worked the Sunrise, he discovered that the ore vein was running north–south rather than east–west. Mining claims were long and narrow, fifteen hundred feet by six hundred feet. He "swung his lines" accordingly on June 24, 1903, and recorded his new boundaries at the courthouse.

In December of 1903, Joe Miljour sold the Violet Jane to Henry Neill for one thousand dollars, who turned around and sold two-thirds of it to his brother John Neill for ten dollars.

On August 30, 1905, the Neills changed the boundaries of the Violet Jane. Joe's lawyer said this is actually the original date for the Violet Jane, since the original claimants had not followed the law in two respects: they did not record the claim within the proscribed time and they abandoned it. So on two counts it did not exist before the Neills claimed it.

The trial droned on all day, a debate of minutia between Joe's lawyer, Frank Mettler, and the Neill's lawyer, Edward Day. It seems a requirement of the legal profession is to love to talk. To this non-lawyer, it seemed they were rephrasing the same questions over and over. Perhaps the strategy was to bore the jurors to such an extent that they would rule in favor of the lawyer who ended their misery. It didn't come to that. After hearing the Neills' lawyer make their case, Judge Bach ruled, there is nothing here, this is a non-suit. The plaintiff, Mr. Lozar, did not prove rights to the land in question; he did not make a *prima facie* case. The case never went to the jury. The jury was dismissed, court adjourned. The Neills won.

The Neills insisted that Joe pay their legal fees. Judge Bach agreed. He ordered the clerk to set the amount that Joe had to pay. Apparently, the clerk chose not to do that. The clerk of court never requested any money from Joe. It is blank in the court records.

You'd think that would have been the end of it. Joe lost. Too bad. But, no, that was not the end of it. Our Joe, our Captain Ahab, would not give up. He kept going. He appealed to the Montana Supreme Court. They would hear the case in the spring.

Joe's Sunrise Mine was only a few miles from Hauser Dam. In early spring, the Hauser Dam collapsed, unleashing the mighty Missouri. A twenty-five-foot surge of water carrying heavy dam debris flooded and wrecked all in its path. Fortunately for Joe, the Sunrise was upstream, his one lucky break in all this.

In June, after a solid month of rain and heavy snow, rivers and creeks swelled higher than ever been before since the birth of the state. A dam near Lump Gulch collapsed, which swelled Prickly Pear Creek, which flowed to East Helena, overflowed its banks, wiped out the bridge, and flooded Main Street.

1908 flood.
COLLECTION OF KENNON BAIRD

Streets in Helena were also inundated, cellars flooded, chicken coops flooded. The city was isolated—no trains, no telegraph, no telephone. The railroads were crippled, "thousands of railroad passengers marooned," said the newspaper. The hotels in Helena were full of stranded passengers. Tracks were washed out, bridges were washed out. If the tracks weren't washed out, landslides covered the tracks with mud. Trains were paralyzed.

A train going from Butte to Helena had to stop short of Basin because the ground underneath the tracks ahead was washed out. The passengers stepped off the train and started walking through the mud toward the tiny town of Basin. A locomotive pulling a caboose crept down the tracks from Basin, picked them up, and took them there. Hundreds of people were stranded in the tiny town. There were no means to get more food to the town.

Three men on that train from Butte were not about to wait around in Basin. They were determined to make it to Helena no matter the high water and mud. They hired a wagon and team of horses to take them to Clancy. In Clancy, they hired a handcar and two men to work it, and off they went up the tracks headed for Helena. They came to a stretch of tracks where the earth was washed out under the tracks for sixty feet. The tracks hung there, suspended in midair, sagging like a rope bridge, or like a roller coaster, but with nothing underneath to hold it up. They stopped, studied the situation, and then one of them walked carefully across the tracks, stepping from railroad tie to railroad tie, to the other side. Now the other four gave the handcar a great big push and down it went, down the little roller coaster of suspended railroad tracks and up the other side where the first intrepid traveler grabbed it. The other four men walked across one at a time, carefully stepping from railroad tie to railroad tie. Back on the handcar, they continued on their way.

I wonder what was so urgent to go through all that to get to Helena.

Streetcar service between Helena and East Helena halted when the floodwaters tore out a stretch of earth twenty-five feet wide and eleven feet deep under the tracks. In no time at all, the streetcar company dispatched workers to build a temporary bridge under the tracks. In only a couple days, the company resumed streetcar operation.

As the people of Helena and East Helena were recovering from this epic flood, the Montana Supreme Court heard Joe's case. To make his *prima facie* case, he had to show that at the time he located the Sunrise

Lode, the ground was not covered by a prior location, or if there were a prior location that said claimant had forfeited the land by failing to comply with the law. (Since the discovery shaft on the Violet Jane had caved in, wouldn't this demonstrate the claim was abandoned and the claimants had not done the annual one hundred dollars of work required by law?) The Honorable Henry C. Smith delivered the court's opinion. The court upheld Judge Bach's decision. Joe lost again.

Mining law was definitely a boon for lawyers. It's no wonder there were more lawyers (fifty-four) than mining companies (forty-four) in Helena at that time.

After John and Henry Neill walloped Joe in court, what did they do with the mine for which they fought so strenuously? Nothing. Absolutely nothing. They obtained the patent for the land in March of 1909, which required paying fees and paying property tax, but otherwise they did nothing with the land. They did not develop the mine any further. There it sat, and there it still sits today, windswept prairie, nothing more.

The following year, 1910, Henry Neill moved to Lewistown, Montana. In 1912, John Neill took a trip to Central America to see the work being done on the Panama Canal. Then he went to Hot Springs, Arkansas. He never returned to Helena. After only a few weeks in Hot Springs, he died. He was fifty-one years old. I found a letter that his brother, Henry, wrote in 1926 to John's son, George, sending him the deed for the Violet Jane and one other patented mining claim. Henry wrote, "I have always believed that there was mineral in those lodes, which if systematically and economically worked would pay."

Joe's legal debacle reminds me of Jarndyce versus Jarndyce in Charles Dickens' novel *Bleak House*. When it comes to litigation, a person can be completely in the right and still lose. And as in the Dickens' novel, one can also lose his health. This happened to young Jarndyce, and it happened to Joe.

"Ma and Pa had quite a thing going for them," Stephie said, "but Papa was not satisfied with the saloon. He decided he wanted to prospect for gold, and every weekend he would load up the wagon and hitched the two horses to it and off they would go, Papa and two other fellows, wagon load contained all kinds of groceries, beer, dynamite, and other things needed for mining. They finally discovered gold and was shipping ore to the smelter and doing well. But like everything else, good things come to an end. The lawsuit cost Papa his health."

If only there had been a sign above the door to the courthouse, hearkening to Dickens' warning about the Court of Chancery, "which gives to the monied might, the means abundantly of wearing down the right; which so exhausts the finances, patience, courage, hope; so overthrows the brain and breaks the heart; that there is not an honorable man among its practitioners who would not give—does not often give—the warning, 'Suffer any wrong that can be done you, rather than come here!'"

17

WHAT ABOUT CAROLINE
AND THE CHILDREN?

IT IS THE DAY BEFORE EASTER. Annie and Mary and Steve and Young Caroline are sitting at the kitchen table cracking walnuts, dropping shells into one bowl, nuts into the other, many going into their little mouths. Stephie is playing underfoot. Baby Francie is in her crib.

Mother Caroline makes the sweet yeast dough. She kneads it. She sets it aside to rise. The children are still shelling walnuts. Walnuts, walnuts, walnuts, she needs two pounds of shelled walnuts. Somebody grinds the walnuts. Not a job for a small child, lest a tiny finger be pinched. Perhaps Annie does it. She is fourteen and old enough. The grinder is affixed to the edge of the table like a vice. She stands at the table and turns the hand crank over and over and over, until the walnuts are smashed and ground to a fine grind. The walnuts must be ground to the finest grind. Any shards could tear the dough. She adds eggs and milk and sugar and cinnamon and melted butter. The children clear away the walnut shells. Mother Caroline throws a huge, clean cloth over the big table, the table they eat at, big enough to seat ten. The cloth covers the entire table and drapes down the sides. She dusts it well with flour. She stretches the dough over the cloth until it is as thin as parchment. Annie and Mary help her. She trims the thick edges. She spoons the walnut filling onto the dough and spreads it with her fingers, being ever so careful not to tear the dough while covering every bit of it with filling. Mother Caroline is so tiny, she must stand on a chair to reach the dough in the middle of the table. Her daughters are taller. Over this, she drizzles a pound of honey and more melted butter. She walks to the long side of the table and lifts the cloth, causing the dough to roll up into a long

131

spiral. This she carefully places in the big roasting pan in snail-like fashion. She lets it rest again. Now she bakes it. The potica (po-tee-tza) is done.

Mother Caroline was a trusting soul, ready to help anyone. She was perpetually cheerful, efficient, practical, and firm.

She was always in the kitchen, wearing an apron, bustling about. She seemed to have boundless energy, and she was so tiny. She made potica for Christmas and Easter. Before the invention of baking powder, cooks used yeast to leaven cakes. The way Caroline made walnut potica, and taught her daughter Annie to make it, who taught me, it is a unique confection between cake and bread. She had a large family and all those boarders, so she made a very large potica and baked it in a big roasting pan, the same roaster she used for the Christmas turkey, which was what her daughter Annie, my grandma, used, and what I use. She also made apple potica and cheese potica, but for those, no yeast. They are closer to strudel.

There was no Easter Break from school, no Spring Break. The Lozar children didn't have far to walk to school. Nobody had far to walk anywhere in East Helena. In the frigid weather—note I didn't say winter, since frigid weather extended beyond winter—the children walked home, shivering, for lunch. Mother Caroline fed them warm red wine and toast. She kissed each child on the top of the head, they bundled into their coats, hats, boots, and mittens, and she sent them out the door, and they trudged through the snow back to school.

The children first attended the East Helena School on Main Street. When the Sisters of Charity of Leavenworth opened St. Ann's grade school in 1907 in a rooming house on Pacific Street, the children went there. The Sisters traveled to the school from their convent at St. Vincent's in Helena. The school was small, so grades were combined, which was not unusual. In 1909, Annie and Mary were in the same room, taught by Sister Mary Louise. There were only thirteen students. Annie and Mary were actually high school age, but attended St. Ann's anyway. Of the thirteen students, four were named Mary, three were named Annie, and three were named Francis or Frances. Young Caroline and Steve, ages eleven and twelve, were in the same room taught by Sister Mary Faber. There were forty-four children in their room. Eight were named Mary, two were named Anna. There was only one Caroline.

By 1910, Mother Caroline spoke English. She still cooked and cleaned for several boarders. Two of the boarders were Joe's cousins from the Old

St. Cyril and Methodius Church, East Helena.
Collection of Kennon Baird

Country. Matt Lozar was fifty-two, married with three children. He'd been in the country fifteen years and was a naturalized citizen. His wife and children were not with him. He worked in the smelter. Cousin Frank was twenty-five and single. He had been in the country three years and did not yet speak English. He also worked in the smelter. There were three other boarders, all from the Old Country; two of them spoke Slovenian but not English. One worked as Joe's clerk in the grocery store. The others worked in the smelter. They identified themselves as Slovenian or Croatian, not Austro-Hungarian.

The neighbors on either side of the Lozars were Slovenian.

Joe joined the volunteer East Helena Fire Department.

In 1911, they finally had a Catholic church in East Helena. It was dedicated to St. Cyril and Methodius, two brothers from Thessalonia who became the patron saints of the Slavic peoples. Stonemasons and carpenters donated their time to build the church. Father John Pirnat, who was Slovenian from the Old Country, supervised the construction. It was built out of native red porphyry and cost $3,450.80 to build.

I wanted to know more about what life was like for my grandmother, Annie, and her siblings, growing up in this frontier smelter town at the turn of the nineteenth to the twentieth century. I found oral histories at the Montana Historical Society, and then I remembered, I already had a wonderful oral history. For this, I thank my American literature teacher at Kennewick High, Laurel Piippo, for giving me the assignment to write

*Lozar children in front of the saloon. Based on the sizes/ages of the children,
I think at least one of the smaller children must be a friend, possibly two.*

my family history. When she did, I wrote to my great-aunts asking about
the family. Aunt Stephie, Grandma's second-youngest sister, wrote me a
wonderful letter. We'll hear directly from her throughout the book.

Letter from Stephie:

> East Helena in those early days was full of excitement. Indians com-
> ing into town. Mama always told about the time she went to Helena
> which was about 3 miles away and in those days it was an all day outing,
> with shopping and what else, it so happened she left Annie, Mary, and
> Caroline in charge of me. I was still an infant, they had me on top of the
> bed sleeping or thought I was and in those days no one ever locked their
> door. I guess Annie must of been about ten years old and Mary nine and
> Caroline seven. They were busy playing in the room and in walks a great
> big Indian chief with all his feathers and all, Annie and the others took
> one look at him and they all scattered to the four winds in fright, leaving
> me to the mercy of the Indian chief, but after tickling me under my chin,
> decided I wasn't going to cry, left. They came for some groceries and as
> they were friendly Indians no one minded them. But E. Helena was real
> Wild West. In those days horse thievery was a very disturbing factor, to
> lose your horse or have it stolen was a fate worst than death.
> Our house was always open house in those days, farmers coming in for
> their monthly supply would stop in and Mama always had bread and ham
> etc. and a glass of beer or whiskey to offer and of course as always in families

East Helena school.
COLLECTION OF KENNON BAIRD

there is always a black sheep. It so happened that this family had two sons
one was a sheriff in Helena and the other became an outlaw. His name was
Jack Haley, but for some reason he took a liking to Papa and when ever he
thought he was safe from the law would stop over to our house and have
himself something to eat and drink and of course as a child I was so interested
in what the older people were talking about and always the stories would
come up about Jack Haley, one day there was quite a to do about him. It
seems he was shot by the sheriff (they had a price on his head) and of course
left him for dead, he played dead, and they all left to get an ambulance or
whatever to take him to the morgue and when they got back to the spot to
pick him up he was gone. What happened was he was only wounded and
being very friendly with the Indians they came and took him to their camp
and nursed the wound. So when he was ok he would come into town for
fun and games, stealing a horse, etc, this one time as I said before the doors
were always open and this one afternoon as Fran and myself trotted into the
dining room, who should be in there seated at the table none but Jack Haley
eating a great big sandwich. It was one of those long french bread cut it in half
long way and he took spoonfuls of raw hamburger and smeared the bread
with that and then poured catsup all over it we all watched in fascination
and then when we recovered our wits we asked him if we could see the gun
shots scars on his leg. He rolled up his pants to his knees and counted about
five holes in his leg. By that time he decided it was time to leave before Ma
or Pa showed up or the sheriff. He was a very wily person. A neighbor of
ours who had a saloon also prided himself on the six white hens he had in his
coop. So foxy Jack goes up to Mr. O'Shea and tells him very confidential that
he knows where he can get six more white hens to add to the six he already

has (Mr. O'Shea knew they belonged to some other owner) but it would cost him $20.00. $20.00 in those days was a fortune, so Mr. O'Shea gives him the $20.00 and Jack brings in six white hens. Mr. O'Shea was so happy he couldn't wait to get home (or didn't care were they come from) to add to his six and when he got home he found out that Jack Haley stole his own white hens and [he] paid $20.00 for them. He was a real honest to goodness horse thief. One day the horses that Papa owned were missing. They had no idea where the horses could of gone as the barn was locked and no way they could of strayed away. Papa was almost going crazy. He didn't know what to do, so who come to Papa's rescue but Jack Haley. He told Papa he knew where the horses were but it would cost Papa $25.00. Papa was glad to pay and get his charger back. It so happened that Jack stole the horses and needed the money—I wish I could remember his face but to this day all I can remember are those gun shot scars in his leg. One could almost put their finger in it. I lost my appetite when I saw him eating the raw meat. I was glad to see him get out of the house.

Mama had quite a way with horses. Mama and Papa had a friend who had quite a ranch and every month she would come to town and fill up on groceries and booze, she loved to drink and after spending all afternoon drinking she was really tipsy, but she didn't have to worry about driving home which was miles away, the horse knew she had a snout full and made his way home ok. One day we all went up to the ranch for some reason or other and it just happened that her son had a very sickly colt on his hands and was ready to

St. Ann School, East Helena.
Annie Lozar is in the second row from the top, third from left.

destroy it as they thought it would never get well. Mama took one look at the colt and told Jimmy that she will buy the colt for 50 cents. He was glad to get the 50 cents and Mama brought him home she nursed it and really gave all the care she could, he got well and grew up to be the most beautiful animal you ever saw. When the circus came to town one day they wanted to give Mama $2000 [maybe she meant $200] for him, but she wouldn't sell, he was quite a pet and always knew when she baked bread as he would kick the screen door until it flopped back and put his nose in the door and then open it and walk in and eat up half the freshly baked bread. One day he was missing for a whole day we looked all over the town for him and couldn't find him so who came to the house no one but Jack Haley tells Mama where Billie was (that was name of the horse). He was up the mountains about 10 miles from town and was about to be shipped out with the wild horses . . . Mama and us kids got into Steve's Ford and drove to where the horses were and sure enough there was Billie in with the others in a large corral. Mama had a halter and a feed oat bag and tried to coax Billie to her. The minute he heard her voice he started to come toward her, but he spotted us kids and went back to the pack so we all hid behind trees so he wouldn't see us and then he finally came to her and she put the halter on him and she had to walk the whole ten miles back home with Billie, Billie was never broken in for a saddle and as a result it was a slow walk back home. We couldn't hitch him to the back of the car as he was a nervous horse so we had to do it Billie's way.

Papa was inclined to be very stout or because as success climbed up he started to have trouble with his stomach and for some reason the doctors couldn't help him or didn't know what to do for him. So Mr. Kessler [the brewer] heard about Papa's illness and made him go to the Kellogg's institute. I don't know if it was a hospital or what. I believe it was in Michigan it's the same outfit that makes cornflakes, etc. Anyway he went and when he came back he was quite slim, but he was so careful with his diet . . . We couldn't eat bacon, pork, butter, if soup was made all the fat had to be skimmed off.

Poor Papa his health was never quite good, too bad, but after losing that mining lawsuit he never was the same . . . Papa had quite a generous streak in him which isn't very good especially if you are in business. Customers would come in and ask for credit and Papa would give it to them as the result no one would pay their bill and there was no way to collect.

I must tell you about the thunderstorms. We were always warned not to be up against a tree trunk don't step on rail road tracks, etc, but we were always lucky when one of those storms came along we would be in the house. I remember I was leaving our house to go to next door and suddenly a flash of lightning streak right across my path. Lucky it didn't do any damage but it was a terribly large blue streak. I guess I was lucky it didn't hit me. Thunder would be so loud it's almost hard to describe it but us kids would run and hide under the bed. Why I don't know.

Mary, Caroline, and Annie Lozar. The girl seated is Mary Rigler, the daughter of friends. This was probably taken on the occasion of Caroline's confirmation.

The winters in Montana were terrific as a child in East Helena we were forever freezing only a pot belly stove to heat 5 rooms. We had to walk to school. It was about 6 blocks away in the snow. A path had to be made and we walked that distance about 4 times a day. No one thought about packing us a lunch but Mama always had a hot lunch waiting for us which consist of hot boiled wine with hot cinnamon buttered toast. On our way back to school our spirits were light and gay but as we neared the school drowsiness began to set in. We couldn't understand why I was half asleep most of the time in school. The summers were almost as bad, it would get so hot you couldn't sleep at night and trying to do your daily tasks was almost agony especially when we had to keep the kitchen stove going to cook the meals. Autumn was the best of them all. The apples would be ready to pick. The trees were changing their color, but going back to summer time it had some good points, we use to go berry picking (it was chokecherries) and we would pack a lunch and away we would go (it seems like it was miles away) and when we got to the spot we would all work like demons to see who could get their pail filled first of course we had to eat them as we went along and as the result our lips, mouth, teeth were pure black and the juice from the berries were also on our clothes. Mama tried to make jelly but for all the delicious food she could cook making jelly was not her forte. She spent hours squeezing the juice from the berries and used pounds of sugar and the end result was pure rubber. It was so rubbery you couldn't spread it with a knife. I always said that Mama invented rubber, she was years ahead of Firestone. It was so hot in the summer we took to sleeping out on the porch. The nights were so silent, one could hear the pin drop. This one hot night I couldn't fall asleep so I tried to listen to the night sound and all I could hear was the steady hum of the electric wires that were strung across the county on the telegraph poles and a sudden thought struck me. As I said I would listen to the older folks talk and somewhere along the line, I heard them discussing the end of the world and one of them said the world will be destroyed by fire. Well that bothered me no end and as I was listening to the buzzing sound of the telegraph wires I said to myself I wonder if one of those wires will catch on fire and keep going until it burns out all the wire and just keep going and going.

East Helena was a pleasant little town it had shady trees on both side of the street in the summer they help shade the street and keep it cool. April or spring was another pleasant time. April showers were quite often and as a result it would bring out the freshness of the air. Lilac bushes also lined the streets and after a spring shower (of course lilacs would be in bloom) the whole town would have the most wonderful fragrance one would want. If one closed their eye you would believe someone spilled a bottle of lilac perfume.

STEPHIE SAID SHE COULD RIDE A HORSE into the prairie as far as she could see and not come to a fence.

Annie and Stephanie Lozar, June 8, 1913.

18

⤫

She Set Her Cap

It seems the Lozar women each had a twin—as far as temperament and personality. Mary and Stephie and their sister Caroline were quiet and reserved. Mother Caroline and Francie were cheerful and lively.

And then there was Annie, my grandma. Annie was unique. She had no twin in any shape, matter, or form. Incendiary, feisty, fiery, full of life, full of vim and vinegar, that was my grandma Annie. She had a sense of fun and mischief but did not cotton nonsense. She told it as she saw it, right between the eyes.

It was still the Wild West to a large extent when Annie grew up in that Montana saloon at the turn of the century. Saloon fights were regular occurrences. She saw one fellow bite off a piece of another man's ear in a fight. I can see Annie laughing while Stephie shrieked. One fight was so bad that Joe pressed charges—assault and battery. The brawler had to pay a fine of twenty-five dollars. Annie was fourteen when that happened.

When she was seventeen (the fall of 1910), Annie and her sister Mary attended Montana Wesleyan University in Helena, a nonsectarian Christian school at Warren and Helena Streets. Annie and Mary were day students. They lived at home in East Helena and took the streetcar to school. The young women who boarded at Mills Hall on North Ewing were advised to bring their own bedding, towels, napkins, napkin rings, and lace curtains. The men boarded in private homes but ate their meals at the ladies' dormitory. Tuition for a nine-week term was $12.50, unless paid in advance, in which case it was $11.25.

The school offered academics, music, elocution, commercial, and English courses. Annie and Mary enrolled in the commercial course. There were fifty-two students in the program that year. I'm guessing that Annie

141

took the bookkeeping course, since she became her father's bookkeeper. The course also included penmanship, business English, spelling, commercial arithmetic, letter filing and manifolding, physical culture, letter and commercial forms, rapid calculation, and actual business practice. It was two terms, each nine weeks.

After that, Annie and Mary attended St. Vincent's Academy. This was the spring quarter of 1911. It was a Catholic school run by the Sisters of Charity, the same order of nuns who taught them at St. Ann's grade school in East Helena. They studied literature, rhetoric, composition, elocution, and typewriting. Both Annie and Mary earned the top grade for deportment.

I couldn't find any record of Annie or her sisters attending Helena High School. While looking into that, I found a biography of the school principal at that time. He studied at Albion College, and at the university in Leipzig, Germany, and at the Sorbonne in Paris—quite a curriculum vitae.

In 1912, Annie's brother, Steve, attended Mount St. Charles High School in Helena. President Taft had spoken at the cornerstone laying ceremony in 1909 while in town to speak at the Montana State Fair. It was a Catholic men's high school and college (now Carroll College). Steve was fifteen and not at all interested in

Bridesmaid Annie Lozar. Years later when she wrote on the back of the picture, she couldn't remember the best man's name (I cropped him out). It was the marriage of Sam Stitch and Mary Schnellar in East Helena in 1910.

St. Vincent's Academy, school Annie and her sister Mary attended in 1911.
COLLECTION OF KENNETH BAIRD

going to school, so he didn't go. I'm told that when Joe found out, he marched Steve all the way from East Helena to Mount St. Charles, Joe driving a team of horses and Steve walking in front of the horses. That was around fourteen miles. It would have taken a good four hours walking. It's hard to imagine that Joe had that much time and patience. Steve didn't attend Mount St. Charles the following year; instead, he worked as a clerk in his father's store. Steve resumed his studies in 1914, but that was the last year he attended. He was seventeen.

The summer of 1914, the war started in Europe.

The New York Stock Exchange crashed on news of Austria-Hungary declaring war on Serbia.

"Markets of the World Demoralized by War," said the *Helena Independent*.

"An unofficial, but creditable report is current in diplomatic quarters that Austria-Hungary has offered to withdraw her troops from Servia and to submit her grievances to an international conference."

That didn't happen.

"Rumored Emperor Josef is Assassinated. Report not confirmed." I hope Caroline didn't see that. She would have been heartbroken. The war was bad enough, but her beloved emperor murdered, how tragic. It wasn't true.

Even so, the news quickly grew worse. "All trade at least for the moment blocked," said the headline on August 4. Half of American copper was exported. Montana was a huge copper-producing state. If copper mines were crippled, how would this domino onto the rest of the state? What about other metals? What about the smelter in East Helena?

The headline on August 8 was gigantic: "Worst Slaughter in HISTORY OF THE WORLD." It was about the Battle at Liege.

While absorbing the shock of what was happening in the Old Country and how it would affect the New World, life went on in East Helena for the Lozar family. Annie attended nursing school in Helena. "That's where she learned her rough language," Dad said, meaning that's where she learned to swear. Annie had her heart set on becoming a nurse until she saw something awful in the hospital, a cancer patient in a very bad way, and decided she didn't have the stomach for it. She quit nursing school and went to work for her father as a clerk in the store and as his bookkeeper.

Her sister Mary worked as a maid for Guy C. Riddell, who was the superintendent at the smelter. She also worked as a clerk in their father's grocery store. Their brother, Steve, ran a saloon with another fellow.

Steve said once when Annie was tending bar, she poured vinegar instead of whiskey for one of the patrons. That may have been a metaphorical telling of the story. She might have poured vinegar alright, verbal vinegar. That would be Annie. She was a spitfire. And that would be Steve to describe her that way. She had all the subtlety of a Mack truck, and Steve liked to joke about her.

*Prickly Pear Band. Annie's brother, Steve, is the handsome guy
in the front row, third from the right, 1919.*
MONTANA HISTORICAL SOCIETY PAC2001-32.1

Annie Lozar, 1915

Stephie wrote in her letter to me, "I do remember your grandmother Annie. She was quite beautiful. She had hair that had that golden touch and the deepest blue eyes and was always dressed in very smart clothes. She was Papa's pet, and she knew it."

Even as a child, I sensed there was a bit of mischief about Grandma L (Annie). I was only fifteen when she passed away, so there's a lot she wouldn't have told me because I was so young. When I asked about the old days when she was young in East Helena, she grinned and said, "Those were the days of real sport." Somehow I knew I was too young to know what she meant. That's what she said when Mom asked too. She didn't elaborate, just grinned.

ON JULY 8, 1915, Annie's sister Caroline had a baby boy. She was sixteen. Annie said, "Caroline got mixed up with an Irishman, and she didn't want to marry him!" It was a tone that did not invite questions. Other than his name on the baby's birth certificate, I could not find hide nor hair of the father in any records. His name was Robert. Young Caroline named her baby Robert. She would never have another child.

Some time after Caroline's baby was born, Annie heard about a European musician who was coming to East Helena. She was keen to meet him. In her twenty-two-year-old imagination, she no doubt pictured him to be tall, slender, dashing, handsome, urbane, much at ease—and he was.

Stephie said, as soon as Annie saw him, "She set her cap for him."

PART THREE

ANNIE AND TONY

19

❦

New York to East Helena

Caroline and Joe and Tony had one other thing in common besides being Slovenians from Austria: within days of arriving on these shores, they were all working, even though none of them spoke English. They arrived, they went to work, they became part of the colorful patchwork that is America. There was no government largesse to help Tony, a war refugee, settle into life in America. He did it himself. Immigrants were expected to arrive with enough money to get a start in life. Immigrants helped each other. They banded together to form ethnic fraternal organizations that provided sick and death benefits. These "friendly societies" were a way of providing insurance that was also social. Taking care of one's own was part of the culture. Members paid dues and checked in on the sick. They celebrated together, they mourned together, they comforted the bereaved. Though there were public hospitals, the safety net was largely local, private, and voluntary.

No one settled Tony. He settled himself. He had to.

Not only did Tony find a job within days of arriving, it was in his chosen profession as a musician. One of his early gigs was performing as a substitute with the Chicago Symphony.

It was truly the land of the free and the home of the brave. Tony and Joe and Caroline and others like them were free to come here and work and start a business. There were next to no encumbrances to do so. Barriers to finding a job, starting a business, hiring people were few or nonexistent. A person didn't need permission from the government to work or to hire people. The message was: welcome to America and good luck. You're on your own, sink or swim. The immigrant had to be brave to attempt it, especially those who did not yet speak English.

Tony's brother, Joseph Leskovar, would soon open his own butcher shop.

The Viennese author I mentioned earlier, Stefan Zweig, told of visiting New York between 1900 and 1910, close to the time Tony arrived. He said he found five jobs in two days. He didn't have a passport. They weren't required. No one asked about his nationality.

When Tony passed through Ellis Island, no official asked whether he was coming for a short visit or to settle here permanently. Not everyone who arrived by ship was planning to immigrate. A lot of immigrants didn't know whether they would stay permanently. Many stayed several years and then went back for good.

It was simple and fluid. Stay as long as you want, leave if you want, come back if you want.

"What happened after you got to New York?"

"Socsur put me up in hotel for three days," Tony said. Socsur was the travel agent through whom Tony's brother, Joe, sent the steamship ticket. Socsur took Tony sightseeing around New York City.

"He show me the whole town," Tony said.

"Then where did you go?"

"I went to Joe in Aurora," his brother in Aurora, Illinois.

"What was Joe doing in Aurora?"

"Butcher. They had a little store."

"Was he married then?"

"Oh yeah. He was married nine years. Then I started play there, orchestra, band, travel around. Oh, I make sixty, seventy dollars per month, just jobs, not steady."

Tony made his declaration of intention to become an American citizen. In doing so he renounced all allegiance to Emperor Franz Joseph of Austria and declared that he was not an anarchist, and he was not a polygamist. (Did anyone ever say, *yes, I'm an anarchist*?) He no longer had to claim he was Serbian. He was safely out of the war zone.

Back then, with the exception of the Chinese, we let in all able-bodied people, as long as they didn't admit to being anarchists or polygamists and had enough money with them to get a start in life; in other words, they weren't sick or impoverished or a "lunatic" and wouldn't immediately depend on charity.

At no time did any immigration officer at Ellis Island tell Tony or his brother, Joe, or any other immigrant how his name should be spelled or change his name. It is a pervasive modern myth that immigrants' names were changed at Ellis Island. Though the ship's doctor wrote "Antoine Leskover" on the passenger manifest, he was always Anton Leskovar and went by Tony. He didn't even know how the ship's doctor spelled his name on the manifest. Life was much more organic. Exactitude in things as mundane as a man's date of birth or the spelling of his name didn't seem important.

"Let's see, I was in the union already," Tony said. "I joined the union in Aurora, the musicians union. That was in 1915, yes. Then I played two weeks with the army, what do you call, militia, Fort Snelling [Minnesota]. They were short musicians, and I was going to substitute for a fellow. I was playing not the bassoon but the clarinet. Two weeks. In the militia. Around a forty-five piece band, full band. We played at Lake Harriet [Minnesota]. After we got through, made trip to Duluth for Elks convention. Then got back and I got a job . . . for three months, thirty-five dollars a month."

Movies back then were what today we call silent movies; the dialogue was written on the screen, the audience could not hear the actors speak. However, the moviegoing experience wasn't silent. A live orchestra accompanied the movie to provide dramatic or comic effect. Movies were on film, the film was stored in cans, and the cans of film traveled from town to town. The orchestra traveled with the movie. The movie company employed local musicians to fill in as needed. Tony performed with silent movies in both capacities.

Tony found himself in Flint, Michigan. I wonder if a movie gig took him there. He went to one of the automobile factories (Buick or Chevrolet) looking for work. He joined the crowd of men massed at the factory entrance. The boss called out, "Any of you know how to paint?" Tony raised his hand. The boss hired him. Truth be told he did not know how to paint, but he knew he could learn, and he needed the work. He painted cars with a beavertail brush. The year before Tony arrived, Henry Ford started paying factory workers five dollars a day for an eight-hour day, a giant leap up from $2.34 for a nine-hour day.

Tony found another gig traveling in the orchestra for a silent movie. This one took him west, quite a ways west, through several states, into Montana, to Helena, and there the movie company went broke.

He went to work using his new skill—painting cars.

"Then I see in paper they are looking for music teacher in Helena," Tony said. "I mean East Helena, bandleader, you know. They send me the ticket. One hundred dollars a month. So I took that job in East Helena."

At Joe Lozar's store, as with other grocery and mercantile stores, the goods were kept behind the counter. The customer would give the clerk a shopping list, and the clerk would gather everything together and put it in a wooden crate. The customer could take the groceries or have them delivered. If the customer and the store had telephones, the customer could call with her shopping list and have the groceries delivered. In addition to being the bandleader for the smeltermen's band, Tony worked part-time delivering groceries for Joe Lozar.

And there he met Annie.

Poor Tony. He went from performing for kings and queens in European capitals to delivering groceries in tiny East Helena, Montana.

But he met Annie.

As for the smeltermen in the band, Tony said, "They was bucking and fighting, those fellows. I see another ad in the Slovenian paper looking for bandleader in Minnesota. They gonna give me one hundred dollars a month, even a job to go on working in a store, yeah, four dollars, that was pretty good, that if I wanna work, that was extra way to make money. I do that job in Minnesota. They send me the ticket. I went to Minneapolis."

And then he came back.

20

Enemy of the State — Again

That will not do, Mother Caroline said. St. Joseph's Day is in March. This is October. You can't name him Joseph.

Though his birth certificate said Joseph, his name became Edward at the baptism. St. Edward's feast day is October 13.

Edward was born October 1, 1916. Naming him after St. Francis would have made the most sense, since his feast day is October 4; however, I can imagine Annie not wanting to give her firstborn the masculine form of her pesky baby sister's name. Annie and Tony's second child was born two years later, on May 8, 1918. He was named Cyril, after one of the saints for whom their parish church was named, St. Cyril and Methodius, the Slavic saints. This was no doubt Mother Caroline exerting her Slovenian cultural influence again, naming the child after the saint of the day, or near the day, or after the saint of the parish church. Annie was born in July, the month of St. Ann's feast day. Her sister Mary was born two days before the Feast of the Birth of Mary. Steve was born a few days after St. Stephen's Day. It didn't always work this way because the saint's name had already been given to another child, but you get the idea.

Annie must have asserted herself at her second son's baptism, or she and her mother arrived at a truce; he was baptized Anton Cyril. He was the baby, so they called him Babe. Year after year no more babies; he would be the baby of the family for nine years. The name stuck. He would be Babe for the rest of his life.

When Annie and Tony married in 1916, Tony had been in the country a little over a year. He had to be here five years before he could become a citizen. Under the law at the time (the Expatriation Act passed in 1907), if an American woman married an alien, she lost her American citizenship.

153

Though Annie had never stepped foot outside the United States, not even out of the state of Montana, the American government decided she must belong to some other nation. When she married Tony, she lost her American citizenship. She was deemed a woman with no country, just a husband.

The law would be repealed in 1922 (the Cable Act) but was not grand-fathered. Annie remained a woman with no country.

Annie had grown up to be the most Slovenian of Joe and Caroline's daughters. Her first language was Slovenian. Her mother taught her fine crochet work, so fine it is lace. She made potica, she made chicken noodle soup from scratch with homemade noodles. She would be the only one of Joe and Caroline's children to marry a Slovenian.

TONY BORE THE CARRIAGE and confidence of a cosmopolitan man, one who appreciated the finer things in life. He was handsome, stately, dapper, with a commanding presence, a man of few words.

Then we have Annie—born in a bar, raised in a saloon full of hardscrabble smeltermen, full of vim and vinegar, never one to hold back a sharp word.

Debonair and sophisticated marries brash and feisty. It was Cary Grant marrying Molly Brown, an uncontrolled conflagration of dynamite and blasting caps.

What could possibly go wrong?

Talented artists, creative souls often march to the beat of their own drummers. They can be larger than life. This can make them difficult to live with.

And there you have Tony.

He was a hard worker. He almost always had more than one job. He was meticulous about any work he put his mind to.

"I played in Helena, in the East Helena band," Tony said.

"You started a paint shop?"

"Oh yeah, I started a paint shop." A car painting shop.

"What kind of shop did you have in Helena? Did you have a shop in Helena?"

"Oh yes. I was connected with the Studebaker there."

"Did you forget how you worked in the smelter?" Annie said.

"Oh, yeah, night shift, yeah."

THE YEAR THEIR FIRST CHILD, Eddy, was born, President Woodrow Wilson was running for reelection on the campaign theme "he kept us out of war." Why

Annie holding Eddy, 1916.

would Americans in 1916 have thought we'd be going to war? Yes, there was
a war in Europe, but there had been plenty of wars in Europe with no serious
talk of our getting into them. Why would we? There was the Franco-Prussian
War in 1870, and those wars in the Balkans I talked about earlier. There was
the Austro-Prussian War in 1866, and Napoleon's wars of conquest. We didn't
get involved, nobody even entertained the idea. Why would it be different
now? Yes, a German submarine commander fired torpedoes at the passenger
liner *Lusitania* and sank her, and innocent passengers drowned, including
Americans, but President Wilson told the Germans to stop firing torpedoes
on innocent passengers, and they did stop. That was a year ago. We didn't go
to war over it. There was a little something called the Monroe Doctrine—you

Europeans worry about your hemisphere, and we'll worry about our hemisphere. Why not stick with that?

Only one month after Wilson began his second term, he sent Congress a declaration of war against Germany.

This was April of 1917. Since we declared war on Germany, that meant we were on the side of France, Britain, Russia, Belgium, and Serbia. Why? Because the Germans invaded neutral Belgium, which started to turn American public opinion against Germany, and became worse after Germany started to sink merchant and passenger ships, in particular the luxury liner *Lusitania*, and then Germany sank American merchant ships, and then the Zimmerman telegram was made public in which Germany tried to pull Mexico into war against the United States.

Austria had nothing to do with any of this but was an ally of Germany. On December 7, 1917, we declared war on Austria-Hungary.

Tony was an enemy of the state—again. He kept a low profile.

To put it another way, when the greatest military might in the world, the German army, invaded neutral little Belgium and started brutally laying waste to the country, destroying cities and executing civilians, international outrage turned from disgust with those who murdered Austrian Archduke Franz Ferdinand, to disgust with those attacking Belgium—which was Germany. Germany was the new bad guy. Even though

Belgian troops with dogs pulling machine guns.
Belgian official photographer

St. Helena Cathedral. This cathedral replaced the Cathedral of the Sacred Hearts of Jesus and Mary. The picture was taken July 3, 1917, three months after we entered the First World War.
Montana Historical Society PAc74-104.GP359. Edward M. Reinig, photographer

Austria was the original aggrieved party—it was their crown prince who was assassinated—Austria was on the side of Germany. Those believed to be behind the perpetrators of the original dastardly deed, the assassination of the archduke, were the Serbs, and they were on the same side as poor little Belgium, the victim. Crazy.

It was a hastily played high-stakes chess match gone horribly wrong.

What was this young man, Tony Leskovar, doing here? He arrived in this country only days after the *Lusitania* was sunk, sending more than one hundred Americans to drown in the frigid north Atlantic. He was of military age. He spoke German. What was he doing here?

He hadn't been here long enough to become a citizen.

Annie's sisters Mary and Caroline were working. Opportunities for young women in East Helena were limited to say the least, but there were jobs in Helena, only a streetcar ride away. Caroline worked as a maid for Dr. Barbour and his wife. The Barbours lived on the West Side in a lovely Queen Anne home with a wraparound porch, just west of Main Street. Dr. Barbour was Sam Hauser's nephew. Mrs. Barbour had an in-law connection to Nicholas Kessler, the brewer from Luxembourg from whom Joe Lozar bought beer for his saloon.

An Englishman living in Montana wrote, "There are no gentry & common people—one is as good as another. Master and maid, mistress & servant meet & shake hands. In fact there are very few servants at all."

In fact, a state report bemoaned the "servant girl problem," the problem being it was difficult to find "adequate domestic help" in Montana. "Housekeepers expect one girl to do the work of three in Europe." Young women would rather work in an office doing clerical work or in a department store, even for half the wages of a live-in maid. "It is quite natural, inasmuch as any woman with a spark of ambition would prefer to choose a position which gives promise of equality and advancement."

Even if Mary and Caroline did not want to work as maids, there were other jobs in Helena.

But Mary did not work in Helena. She left. She went to Great Falls. She worked as a clerk at the Bee Hive and roomed at the Hotel Ben. Why did she leave? What did Great Falls offer that Helena didn't? Young Caroline also left. She went to San Francisco. Was it a sense of adventure, wanting to spread their wings? Or was there another reason they left? Did it have something to do with one Will Campbell?

FAREWELL, JOHN NEILL
HELLO, WILL CAMPBELL

"Austria, Turkey and Bulgaria Are to Sever Relations With the United States"

"Scores of Teut Suspects to go to Cells, Horde Being Watched!"

"Thousands of Aliens Have Been Put Under Close Surveillance"

Those were the front-page headlines in the Helena paper the day after the United States declared war on Germany (*Helena Daily Independent*, April 7, 1917).

Sixty alleged "ringleaders in German plots, conspiracies and machinations" were arrested across the land, all of them civilians. "Bail will be refused in each case . . . the entire group will be locked up."

"For the first time in more than a century, arrests of alien enemies under the attorney general's order will be made without reference to the courts. The president is empowered to adopt this course in time of war under an act of Congress passed in 1798 and not invoked since the war with Great Britain in 1812."

The government was prepared to challenge any *habeas corpus* petitions.

Germany required young men to do military service. Once they finished, they were automatically reservists. They had no choice. This was also the case for Austrians. That meant our Tony was an Austrian reservist. Thousands of such German reservists in America were put under surveillance by the Secret Service and the Bureau of Investigation.

In contrast to those headlines, the paper's editor, Will Campbell, reminded readers that between 1840 and 1850 many Germans immigrated to the United States and assimilated. "They became part of the bone, blood, and sinew of the nation. . . . It would be a crime and a dishonor to our nation to look upon or treat these people as other than our loyal fellow Americans."

Shortly after John Neill died, his family sold the newspaper to a group of prominent Democrats. They brought in Will Campbell as publisher and editor. He was from Nebraska. He had been doing publicity for the railroads, trying to entice easterners to venture to the West and attempt dryland farming. He was a Republican. He checked the prevailing wind and switched to Democrat. In time, he would own the paper.

On June 7, 1917, the paper reported that there were one hundred and sixteen enemy aliens in Lewis and Clark County.

Almost since the war started, Americans were reading about German atrocities against Belgian civilians.

The July 8, 1917, editorial, I assume written by Will Campbell since he was the editor, talked about efforts made by the German government in 1902 to foment civil war in the United States. It said the German government had urged German-Americans to rise up and take over on behalf of the kaiser. If you were sitting in your kitchen in 1917 and read only that far, you'd be pretty upset. Enraged. Today you might say, I don't remember learning that. That's because it didn't happen. The editorial went on to say, "Though appearing in a satirical publication this is a serious and timely exposure of Teutonic deceit and the diabolical attempts to turn the United States over to the authority of the Prussian militaristic regime." Since the Zimmerman telegram, in which Germany tried to convince Mexico to go to war against the United States, had been released a few months earlier, this sort of story fed into fears of sinister plots authored by the kaiser and the German government, even though this bit about fomenting civil war in 1902 was completely made up.

Back in July of 1916, the year before we entered the war, German saboteurs blew up Black Tom Island in New York Harbor. This was where munitions were transferred from rail to ships bound for France and Britain. The Germans naturally wanted to cut off this supply route. The explosion obliterated the island, blew out windows in Manhattan, tore holes in the Statue of Liberty, and woke up people in Maryland.

Because of the effective British blockade of Germany, though we were officially neutral, we couldn't sell munitions to Germany.

The next month, August of 1916, still before we were in the war, President Wilson created the Council of National Defense, the purpose of which was to coordinate industries and resources in the event of war, to ease mobilization. Yes, you have that right. He did this while he was campaigning for reelection on the slogan that he kept us out of war. The national council spawned state and local councils of defense. In Montana, the state Council of Defense was headed by Governor Stewart, but the most influential member was newspaperman Will Campbell.

Early on, the council busied itself with trying to increase food production, as if farmers didn't already do that. After we declared war, their mission morphed from facilitating mobilization to promoting loyalty, and with great vigor. This they could sink their teeth into.

If you weren't gung-ho about the war, you'd better keep it to yourself. You better buy Liberty bonds, you better not be caught eating meat on meatless days, you better not be suspected of being a slacker, you better not be suspected of any warm feelings toward anything German.

Will Campbell called German "the most despised language in history."

Americans now ate "liberty cabbage," not sauerkraut.

Before long, it wasn't enough to support the war, you must tell on anyone who might disagree. Disagreeing with the war meant you were disloyal. This could be considered criminal behavior. Anti-disloyalty fever swept the land.

Will Campbell and his associates set to work rooting out pro-German spies and slackers and any inkling of "pro-Germanism." This went on throughout the country, but in some places it was more virulent than others. Helena, Montana, was one such place, due in large part to one Will Campbell.

In August of 1917, U.S. marshals arrested Justice of the Peace John Langdon of Marysville because his neighbors said that he said he hated England, he hoped England would lose the war, Germany was in the right, and the United States was in the wrong. He was an elderly curmudgeon from Ireland who was an American citizen and had lived in this country for a very long time.

My Irish great-grandfather said much the same, but he lived in Butte, an island surrounded by land, a world unto itself. He was not arrested.

The same day the story about Justice of the Peace Langdon appeared in the paper, Will Campbell ran this headline on the front page: "Airship Seen Flying Above Helena. Have German's Spy Post Near Here?" The article led off: "Is there a German observation post nestled down in some secluded nook of the Rockies adjacent to Helena?" A couple who were up late, much later than most in Helena, claimed that they saw "an airplane of curious design . . . hovering over the city." In the dark, they saw this. There were no lights on airplanes in 1917. Pretty dangerous to be flying an airplane in the Rocky Mountains at night, with no radar, no lights, never knowing when a cloud would slip in front of the moon, if there was a moon. They said the plane crashed in a swamp near Hamilton, but it was so remote, it couldn't be investigated until it froze over. How convenient. Oh, and they said the plane was silent, it made no noise. Remarkable. A stealth prop.

First off, no one had as yet flown across the Atlantic. Lindbergh's historic flight was still ten years off. Second, Hamilton is a hundred miles from Helena as the crow flies.

Did anyone actually believe this?

The next day the paper showed a picture of New York City in ruins, skyscrapers toppled, smoke billowing from the wreckage, ships in the harbor sunk. The headline read, "EXTRA! 2000 killed in German Air-Sea Raid on New York!" "What will happen when Kaiser's u-boats and battle planes Strike at the U.S." Upon closer inspection, one could see it was not a photograph but an artist's rendering. Yellow journalism at its worst. I wonder how many people read only those headlines, didn't read the caption and article, and believed that really happened.

I have researched the First World War extensively. I knew that no American city was attacked. But when I stumbled across that picture in the newspaper, I was taken aback. It looked so real.

"How soon will the Germans raid New York City from sea and sky?" asked Campbell in his editorial.

Campbell offered one hundred dollars to the person who could find the suspicious airplane that two of his reporters were sure they heard. This one not so silent.

"Are Germans about to bomb the capital of Montana?" he asked.

When I read all those outrageous things that Will Campbell put in the paper, I thought he was just some charlatan opportunist trying to sell more newspapers. No one in their right mind could actually believe all that, so I thought. Then I came across this: "It is, therefore, an effort in the interest of Germany to turn the United States into a larger Belgium—an easy prey for Germany whenever Germany desires to seize it." No firebrand newspaperman said that. Oh no. Former president Theodore Roosevelt said that. Actually he wrote it before we entered the war, before German Foreign Minister Arthur Zimmerman wrote his fateful telegram trying to foment war between us and Mexico.

Politicians from across Montana convened in Helena for the legislative session and decided to codify this anti-disloyalty fever with passage of the Montana Sedition Act. That was in February of 1918.

The legislature gave the Council of Defense the authority of an elected body. Anyone who dared disobey the council could end up in jail—for a year. Now Will Campbell not only had the power of the press, he could throw you in jail.

In March, people burned German textbooks in the street in Lewistown.

In April, at Campbell's insistence, the Montana Council of Defense forbade use of the German language in schools and churches and banned German books from public libraries.

German books were burned across the state, from Great Falls to Miles City.

Even after the war ended, Campbell still wanted to ban the German language. Keep in mind, we are talking about the First World War, not the Second.

The politicians in Washington cast their collective gaze across the land to the west, saw what was happening faraway in Montana, liked what they saw, and decided to do the same. They took the Montana Sedition Act and put a federal stamp on it, essentially copying it. The Federal Sedition Act passed and was signed by President Wilson in May of 1918. President Wilson created the Committee for Public Information, a war propaganda organ encouraging Americans to tell on each other, to tell on any suspected spies or slackers or German sympathizers, any sign of disloyalty.

Many men went to prison under the Montana Sedition Act, convicted by the testimony of tattletales repeating chitchat. Most of those convicted were born in Germany or Austria, but not all. While in Red Lodge, a hapless American-born traveling salesman from San Francisco started mouthing off about the war, about how ridiculous the food regulations were, and that Americans had no business boarding the *Lusitania* since it was carrying wheat to England, which meant it could be sunk by German torpedoes. For saying all that, he was arrested, charged, and convicted of sedition, and was sentenced to seven-and-a-half to twenty-one years in the Montana State Prison.

Being opinionated became a crime.

An Austrian rancher near Miles City said the war was none of our business, and we had no business sticking our nose in it. Off with his head, said the Red Queen. Well, not quite. He was sentenced to three to six years and ended up serving eighteen months. But since he died four months after he was released, perhaps the Red Queen did have her way.

Sedition "is the most heinous act that a citizen of this country can commit," declared the deputy county attorney in Helena.

Any man accused of sedition should be taken out and shot at dawn, said his boss, the county attorney.

Some saloon owners would not allow talk about the war on their premises. I wonder if Joe Lozar was one of them.

Will Campbell was relentless. "YOUR NEIGHBOR, YOUR MAID, YOUR LAWYER, YOUR WAITER MAY BE A GERMAN SPY."

Your maid.

Young Caroline Lozar, Annie's sister, worked as a maid for Sam Hauser's nephew, Dr. Barbour, and his wife. Did it become untenable for the Barbours to employ her, the daughter of a German-speaking couple from Austria? Did Will Campbell's vitriol make life miserable for Young Caroline and her sister Mary?

Mary and Caroline were twenty-three and nineteen. Such pressure, such venom from official sources, such public shaming based on identity, can be unbearable for anyone, but especially for the young and unattached.

They left.

Mary went to Great Falls. Caroline fled to San Francisco.

22

THE WHOLE KIT AND CABOODLE

HE LOST IT IN A CARD GAME—that was one story I heard. It's an old Montana saw but quite out of character for Joe to be that reckless—a wife and children to support, and he would toss away their home and livelihood in a card game? Nevertheless, I sleuthed that tale to see if it were true. It wasn't. Had it been true, the county deed book would have shown his selling it for a dollar. It doesn't. It didn't happen. He never sold the house or the saloon or the grocery store—ever. I'm guessing someone said it as a way of not saying what happened.

"Papa's business was going from bad to worse and he was ailing. . . . He couldn't collect the hundreds of dollars that the customers owed him." That's what his daughter Stephie told me.

Annie was brutally frank: "The Irish didn't pay their bills!"

Joe did have to go to court to get a customer to pay her bill. Just as the sheriff was about to impound her property, she and Joe settled. She was not Irish.

I also heard that Joe was grub-staking miners.

Those could all be pieces of the same sad story.

As I mentioned earlier, people didn't pay for groceries and whatnot right away. They bought on credit, the merchant kept track, and the customer paid the bill at the end of the month. It was incumbent upon a successful merchant to hold the line on credit. Frank Gorsich, the Slovenian butcher in town, said he would allow only so much credit and then if the customer didn't pay, he wouldn't give any more credit until he paid. Apparently Joe was a soft touch. That's what Stephie said. The bills owed to him stacked up.

People not paying their bills can happen any time. The lawsuit with the woman who wouldn't pay her bill was way back in 1903. What happened in the ensuing years to cause Joe's financial house to crumble?

165

He still suffered from that lingering ailment—gold fever. That didn't help. You'd think losing the lawsuit might have cured him, but no, not in the least. He was undaunted. The siren would not relent. Captain Ahab to the end. Hope springs eternal for a man with gold fever. Joe would not give up. Low-grade ore could lead to high-grade ore. It did for others, it could for him. One month after he lost the claim jumping lawsuit against John and Henry Neill in district court, before the case went to the Montana Supreme Court, he claimed four, yes, four more mines in the Mitchell Gulch area southeast of East Helena. These were in Jefferson County, not far from the once vibrant mining district around Clancy. Joe named his new mines the Hecla Nos. 1, 2, 3, and 4 Lodes. In 1912, he claimed the Larjorn Lode next to the Hecla No. 2. In all those mines, he found gold, silver, and copper. But was there enough good ore to make the mine profitable? That was always the question and the risk. All told, Joe had eight mines: the Atlantic, the Sunrise, the Alice and Lorna Doon, the Hecla Nos. 1, 2, 3, 4, and now the Larjorn Lode. I have the tunnel survey he commissioned for one of those mines in October of 1915. It showed 270 feet of tunnels. If he did that much work on all of them . . . oh my, that is expensive. As the song goes, "another day older and deeper in debt." If only he hadn't gone into debt to do all this.

"Of all those expensive and uncertain projects which bring bankruptcy upon the greater part of the people that engage in them, there is none perhaps more perfectly ruinous than the search after new silver and gold mines," wrote Adam Smith in *The Wealth of Nations*.

Yes, gold fever gripped him, the siren song of the Big Bonanza, the search for the Mother Lode, it was there, buried treasure, under the earth somewhere; with hard work and luck it was only a matter of time before he found it. Mining gobbled up his money like a voracious beast—buying lumber to

Stephie wrote on the back: "This is the entrance to the tunnel of Papa's mine. Your great grand uncle Steve pushing the tram." On the front she wrote: "Steve at the mine Mitchell Gulch."

timber the shafts and tunnels, hiring miners to dig the tunnels, buying air pipe, tools, mules to pull the heavy wagon loads of ore to the smelter, hay to feed the mules, groceries to feed the miners. Even if he weren't in poor health, he couldn't possibly mine all those mines himself. He had to hire help.

Meanwhile, the stack of bills owed to the Lozar store kept mounting.

Eight gold mines and a saloon and a grocery store weren't enough. Joe and two men from Helena filed a coal declaratory statement on some land out in Granite County. A coal declaratory statement was a way of claiming public land believed to contain coal. It turned out the land had already been claimed by someone else under the Homestead Act. Never one to give up on anything, Joe appealed. It dragged on for almost two years. The Land Office still denied his claim. I found out about this by accident. Who knows what other land deals he was into that I didn't find. While he was doing all this, who was minding the store?

His cousin Peter Lozar did until he died of consumption in April of 1907.

Up until 1907, Joe owned all his property—the saloon, the store, the house—free and clear, no mortgages. On November 1, 1907, two months before he went to court against John and Henry Neill in the claim jumping lawsuit, Joe took out a chattel mortgage on his livestock. As far as I can tell, this was the first time he went into debt.

Nine years later, in December of 1916, he mortgaged the property—all of it. Why?

I searched the county tax books for clues. Joe was never delinquent on his taxes. He routinely overpaid his property tax. In 1910, his property was worth $3,175. This included the saloon, the grocery store, the house, the merchandise, the carriage, two mules, harnesses, and two cows.

This was in the days before income tax and sales tax and social security and Medicare withholding. For Joe, his property tax and business tax were it. The property tax was levied on all significant property, not only the land and house, but also livestock, wagons, and so on.

What else was going on to contribute to his financial demise? Did people steal from him?

Back in 1904, Joe leased farm equipment on his ranch to Henry Rohde [or Rhode], a German immigrant from Bremen who also lived in East Helena. Rohde agreed to buy the goods but never did. Joe asked him to pay up or return the goods. When Rohde refused, Joe had no choice but to go to court. He filed a complaint in Jefferson County. The court ordered Sheriff Gibson to retrieve Joe's property from Rohde and return it to Joe.

The property Joe was trying to recover was worth four hundred and fifty dollars. This included eight scythes, a grindstone, three picks, chains, two wood augurs, two blacksmith rasps, a monkey wrench, two hatchets, a cook stove, cooking utensils, dishes, two lamps, one hand hay rake, two sets of work harnesses, three horses, a mule, a plow, two calves, four scythe handles, a blacksmith's vice, three shovels, a hay rake, two iron drills, three hundred feet of rope, two axes, two nail hammers, an alarm clock, two lanterns, a hay fork, a wagon, and two rain coats.

All Sheriff Gibson could find and return to Joe were a harness, a grindstone, the blacksmith vice, one rake, two small chains, and a mare—only a fraction of Joe's property.

Wait a minute, you say. What's this about Joe's ranch? What ranch? That was my reaction too when I stumbled across this in the court records while looking for something else. The court records said all this property was on Joe Lozar's ranch known as Joe Kastner's Place, on Maupin Gulch Creek. The following month, the federal government charged Joe with mending a fence on three hundred and fifty acres of public land on Maupin Gulch Creek. Yes, the fence mending fiasco. Henry Rhode [Rohde] and his wife were witnesses in the fence mending trial.

All of that was unfortunate, but it happened years before Joe started to mortgage his property.

Was there something else going on, forces beyond his control?

Well, yes, another panic. The Panic of 1907.

Historians trace the first rumblings leading to the Panic of 1907 to the huge earthquake that struck San Francisco in April of 1906. The quake caused a fire, the fire burned so hot the bank vaults could not be opened for some time. Much money was needed to rebuild The City. Money was in demand. Money became expensive. The result was tight money—a shortage of available credit—which made it expensive to borrow, meaning high interest rates for borrowers. This rippled across the country. With money commanding high rates, why risk owning stocks? Cash became more attractive. People sold stocks for cash to loan out at high rates. Insurance companies sold stocks because they needed cash to pay off enormous claims resulting from the earthquake. This spurred a sell-off in the market. Stock prices slid downward. Insurance and railroad stocks were hit especially hard. When the stock price plummets, the market value of the company drops. This can make it more difficult for the company to borrow money. In March of 1907, in only a matter of days, mining stocks tumbled 14.5 percent. Other industries saw worse drops. This was on top of the 7.7 percent slide that began in September. The downward slide continued, as if the stock market were on a sled that hit a patch of ice, which threw it out of control with nothing to grab onto as the hill grew steeper and steeper.

The values of ores mined in Montana crashed: gold dropped 26.5 percent, silver dropped 23 percent, lead dropped 22 percent. (This was from 1906 to 1907.)

"Money is commanding such high rates that it is impossible to float even gilt-edge securities at the low figures." This from the March 23, 1907, issue of the *Commercial and Financial Chronicle*.

Now comes Fritz Heinze, the most notorious and colorful of Montana's Copper Kings. This swashbuckling mining buccaneer made millions, mainly in court. He was said to have "the torso of a Yale halfback" and to have lived alone in a log cabin when he first came to Butte, or so said *McClure's* magazine. It sounds romantic, but I bet he lived in a boardinghouse. I had to check. In the early days before he made it big, he lived in Mary Rutledge's boardinghouse at 42 Main Street in Meaderville, next to Butte.

In his pitched battles in the War of the Copper Kings, Fritz Heinze fought fierce foes—two of the biggest companies in the world: Amalgamated, which was the holding company of the Anaconda Copper Mining Company, and the mighty Standard Oil. He walked away from that fight unscathed and wildly rich. However, as metal prices continued their precarious slide downward in October of 1907, things were looking grim for the swashbuckling Fritz Heinze. He and his brother, Otto, tried to rescue the stock of their company by cornering it, meaning they secretly bought their own stock to run up the price. The idea was then to sell and cash in. It was a risky venture, a game of chicken, but he was a moth who loved to fly close to the flame. Some historians say Amalgamated and Standard Oil manipulated the stock and spread vile rumors on Wall Street to punish and take down the buccaneer. If they did that, and if that was their intention, it worked. The stock cornering scheme went horribly wrong. The stock price of Heinze's company plunged from sixty dollars to ten dollars, which caused a run on his bank and took down his company and his brother's brokerage firm. When word got out that the esteemed Knickerbocker Trust Company was mixed up with Heinze, there was a run on that bank, and it failed. Heinze was wiped out. The president of the Knickerbocker Trust, Charles Barney, shot himself.

This prompted a run on any trust (a type of bank) associated with Fritz Heinze and Charles Morse, who was his accomplice in the cornering scheme. Other banks were reluctant to lend money, lest they face a run on their deposits. Interest rates skyrocketed. Brokers couldn't borrow money to buy stock. The stock market crashed. In three weeks the New York Stock Exchange dropped fifty percent.

This was the Panic of 1907.

Added to this, politicians were inflicting uncertainty on the markets. President Theodore Roosevelt's Justice Department sued scores of corporations. The financial press called him "the irritant." Even at ridiculously low prices, it was difficult to lure investors because of this uncertainty. Jack Morgan, Jr., son of J. P., wrote to his partners in London, "There is a tremendous productive capacity in this country, . . . this productive capacity has not been one whit reduced by the colic we have all been having."

Mining and railroad stocks were walloped. Some mines in Montana shut down for several months. Any time mining is hurt, smelters are hurt. All this had to hurt East Helena, a one-shop smelter town, which hurt Joe's business.

Conrad Hilton wrote of his father's predicament at that time. He owned a mercantile in New Mexico. Prices dropped below what he had paid for the goods. "Money simply didn't exist in the fall of '07. He lost a lot. He owed a lot. He could sell nothing or, if he did, he was forced to extend credit he couldn't afford. We were certainly in a fix."

As was my great-grandpa Joe.

On November 1, 1907, Joe took out that chattel mortgage on his five horses, three cows, three calves, and sundry personal property. This was collateral for a one thousand dollar promissory note. He borrowed the one thousand dollars from a fellow name Joseph Pirnauer. From all I could find, this was the first time he borrowed money. He had owned all his property free and clear; now he was in debt.

Just as things were starting to turn around, then came the massive flood. That was in June of 1908. "Just at the moment of recovery, floods created great damage to railroads which retarded opening the smelters for months."

One needs cash reserves, not debt, to weather such storms.

Like a blind guide, Joe's luck kept turning the wrong way. His collateral on that one thousand dollar note started to erode. One horse became crippled. The mare died of overwork. The colt disappeared. The cow and calves disappeared. So much for Joe's collateral. Things did not look good for Joe.

Pirnauer said Joe was insolvent and insisted that Joe sell his remaining property at auction to pay off the note. Joe's lawyers, Galen & Mettler, said this was not true; Joe was not insolvent.

By 1910, Joe had only two mules and two cows. That I know because they were listed on his tax assessment. Again, he overpaid his property tax.

On March 25, 1911, Joe and Pirnauer renegotiated the debt. Pirnauer owed Joe money for his outstanding bill at Joe's store. They agreed that now Joe owed Pirnauer $550.

It seems Joe recovered from all this. Life hummed along with no more borrowing money. He sold lots of whiskey, lots of groceries, and he did a lot of prospecting.

Then that other historically seismic event happened. On July 28, 1914, Austria-Hungary declared war on Serbia. Germany allied with Austria. France and Russia allied with Serbia. Britain jumped in to protect neutral Belgium, which put them on the same side as France. This would soon be called the Great War, the World War. Today we call it the First World War. Though we were as yet not in it, sparks from such a monstrous conflagration immediately spread all the way across the Atlantic to New York and across the land. The world situation was so volatile that the price of metals could not be quoted. How does one run a smelter or a mine without knowing the price of metals? The New York Stock Exchange closed to prevent a crash. The fear was that Europeans would dump their American stocks for cash and buy gold.

Yankee ingenuity quickly stepped in and a market opened on the "curb" on New Street. It was called the New York Curb Market. People with cash resumed buying and selling stocks. It wasn't the full New York Stock Exchange, but it was something.

The New York Stock Exchange remained closed for four months. This was unprecedented.

Silver mining fell off a cliff when Europeans quit buying it at the outbreak of war. Copper was throttled. Lead seemed to hold its own. Mines in Idaho continued to send ore to the East Helena smelter for processing. Those running mines and smelters were in rough seas. Lead demand picked up, lead for bullets for France and Britain.

Joe seemed to weather this storm. Back in 1906, he lost his brand when he mortgaged the livestock. In August of 1916, Joe registered a new brand for cattle (left rib) and for horses (left shoulder). That meant he could once again afford to buy livestock. Things were looking up.

Oh, but not for long. That December, Joe and Caroline took out a mortgage on their property—all of it—the house, the saloon, the mercantile, the whole kit and caboodle. It was with the East Helena State Bank and was for $1,500 to be paid in one year at eight percent interest. Caroline marked her X on the legal documents; she still didn't know how to sign her own name. Five months later, on April 5, 1917, they borrowed an additional $800 on the property, also to be paid in one year at eight percent interest. The next year on February 20, 1918, they borrowed $800 on the property from Frank Klemenc. On July 5, 1918, they borrowed $516.50 from Joseph Sasek. They now owed a grand total of $3,616.50 on the property. They were buried in debt.

Joe made payments, but not nearly enough.

If only he had Shakespeare's Polonius to advise him: "Neither a borrower nor a lender be: For loan oft loses both itself and friend; and borrowing dulls the edge of husbandry." I wonder if that was it in a nutshell. Everything seemed to be going great until Joe started borrowing money. He built up that business with cash, bought all that property with cash, then years later, he started borrowing money. If Joe borrowed money so he could spend more time prospecting, it meant he wasn't minding the store; whoever was minding the store sold too much on credit. Perhaps all that borrowing made matters worse, as Shakespeare wrote, it dulled "the edge of husbandry." Perhaps he felt he didn't need to take as much care with minding the store and saloon since he had all that borrowed cash to play with. Soon it was all gone.

And then there was the matter of Joe's sister Anna.

Anna arrived from the Old Country around the time Joe and Caroline married in 1892. Caroline said she brought a young woman over from the Old Country to help with the boardinghouse, but the girl ran off and got married. I wonder if that were Anna. She helped Caroline run a boardinghouse until she ran off with a miner from Butte. To put it another way, she met a fellow Slovenian countryman, John Kogar, and married him at the cathedral in Helena on November 15, 1894. They settled in Butte, the copper metropolis south of Helena. I've seen the name spelled Kogar, Kozar, Kozier, Cozier, Kozar. Eventually the Kogar spelling stuck. It is pronounced ko-shjar.

Anna was twenty-one, and John was twenty-four when they married. One year later, their daughter Mary was born. Anna bore two other children who died as infants. One was stillborn.

In 1900, John and Anna Kogar started borrowing money on two lots

Joe Lozar, his sister Anna, Karolina Lozar, circa 1892.

on Plum Street in East Butte. In 1900, they borrowed seven hundred dollars on one of the lots from Margaret Jones, which they paid off in a year. I'm guessing that John built a house on one of the lots and borrowed against it to build a house on the other lot, which was in the next block. In 1901, they borrowed six hundred dollars on the other house from William Monaghan, which they paid back in four years. In 1902, they borrowed one thousand dollars from Kate Wheeler, and paid it off in a few months. What is odd about all this, at least by today's standards, was they didn't officially own the two lots until 1902. This means they were borrowing money against property they didn't legally own. The previous owner was Centennial Brewing Company. John and Anna Kogar paid the brewing company one dollar on July 30, 1902, for the two lots.

In 1903, they again borrowed one thousand dollars from Kate Wheeler and paid it off in a few months. On September 21, 1905, they borrowed twelve hundred dollars from W. D. Wallace.

Then tragedy and sorrow struck—Anna's husband, John Kogar, died on October 26, 1907, of meningitis. He had been sick seven days. When asked the names of John's parents for the death certificate, Anna said she didn't know.

Here was Anna, a thirty-six-year-old widow with a twelve-year-old daughter. She did not speak English, she could not read or write, and she still owed W. D. Wallace twelve hundred dollars. She paid it off in February of 1909. I wonder if the money came from Joe and Caroline. On July 20, 1909, Joe bought those two houses on Plum Street in East Butte from his sister for $716. Anna still lived in one of the houses and rented out the other.

On August 16, 1917, Anna bought the two houses back from Joe for one dollar. So Joe effectively gave her the $716. Joe was already in a financial pickle. He needed the money. He was falling deep into the abyss of debt. A year later he would lose everything. It's a good thing those properties were not in his name, or else he'd have lost them too.

Between the time Joe bought the houses from his sister Anna and she bought them back for a dollar, Anna had remarried and was in the process of getting a divorce.

Dad always referred to Anna's second husband as Old Man Ulsher. His name was Andrew. He was a fellow Slovenian from the Old Country and was a widower with three young children when he married Anna. His first wife, Katherine, died when their youngest child was only two.

Old Man Ulsher lived in a log house in Bison Canyon in Elk Park and had a stone quarry there going back to 1889. One of his customers was the streetcar company in Butte, which hired him to cut granite stones for Park Street and Broadway.

When Anna married Old Man Ulsher, he was in the middle of suing the Great Northern Railroad. He hired a young, ambitious, up-and-coming lawyer named Burton Wheeler to represent him. Andrew said an employee with the Great Northern damaged the derrick he used to lift stones out of his quarry and ruined it. He lost a large contract because of that. He claimed nineteen hundred dollars in damages. This dragged on for two and a half years. By the time they reached a settlement, Wheeler had been named U.S. District Attorney. He would go on to become one of the most powerful senators in Washington.

It seems that Anna's marriage to Old Man Ulsher lasted about five minutes. They married in January of 1912, separated in April of 1914, and were divorced in March of 1918.

She went back to using her first husband's surname—Kogar.

"Mama and Papa were quite upset over the divorce, as it was the only one in the family," Stephie said.

To what extent did Joe support his sister and her daughter through all this?

By this time, we had entered the First World War. Conrad Hilton wrote, "The war . . . played havoc with the mercantile business and Father took a substantial loss before he gave up and sold out."

Joe didn't sell.

Now it was the summer of 1918. Prohibition loomed like a dark, ominous cloud. It would go into effect in Montana in a few months. Most of Joe's income came from the saloon. Possibly those who held the mortgages on Joe's property figured, if Joe can't pay now, he won't be able to pay later when his saloon is shut down by Prohibition.

On August 14, 1918, the court ordered that all the Lozar property in East Helena be sold at public auction to pay off the mortgages.

23

EAST BUTTE

BEFORE ENGINEERS HARNESSED the mighty Missouri for electricity and before use of natural gas was omnipresent, people burned coal and wood in their stoves. Industry burned coal to run machinery. Smelters burned coal to heat the furnaces. The mines burned coal to create steam to drive the hoists that lowered the miners into the mines and brought them back up again. Measures to clean the resulting soot and smoke were primitive or nonexistent. The prevailing wind in Montana is from the west. The wind blew that soot and smoke east. So the preferable, cleaner place to live was west of industry, west of the mines, upwind. The West Side became the fashionable part of town. We see this in Butte and Helena; those nineteenth-century mansions and finer homes were on the West Side. The East Side was the humbler side, the rougher side. But my relatives didn't live there. They lived east of the East Side.

Not only were they east of the East Side, they were east of Butte. "You lost your reputation when you moved to Butte," Annie said. She and Tony stayed in East Helena.

Joe and Caroline had lost everything except each other. They moved their family to East Butte, the Slavic enclave next to Butte.

The town seemed drab and gray to their young daughters Francie and Stephie.

They were living on the other side of the tracks, east of arsenic-laden Silver Bow Creek. East Butte was a world apart from a town that was itself a world apart.

Looking to the west from their new home, Caroline and Joe beheld the city of Butte, the largest city in Montana, the mile-high copper metropolis climbing ever more up the mountain and burrowing down deep into the

176

earth, a mountain studded with gallous frame after gallous frame, each towering over a mine shaft—the Neversweat, the West Colusa, the Original, the Tramway, the Pennsylvania, the Speculator, the Granite Mountain, the Bell, the Black Rock, the Leonard, the Lexington, the Mountain Con, the Elm Orlu, the Modoc, the Tuolumne, the Diamond, and the list goes on and on, miners in each mine pulling rich copper from the richest hill on earth, providing fodder for the nation's, actually the world's, industrial growth. It was a Runyonesque town dominated by the mighty Anaconda Copper Mining Company, a metropolis built on copper. She looked tarnished, but she had tremendous value, a tarnished treasure she was.

Butte was a twenty-four-hour town where gambling and prostitution, though illegal, persisted unfettered amid a patchwork of ethnic enclaves alongside a cosmopolitan, fashionable, bustling uptown. Cowboy detective Charlie Siringo called Butte "the cradle of anarchy." Even so, it was said, "the people are very kind but there will be frost and snow till June."

Yes, Butte was the big town from which the hamlet of East Butte drew its name. East Butte had been called Pittsmont, taking its name from the Pittsmont Mine and Smelter. After dark when the smeltermen dumped the hot slag on the slag dump, it looked like fireworks rolling down a mountain.

In the years leading up to the First World War, Montana produced one-fourth of the copper in the United States, and we were a big exporter.

Pittsmont Mine and Smelter, East Butte
WORLD MUSEUM OF MINING 32-01297 ©WORLD MUSEUM OF MINING

Butte, Montana, looking east.
WORLD MUSEUM OF MINING 28-00367 ©WORLD MUSEUM OF MINING

Pittsmont Mine and Smelter, East Butte
WORLD MUSEUM OF MINING 29-0052B ©WORLD MUSEUM OF MINING

West Colusa Mine, Butte, Montana.
Butte-Silver Bow Public Archives, 40.051.01. Smithers, photographer

After markets recovered from the initial shock of the war, copper mining boomed. From 1915 to 1916, copper production in Butte increased twenty-nine percent.

"At the outset of hostilities England had found herself practically without any supply of copper and we were forced to provide it," wrote the company biographer. Butte had plenty.

When Joe and Caroline and the children arrived in the summer of 1918, the United States was in the war and Butte was booming.

Now at age fifty-four and in poor health, Joe Lozar was starting over. He went to work in the mines, not his own mines, the mining company mines. Underground, hard-rock mining is difficult physical work at any age. He started at the Pittsmont Mine in East Butte. He and Caroline and the children lived with Joe's sister Anna and her daughter, Mary, who was twenty-three. Caroline and Joe's youngest daughters, Stephie and Francie, attended the Harrison School. Stephie was thirteen, Francie was ten. Young Caroline's son, Bobby, was three.

24

❦

WAR OVER

JOE AND CAROLINE'S SON, STEVE, was inducted into the Army in September of 1918. He didn't make it to France, but you'd never know it by the way he was feted when he returned. Every bar in East Butte gave him a drink on the house, so he stopped in every bar. He made it to the house and passed out on the porch. His little sisters Francie and Stephie dragged him inside and shoved him into the bathtub.

On November 11, 1918, the "war to end all wars" ended. I wonder how Joe and Caroline and their Slovenian and Croatian neighbors felt about their homeland being vanquished. My guess is many just shrugged. They identified with their tribe. They were Slovenians and Croatians born in lands that had been ruled by Austria-Hungary. Caroline was different. She had lived in Vienna.

Tony and Annie and the children were still living in East Helena when the war ended. Only four years after Tony left the Austro-Hungarian Empire with her ruling Habsburgs behind, so too did the world, a dynasty ended, an empire shattered, dismembered. In June of 1919, leaders of the warring countries signed the peace treaty in the resplendent Hall of Mirrors in the Palace of Versailles, an auspicious setting to formally end a brutal, long, horrible war. The treaty vanquished the vanquished further by dismantling the Austro-Hungarian Empire. The Slovenian-populated duchies of Carniola and Styria, from which Joe, Caroline, and Tony hailed, became part of the Kingdom of Serbs, Croats, and Slovenians. Tony was unhappy about his homeland being united with Serbia. He was very unhappy that Trieste was taken away and given to the Italians. The British made sure the Italians got Trieste. That was the deal the British made with the Italians to pull Italy into the war on the side of Britain and France.

180

More Slovenians lived in greater Trieste than in any other city including Ljubljana (now the capital of Slovenia). President Wilson's Fourteen Points promised "self-determination," but whose self-determination? Mine or my neighbor's? The Slovenian farmer on the hill or the German blacksmith down the road or the Italian merchant in town? Not so simple. In 1910, though the majority of the people in Trieste were Italians, when you included the environs there were 421,000 Italians, 160,000 Croatians, and 320,000 Slovenians, more Slavs than Italians. Even so, Trieste went to Italy. That was the deal.

"Treachery," Tony said.

The war had been hard on Caroline's friends in Vienna—food shortages, and long lines to buy what food could be found. Farmers such as Joe's brother and Tony's mother and sister had it easier. They grew and raised their own food.

Austrian novelist Stefan Zweig said the war brought to Austria poverty, hyperinflation, riots, loss of civil liberties, enslavement to the state, insecurity, suspicion, and before long—the Brown Shirts.

In Butte, when the war ended, so did all that war demand for copper. Butte's economy teetered on the edge of a cliff.

25

FIRE

KIDS WERE SMOKING in the hay loft and set the town on fire—that's what Stephie said.

Someone threw out the ashes from the stove while they were still hot, which ignited the dry grass—that's what the butcher Frank Gorsich said.

It started during the noon hour on August 19, 1919.

As soon as she saw the flames, Annie grabbed Eddy and Babe and Tony's bassoon and ran out of the house.

A strong west wind fanned the flames and blew the fire into the business district of East Helena. Two gasoline storage tanks exploded. The fire engulfed stores that sold bullets. They exploded. The East Helena volunteer fire department assembled and valiantly fought the fire. Citizens formed a bucket brigade to help douse the flames. They pumped water from wells. There was no city water. When it was over, fifty homes and many businesses and barns had burned down. Two blocks on the south side of Main Street burned to the ground. What had been Joe and Caroline's store and home were destroyed. Only the stone saloon survived. Even though they had been gone for a year, people still referred to it as the Lozar store and Lozar Hall. One hundred and twenty people were homeless. The Salvation Army arrived with sandwiches. The Red Cross and YWCA found beds for those burned out of their homes.

Most of the homes were insured.

Tony and Annie rented their house. It survived. The town was a mess.

Main Street during the East Helena fire, August 19, 1919.
MONTANA HISTORICAL SOCIETY PAc93-14.4. THOMAS LESLIE LYLE, PHOTOGRAPHER

East Helena fire, August 19, 1919.
MONTANA HISTORICAL SOCIETY PAc93-14.7. THOMAS LESLIE LYLE, PHOTOGRAPHER

Main Street looking east, East Helena, after the fire.
MONTANA HISTORICAL SOCIETY PAc93-14.9. THOMAS LESLIE LYLE, PHOTOGRAPHER

Belongings of residents after the fire.
MONTANA HISTORICAL SOCIETY PAc93-14.6. THOMAS LESLIE LYLE, PHOTOGRAPHER

Eddy and Babe.

26

∽

Recruited

Six guys get together in a saloon in Butte and form a band. It didn't quite happen that way, but close. As with any successful enterprise, somebody had to be the driving force.

Tony said, "1919, after the fire, yeah, what you call ACM Band picked me up. Sam Treloar. I get you all the work you want, if you move to Butte. So I did."

In May of 1919, a few months before the fire, Tony received a letter from Sam Treloar, the bandmaster of the Butte Mines Band. He was trying to recruit Tony to move to Butte to play in the band. Here was Tony, a classically trained bassoonist who had performed with great orchestras in Europe. What a find. Competent bassoonists were rare enough let alone one with Tony's talent and experience. Sam Treloar would have been a fool not to recruit him, and Sam Treloar was no fool.

Sam Treloar immigrated to this country from Cornwall when he was a teenager, around 1885. His mother had died. He and his father and two brothers ended up in Butte. The bandmaster at the Alice Mine Band recruited Sam to play solo cornet. When that band folded, he went to work for the Boston and Montana Mining Company. The superintendent, Captain Couch, was also from Cornwall and was a friend of Sam's dad. He said he would support forming a brass band. Sam was the man to do it. I hear tell, one of the reasons the mining companies were happy to form bands was that it kept at least a few of the miners out of the saloons so they'd show up for work. When you think of how many miners there were, and only a few men in a brass band, I doubt that was the reason. Captain Couch said it was to provide entertainment for the miners and their families. That makes more sense.

Sam Treloar formed the Boston and Montana Band in October of 1887. The mining company paid for it. The musicians all had day jobs, including Sam. The foremen put the musicians on day shifts in the mines, so the band could practice in the evenings.

Their first rehearsal was said to have been in a log cabin in Meaderville. Didn't everything begin in a log cabin in Montana? It could be true, it could be legend. The number of band members grew and the audiences for those rehearsals grew so large that they had to move to the Knights of Labor Hall. In 1890, the band members chipped in and bought their own rehearsal hall across from the Leonard Mine.

When Amalgamated, the holding company of the Anaconda Copper Mining Company, bought the Boston and Montana, it became the ACM Band.

The band performed for the Democrat National Convention in Chicago in 1896 and in Kansas City in 1900. William Jennings Bryan was nominated as the party's candidate for president, but he did not attend the convention, so on the way home, when the train stopped in Lincoln, Nebraska, the band members went to his house and performed a gentle serenade out front in the square.

In 1902, the band won a national competition sponsored by the Elks in Salt Lake City. When they went to Denver to compete in 1906, they marched into saloon after saloon performing all the while, creating buzz all over Denver about this great band. They won. The people of Butte went wild in celebration every time the band won a competition.

Sam Treloar was a busy man. He started out working in the mines and later leased mines, bonded them, and sold them. He organized the musicians local. He served in the state house. All the while, he was the bandleader.

When he heard about the talented bassoonist in East Helena, Sam set out to recruit Tony Leskovar. Sam asked Tony to perform with the band in Deer Lodge and Salt Lake City. Tony responded by telegram on June 6, 1919: "Letter received accept engagement will arrive Deer Lodge Thursday morning 10:30." There he joined the thirty-four members of the band to perform for the reunion of veterans of the Grand Army of the Republic (the North in the Civil War), the Spanish American War, and the World War. Three days later, Tony joined the band in Butte. All thirty-five band members "voluntarily serenaded the Finlen, Thornton, and Butte Hotels" and then took a special streetcar to the Northern Pacific Depot, performing all the way, where they joined the Rotarians of Montana on a special train to Salt Lake City to attend the Rotary convention. They arrived in Salt

Lake City at 10:15am and paraded to the Hotel Utah. Each day, they gave concerts at the hotel, McDonalds Candy Factory, and Walkers Store, and they performed at Fort Douglas for wounded soldiers who fought in the World War. All these performances "were appreciated, winning name and fame for Montana."

In September, Tony performed with the band at the state fair. The band secretary assured the directors of the fair that the ACM Band "will give all Patrons of the Fair the best one hour concert each day they ever heard at any fair." They performed for a concert and dance each evening at the city auditorium during fair week. Tony earned thirty-two dollars for that gig.

The trip to Salt Lake troubled Sam Treloar. People in Salt Lake assumed the band was from Anaconda, because of the name, the ACM Band, which stood for Anaconda Copper Mining Company. The band was from Butte, not Anaconda. The name had to be changed to show that the band represented Butte. The name was changed to the Butte Mines Band.

Sam Treloar engaged Tony again to perform with the band, this time in Roundup. "Anton Leskovar bassoon player living at East Helena met the Milwaukee train at Lombard making 32 men." Treloar secured Pullman sleeper cars for the band and reserved a drawing room.

At 10:30am, the band gave a concert from a bandstand on Main Street. At 11:30am, Governor Stewart gave a speech welcoming returning soldiers, sailors, and Marines from the World War. Another man gave a patriotic speech, followed by lunch, a parade, and athletic sports. In the evening, the band gave a short concert at the bandstand on Main Street, and then played "necessary and appropriate music" for two hours of dancing. An entire block on Main Street was packed with dancers.

Tony earned thirty dollars for that gig. This was good money.

"A. Leskovar Bassoon player telephoned he had quit Helena and intended locating in Butte permanently, he was looking for a suitable location to establish an auto paint and finishing shop. Later he called in person to talk over details and secure information on condition . . . he intends locating here as early as possible, work at his trade and attend to the band work." This was written in the band minutes of November 2, 1919.

The next day Tony arrived in Butte for rehearsal after which he began to look for a location for his car painting business.

"Where did you go when you first came to Butte?"

"We stayed with old folks," Tony said, meaning Annie's parents, Joe and Caroline.

Sam Treloar, founder and bandleader of the Butte Mines Band.
Butte-Silver Bow Public Archives PH316_006_003

Sam Treloar went to great lengths to secure work for band members. He asked the powers-that-be in the mining company to have a man transferred from the smelter in Anaconda to a job in Butte so he could play alto saxophone. Sam was particularly keen that the solo cornet player be transferred to Butte. He arranged a job for the oboe player, George Wrightson, as a machinist at Silver Bow Automobile Co.

Butte Mines Band. Tony is in the front row, fifth from the left.
Butte-Silver Bow Public Archives PH255. Smithers, photographer

Sam Treloar was a master bandleader and marketeer. He was great at drawing attention to the band. Here they are performing on a sidewalk.
Butte-Silver Bow Public Archives 22_063_03. Smithers, photographer

"Arranged for Mr. Leskovar bassoon player auto painter and finisher to confer on a place for partnership with Mr. Pierce and McGrew . . . with Leskovar as manager."

Sam Treloar told Tony, if he joined the band and moved to Butte, he'd get all the car and truck painting work for the ACM—the Anaconda Copper Mining Company, the company that owned almost all the mines in town and funded the band. Treloar made good on that promise. Tony worked for himself in the car painting business. He said, "If you work for yourself, you always have a job."

Only a few months after Tony settled his family in Butte, he was able to buy a used 1917 six-cylinder Touring Studebaker for $778. Not bad. He was doing well. He made a down payment of $300 for the car and agreed to pay off the rest in one year. Monthly payments were at twelve percent interest. As far as I know, this was the first time, and one of very few times, he went in debt.

Even with the war demand for copper falling off a cliff, Butte had the largest payroll in the country for a city of its size. Day's pay for a miner was $5.75. Contract miners could earn more. When Tony traveled with the band, he made $6 a day.

Tony traveled with the Butte Mines Band to Portland to perform for the Shriners. They performed for folk dancing and the Safety First Picnic and Miners' Field Day at the Columbia Gardens, the wonderful amusement

Butte Mines Band performing at the Columbia Gardens

Butte Mines Band performing at the Columbia Gardens, August 1924.

park up the mountain from East Butte. They performed for the farmers' picnic in Deer Lodge. The Serbs hired the band to play for a funeral. The band escorted Marshal Foch, the French hero of the World War, during his visit to Butte. They performed for parades. They performed whenever anything significant was happening in Butte, including visits from the president or a presidential candidate.

Tony would become president of the band.

For their summer concert season, the band played twenty performances every week. I found programs for their 1922 season. They performed on Galena, west of Montana Street. The concerts were from seven thirty to nine thirty in the evening. Every concert was different, completely different. On June 15, they performed a waltz suite by Lehar, a medley of Gilbert and Sullivan operettas, and more. At each concert, they performed nine pieces. The next week they performed the overture from *Tancredi* by Rossini, Welsh songs by Godfrey, and more. The next week they performed *The Merry Widow* by Lehar, Irish songs, a waltz suite by Hall. "Windy Willie" by Loscy, a zippy ragtime tune, was described as a "trombone blizzard" in the program.

The band wore spiffy uniforms. From time to time, Sam Treloar had to order new caps or have a uniform repaired. A letter in June of 1919 attached to an invoice from the company in Columbus, Ohio, that provided the caps said there was a ten percent luxury tax on the caps. It was a war tax. The war was over; the tax lived on. The owner of the company urged Sam to write to his congressman if he agreed that the tax was ridiculous.

Whether Tony was performing for kings and queens in Zurich and Paris or for miners and their families at the Columbia Gardens in Butte, he performed at his utmost. The consummate professional, he was. He never stopped practicing until the day he died.

Annie and the children attended every performance.

Tony was a member of two unions: the painters' union and the musicians' union. The handbook for the Butte Musicians' Mutual Protective Union listed their pay scale. The handbook I found at the Butte Archives was for 1910. If it hadn't changed much, Tony earned six dollars to perform with the Butte Mines Band at a picnic. This included the parade to and from the depot. The handbook stipulated that they be dismissed by six o'clock in the evening. For a Fourth of July picnic, he earned double, twelve dollars. For the Fourth of July parade, he earned ten dollars. For the Labor Day Parade, the Decoration Day Parade, the Washington's Birthday Parade, the St. Patrick's Day Parade, the St. George's Day Parade, he earned five dollars. For parades that went beyond the city limits, he earned seven dollars and fifty cents; for a political convention, five dollars; for a four-hour concert, five dollars; for a seven-hour concert (three hours in the afternoon and four hours in the evening), seven dollars and fifty cents.

Tony and Annie rented Joe's sister Anna's rental house at 117 Plum Street in East Butte, one of the two houses Joe bought and gave back to his sister. They lived there with Joe and Caroline and the children. That made four adults—Joe, Caroline, Annie, and Tony, and five children— Stephie (age fifteen), Francie (twelve), Bobby (four), Eddy (three) and Babe (eighteen months)—nine people in one very small house.

Joe's sister Anna lived in her other house on the next block at 45 Plum Street. Her daughter, Mary, was twenty-four years old. Neither Anna or Mary worked outside the home. Anna had a boarder, a fellow called John Zufertz. He was forty-two years old, also Slovenian. As far as I know, his wife and children still lived in the Old Country. He was a miner who had been in the country twelve years.

The neighbors were the Flanicks, a Slovenian family with eight children; the Bensons from Sweden; George and Agnes Stafac who were Croatian; the Bakers from Missouri, who must have felt like foreigners in their own country. Mary Shubitz, also a Slav from Austria-Hungary, ran a boardinghouse. Pete Gergorich, who was Slovenian, was one of her boarders, as was Kurt Dawich from Dalmatia, and Peter Cauch, another Slav from Austria-Hungary.

Now with Prohibition the law of the land, Caroline resorted to making her own liquor. She filled a big copper double boiler with sugar and fruit and whatnot. She dumped the leftover mash by the slag dump next to the Pittsmont smelter. Cows would wander over and eat the mash and bloat up with gas. The owner would poke the cow with a knife to relieve the gas.

Speaking of Prohibition, you never know what you'll find by accident when digging into the past. While looking up Tony's car painting business in the Butte city directories, I stumbled across the list of "Soft Drink—Cigar" establishments. Yes, soft drinks and cigars, don't we always associate those with each other? Some of the businesses on the very, very long list were the ABC Bar on Wyoming Street, the Milwaukee Bar on Montana Street, and the Tivoli Brewery Saloon southwest of town. I didn't count but there were a lot of them. Yes, all these were listed as soft drink parlors, the Prohibition-era euphemism in Butte for a saloon. A soft drink parlor brewery. A soft drink parlor bar. There was probably not a soft drink to be found in any of those places. Word was the saloon owners paid off the cops.

In June of 1920, Caroline and Joe heard from their daughter Caroline in California. She had gotten married. Her husband's name was John William Davis. She was twenty-one, and he was twenty-four. She had been living in Oakland. They settled in San Francisco. He worked as a machinist in the shipyard. Her son, Bobby, now four, remained in Montana with Joe and Caroline.

Tony and Annie and the children, Eddy and Babe, moved into a rental house at 2111 Redwood in McQueen, which was north of East Butte. The house was only five blocks from where Joe and Caroline lived.

Annie with Eddy and Babe at the
house in McQueen, 1920.

Annie with Eddy and Babe, August 1921.

Tony rented space for his car painting business on East Galena in Butte, near The Line, known in other cities as the Red Light District.

A few months later, Tony and Annie moved back to East Butte and rented a one-bedroom house at 210 Cherry, only a block from Joe and Caroline.

His car painting business was humming along, he enjoyed performing with the band, and things were about to get even better for Tony.

Annie with Eddy and Babe, 1922.

Out for a drive, stop for a drink — Tony, Annie, Eddy and Babe.
That might be Francie on the right.

27

HIS GLORY DAYS

There is nothing so warm and moving as the sight of a symphony orchestra. The romantic lights of their music stands, the tuning up and the sudden silence as the conductor makes his entrance.

—Charlie Chaplin

THE MUSICIANS TAKE THEIR PLACES in the orchestra. Scattered strains of violins and woodwinds fill the auditorium as the musicians warm up. All fall silent as the conductor walks to the podium. He lifts his ebony baton, the strains of Tchaikovsky's *Pathetique Sypmphony* pour forth.

The conductor is Tony Leskovar. It is September 24, 1921, the first performance of the Butte Symphony Orchestra, founded by Henry Francis Parks. On May 18, 1922, the day after Tony's thirty-fifth birthday, anyone with a radio within a thousand miles can listen to the live performance. It is a benefit concert for the Salvation Army Boys' Band.

There were forty musicians in the orchestra. Many were amateurs. Henry Francis Parks said Anton Leskovar was most instrumental in maintaining regularity of rehearsals. That's a polite way of saying that Tony was very strict. He was a professional.

Did Tony hold an affinity for Slavic composers? He was a boy when Tchaikovsky died of cholera after sipping an unfortunate glass of water in St. Petersburg. Or did he prefer Austrian composers? His selections would indicate a split, we see Mozart, we see Tchaikovsky. And Tony was forward looking—he included pieces by composers of his adopted country. He also chose pieces by Grieg (Norwegian) and Sibelius (a Finn) and Berucci (Italian).

"Those were his glory days," Annie said.

Butte Symphony Orchestra, Tony Leskovar conductor, 1921.

ANNIE'S FATHER, JOE LOZAR, worked as a miner at the Pittsmont Mine in East Butte. Then he worked at the West Colusa in Butte.

Joe's gold fever would not abate despite his declining health. Gold fever consumed him; perhaps that's why the disease that killed so many miners was called consumption. His mining, his litigating, his grub staking miners, all of it consumed him, consumed his health and his money. Even so, he and his son, Steve, and Tony prospected for more mines. In January of 1920, yes, cold, frigid, snowy January in the Rocky Mountains, the three of them claimed the Barger Lode and the Brook Lode in the Corral Mountain area of Jefferson County, north of Butte.

Then in April of 1921, mining in Butte came to a screeching halt. The Anaconda Copper Mining Company had stockpiles of copper because of government dictates during the war and not enough buyers due to the severe economic depression that followed. Most of the mines shut down. It was the worst shutdown since 1893.

"Papa's health was getting worse all the time," Stephie said. "He couldn't work so Mama went to work for the Butte mines working nights as a janitress.

Mr. ANTON LESKOVAR, Conductor

From concert program, November 24, 1921.

Any other kind of work was scarce. The money she got helped keep the wolf from the door, and I can't remember that at any time we went hungry, our wants were very few so it seems. Yet we had plenty of food and all."

Caroline still couldn't read or write. She had an ailing husband and three children to support—Stephie, Francie, and her grandson Bobby.

I suspect Caroline was saying a lot of Hail Marys as she swept and scrubbed the floors of the East Butte Mining office.

On Annie's twenty-ninth birthday, July 2, 1922, her father died. Joe was fifty-nine years old. He died of pulmonary tuberculosis, more commonly known as miner's con (consumption). He had been under a doctor's care for two months and died at the Murray Hospital.

When asked Joe's date of birth for the death certificate, Caroline replied in her Slovenian-German accent, "I don't know."

Annie was heartbroken to lose her father.

Annie Leskovar and her sisters Francie Lozar and Caroline Lozar Davis in the front yard, 210 Cherry in East Butte, taken after Joe Lozar's funeral. July 1922.

The wake was at Annie and Tony's house. The funeral Mass was at Holy Savior Catholic Church. Joe was buried at Holy Cross Cemetery.

One of the managers at the mining company where Caroline worked wrote to a building and loan company in which Joe had invested. He inquired about dividends that should now go to the widow Caroline. The company was bankrupt.

28

SEATTLE

SIX WEEKS AFTER JOE LOZAR DIED, Tony received a letter from the orchestral manager of the Coliseum Theatre in Seattle. He offered Tony the position of bassoonist for fifty dollars a week. That was good money in 1922. He would work six hours a day, six days a week. Hours in the pit would not exceed twenty-four hours per week.

Tony closed his car painting business, quit the Butte Mines Band, packed up the family, and off they went to Seattle in that 1917 Studebaker.

Long road trips were a novel idea in 1922, if not outlandish, if not downright crazy. The first time a family ever dared drive across the country in a car was only fourteen years earlier, and they brought a mechanic with them. The car was a step up from a covered wagon but not yet a big one. At least they didn't have to feed and rest animals, but it was still slow. Some military convoys inched along at only six miles per hour. Roads between towns were not yet designed for cars; they weren't paved with asphalt or concrete. They were more like trails, just dirt. This included mountain passes, narrow dirt roads of packed dirt with steep cliffs off to the side. Tony had to cross several mountain passes on the way to Seattle. "Camel's Hump was the worst," he said. "There was switchback. I had to back the car to make the turn." He had to back up and go forward a couple times to make each switchback turn. To attempt this drive in 1922, having to cross two daunting mountain ranges, the Rockies and the Cascades, and a blazing hot desert with a wife and two small children, a person had to be intrepid or insane. Cars broke down all the time. The civilized mode of travel back then was by train, but, no, that wouldn't do, Tony wanted to drive. He'd be his own mechanic when the car broke down, which it did, repeatedly. He'd figure it out, and he did. He had to bring gas. There weren't gas stations at regular intervals along the way. He brought water for when the car overheated, which it did. He brought extra tires for when they got a flat, which they did, repeatedly. This Studebaker was a big car. It could take seven passengers. Tony stacked their suitcases on the backseat. Annie draped a blanket over the suitcases. Eddy, who was five, and Babe, who was four, sat up there and napped much of the trip. Tony taught Eddy how to patch tires, which Eddy did from his perch on the suitcases in the backseat. Annie brought food. They camped out along the way in a tent. The car came with roller beds. The gas tank on the Studebaker held fifteen gallons. The car could go about ten miles to the gallon.

The letter offering Tony the job was mailed on August 19, 1922. The job started September 2, so they must have left right away. Today that trip is six hundred miles. Even though it was August, you never know when you will run into bad weather in the Rockies, and there was no car radio to warn of bad weather. Rain on those mountain passes can be worse than snow. Cars were uncomfortable with hard seats, bumpy roads, no serious shock absorbers that today we take for granted. I am going to take a wild guess that Annie was not happy about this trip.

When they pulled into Kirkland on the east side of Lake Washington, it was dark and foggy. "My gosh, I hardly could see," Tony said. "We went slow."

They rented a house in the leafy Seattle neighborhood of Green Lake.

Tony performed in the orchestra at the Coliseum Theatre at Fifth and Pike in downtown Seattle. When it opened in 1916, it was called "the world's largest and finest photoplay palace," a photoplay being what we now call a silent movie. The theater was lavish; calling it a palace was no overstatement. The outside was white terra-cotta in the neoclassical style. The inside was ornate with goddesses and gargoyles and a giant lion's head overlooking the audience. (For those of you who don't remember it being so lavish, it was remodeled, some might say de-modeled, in 1951.) There was a large smoking room for men. The ladies' restrooms were quite large, lounges actually. There was a playroom for children. A gorgeous curtain covered the screen, with immense valances above and on the sides. The seating capacity was around two thousand, which included a very large balcony. It was said that the musicians were the highest paid in the country. Why wouldn't Tony want that gig.

As in Butte and Helena, Tony supplemented his income painting cars, and he took any additional music gig that came along.

"Three times I make a trip to British Columbia," he said. "What do you call that town?"

"Vancouver."

With all the greenery around the porch, I'm guessing this is the house they rented in Seattle. Annie, Tony, Eddy (taller), and Babe, 1922 or 1923.

"Vancouver, yeah, twenty-five dollars and transportation, play half hour, two French horns and bassoon. I still remember, eleven o'clock we got on the boat, seven o'clock in the morning we get to Vancouver. We had sleepers. Cabin. Back the same way. Leave eleven o'clock on Monday. Tuesday morning seven o'clock, we were in Seattle. Two o'clock in the afternoon we play in Seattle. Afternoon and evening. It was quite a job."

They were doing well. It was a good living for the family, but Annie didn't like it. She didn't want to stay in Seattle. She didn't want to leave Butte in the first place. She complained and complained. Tony put Annie and Eddy and Babe on the train back to Butte. He followed in the car. They weren't even a year in Seattle.

By April of 1923, Tony was again performing with the Butte Mines Band. In June, they performed for President Harding during his visit to Butte.

The other big development in 1923 was when the Anaconda Copper Mining Company bought the Chile Copper Company. It was the biggest transaction on Wall Street to date.

Tony and fellow musician George Wrightson at a Butte Mines Band concert, Columbia Gardens, August 1924.

Eddy, Babe, Tony, Annie, and Tony's sister-in-law, Anna, visiting from Racine, Wisconsin. You will get to know her in Chapter 35. They are at the Columbia Gardens for a Butte Mines Band concert, August 1924.

Eddy, Tony, Babe, Tony's sister-in-law, Anna, at the Columbia Gardens

*An excursion to Elk Park outside Butte. Tony's sister-in-law, Anna,
is frying bacon. Annie is at the far right in the bottom picture.
The boys are Eddy and Babe. August 1924.*

Annie, Tony's sister-in-law, Anna, and Eddy, 1924.

Perched on a rock. Annie, Tony's sister-in-law, Anna, Eddy and Babe.

Tony, Eddy, Tony's sister-in-law, Anna, and Babe. 1924.

Tony rented a house at 2309 Hazel Street in McQueen. Later, they moved back to 210 Cherry in East Butte. The rent was fifteen dollars a month. Tony never had to mow the lawn back then. There was no lawn, just dirt.

He went into business with a fellow named Ray Harrington, an automobile painting shop they called Galena Auto Painting at 17 East Galena.

Tony then started his own business at 115 West Galena, which he called Central Auto Painting. He rented the space. He hired a Swiss-German taxi driver named Carl Matter and taught him to paint cars.

On July 22, 1924, several inches of snow fell on Butte.

Some neighbors in East Butte kept livestock. Annie and Tony didn't. Though Tony grew up on a farm, he left that life far behind for good.

Son Eddy said about the neighbors, "They would buy a whole hog and butcher it. They rendered the fat for lard and made pickled pigs feet. One of the neighbors had a smoke house and smoked bacon and ham."

Another neighbor hunted elk, and that's what they lived on all year.

A professor of music in Bozeman named Joseph Adam wrote to Tony. He had recently formed the Montana State Symphony Orchestra and wanted Tony to become part of it. Joseph Adam was also an immigrant from Austria. He had been orphaned at age fifteen. He came to this country and later returned to Austria and studied at the Imperial and Royal Conservatory of Music in Vienna.

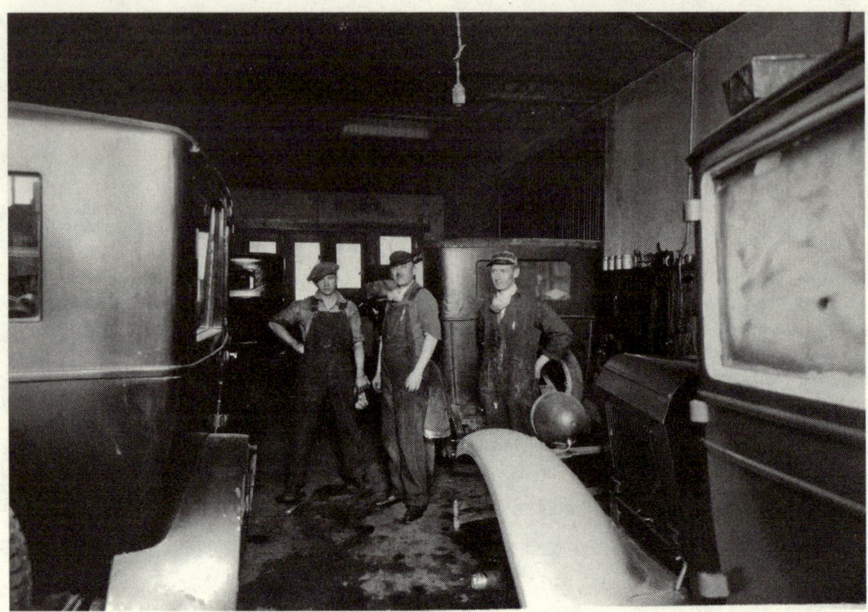

*Central Auto Service. Tony is in the middle. One of the men is Carl Matter.
Someone wrote on the back: "1925. Central Auto Service Smart Alek,
115 West Galena—Business Very good."*

He came back to the United States and was drawn to the west, to Montana. He convinced the Bozeman Chamber of Commerce to send letters to the one hundred wealthiest people in Montana beseeching them to become "Founders of the MSSO," the Montana State Symphony Orchestra. As an incentive, Joseph Adam listed the credentials of members of the orchestra: "Mr. Anton Leskovar of Butte. Formerly bassoonist with a symphony orchestra in Austria, former conductor of the Butte Symphony Orchestra. He played for me and am convinced that neither Minneapolis nor Portland has a better one. A real find!"

Mr. Adam's solicitation was a success. His plan was to take the orchestra on tour.

He offered Tony fifty to sixty dollars a week with no more than twelve concerts each week. The tour would last two to three weeks. Tony's hotel and transportation would be provided. Day's-pay miners in Butte were making around thirty-four dollars a week.

About the tour (in the fall of 1926), Tony said, "Small orchestra. We go to Bozeman, Livingston, Red Lodge, Billings, Miles City, Sidney, Poplar, Glasgow. Adam was the head of it. Father Lesha was his teacher. Catholic priest was his teacher, Bavarian. He was playing string bass the whole way. Let's see, Glasgow, Shelby, Havre, Great Falls, yes, we went from Butte to Helena, Great Falls, Kalispell, Polson, Missoula, Butte, Anaconda, Deer Lodge, Helena, and Great Falls, then we quit in Great Falls. We went to Lewistown, then back to Bozeman. But that wasn't bad, ten dollars a day and what you call, transportation. All I paid was my meals out of the ten dollars. It was a great tour by golly."

"Did you play every day?"

"Yes. We even play in Fort Benton, up north from Great Falls, Fort Benton, yes. We always traveled by train."

The tour was covered nationally by several magazines, including *Sunset*, *Time*, and *Musical America*.

I got a kick out of how *Time* magazine told the story. This was in the February 28, 1927 issue:

Brave Joseph Adam, professor of music at the state college, had the foolhardy intrepidity to offer the privilege to the native sons of becoming founders of the Montana State Symphony at $10 apiece. Rawboned Montaneers smiled, argued, complained, joined up.

The professor rounded up talent and discovered a first class bassoon player, formerly with the German and Slavic Philharmonic in Laibach, Austria, sawing wood for new garages in Butte; one of Finland's best clarinets coal-digging in Red Lodge; an able violinist in a Helena high school. Additional products were imported.

He then hopped into his car and canvassed the state for moral support as well as program advertising. Local gentility encouraged but the potential box-office pyatrons remained contemptuous. The first rehearsal was held last fall. In order to allay suspicion such more popular numbers as "The Merry Wives of Windsor," "Peer Gynt," and Sousa's "Gridiron Club March" were promised.

The opening night in the metropolis of Bozeman, Mont., dauntless Adam coughed away timorousness, tapped his baton, swung into full-rounded and accurate melody. The audience frowned in puzzlement, paid polite attention, learned to like it.

The applause was sensational. Last week the troupe finished a 42-performance run through 24 cities spread over 3,500 Montana miles completed in 36 days. Pioneers never lack for new fields to conquer.

A man in Miles City didn't appreciate how Montanans were characterized. Here is his letter to the editor, which appeared in the March 21, 1927, issue of *Time:*

Sirs:

It is difficult to express to you how intrigued we are to be dubbed "Mountaineers" in an article concerning the newly formed Montana Symphony Orchestra published in TIME, Feb. 28.

Doubtless you are that New Yorker who asked how far west of Buffalo one began to see the Indians. . . .

After reading your article, one gets a big picture of musician Joseph Adam, trembling, but courageous, facing an audience of long-bearded, rawboned (your own word), two-gunned, tobacco-spittin' individuals, booted and spurred and clad in chaps and ten-gallon hats, smelling unpleasantly of cattle. They have the noose ready and the tree all picked out in case Director Adam fails to please.

Adam, dauntless, surprises them; they swallow their tobacco, are taught to like it, although still in stupendous puzzlement. Pardon me if I say you're all wet.

In Miles City Professor Adam and his orchestra were greeted not merely with politeness, but with pleasure. People here were in sympathy with the movement. The auditorium of the high school (by the way, did you know that our school buildings are listed among the best in the country?) was comfortably filled. Professor Adam's talk, explaining the organization and finances of the orchestra, was loudly applauded. Pledges to purchase tickets for the next concerts were circulated. Signing was brisk. . . .

Professor Adam could hardly feel encouraged or complimented by your article, nor do we double up in excruciating joy to learn that we are musically a lummox.

DULANY TERRETT

Miles City, Mont.

The editor of *Time* couldn't let that go:

Let Subscriber Terrett reread the article which has galled him. TIME did not mention spitting, noosing, chaps, hats, cattle. TIME noted Professor Adam's orchestra as something by which 1926–27 will be remembered musically. —ED.

Joseph Adam asked Tony to play the bassoon for two performances of the comic opera *The Chimes of Normandy* by Planquette, to be performed by the Looters Club of Montana State College. Adam was the musical director. It was an eighteen-piece orchestra. The costumes and scenery were rented from an outfit in San Francisco. Adam offered Tony free

Montana State Symphony Orchestra. Tony is to the immediate left
of the drummer. Conductor Joseph Adam wrote on the back of this
picture: "To Mr. Antone Leskovar, the reliable and efficient bassoonist
of the Montana State Symphony Orchestra, in remembrance of the
first state-wide concert tour, Oct.-Nov., 1926."
LESKOVAR FAMILY COLLECTION

transportation, lodging, meals, and six dollars a night. The dress rehearsal
was on Easter Sunday. He knew that Tony was director of the choir at
Holy Savior Church.

> Please let me know at once your financial demands. . . I feel that on that
> particular day you are tied up with your Church-Choir in Butte, so
> would feel perfectly satisfied if you could be with us at least on the two
> performances, Monday and Tuesday. The music is easy to play and you
> are well acquainted with my way of directing, . . . Please let me know
> at once, so we can advertise your coming, and send you railroad-ticket.
> With best regard, also to Mrs. Leskovar, I remain, sincerely yours,
> Joseph Adam

MOTHER CAROLINE HAD ALREADY moved away by the time Tony and
Annie's third son was born in November of 1927. Annie named him Joseph
after her father even though it wasn't St. Joseph's month. Eddy was now
eleven, and Babe was nine.

Annie with Eddy holding new baby Joe, March 1928.

Eddy and Babe attended the Harrison School, a short walk from the house. For breakfast, Annie made fried cornmeal (polenta) mixed into scrambled eggs with bacon, or cornmeal mush, or cornmeal pancakes, or they might have Corn Flakes.

One day while wandering through the dirt fields around the neighborhood, Eddy picked up something and brought it home, and played with it in the front room, and left it on the floor. Annie, always the neat housekeeper, picked it up and threw it in the stove. It was a wood-burning

Annie.

stove. People routinely threw trash into the fire in the stove. Thank God, she promptly left the kitchen and nobody else was there. It exploded and blew the metal plates off the burners. It was a blasting cap. She called the ACM (the mining company) and let them have it for leaving such things around. (No doubt, the mining company didn't leave it around. Somebody pinched it.)

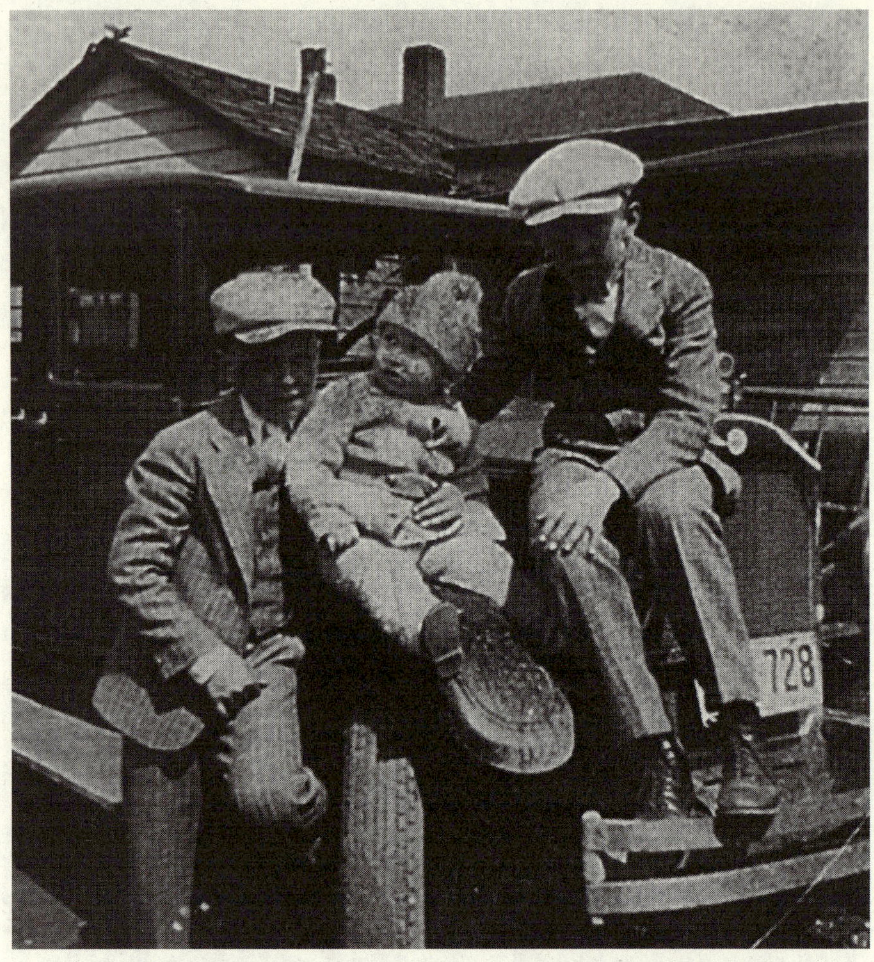

Joe at seventeen months with Babe and Eddy, March 1929.

Another time Eddy picked up a can-shaped thing. It had water in part of it. He lit a match and it burned off his eyebrows. It was the carbide can for a miner's lamp.

One year six kids were playing with dynamite on New Year's Eve. It exploded and all were killed.

PAINTING CARS HELPED PAY THE BILLS, but music was always Tony's first love. He jumped at any chance to perform. When the silent movie *Ramona* came to Butte, Tony performed with the orchestra.

Joe on running board.

*Confirmation day for Babe and Eddy, June 12, 1930.
With little brother Joe.*

*Jo Fouty (Zelda and Steve's daughter), Annie Leskovar, that might be Babe
behind Annie, blond boy next to her is Joe, Zelda and Steve Lozar,
I think that is their son, Buddy, next to Steve.*

Shortly after Tony arrived in this country back in 1915, he made a
declaration of intention to become an American citizen. In doing so, he
renounced allegiance to the emperor of Austria. He had to be in the country
five years to become a citizen. He didn't get around to becoming a citizen
until 1932. By that time, the first declaration of intention had expired,
so he had to make another one. This time he renounced allegiance to the
Kingdom of Serbs, Croats, and Slovenians, a country that did not exist
when he lived in the Old Country. When the heads of state of the winning
nations at the end of the First World War re-drew the map of the world,
one of the countries to which they gave birth was the Kingdom of Serbs,
Croats, and Slovenians, which included Tony's homeland.

Tony and Carl Matter and Anthony Marziak incorporated the Butte Auto
& Painting company in January of 1931. On March 3, it was eighty degrees in
Butte. Two days later, a blizzard hit the Rockies. This would parallel how things
went for Tony over the next few years, boom and bust, hot and cold, really cold.

Let us recall what else was going on at this time—the Great Depression.
The mining company in Butte was shutting down entire mines. Wages
dropped precipitously.

Tony lost his partners. One ended up in the state hospital for the insane
in Warm Springs. I don't know what became of the other fellow.

Tony became an American citizen the next year, 1932.

Five years later, in August of 1937, Annie petitioned the U.S. government for citizenship. Mixed in with her citizenship papers, I found a scrap of paper on which she had written: "Have lost my citizenship—through marriage—to regain my citizenship I had to get re educated—." Where the form asked her race, she wrote "Slovenian." She said she was married October 10, 1915. She regained her American citizenship in March of 1938. She was forty-four years old. Sam Treloar was one of the witnesses. The article in the paper announcing her citizenship said she had previously been a citizen of Yugoslavia, a country that she never visited, a country that did not exist when she was born nor when her husband lived in Europe, a country that did not claim her.

I NEED TO PICK UP A LOOSE END and tell you what happened with Annie's aunt Anna (Joe's sister) and Anna's daughter, Mary. Back in 1918 when Anna and Old Man Ulsher were in the middle of divorce proceedings, Anna borrowed six hundred dollars on her two houses on Plum Street in East Butte. Four years later, her daughter, Mary, married Victor. Anna

Annie and Tony.

paid off the loan eleven days after Mary married Victor. That was in May of 1922. Mary was twenty-six. Victor was forty-six and worked for the railroad. He had been married before. His first wife was Nora. Then he married Myrtle, and she died. Then he married Marie, and she died. Then he married Annie's cousin Mary Kogar, and he died—in the insane asylum. What happened?

In 1906, when Victor was thirty-one years old, he married Nora. She was a very young divorcee. I don't know what became of her, whether she ran off, or they divorced, or she died. I could find no record of divorce and no death certificate. I think she might have gone back to her maiden name and had a cattle ranch outside Livingston. Some vague clues led me to think that. All I know for certain is the marriage was brief because Victor married again four years after he married Nora. He married Myrtle in Livingston. She was divorced with three grown children. She died three years later of liver cancer. She was forty-six. Then he married Marie. She had never been married. They lived at 411 East Calendar Street and later at 106 South Fifth Street in Livingston and had several boarders, all teachers. Victor was now a conductor for the Northern Pacific. One year after they married, Marie bore him a son, and then in 1921, she died of peritonitis from a pelvic abscess caused by a miscarriage. She was thirty-five. Then Victor married my grandma Annie's cousin Mary Kogar. They married at St. Mary's Church in Livingston. Victor's son was four years old. They moved to East Butte and lived with Mary's mother, Anna Kogar, at 45 Plum Street. Mary was barely married to Victor when he became sick, horribly sick, from a horrible disease. Three years later, in 1925, he was committed to the state mental hospital at Warm Springs. He died four years after that of "exhaustion of general paralysis of the insane," the late manifestation of a bacterial disease with a decades-long incubation period, a horrible way to die.

Meanwhile, across the Atlantic, Alexander Fleming had discovered a mold that killed bacteria. That mold is penicillin. It wasn't in time for poor Victor. There was no cure for him.

Mary was also in poor health when Victor was committed to the insane asylum. She suffered from Addison's disease. The county auditor concluded, because of her poor health, she couldn't work and needed help. She received pauper's aid for a short time. Her health improved somewhat, and she worked as a maid for a family. When Victor died in June of 1929, it seems her money problems were over, which makes me think she received a widow's pension from the railroad. In November of 1930, Anna and Mary started loaning money: six hundred dollars to Roy Redlich on a house in the Leggat Foster Addition, five hundred dollars to Catherine Auxier on a house in the Fausetts Addition, six hundred dollars to Stewart Downey on a property in the Floral Park Addition, thirteen hundred dollars to Park Lawthar on a house on Noyes Street. This brings us to 1931. The country was in the Great Depression, but apparently not Anna and Mary. They were now the loaner, never again the borrower would they be.

Right after Victor died, Mary and Anna took in a boarder, a Slovenian miner named John Jeroni. He was a good looking guy. The tongue-wagging neighbor ladies deemed him the "Star Boarder." John and Mary obtained a marriage license in 1931, but I found no marriage certificate to go with it. However, when she died of Addison's disease in 1951, the death certificate said he was her husband.

29

⁓

I'm Leaving this One Horse Town

"After Papa died, a friend of Mama asked her if she would be willing to open up a boardinghouse in East Helena," Stephie said. "So this friend had a great big house which was offered rent free. The work at the Butte mines as a janitoress was back breaking so she decided to take the offer. She really could cook delicious meals."

So Mother Caroline took daughters Stephie and Francie and grandson Bobby back to East Helena. They left East Butte around the same time that Annie and Tony returned from Seattle.

Francie was cheerful like her mother and full of fun, easy to laugh, the rambunctious youngest child now grown into a teenager. One night Mother Caroline yanked her off the dance floor when she thought Francie was dancing the Charleston with too much vigor with a tall, handsome man. The world would soon know him as Gary Cooper.

Bubbly Francie was a popular bridesmaid—in May of 1925 and again in October. Mother Caroline was friends of the parents. The paper tells us that Caroline attended the bridal shower.

Francie went back to East Butte to work as a bookkeeper. Stephie went with her though she hadn't yet found a job. They lived with Annie and Tony. Mother Caroline stayed in East Helena running the boardinghouse.

Francie and Stephie didn't stay long in East Butte. They went back to East Helena and lived with their mother.

We hear what happened next from Stephie:

Anyway we stayed in East Helena until I decided I wanted to go to California. We knew that Caroline [her sister] was already living there (in San Francisco) and figured we would not be lost. How it came about was one day I happened to meet a lady that just came from SF and somehow or

222

other the subject of carrots come up. I don't know if I went to the garden to dig some out for dinner but I mentioned how hard it was to grow them in East Helena. Oh she said out in California they grow wild all over and on the curb of the sidewalks, etc. Well that intrigued me no end. I wanted to see those carrots so one day I said to Mama I'm going to San Francisco. I didn't know how I was going to go there, but I knew I was going (at that time I forget about the prediction) but in the meantime before I met this lady from SF, I happened to go to a party and at this party was a woman who told fortunes. I decided to have her tell me mine. All I could remember was she said I was going to live where there was a large body of water and to let my mother go first otherwise if I went first I would have to come back to East Helena and stay. I'd be very unhappy. I couldn't imagine where the big body of water could be located. I thought maybe one of the lakes outside of Helena. Finally Mama thought it was a good idea to go to SF. Frances went first, then Mama, and after I closed the boardinghouse and all, I left for San Francisco and it was one of the best moves of our lives.

ONE DAY WHEN SHE WAS ALL OF NINETEEN, Francie declared, "I've had enough of living in a one horse town!" and off she went on the train all by herself all the way to San Francisco. She lived with her sister Caroline and Caroline's husband in a flat in a beautiful Italianate building with bay windows at 1350 Sutter Street, west of Van Ness. Francie worked as a packer at the MJB Coffee Plant where Young Caroline was forewoman.

Annie Leskovar, her sister-in-law Anna Leskovar, and Caroline Lozar,
East Helena, August 1924.

Stephie Lozar, East Helena, August 1924.   *Francie Lozar and the horse.*

A what-people-are-doing column in the Helena newspaper said, "Mrs. Lozar went to visit her daughters in San Francisco." That was November 24, 1926. She took grandson Bobby with her. She was fifty-seven years old.

Stephie was next.

Francie and Stephie were awestruck seeing San Francisco for the first time: the Bay, the fishmongers, the ocean, the mighty ships, the moist air, the fog. And the flowers, all year long there were flowers. Mother Caroline, the former Viennese cook, was right at home in the big city.

A man named Anton Belin had been living in San Francisco and managing a restaurant. He was born in the Slovenian part of Austria around 1882. He immigrated in 1898. I can't help but wonder if there was a connection to Caroline's father. I also found an Anton Belin in Calumet, Michigan, the town where Caroline met Joe. He was also an immigrant from Austria.

By 1928, all of them—Mother Caroline and grandson, Bobby (who was thirteen); Young Caroline (who was thirty and was Bobby's mother) and her husband, John (thirty-three); and Stephie (twenty-four) and Francie (twenty-one) were living at 129 Castro, near Buena Vista Park. It was quite a climb uphill to get there, but it was actually a house, much bigger than their half flat on Sutter.

When I asked one of Mother Caroline's future sons-in-law what she was like, he said, "With all those women in one house, somebody had to be in charge."

Francie and Stephie worked as telephone operators, connecting calls with cables on a switchboard. They knew who was talking to whom, and if the operator listened in, the callers would never be the wiser. I'm not saying my great-aunts Francie and Stephie ever did that. But the fact that they knew from firsthand experience that this was not uncommon could explain some of Stephie's strange behavior later.

Francie was the lively one, always talking and laughing. Stephie was the quiet one, the reserved one, who sat back and took everything in. They were different in every way, yet very close and always would be.

The next year, 1930, the family moved down the hill to a flat at 2341 Market Street, and the year after that to 2517 Polk in the heart of Russian Hill. The rent was thirty-five dollars a month. Caroline's husband worked as a machinist in the shipyard. Somewhere along the way he disappeared from their lives. I couldn't find a death certificate. I don't know what happened.

Everywhere they lived in San Francisco, Mother Caroline could walk to daily Mass. She loved that. She was always early for Mass.

Their next-door neighbors on Russian Hill were from Ireland; the husband of one was from California. A few doors down, the husband was from Germany, the wife was from New York. Then another couple, the husband was from England, the wife from Nova Scotia. A little farther up the block lived the Gagganos from Italy, and then a family with the husband from Italy and the wife's parents from Italy. Then another couple, the husband was from Poland and the wife from California, and then a woman from Montana and her husband from New York. It was a hodgepodge, much like Butte. Just about everyone was from somewhere else or their parents were.

Friends invited Francie over to play bridge. She said she didn't know how. The wife said, "Don't worry, every time it's your turn, just pass." The other guest was a gentleman named Ray Waters, a native of Iowa who grew up in California. Every time it was Francie's turn, she said, "Pass," no doubt followed by a laugh. Ray was an accomplished bridge player, and he couldn't understand why she kept passing when she had such great cards. Ditzy card playing did not dissuade him. Ray fell hard for the bubbly, stylish Francie, who burst out laughing at the least provocation. They ran off to Reno to get married. It was the daring, fashionable thing to do in those days.

Francie joked that they didn't have the silver engraved in case it didn't last. They married on September 15, 1934, two days before her twenty-seventh birthday. Ray was already twenty-seven and had a good job. He earned enough money that he and Francie didn't live with Francie's mother and sisters. Francie and Ray lived in their own apartment on Green Street. It was modern with garages on the ground floor and only two blocks from Francie's mother and sisters.

Once when Francie was mad at Ray, she stormed out of the house and marched straight home to mother. Mother Caroline said, "You're not coming here! You're married. Go back home to your husband!"

Francie and Ray Waters.

In the back are Francie, Bobby, and Stephie Lozar.
In front of them are Caroline Lozar and Caroline Lozar Davis.
Golden Gate Park, San Francisco, February 1927.

Francie Lozar Waters and Annie Leskovar, East Butte, June 1936.
Someone wrote on the back: "I think you're awful cute here."

Francie back in East Butte for a visit, June 1936. Left: *Here she is with her nephews Babe and Eddy Leskovar. She wrote on the back: "I certainly didn't ever expect these two lugs to out grow me. I look like a shrimp."* Right: *Francie and nephew Joe Leskovar.*

Francie quit her job when she and Ray married, fully expecting children would be arriving.

One day she suffered severe abdominal pain. Ray took her to the hospital. The surgeon came out to ask Ray's permission. Ray said, yes. That was the cryptic way Uncle Ray told me the story. I asked him what happened, but he didn't elaborate. Uncle Ed (Eddy) told me that Aunt Francie had appendicitis, and the doctor did a hysterectomy. I didn't understand the connection. A few years later, I had a ruptured appendix. Then I understood what most likely happened. Sometimes when the appendix ruptures, it seals itself to another part of the body. The body is trying to protect itself. In my case, the appendix stuck itself to the colon. Even with the benefit of a CT scan, my surgeon didn't know this had happened, only that it had ruptured, until he went in to remove the busted appendix. He had quite a time dislodging the appendix while saving the colon. I was in surgery much longer than anticipated. Francie's appendix must have ruptured and stuck itself to an ovary. Perhaps the only way the surgeon could save her was to do a hysterectomy.

No babies. Francie went back to work as a telephone operator.

30

Teddy Is Born

It was August 15, 1933, in the middle of a raging blizzard, eighteen inches of snow would fall on Butte, Montana, that day, somehow Tony managed to drive Annie all the way from East Butte across Butte up the hill to St. James Hospital. There she gave birth to a boy. Annie and Tony named their fourth son Theodore Sebastian and called him Teddy. Sebastian was Tony's middle name. Their eldest son, Eddy, was almost seventeen, Babe was fifteen, Joe would be six in November. Their tiny house at 210 Cherry had one bedroom.

Teddy was the youngest son of the youngest son. Tony was forty-six years old when Teddy was born. Annie was forty, the same age as Tony's mother when Tony was born. Teddy wouldn't remember his mother's hair being anything but gray.

When Teddy was still a baby in arms, Tony and Annie took him to Elk Park outside of Butte for a picnic with friends. Young and old held up glasses of beer in a toast as they posed for a picture. Perhaps they were toasting legal beer since Prohibition had finally ended. I know this because I found the picture in an album Annie made for Teddy with pictures of his life. She wrote 1934 on the picture. Annie is holding Teddy and has a huge smile on her face. I didn't notice until I scanned the tiny picture and saw it blown up on my computer screen—she was giving Teddy a sip of beer.

According to Annie's brother, Steve: "When Teddy was a baby, we were in the car, and Teddy started to cry, and Annie says, 'Stop the car! Stop the car!' and Tony stops the car, and Annie gave Teddy whiskey. [Steve laughed.] The kid didn't draw a sober breath before he was twelve."

No doubt Annie put a dab of whiskey on Teddy's gums when he was teething. Steve knew that, but he didn't miss a chance to make a joke about his sister.

Nazdravje! *Look closely and you can see Annie giving Teddy a sip of beer. Elk Park, north of Butte, 1934.*

Teddy began life in the Bohunk enclave of East Butte. "I grew up in a very unusual neighborhood in a very unusual town," he said.

Bohunk, you say—what is that? In Butte, people of Slavic descent called themselves Bohunks. Growing up hearing that I never thought about the origin of it until now, so I looked it up. "Bo" is from Bohemian (Czech, not paleo-hippies) and "hunk" is short for Hungarian. It came to mean people of central European descent, mainly Slavs. It could be a term of identity or a term of derision, depending on who was saying it and the tone of voice. It was used all over the country, not only in Butte.

It was a spring tradition for the students at Butte High to celebrate Bohunkus Day by skipping class and marching uptown.

So yes, Teddy was raised in the Bohunk enclave of East Butte, a tiny hamlet east of the East Side full of high-strung Balkan peasants. That might be an exaggeration; some say the Slovenians are not Balkan. Most of the neighbors were Croatian, definitely Balkan. The neighborhood to the north called McQueen was full of Serbs, also Balkan, all Bohunks.

East Butte was full of people from a paternalistic culture with headstrong women. Everybody was bossy. If Teddy was into mischief, the nearest mother would scold him, and Annie would know about it before he was home. Whenever Teddy was playing in the street with his friends, one of the neighbor ladies would yell at them to quit playing in the street, even when Tony was the only one in East Butte who owned a car.

A neighbor lady came to the house to ask Tony to take her to the hospital. She was bleeding. He took her.

Years later when neighbors had cars, one of the neighbor ladies had parked on a street uptown. A cop parked his motorcycle behind her. She didn't see it and backed out and knocked it over. She jumped out of the car and bawled out the cop—what did he think he was doing parking behind her? He jumped on his motorcycle and took off.

When she took her driver's test to get her license, after the test she didn't get out of the car. She didn't know how to undo the seatbelt. She had never used it.

Within East Butte there were the Uppers and Lowers. Annie and Tony and their four sons lived among the Lowers, who were vastly superior to the Uppers. Even a poor neighborhood can enjoy the luxury of snobbery.

The Uppers weren't particularly uppity, no one could afford that, but they had the unfortunate fate, alas, not to be Lowers.

When asked about someone from East Butte who had become quite successful, Ted said he knew the name, but that man's parents didn't want him associating with other people from East Butte. I asked why.

"They were Uppers," he said.

They weren't as good as Lowers?

"No. For our generation there was a lot of feud between the Uppers and Lowers. The Lowers were mostly all Bohunks. The Uppers were a mixture."

Teddy, May 1935, in their front yard at 210 Cherry in East Butte.

Ted talked about the Uppers and Lowers with a mischievous grin and glint of humor in his eye. It was an important distinction in a neighborhood populated by Bohunk peasants and their offspring, a neighborhood comprised of only a few blocks, perhaps a type for age-old European rivalries.

TEDDY IS AROUND FOUR. Annie is in command of the camera. Teddy, stand still so I can take your picture, she says. He won't stand still. Tony goes down on one knee. He hands Teddy the whiskey bottle. Teddy hugs it like a Teddy Bear. He leans against Tony and smiles, all the while clutching the whiskey bottle. Tony tells Annie to move so her shadow won't be in the picture. She doesn't listen and takes the picture. Later she writes on the back: "Tony & Baby holding bottle of whiskey only way we could snap his picture he was not feeling well—account of vaccination. This was taken going home. Labor Day."

TEDDY GREW UP in the middle of the block at 210 Cherry Street in East Butte. There was a bar on the corner to the east. There was another bar a block and a half to the west. Francie Spehar's bar was on the next block over on Plum.

The Cash family lived next door to the Leskovars. They were Slovenian. Cash is the anglicized spelling of the Slovenian name Čož. Other neighbors were John and Johannah Gregorich who were Croatian; Mollie Pace was from Pennsylvania; the Rozichs were Slovenian; Tom and Mary Gergurich were Croatian; Mary Malesek was Slovenian; the Flaniks were Slovenian; the Orliches were Croatian; and the Kasicks. Those ch-ending names are anglicized; in Slovenian and Croatian they end in č, which is pronounced ch.

In one family, the husband and wife didn't speak to each other for years. He did something, and she was mad at him. At the end of his life when he was sick and bedridden, she took care of him.

When Teddy was a little tyke, Mrs. Cash would send him to the corner bar with a lard bucket to buy beer for her. He had to stand on the bar rail to be able to reach to put the bucket up on the bar. While the bartender filled the lard bucket from the tap, Teddy checked the slot machines and phone for change. The bartender handed the bucket of beer to Teddy. The lard bucket had a metal handle and no lid. Teddy would walk home swinging the bucket round and round, fast enough that the beer didn't fall out when upside down. He would walk into Mrs. Cash's house and put the bucket on the table, full of foamy beer, and she would ask Teddy, "Do you want a nickel or a glass of beer?"

"I'll take the glass of beer," he said. It was a small glass.

Mrs. Cash was a widow with three grown children living with her. Frank was a miner, Mary was a waitress, Joe was a busboy. In 1939, during the Depression, Mary made more money in a year as a waitress (nine hundred dollars) than Tony did (eight hundred dollars). The Cashes raised pigs in their yard. One day the pigs got loose, and Teddy and his friend Bobby tried to wrangle them back to the yard. They only scared the pigs.

Annie would send Teddy to the corner bar for a quart of beer and a Hershey bar. They'd have it together, beer and a Hershey bar.

*Teddy with big brothers Babe and Eddy in their front yard
at 210 Cherry in East Butte, May 1935.*

Annie with Teddy, May 1935.

LEFT: *Tony and Teddy, June 1936.* RIGHT: *As for Teddy clutching the whiskey bottle, Annie said, "It was the only way we could get him to stand still." September 1937.*

Nobody had a refrigerator, everybody had an icebox. The ice man came through the neighborhood selling blocks of ice to put in the icebox to keep food cold. Peddlers and other tradesmen walked door to door selling their wares. A man used to walk through the neighborhood with a pony and a camera. He'd take a child's picture on the pony—for a fee, of course.

Annie and Tony had a telephone installed at the house. Nobody had their own line, all were party lines, meaning several families shared the same line. A person could pick up the phone and listen in on other people's conversations.

"LET'S GO," SAYS TONY, and they all climb into the car and drive to Elk Park. Along the way, Tony stops to fill bottles with spring water at the fountains hewn out of granite along the highway. Annie wants to take a picture. Joe sits on the bumper of the car. Tony sits on the low stone wall along the highway. Teddy climbs on his lap. The mountains are behind them. Annie takes the picture.

Ice peddler.
WORLD MUSEUM OF MINING 03159 ©WORLD MUSEUM OF MINING

Leskovar home at 210 Cherry in East Butte, 1938.

Annie and Tony didn't go to Mass, but Catholicism was part of Slovenian culture. Hence, Teddy received his First Communion at Holy Savior Church, as did his three brothers before him. Before First Communion, children made their First Confession.

It is the day before Easter. Teddy and Joe are sitting at the kitchen table cracking walnuts, dropping shells into one bowl, nuts into the other, many going into their mouths. Annie throws a cloth over the oak pedestal table in the front room. She flours it. She makes the dough. She makes the filling. She stretches the dough until it is thin as parchment. She carefully spreads the filling of ground walnuts, honey,

Joe, First Communion, May 1935.

Holy Savior Church, East Butte.

brown sugar, white sugar, butter, cinnamon, eggs, and milk over it with her fingers. She picks up the edge of the tablecloth and rolls up the potica. She winds the six-foot-long roll of dough into a snail shape in the big turkey roaster. She lets it rest. She bakes it. The wonderful aroma of gently roasting walnuts fills the kitchen.

She takes the food they will eat on Easter to Holy Savior Church to be blessed by Father Pirnat: ham, sausage, hard-boiled eggs, radishes, green onions. Easter is a big celebration.

Months pass and now it is Christmas. Annie makes potica. A package arrives from Uncle Joe and Aunt Anna in Racine, Wisconsin. It is klobase (sausage). The present tucked under the tree for Teddy is a toy cannon. It fires little wooden balls. Babe and Eddy commandeer it and shoot the ornaments off the tree until the cannon breaks. Then they give it back to Teddy.

THE RENT FOR THEIR TINY HOUSE at 210 Cherry was fifteen dollars a month in 1930. By 1936, well into the Great Depression, the rent jumped to twenty-five dollars. The owner told Tony he was going to sell the house; they'd have to move.

"Why are you selling the house?" Tony asked.

"To buy a car," he said.

Tony went to Joe Wilson, the Chrysler Plymouth dealer, and worked out a trade—he'd trade his paint work for a new Plymouth. Wilson agreed. Tony told the man who owned the house, "I'll trade you this car for the house." He agreed. That is how Tony and Annie came to own the house at 210 Cherry Street.

When you walked through the front door, you were in the front room. There was a sofa (davenport) and chair, a round oak pedestal table and chairs, the piano, and above the mantle, the large portrait of Mother Caroline when she married, the picture of her that is on the cover of this book. There was a wood stove for heat. To the right of the front door was the door to the bedroom, which connected to the bathroom, which connected to another small room, which connected to the kitchen and the front room. The house had no halls. There was a small enclosed porch off the kitchen. The kitchen had a wood stove, which later burned coal. For a time, theirs was the only house in the neighborhood with an indoor toilet.

The door to the root cellar was outside. It had slanted doors like the ones in *The Wizard of Oz*, where Auntie Em and the hired men went to flee the tornado.

Joe and Teddy, May 1938.   *Teddy and Joe.*

Tony built a garage out back on the alley. He hung sausages in the garage. He'd scrape the mold off and eat the sausage.

Eddy and Babe were grown up by the time Teddy was old enough to remember. They were closer in age to their aunt Francie than to Teddy. Teddy was eight when Eddy and Babe got married and left home. Teddy would be closest to Joe, who was almost six years older.

One night Joe was watching the radio. Yes, before TV, people watched the radio. It was a big stand-up radio. Annie told him to go out to the shed and get kindling and coal for the fire in the stove. This was Joe's regular chore, but a boy engrossed in a radio show had to be reminded. The shed was out back on the alley next to the garage. The walls of the shed were covered with cardboard, no drywall or sheetrock. It was dark, so Joe tore a bit of cardboard back from the wall and lit it with a match, so he could see. He did this every time. He chopped the kindling and gathered it up and picked up some coal and blew at the flame and went back into the house and resumed watching the radio. A little while later, he heard *rrrrr rrrrr*, the siren of the dreaded East Butte Volunteer Fire Department. He and Tony looked out back. The shed was ablaze.

The shed burned down, but fortunately not the garage, not the house, and Tony had insurance.

The East Butte Volunteer Fire Department used an old surplus fire truck that had a pump to draw water out of a river, which they didn't need since there was no river and there were fire hydrants in East Butte. But for some reason, when a neighbor's shed caught fire, they thought they needed the pump. They hooked up the hose to the fire hydrant and the pump, aimed the hose at the fire, opened the fire hydrant, turned on the pump, and blew the roof off the shed. "There were boards flying all over the place," Ted said.

A particularly fastidious woman wouldn't let the East Butte Fire Department into her house when her kitchen caught fire. She was more worried about their wrecking the house than the fire.

Nearby McQueen also had a volunteer fire department. A gas station in disputed territory caught fire. The East Butte Volunteer Fire Department showed up on one side. The McQueen Volunteer Fire Department showed up on the other side. Each insisted it was their fire. The two fire departments hooked up their hoses and streamed water over the fire onto the other fire department, dousing each other with water, while the gas station in the middle burned to the ground.

By and large, East Butte was a neighborhood of people of humble means who kept their yards and houses neat and tidy. If someone's yard was messy, the East Butte Fire Department took it upon themselves to clean it up.

When a neighbor was short on cash, he might borrow money from Larko. There was always collateral involved. If they didn't pay, Larko kept the property. It was an informal pawn operation. When he took a trip to California, he asked Tony to keep an eye on the property he had stored in his garage. Everything had a price tag on it.

Mining scaled way back during the Great Depression of the 1930s. The Pittsmont Mine and Smelter in East Butte closed for good. People pulled wooden boards from the fence around it and used them to heat their homes.

The year after Teddy was born, 1934, the few miners who were working went on strike, a wildcat strike. The Butte miners had unionized early on, back in 1878, but there had been no miners' union since the riot in 1914. One of the neighbors crossed the picket line and was deemed a scab. A crowd gathered at his house and burned a dummy in effigy to scare him into not working. He may well have been a pumpman. If the pumps didn't operate, the mines would flood and be ruined.

That strike lasted four and a half months. In the end, the miners had a five-day week and their union back. Twenty years of open shop were over.

ONE OF THEIR NEIGHBORS in East Butte was Bluebird, so his wife was called Annie Bluebird. Another was Goldie, so his wife was Mary Goldie. I asked Ted why they were called Bluebird and Goldie. He didn't know. He was a kid. What one grows up with, one tends to think of as normal. Having neighbors called Bluebird and Goldie seemed normal.

"It probably wasn't until after I got married I learned Mary Goldie's name was Mihelich," Ted said.

Bluebird was Old Man Lubick, his friend Bobby's dad.

When Ted talked about the neighborhood, it seems all the women were named Annie or Mary. "Were there any mothers in your neighborhood not named Mary or Annie?" I asked. He shrugged. I asked his friend Chuck Flanik. He wrote back:

Adding to your list of Anns and Marys, please add Ann Carveth (lived on Plum Street), Ann Metully (my sister), Mary Mihelich (lived on lower Plum Street), Annie Kranitza (Plum Street), Mary Gergurich (Cherry Street owner of 156 Club), Mary (Gip) Orlich (Don Orlich's mother), Mary (Legs) Orlich (Don Orlich's aunt), Mary Chabai (my next door neighbor when your dad was just getting out of diapers), Annie Gergurich on Cherry Street two houses from your dad's), Annie Cash (your dad's next door neighbor then moved to Las Vegas with husband Butch Lee in gambling), Ann Marinovich (Pinkie Marinovich's mother), Mary Oreskovich (lived next door to Harrison School), Mary Laurich (upper East Butte later girlfiend of George Snookie Gergurich after his wife Riva died), Annie Stefanac (Plum Street near the HiHo Lounge, Mary Rozic (next door neighbor), Annie Leskovar, and Mary Flanick (school teacher lived on Plum Street). I'm sure there are few more, but memory fails at this point.

As for nicknames, Ted said, "Let's see, in Chuck's house there were Feet, Pasty, and Pork."

Laughing, I asked, why were they called Feet, Pasty, and Pork?

"I don't know."

I asked Chuck.

During the years prior to WWII, nicknames were quite common throughout Butte and probably the nation. Why this occurred I have no idea. Maybe because there was no TV and and fast moving cars.

Joseph (Feet) Brozovich was my stepbrother who wore a size 11 shoe. Don Orlich wears a size 14.

Frank (Porky) Flanick was my full brother was 6'1", muscular and played football.

Why the difference in the spelling of our last name is another story. When Frank was drafted in 1942, the Army spelled his last name "Flanick." His attempt to have the spelling corrected, was not a serious issue (more important matters were at hand) and after 4 years in the Army the spelling remained the same until he died.

Peter (Pasty) Metully was my brother-in-law married to my sister Ann Brozovich. My father died when I was 5, and Pasty assumed the role of a surrogate father. I was very blessed. The nearest I came to a nickname was Chuck but not Charlie.

McQueen Additon was the home of many more and unusual nicknames: Big Eye, Brown, Peachy, Long John — all in the Petriz family.

In the Orlich family there was Greek, Lefty, Legs, and Gip. The list goes on and in a few more years this history will be lost forever.

Not if I have anything to do with it.

MISSING FROM CHUCK'S LIST of nicknames was the one Annie gave to one of the neighbor ladies: the Baby Elephant. That was not a widely known nickname.

Annie's generic nickname for a little boy was Buster, as in Buster Brown. When she saw a neighbor's baby boy, she attempted to say, "There's a little Buster," but instead, out came another word beginning with a B. Oh, Annie.

Chuck's dad died of tuberculosis. He became sick shortly after Chuck was born. The county authorities took Chuck's dad to the sanatorium in Galen. Chuck only saw his dad waving from the window when his mother went to visit him. Adults could go inside but not children. That is the closest memory he has of his father, waving from a second-story window.

After grocery shopping on Saturday mornings, Teddy and Annie would sit and watch the opera on the radio.

Joe slept in the garage in the summer. It was still cold at night. Annie would heat a brick in the oven and wrap it in newspaper and put it at the foot of his bed.

"She was a very attentive mother," Joe said.

Teddy slept in the small room off the kitchen. It was so cold he could see his breath. He didn't dare move, the sheets were ice cold. Tony would come into the kitchen early in the morning and light the fire in the stove. He'd close the door to the little room where Teddy slept. This was no doubt so as not to wake him, but it also made the room even colder.

Milk was delivered and left on the porch. Milk was not homogenized back then, so the cream was on top. Joe always hurried to drink the cream off the top. "The quick and the hungry," Ted used to say. Big brother Joe was the quick. He'd grow to be six feet six. Teddy was the hungry. He would grow to be the same height as Tony, five feet eleven. When it was really cold outside, the milk froze and expanded and the cream rose and pushed the cap off the top. Joe was eating unsweetened iced cream.

There were no houses across the street, just railroad tracks and dirt. On bitter cold nights, which could mean thirty or forty below in winter, Ted said, "It sounded like the trains were barreling right through the house."

ONE NIGHT AT DINNER, Joe was teasing Teddy. Teddy tired of it and picked up his plate and hit Joe over the head with it. That crack in the plate would forever remind Teddy of what he did. He didn't feel good about it.

Eddy and Babe called their parents Annie and Tony. Joe and Teddy called them Ma and Pops.

Joe would take little brother Teddy on the streetcar uptown to the paint shop. He'd ask Tony for a nickel. Tony called him "Give-Me-Nickel Joe." He could buy a Pepsi and a Hershey bar with a nickel.

"I don't remember being around Pops much when I was a kid," Joe said. "And when I was a teenager, I was out all the time. When I was a kid, he'd come home for dinner, and then go back up to the shop to work on the books."

ANNIE HAD A HOME CURE for everything. When one of her sons was sick, she'd put her hand against the cold wall, let it get cold, then put her hand on his forehead to see if he had a fever. Of course he did. The cure for a fever was eggnog, which was a beaten raw egg with brandy. Teddy liked that cure. Edith Stein, the nurse in Austria during the First World War, said they gave the sickest typhoid fever patients a beaten egg mixed with cognac. That's the old way of making eggnog, with no milk or cream.

The cure Teddy feared most was her cure for the common cold: mustard plaster smeared over his chest. This was to draw out the poisons, meaning whatever was making him sick. It was dry mustard mixed with water. It burned like a son-of-gun, so she followed it with Vick's Vapor Rub to sooth the burn. One time she burned herself pretty badly.

"You didn't want to tell Ma you were sick," Ted said. "She'd give you mustard plaster."

Did it burn your skin?

"Yes. There were no hypochondriacs. Ma would say, 'Are you sick?' No!"

Another cure she used for a cold was a hot toddy of hot tea, honey, cognac, and lemon.

She put a piece of onion on a bee sting.

She put apple cider on sunburn and ordered a cold bath.

She must have believed the ads in the paper that claimed sarsaparilla was the cure for blood, liver, kidney and bowel ailments; she drank it.

Annie made a medicinal tea for Teddy out of a weed called palum. I looked it up. It's a "drastic purgative." Ted said it was awful. "You never admitted you were sick around Ma."

Even after Joe was a grown man and married, one day he was talking to Annie on the phone and she heard him sniffling and concluded he had a cold, and she said, "I'll be right over with a mustard plaster!" Joe said, "Ma, you don't have to do that anymore. I'm married." She came over anyway and smeared a mustard plaster all over his six feet six chest. Even after they were married, they didn't want to tell Ma they were sick.

One time she put an onion plaster on her sore throat, and it left burns on her skin.

When all else failed, she used whiskey.

The first time Teddy remembered going to the doctor was when he drank the Easter egg dye. The second time he was in grade school. He had a boil behind his ear. Tony took him to his friend who was a doctor. This doctor had invented something and lived comfortably off the proceeds. He didn't normally see patients but kept his office as a place to go to get out of the house. He led Tony and Teddy into his office, took a glass vial off the shelf, blew the dust off it, took the needle out, and with nothing to numb the pain, lanced the boil and pulled out the core. Teddy said it hurt like the dickens. This was around 1946 when Tony was down on his luck; I'll tell you more about that later. The doctor didn't charge Tony, he knew he didn't have the money. Those were the only two times Teddy remembered going to the doctor as a child. People didn't go to the doctor unless they were sick or hurt. If your mother couldn't remedy the problem, she asked a nurse she knew. If it was beyond the nurse, then she might call the doctor.

Late in August, Annie remarked to Teddy, "Didn't you have a birthday a couple of days ago?" She was not one to stand on ceremony.

PROUST WROTE OF A FRENCH VILLAGE in which seeing "a person whom one didn't know at all was as incredible a being as any mythological deity." One could say the same thing of East Butte. Everybody knew each other. Annie knew everything that was going on. Ted said, "Ma knew what I was going to do before I did it."

ANNIE IS GOING VISITING, which she does often, or someone visits her. It is one of her favorite pastimes. She takes Teddy. They walk into the neighbor's house. She doesn't knock. Nobody knocks. Nobody's door is locked. They just walk in. Annie tells Teddy, "Sit in that chair and be quiet." He does.

He starts driving when he is around nine years old. Annie never learns to drive, so Teddy drives her to the store. He sits in the car and waits, and waits, and waits, and finally goes inside and finds her visiting.

Tony and Annie went visiting on Sundays. They dropped in, or friends dropped in to see them, nothing planned, nothing scheduled, they simply dropped in. They drank red wine and visited. Amazing that they didn't all go visiting at once, and then no one was home because they'd all gone visiting.

From time to time, they drove up to East Helena to visit friends. It took the whole day to drive there and back. The car would break down. Tony would get out, work on it, get it running, they'd continue on their way. Tony always kept a shovel in the trunk of the car. He never knew when he might have to dig out the car, be it stuck in snow or mud, and snow could come any time.

They went up there to visit after the earthquakes that struck Helena in 1935: a 5.9 in the middle of the night of October 11, a 6.3 on October 18, a 6.0 on October 31, and a 6.0 on Thanksgiving. The saloon that Joe Lozar built still stood, while many granite buildings in Helena, including the new high school, tumbled. Quake refugees were living in a tent city.

Around the same time, Tony was on the welcoming committee to greet Archbishop Rozman of Ljubljana, Yugoslavia. When asked about another European war, the archbishop said he thought the possibility was remote. The memory of the last war was so fresh. No one would start another war. Though the Italians were fighting in Ethiopia, he doubted England would attack Italy.

One time when they were driving to East Helena, Joe and Teddy were in the backseat. Teddy was pretty small. Joe kept saying to him, "Tell them you're hungry," and Teddy kept saying, "No." So Joe hit him, and he started crying. Annie said, "What's the matter with Teddy?! What's the matter with Teddy?!" Joe said, "He wants a hamburger."

They used to visit their friends who owned Smith's bar. The grown-ups drank whiskey and beer at one end of the bar; the kids drank milkshakes at the other end.

Tony always brought spare tires. At least one was sure to blow out on the drive, even though it was just a day trip. Those spring water fountains carved into the granite along the highways were not only convenient for a refreshing drink, but also to cool the car radiator.

Joe started driving on his own when he was around twelve. Tony let him take his truck. "I would take Teddy for a drive," Joe said. One day they drove out to the airport to look at the planes. "I put Teddy on my shoulders and walked all the way to East Butte." He had blown out the tires. Tony didn't get mad. Annie didn't get mad.

A FAVORITE PASTIME was to drive up to Elk Park for a picnic with friends. Annie packed a delicious meal. Tony brought wine. Somebody played the cordeen (button accordion). This particular picnic Teddy was pretty small. "Joey, watch Teddy," Annie said. Later she asked Joe, "Where's Teddy?" Joe shrugged. There was a fast-moving creek nearby. Panic set in. All started searching, terrified that Teddy had fallen into the icy swift waters. Then Joe remembered that he didn't feel like watching Teddy, so he locked him in the woodshed. He told his parents, and there they found him sitting calmly on a block of wood.

Annie loved to gamble, which was still illegal but wide open in Butte. The mother of a friend of Teddy's ran a casino. She paid the cops one hundred dollars a table every month.

"Ma used to drag me there—the Board of Trade, the M&M, the 30 Club," Ted said. "She played what they called Chinese lottery [keno]. At the 30 Club you go through the door, there was a jewelry store—just a counter with everything covered with dust. The next room you went through a door, there was a ring of slot machines. The next room was keno. It was huge."

Teddy on Tony's lap. Joe is leaning against the car.

Tony is in the middle, holding Teddy's knees, Annie is to the right, then Eddy, then Joe standing on the stone wall. I don't know who the other people are. They were on their way to or from a picnic at Elk Park, north of Butte.

Louise and John Lousen's twenty-fifth wedding anniversary, May 30, 1935, Elk Park. Tony and Annie are the second and third from the right, standing. Annie is holding Teddy. The Lousens are friends from the Old Country and future in-laws.

Stopping for a picnic along the way. Annie, Babe, Tony, Teddy, Joe, May 1938.

31

⁂

TONY'S MINES

I WOULDN'T SAY THAT TONY was afflicted with gold fever to the extent of his father-in-law, Joe Lozar, but it was hard to live in Montana back then and not give it a go. Why not? He never went into debt to do it. He didn't mortgage his house. He didn't fall into Joe's folly.

In June of 1932, Tony discovered and posted the Brookside Quartz Lode. This was north of Butte, in Elk Park. He dug a tunnel at the point of discovery. It was six feet wide, eight feet high, and twenty feet long, and sloped down. It was ten feet below the surface at the end. He discovered a well-defined vein bearing gold, silver, and iron. He dutifully posted his claim and recorded it at the courthouse in Boulder, the seat of Jefferson County. All this he did in accordance with mining law.

Tony knew there was ore at that spot even before he proceeded to dig. The mine was on Highway 91, the highway between Butte and Helena. When the workmen excavated the land to build the highway, they uncovered ore veins. In other words, they created outcroppings. John Jeroni, the miner who lived with Annie's aunt Anna and cousin Mary, helped Tony find the right spot to dig.

Over the next few years, Tony dug another ten feet of tunnel. He sank a shaft sixteen feet deep. He dynamited the rock to put in four hundred feet of road to access his mine, and built a fifty-foot bridge over the creek. He hired workmen and miners; Eddy and Babe helped too, and son Joe when he was big enough. One time Tony and Joe were on their way home from the mine; Tony was driving a pickup truck with a trailer on the back. They ran out of gas just outside of Butte. Tony coasted the truck downhill. He told Joe they would both jump out to lighten the load so the truck would coast down into Meaderville where he could buy gas. Joe jumped out too

249

soon and fell and broke his finger. He stood up and slapped it back. "Don't tell Annie," Tony said.

The Mining Act of 1872 required that a claimant do at least one hundred dollars of work every year on the mine to maintain the claim. Tony documented that he did so in affidavits he filed at the courthouse. Naturally, he couldn't work on it all the time. He had his car painting business, and he performed with the Butte Mines Band. Nevertheless, he did the required one hundred dollars worth of work on the mine every year.

The Mining Act also said that claimants "shall have the exclusive right of possession and enjoyment of all the surface included within the lines of their locations."

Tony's mine was at the mouth of Sawmill Gulch, about eight miles south of Basin and a quarter mile north of Old Man Ulsher's claim, yes, the Old Man Ulsher who had been married to Annie's aunt Anna Lozar Kogar Ulsher. He and Tony were friends. Old Man Ulsher lived in Elk Park, near his stone quarry. In the winter, he would kill an elk, clean it, cut off what he needed and leave it in the snow. He'd go back and cut off another piece of meat when he needed more.

Young miner Joe at the entrance to Tony's Brookside Mine.

I think this is John Jeroni, the miner who helped Tony locate the lead and who lived with Annie's aunt Anna and cousin Mary.

Tony at his gold mine.

Old Man Ulsher's granddaughter Molly Gill told me she remembered Mr. Leskovar as the "elegant man" who visited her grandfather. "He radiated a lot," she said. "He had a presence. He stood up straight. We kids looked forward to seeing him." She said he spoke English well.

This day Tony took Teddy with him, which he did often. After greetings and pleasantries, Old Man Ulsher picked up a jug of beer, slapped the bottom hard, and the cork flew out and stuck in the ceiling. Teddy looked up and saw many corks stuck in the ceiling and pockmarks where corks had stuck and fallen down. Then Old Man Ulsher swung the jug over his shoulder and poured a glass of beer for Tony and a little one for Teddy. Teddy was in grade school. After a long conversation in Slovenian, Tony climbed into the backseat of the car, stretched out and took a nap while Teddy drove home along the narrow old road that hugged the mountain.

This was repeated on every visit. Teddy was twelve when Old Man Ulsher passed away.

"I remember Pops had me driving," Ted said. "I had two pillows, one I was sitting on, one behind my back."

IN FEBRUARY OF 1938, the United States of America sued Tony for trespassing on public land, namely, for having the audacity to be on his own mining claim, the Brookside. Besides the fact that Tony claimed the mine in accordance with the law, I have to ask the obvious question: if it is public land, how can a member of the public trespass on it? Tony legally claimed land under the Mining Act of 1872. The government said Tony built a cabin on his mining claim. That was true. I could not find anything in the Mining Act of 1872 that said a miner was forbidden from building a dwelling on his claim. If a miner did not build a cabin at his mining claim, how on earth could he do any prolonged work on it and where would he store his tools out of the weather? Mining claims were remote. Was he always to live in a tent? In Montana? I bet Tommy Cruse built a place for himself to live in at the Drumlummon, which he worked for eight long years before he struck his gold bonanza. A tailor named William Oertel, who lived in Butte, worked his mining claim for forty years before he finally struck a rich vein in 1924. It was near Marysville, which is a long way from Butte. William Oertel had to have built a little cabin up there. Perhaps those claims were nowhere near the highway and were not ideal picnic spots, which Tony's was.

Tony did build a small cabin for himself and his workers to stay in while working the claim. There was a nice home in the area, but it was not Tony's. The court records include a picture of Tony's cabin and this other home that it called his "summer home," which it was not and is laughable. The house in the picture looks nicer than his house in East Butte. Tony couldn't afford a "summer home." He had a business to run in Butte. I haven't been able to figure out whose house it was. On seeing the picture, Ted said it was not his dad's cabin.

The government also alleged that Tony built a dance floor near the claim. Tony said he did not. It would be my guess that whoever built the nice house, the "summer home" as the government called it, also built the dance floor. With nary a scintilla of evidence, the government insisted that Tony built it. The government said Tony invited his friends there. That was true. It was a nice area. The Fireman's Picnic was held there.

Tony's cabin at Elk Park. Annie wrote on the back, "Everybody eating lunch at this moment." July 4, 1935. A picture of the side of the cabin was the government's Exhibit 2 in the lawsuit.

Tony serving drinks at the cabin at Elk Park.

Annie in the foreground, picnic at Elk Park. One of several picnic tables.

*The dance floor at the Brookside Lode. The government's
Exhibit 4 in the lawsuit.*

Tony must not have been too discomfited by the lawsuit, for in June of 1938, he claimed another mine, which he named the Cedar. It was next to his first mine, the Brookside.

The case of the United States of America versus Anton Leskovar came before the court on December 3, 1938. There was no jury. The judge would decide.

The mining engineer, whom Tony hired, testified that he took samples from inside the tunnel. He said the assay showed enough gold and silver for a prudent man to justify spending time and money developing the claim.

The government geologists said, yes, they found ore in Tony's mine, but not much. I will again point out that this was the case with mining claims. The prospector didn't strike the mother lode immediately. It could take years of mining and a tremendous amount of hard work. Only part of the transcript was in the court records, so I don't know if Tony's lawyer made that point. Decades later, Tony's son Joe hired a lawyer to look at the court records. "Your father did not have a good lawyer," was all he said.

It was essentially an eminent domain case. The Forest Service said it wanted the land for "a place of recreation for the general public." Tony's mining claim at that spot prevented "forest officials from using the area as

This picture called "Summer Home" was the government's Exhibit 5. This house did not belong to Annie and Tony. I don't know whose house it was.

Elk Park, cabin down below the highway leading back to Butte.

a public camp ground." Out of the vast Deer Lodge National Forest, thousands of square miles, the Forest Service had to have this particular spot. The judge decided that Tony never found enough ore to be of commercial value and by judicial fiat, declared Tony's mining claim void.

The government took Tony's mine away and billed him for doing it. The court ordered him to pay the government's court costs.

"It's still the Wild West," Tony said, "but now they use dollars instead of bullets."

32

East Butte Owls

"Was it on the tracks, on an old abandoned siding?" I asked.

"It wasn't anywhere near the tracks."

"It was out there in the middle of a field—a boxcar? How did it get there?"

"I don't know," Ted said.

It was just sitting there, an old wooden boxcar on an empty piece of dirt; no one knew how it got there. No one knew who owned the land, if anybody. It didn't seem odd that a boxcar was sitting in the middle of usually frozen prairie. It seemed normal. To call it prairie sounds too romantic. It was a dirt field, empty save for the old abandoned boxcar, expropriated by Teddy and his friends as their clubhouse. The boys called it their shed. There was an owl painted on the side. They were the East Butte Owls.

Teddy was the youngest Owl. The rest were in grades ahead of him at the Harrison School. They were Don Orlich, Chuck Flanik, Bobby Lubick, Stevie Casick, Don Meglan, Buddy Worth, and Pinky (Pete) Marinovich. The school was close by. They walked home for lunch.

Their playground was the slag dump from the old abandoned Pittsmont Smelter. The slag was black as coal and huge, several stories high. Slag is what is left over from the smelting process. In Britain, they call it a slag heap, which sounds poetic, almost charming. Dump is more to the point, for a dump it was. It was covered with pigeons until one of the neighbors shot them all.

When the Leskovars looked out their front door at 210 Cherry Street, they beheld the magnificent beauty of the Rocky Mountains. When the neighbors behind them across the alley on Plum Street looked out their front door, they beheld a wall of black slag. The beauty of the Rockies, the reality of mining, there to behold in East Butte.

*Pittsmont Mine and Smelter in East Butte. The street facing the
slag dump is Plum Street. Cherry Street faces the open field and
railroad tracks, which are difficult to see in the picture.*
WORLD MUSEUM OF MINING 09708 © WORLD MUSEUM OF MINING

The slag was hard, rock hard. One side was a wall of hard slag, the other
side was sand. The boys would climb up the sand. The walls at the top of
the slag dump were the ramparts of their imaginary fort.

When they weren't climbing around on the slag dump, Teddy and
his fellow Owls scrounged around the railroad tracks and roundhouse
looking for all manner of fun things, such as coal to build a fire to keep
warm in the shed.

The railroad roundhouse was at the turnoff into East Butte. A Japanese
man who worked there put in a beautiful garden, a touch of beauty in an
otherwise bleak setting.

One day Teddy and the Owls found a bunch of flares. They climbed
up on top of the slag dump, which was about three stories high, spaced
the flares around the perimeter, and set them off. The neighbors were very
impressed. They thought the chamber of commerce did it.

When they tired of the slag dump, they sat on the bench outside the
corner bar and played bomber with cigarette and cigar butts they found
lying around. Teddy would slip inside and check the slot machines for
change. Around the Fourth of July, the boys opened the door to the bar
and threw lit firecrackers inside.

In winter, they found an old car hood and used it as a sled to slide down the sandy side of the slag dump.

Spring was marble season for the boys. In summer they played Kick the Can.

When it was time for dinner, Annie opened the door and yelled, "TEDDY!" and he came running.

He always ran home when it was time to watch his favorite radio show.

Teddy started working for his father in the paint shop when he was a young boy. He swept the floor. One day, maybe more than one, Tony "took an ornery turn" and wouldn't pay him. A friend of Tony's was there and said, "I'll pay him." Tony relented and paid Teddy.

The Boom-Ni-Ga was about a block from the Leskovar home. The real name was Narodni Dom, which means "people's house." One of the lodges owned it. It was a big place. The kitchen and banquet room were in the basement. On the main floor was a dance hall with a stage and a bar, a very big bar. Boom-Ni-Ga means "hit 'em." The other nickname for the place was "bucket of blood." Lots of fights there. Teddy's friend Don Orlich and his family lived in the back. They were caretakers for the place. Chadonich's grocery store was in part of the building.

There was a dance there every Saturday night during the winter, sponsored by one of the lodges or the volunteer fire department or some other group.

Somebody is playing the cordeen in the Boom-Ni-Ga. Annie is there, slapping her knee and whistling through her teeth. The earthy scent of klobase wafts in from the kitchen.

Annie loved to polka at the Boom-Ni-Ga.

"Downstairs was a banquet room, that's where they cooked the sausages," Ted said.

"Did your mother ever cook klobase in onions and beer?"

"If Ma was cooking with beer, she was drinking it."

An advertisement for American Beer, which was bottled in Great Falls, was directed to the "Woman of the House." It said: "Upon her often falls a heavy burden, the daily routine of housework, the care of the children, the shopping, the social duties. Small wonder that she often sustains a 'breakdown' and must receive medical assistance. Such a result may be avoided by moderate use of AMERICAN BEER."

No argument from Annie on that score.

When a couple from East Butte got married, the wedding was at Holy Savior, one of ten Catholic churches in Butte, and the reception was at the

Boom-Ni-Ga. Teddy and his fellow Owls would scurry over. They'd tie tin cans to the back of the groom's car and beat on the cans and on metal garbage can lids with sticks, making the biggest racket they could. Out would come the groom, and he'd toss a handful of coins to them. The boys would scramble after the coins. This was an East Butte shivaree.

Annie and Tony were active in their respective lodges (Slovenian fraternal organizations). Tony's provided sick and death benefits. Annie was a member of the Western Sisters Lodge. They met at the Boom-Ni-Ga. The ladies elected Annie recording secretary and later president. Tony was elected president of his lodge. All this was reported in the Butte paper.

Annie was also active in the parent committee at Teddy's school, the Harrison School. She helped organize the Founders Day celebration. She brought refreshments for the parents' meetings at the school. One item on the agenda was improving the children's ice skating rink. She was in charge of the pageant Rainbow Flame. She kept busy, and it was a way to socialize. She knew everything that was going on, all the gossip.

She had a book on the Palmer Method, which she studied and practiced.

Annie is in the front row, third from the right, 1937.
I don't know what this gathering is.
HEISER, PHOTOGRAPHER

It seems having beautiful penmanship was considered a virtue. Both of my grandmothers did.

She listened to shortwave radio in bed before she went to sleep.

One day son Joe was teasing her, and she chased him outside with the broom. She was standing in the doorway at the backdoor looking for him. He ran around the house and inside the front door and came up behind her and said, "Boo!" She jumped, startled, and cracked up laughing.

Teddy would walk over to a fellow Owl's house. He wouldn't go to the door; he'd stand on the sidewalk and yell, "DO YOU WANT TO COME OUT AND PLAY?" And his friends would do the same at his house.

In winter, the Owls hooked up a hose to the fire hydrant and flooded their ice skating rink, which was at the corner of Plum and Garfield. They didn't want cars to run over the hose, so they took it upon themselves to reroute traffic. The county plowed the area, and the boys took it from there. The rink was sixty feet wide and one hundred and twenty feet long. Ice skating and maintaining the rink were great ways for boys to burn up energy during the long frigid Butte winter. The boxcar that was their shed was next to the rink. One of the Owls, Chuck, told me he figured the Northern Pacific put it there so the kids would have someplace to change from their boots to their skates.

Teddy and Don Orlich would slip into Chadonich's grocery store and try to make the slot machine skip. One day they went behind the store and pulled up weeds and threw them up in the air so dirt would get into the air vent. This made Chadonich mad.

"At Chadonich's they had these wooden boxes," Ted said, "and people would call in what they need, [and Chadonich would put the groceries in the wooden crate] and Ty Cobb would take his panel truck out and deliver groceries. We used to call him Ty Cobb. That's the only name I knew him by."

In the winter the boys would hang out at Chadonich's. They'd gather around the radiator to keep warm and talk.

A candidate for office would say, "Give me a scratch," which meant vote for me. One day a man gave Teddy a bunch of political fliers and told him to hand them out. He walked into Francie Spehar's bar. She looked at them and threw them in the fire.

Francie Spehar took over the bar around 1920, after her father died; she was twenty-five years old. It was always known as Francie Spehar's bar, even after she married. I never did hear what her married name was, so I looked it up. It was Puhek.

She grew up over the bar with her six sisters and a steady stream of boarders, Croatian and Slovenian miners. Her parents were from the Croatian part of Austria-Hungary. She and her sisters were born in Montana. Francie and her husband didn't have children, so after her sisters moved out, she rented out those rooms. She charged a dollar a night for the room and sixty cents for breakfast. Breakfast was fruit, bacon and eggs, and hotcakes.

In the fall, an Italian man would drive through East Butte with a truckload of grapes. People flagged him down and bought crates of grapes. Ted said, "Everybody in East Butte made their own wine except Pops. When Stevie built his house, he made sure part of it was dirt, and that was where he made his wine."

The Boom-Ni-Ga was decorated with clusters of grapes every October.

MEANWHILE OVER ON WALNUT STREET, the pretty widow Aila Thompson admonished her children not to go past the yellow bridge. Way past that bridge lay the railroad tracks, and the roundhouse, and East Butte.

*Annie and Teddy in the front room
at 210 Cherry, 1940.*

*Teddy on the right,
First Communion.*

Joe and Teddy.

Tony, Joe and Teddy, St. Mary's Lake, Glacier Park,
August 10, 1940. The family enjoyed Montana's beauty.

33

ANOTHER WORLD WAR

It was a war to end all wars. [First World War, the one that ended in 1918.] Well, it wasn't, so what've you got to be so smug about!

> —*Upstairs Downstairs*, 2010–2012

Each one hopes that if he feeds the crocodile enough, the crocodile will eat him last.

> —Winston Churchill, 1940,
> when he was Britain's First Lord of the Admiralty

LEGEND HAS IT, Georges Clemenceau said he wanted to be buried standing up facing Germany. He knew they'd be back. He was a young man when the Prussians invaded France in 1870. He became prime minister of France for a second time after the Germans invaded during the First World War. He was dead now.

Only a few weeks after Teddy was born in 1933, Tony saw this ferocious headline in the newspaper: "As Hitler Rants of Blood."

Hitler spouts fire before his shouting, cheering Nazi partisans, delirious with political victory, the French premier solemnly goes out to inspect the new military defense line of steel and concrete that stretches for 125 miles along the German frontier and pronounces it adequate. Little Austria augments her pitiful standing army of 22000 men with 8000 recruits . . . It's about as discouraging a picture as has been painted for the world to study at any time since the 'war to end war' was brought to its inconclusive termination. As a matter of fact, this present world picture would indicate that the terrible war of 1914–18 was but the prelude to a struggle for mastery of titanic proportions unparalleled by anything known to history.

[*Montana Standard*, September 4, 1933]

How sadly prescient.

Just before Teddy turned two, Tony picked up the Butte paper and read about the Nazi crackdown on Jews, Catholics, and Protestants.

Anti-Jew Directing Campaign . . . Mass arrests of Roman Catholic clergymen were predicted today in the new Nazi drive against the church . . . Developments in the long, determined fight of Protestant clergymen to prevent Nazification of their church were awaited with interest and, by those involved, with apprehension.

[*Montana Standard*, July 20, 1935, page 13.]

This did not make Tony homesick for the Old Country.

In 1933, the leader of the National Socialist Party became chancellor of Germany. That man was Adolf Hitler. He started secretly re-arming Germany. This was in violation of the 1919 peace treaty at the end of the First World War, the Treaty of Versailles.

In 1935, Hitler threw off all secrecy and brazenly continued his military buildup. He instituted conscription. All this was in violation of the Treaty of Versailles.

In March of 1936, he took the Rhineland, also in violation of the treaty of Versailles.

Did France and Britain forget that they won the war? Easy to do, so many men killed or maimed, so much of France obliterated.

Now Hitler aimed his sights on Austria, also in violation of the treaty.

How many times over the centuries had Austria and Prussia been at war with Prussia as the aggressor. Back in the eighteenth century there was the War of Austrian Succession. Who started that one? Not Austria. The age-old continental European rule called the Salic Law said that only a male heir could succeed the throne. Charles VI, emperor of the Holy Roman Empire (later called Austria) had only daughters. He believed that his eldest daughter, Maria Theresa, was perfectly fit to rule, and why shouldn't she? He made a new rule; he was emperor after all, he could do that. His new rule, aptly called the Pragmatic Sanction, said his daughter could succeed him as empress. When he died in 1740, Maria Theresa assumed the throne. Prussia saw it as a good excuse to go to war and grab a piece of Austria, which they did and took Silesia.

And yet we were supposed to believe, or I should say the rest of the world was supposed to believe, that the Austrians wanted to be united with Germany all along, and Hitler was doing them a favor. If that were so, why did he need to go in with tanks and disperse thugs to terrorize the Austrian people? Let's recall what happened. The 1919 treaty that effectively ended the First World War, the Treaty of Versailles, forbade unifying Austria and Germany. In the 1930s, Nazi Brown Shirts terrorized the German people and the Austrians, softening them up, like a bull being poked repeatedly by the *picaderos*, the animal so weakened it can't fight back, it can only submit, ready for the kill. In 1932, Austria outlawed Nazi demonstrations. The next year the Austrian leader, Chancellor Dollfus, dissolved Parliament. The next year the Nazis murdered him.

The new chancellor, Kurt Schuschnigg, tried negotiating with Hitler. That was a disaster.

Hitler demanded that Austria and Germany be unified, which was forbidden by the treaty. Austrian Chancellor Schuschnigg scheduled a vote of the Austrian people. The question on the ballot would be whether the two countries should be united with Hitler as leader. Rather than wait for the vote, Hitler finagled a coup; Nazis stepped in and forced Chancellor Schuschnigg to resign. The vote was called off. The next day Hitler invaded Austria with tanks. The Gestapo arrested Schuschnigg.

Nazis spread "bloodshed and terror" across Austria.

France and Britain wrung their hands.

One month later, Hitler called for a vote of Germany and Austria. One hundred percent "voted" in favor of Hitler as leader and that Germany absorb Austria, which had already happened. Actually, it was 99.7 percent. Only one or two dissenting souls among millions of people. When do 99.7 percent of the people in any country ever agree on anything? The myth endures to this day that the Austrians wanted to be part of Germany. Really? It stretches credulity to the snapping point to believe one hundred percent of any people ever support a political leader unless there is a gun to their heads. It can only happen if those people are not free and are terrorized.

Where did this idea come from that Austrians always wanted to give up their sovereignty and become part of Germany? From pervasive and pernicious Nazi propaganda, that is how.

If the Austrians were so keen on joining Germany, why the troops? Why arrest the Austrian chancellor? A simple signing ceremony would have sufficed. It was an invasion, an invasion of a country that had been disarmed by the Treaty of Versailles. The invader Nazis ignored the treaty, and the winning powers were either still recovering from the horrors of the last war (France) or didn't have the stomach to stop them (Britain under

Chamberlain, before Churchill) or thought this was a European problem, not our problem (us—the United States).

Then it was on to the Sudetenland. The leaders of Britain and France gave it to Hitler. They rationalized, if we give the crocodile something to eat, he will leave us alone.

The wounded, battered, ignored Treaty of Versailles was now dead, dead and gone, and with it, peace.

In January of 1939, Hitler signed a nonaggression pact with Stalin.

In February, the pope died.

In March, Hitler took the rest of Czechoslovakia. He took part of Lithuania.

France and Britain now realized that attempts to appease the crocodile only made for a hungrier more ferocious beast. They decided to stand up to Hitler. They promised to defend Poland, sort of.

On September 1, 1939, Germany invaded Poland. France and Britain declared war on Germany. The Second World War had officially begun.

BUTTE WAS A ONE-SHOP TOWN—mining. Mining was walloped by the Great Depression, but in 1935, it started to claw its way out, but in fits and starts. Ores are precursors, they are fodder for manufacturing, they are at the leading edge of economic growth. The U.S. economy was largely one of manufacturing. Orders for Butte copper increased in 1935, again in 1936, way up in 1937, then whoa, pull back on the reins, and a big drop in 1938, back up in 1939 and again in 1940.

Tony earned around $800 dollars a year between his car painting business, Central Auto Painting, and every music gig he could find. He worked all fifty-two weeks. Day's pay for the Butte miners was around $5.85. They had a five-day week, so a day's-pay man who worked every week could make $1,521 a year. Contract miners could earn more.

A huge change came in April of 1940 when Tony became the Willys dealer. Now he sold cars in addition to painting them. He named the business Willys Central Auto Service. His grown sons Eddy and Babe worked for him. Eddy was twenty-three. Babe was twenty-one. Joe was twelve. Teddy was six.

Later that year Willys won a contract with the U.S. Army to build a new kind of vehicle—the jeep.

Tony had to go all the way to the Willys factory in California to get a car. He'd take the train down and drive the car back.

*Tony's shop, Central Auto. Annie wrote: "The back shop—where
Eddy & Babe do the work. Ed paint—Babe repair cars & fender.
Body fender repair & auto painting."*

*Annie wrote: "Tony preaching to me." November 14, 1940.
On another picture taken at the same time, she wrote:
"Tony polishing or wiping dust off the Americar. Willys car 1941."*

Willys introduced the very patriotic sounding Americar.

Tony ran an ad in the paper offering a brand-new Willy sedan for $725, a 1933 Dodge for $95, and a 1937 Willys coupe for $265.

Meanwhile, the crocodile gobbled up Denmark and Norway.

On May 10, 1940, Hitler attacked Luxemburg, the Netherlands, Belgium, and France. That very day, the British House of Commons chose Winston Churchill to be prime minister. On June 4, Churchill delivered his famous speech over the radio: "We shall fight on the beaches, we shall fight on the landing grounds, we shall fight in the fields and in the streets . . . we shall never surrender . . . until, in God's good time, the New World, with all its power and might steps forth to the rescue and the liberation of the old."

Never surrender.

That received considerable attention in the Butte papers, indeed, in papers across America. An editorial in the *Montana Standard* of June 6, 1940, said if Britain is overrun and never surrenders, as Churchill said, the British government will surely move to Canada, bringing the war to our doorstep. Any aggression against Canada would involve the United States on the side of Canada. "The terrible blow which may destroy Great Britain can fall with breathless rapidity. America must make its decision now to meet such a possible eventuality. We can hardly bring ourselves to realize in this country the terrible import of the situation in Europe."

"Italy Warns U.S. Not to Take Sides," said the headline the next day. A firebrand editor in Italy, a supporter of Mussolini, said the United States had no duty to save the Old World.

The U.S. Navy made fifty airplanes available for France and Britain. The House Appropriations Committee voted more money for defense.

The next day the *New York Times* called for "universal compulsory military training." President Franklin Roosevelt said he read the first paragraph and liked it.

The day after that, Senator Burton Wheeler, Democrat of Montana, set out on what was expected to be a keep-us-out-of-war tour.

A Massachusetts congressman said Republicans can be counted on to support "all real defense measures" while they "naturally resent efforts to make national defense measures vehicles for granting dictatorial powers to the executive."

Off in France, General Petain, now vice premier, bemoaned: "Too few allies, too few weapons, too few babies." Though France had been on the winning side in 1918, her spirit had been mortally wounded, as had Petain's.

France fell the next day, June 21, 1940.

Britain stood alone defending the ramparts of liberty and decency.

The Alfred Hitchcock movie *Foreign Correspondent,* starring Joel McCrea, was released in August. The movie's thinly veiled message warned of the Nazi menace without calling it by name.

On September 7, the Nazis started bombing London.

On September 16, President Franklin Delano Roosevelt signed the Selective Training and Service Act. This instituted the first peacetime draft in American history. All men, whether a citizen or not, age twenty-one to thirty-five, had to register for the draft.

Draft registration began one month later, on October 16. That same day Paramount Pictures released *Arise, My Love,* with Ray Milland and Claudette Colbert. This movie had an overt pro-interventionist message, a clobber-you-over-the-head overt message, not veiled at all.

Eddy and Babe dutifully registered for the draft. Unlike in 1917, there were no draft riots in Butte, no disturbance whatsoever. It's harder to get people stirred up when involvement in the war is theoretical rather than real. Europe was at war, but we weren't. If we did get in it, of course we'd be on the side of Britain. Hitler was the enemy. In 1917, the Irish were upset that we were on the side of Britain. Now Ireland, except Northern Ireland, was an independent country. She was no longer part of Britain. That objection was gone. In 1917, the Finns were upset that we were on the side of Russia. Hitler and Stalin had signed a nonaggression pact, so Russia, now the Union of Soviet Socialist Republics, was on the side of Germany. The old objection of the Finns was gone. They couldn't know that the crocodile would bite Russia the next year.

There were stories in the Butte paper about precautions being taken against sabotage at a military aircraft plant in Baltimore. This was in November of 1940, more than a year before Pearl Harbor.

There were more notices about the draft.

Newsreels at the movies were about the war.

In June of 1941, Hitler invaded the Soviet Union, so much for a non-aggression pact with a crocodile.

TONY AND ANNIE'S ELDEST SON, Eddy, married Louise Lousen at Immaculate Conception Church on October 4, 1941. Not only were Louise's parents Slovenian from the Old Country, they were from Carniola, the same Austrian duchy as Annie's parents, Caroline and Joe. The Lousens lived on Platinum

*Picnic at Georgetown Lake. Going right to left, at the far right standing
are Babe, I don't know who that woman is, then Eddy and Louise and
Tony, September 1937. Eddy and Louise married in 1941 when he was
twenty-five and she was twenty-one.*

Street on the West Side, far from East Butte in every way. Louise's father was
a tailor. He and his brother ran a clothing store at 201 East Park.

Eddy was listed as a man with dependents in an article about the draft.
Babe was listed as 1-A, which meant fit for immediate induction.

Keep in mind, we were not in the war yet, but men were being drafted.

As I came across all this, I found myself continually double-checking
dates. I thought these stories must have been after Pearl Harbor, but they
were not. They were before we were in the war. The same with those
movies. I can't believe this was all organic. It appears there was a concerted
effort to get the country used to the idea of going to another war in Europe,
to put the American people on a psychological war footing long before
we entered the war.

"When Ma went visiting when we were kids, we just sat," Ted said.
"There was no running around. We just sat. We couldn't even use the restroom. We had to sit and listen to them gossip. They'd give us wine. This
was in 1940. We were at Severinskys and they were giving me wine. Babe
was supposed to report for the draft, and I'm sitting there half smashed,
and thinking, naw, he won't get drafted. I was seven years old."

Annie and Tony's second son, Babe, married Kay Severinsky at Holy
Savior Church on November 16, 1941. Father Pirnat officiated. Kay's

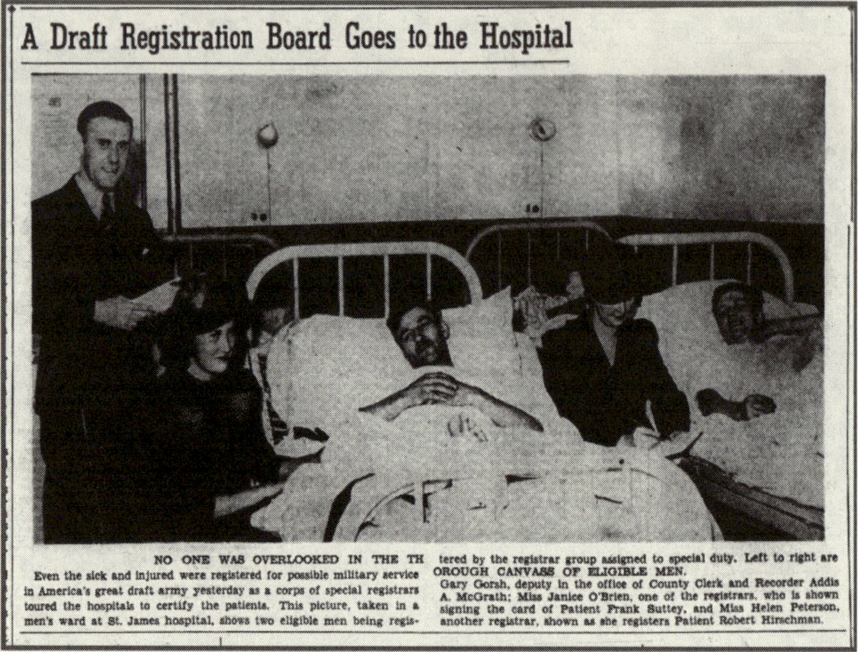

A Draft Registration Board Goes to the Hospital

NO ONE WAS OVERLOOKED IN THE THOROUGH CANVASS OF ELIGIBLE MEN.

Even the sick and injured were registered for possible military service in America's great draft army yesterday as a corps of special registrars toured the hospitals to certify the patients. This picture, taken in a men's ward at St. James hospital, shows two eligible men being registered by the registrar group assigned to special duty. Left to right are Gary Gorsh, deputy in the office of County Clerk and Recorder Addis A. McGrath; Miss Janice O'Brien, one of the registrars, who is shown signing the card of Patient Frank Suttey, and Miss Helen Peterson, another registrar, shown as she registers Patient Robert Hirschman.

Montana Standard, *October 17, 1940.*

parents were Slovenian from the Old Country. Her father was a miner. They lived on Fir Street, near Annie and Tony.

"There were five girls [in the Severinsky family]," Ted said. "I remember they were all working and they had to give their checks to the mother. Mother was Slovenian. Father was Slovenian."

As for Eddy and Babe marrying daughters of Slovenian immigrants, Ted said, "That was the way it was supposed to be."

TONY TOOK JOE AND TEDDY with him up to Elk Park. He stopped to fill bottles with spring water, then drove up to the cabin. The first thing Tony did when setting out for a walk in the forest was to find a long stiff branch that would make a good walking stick. He found such a stick. He and Joe and Teddy walked through the forest, then back to the cabin. Tony turned on the radio. It was Sunday, December 7, 1941. They heard the news about Pearl Harbor.

"How did your father react when he heard the news?" I asked.

"No reaction. He didn't say anything."

"How did your mother react when you got home?"

"They went visiting to talk about the war."

"Anything else?"

"Ma put paper over the windows where I slept," a precaution against air raids.

Then the next bombshell dropped. President Roosevelt ordered what he deemed to be nonessential civilian manufacturing to cease. By presidential fiat, American industry would be put on a war footing—all of it. All manufacturing would be for the war. No cars or trucks could be built to sell to civilians. Car and truck manufacturing stopped on February 22, 1942. Sales of cars in stock and delivery of cars on order were frozen. Tony couldn't sell the cars he had in stock without getting permission from the government. He could sell cars only to those the government deemed essential drivers.

There went much of Tony's livelihood, the rug pulled out from under him. Willys switched to war work and nothing but war work. They had no choice.

"[B]igger businesses tended to do well, for they were the ones who became government partners," wrote historian Amity Shlaes in *The Forgotten Man*. Tony was small fry, the Willys dealer in Butte, Montana; he was the Forgotten Man. He did not do well. No more Willys franchise, and he didn't get a penny for it. In Austria, when the army used a farmer's land, the army paid the farmer. Tony knew this because he negotiated terms with the farmers when he was in the army.

Now in April of 1942, Tony had to register for the draft. He was fifty-five years old. Men as old as sixty-five had to register. This was the wartime draft.

Tony was paying his son Eddy thirty-five dollars a week. Sometimes Tony didn't sign his check on time.

A fellow named Dick Cloak had been a drummer in the musicians union. Tony hired him in the paint shop and taught him to paint cars. "He used to work for us, good kid," Tony said. Dick Cloak moved to Seattle, took a job with Boeing using the painting skills he learned from Tony, and became the paint superintendent. He told Eddy he could have a job anytime. Eddy and Louise moved to Seattle, and Eddy went to work for Dick at Boeing. Boeing was building airplanes for the British Royal Air Force and was gearing up to build planes for the U.S. Army Air Forces. The shipyards were also busy.

Eddy made sixty cents an hour at Boeing.

Babe was drafted in May of 1942, but he didn't go. He was working in the Anselmo Mine. Miners were exempt. Mining was war work.

Babe earned around five to six dollars day's pay in the mines. The miners in Butte had an eight-hour day, so Babe was making sixty-three to seventy-five cents an hour.

As for Tony's family in the Old Country, back in 1918 as the First World War was ending, the Slovenians and Croatians threw in with the victorious though vanquished Serbs and proclaimed themselves the State of Slovenians, Croats, and Serbs—a country of southern Slavs, which was exactly what the assassins of the archduke wanted. This was formalized by the Treaty of Versailles, which created the Kingdom of Serbs, Croats, and Slovenians, carved from the corpse of the former Austro-Hungarian Empire and united with Serbia. In 1929, the Kingdom of Serbs, Croats, and Slovenians renamed itself the Kingdom of Yugoslavia.

Now the Second World War has begun. The Nazis invade the Kingdom of Yugoslavia.

German soldiers shot one of Tony's cousins right in the doorway to his home. They expelled Tony's cousin, Franc, and sent him far south. His wife did not survive the ordeal. After the war, Franc walked home, four hundred miles he walked home.

"Some dirty work, the Germans did," Tony said. "The oldest, Franc, he was kicked out by the Germans. They shot his son right in the doorway. The German army invade, Hitler's army. They shipped him down way south, oh some three or four hundred miles close to Serbia. His wife was always sick, kind of weakly like. Tuberculosis or something. She died down there. He came back home on foot after it was over. They are bitter against the Germans. Oh, yeah. Some dirty work, the Germans did."

"They put the dummy on trial," Irene at the Butte Archives told me.

"Then they burned it?"

"Yes, but first they chopped the head off."

Mesopust is the Slovenian and Croatian pre-Lenten festival, Carnival or Mardi Gras in other cultures. The first time I saw a picture of Mesopust in Butte, I thought, how sad, the women looked so homely. As I looked more closely I realized, they were men. It was a mock wedding and a trial. Men played all the parts. The *Anaconda Standard* described the 1921 Mesopust: "Will have Singing, Dancing, and the Decapitation of Sin." The greatest sin of the year will be put on trial. Sin's mother will weep, sin will be found guilty, and then off with its head and burned to ashes.

Sin or evil was represented by the dummy. One year during Prohibition, the sign on the dummy said bootlegging. During the First World War, one year the dummy was the kaiser. One year it was avarice. The dummy was put on trial, found guilty, and sentenced to death. Evil was vanquished.

"They had a dummy sitting in a chair—Hitler—and they beat him," Ted said recalling one Mesopust when he was a boy. "In East Butte, they didn't cut off the head and burn the dummy. They just beat it. It was hard when they were all talking Slovenian. I'd lose interest quite fast. I'd just go down and have another beer."

CAR PAINTING WORK WAS SPARSE during the war. What good were Annie and Tony's ration coupons if they didn't have money to buy anything. Sometimes there was no food in the house, nothing at all. Annie and Teddy would search the house for loose change.

When Annie had cornmeal, she made polenta. Polenta for breakfast, polenta for lunch, polenta for dinner. Plain polenta, made with water and

Mesopust 1945 at the Narodni Dom (Boom Ni Ga) in East Butte.
Annie is in the front row, fifth from the left. Hitler and Mussolini
are the dummies to be condemned.
ZUBICK, PHOTOGRAPHER. FOUND ON PAGE TWENTY-TWO
OF *BUTTE'S CROATIAN-SLOVENIAN AMERICANS* BY ANN STAJCAR SIMONICH.

Tony practicing the bassoon in the front room at 210 Cherry, 1942.

Front room of Leskovar home at 210 Cherry in East Butte, 1941.

a little salt. For breakfast, she fried it and they poured Karo corn syrup on it, or they ate cornmeal mush.

As bad as things were, Tony didn't want Annie to work. He thought it was a disgrace to be supported by his wife.

One day during the war when Tony was particularly down on his luck, Annie read her horoscope. It said, "This is your lucky day." She walked to the front door and yelled, "TEDDY!" He came running home. They pulled up the cushions of the davenport and looked for change. She sent Teddy to the corner bar to check the slot machines and phone for change. Then off she went with Teddy in tow straight to the 30 Club, the pretend jewelry store that was a gambling speakeasy. Annie and Teddy walked past the dusty counters with a few pieces of token jewelry and straight to the back to the real business. Annie played bingo. She won sixty dollars. Then off she and Teddy went to the M&M, a saloon on Main Street. She played bingo. She won sixty dollars. Then off they went to the Board of Trade. She played the Chinese lottery (keno). She won sixty dollars. After that, she always read her horoscope, but lightning did not strike twice.

A man approached Annie about joining the Fifth Column, a subversive organization of Nazi sympathizers. She cussed him out up one side and down the other.

Tony went to all the car lots in town to rustle up work. He didn't have enough work to hire help in the paint shop. Joe worked there after school. He was in high school.

Tony was having a hard time paying the rent on the building he leased for his car painting business. The rent was one hundred dollars a month. He asked the owner for a break on the rent. The landlord dropped it to seventy-five dollars a month. Even that was tough. For two months in 1944, he couldn't pay. The company that owned the building was out of New York. They brought suit for nonpayment, but somehow they worked things out and the case was settled.

Some days all they ate were pancakes. Pancakes for breakfast, pancakes for lunch, pancakes for dinner.

"Teddy, are you ill?" No, he always looked like that. He was malnourished.

Steve and Zelda arrived with a carload of groceries.

34

∽

STEVE AND ZELDA

Letter from Zelda:

Great grandfather Francois Morigeau (Frenchman) born in Montreal, Canada, was a free fur trader all over northwest US and southern Canada, he worked for a while for the Hudson Bay Co., but was mostly a free trader, he also was very religious . . . He married Isabell Mctaler [MacTaylor] Indian & Scotch. They lived in Colville, Wash, they had a large family. My grandfather Alexander Morigeau was one of this family. He made his money by trapping all kinds of animals from Washington Territory to the Big Hole south of Butte. He settled on the Jocko River south of Arlee. Here he met my grandmother Rosalie Finley Morigeau Indian and French. They farmed and raised cattle on the Jocko on the Flathead reservation.

9 children was born to this family and my father Eli Morigeau was one of this family [born in 1875].

My mother Nancy Cameron Morigeau was born in Canada [around 1880]. Her father was a Scotchman named Jack Cameron. Mother Justine Bouneau Indian, French. Her father was a trader between McCloud, Canada, [Fort MacLeod on Old Man River in Alberta] and Fort Benton, Montana, she came to this country and was placed in the sisters boarding school at St. Ignatius and after leaving school she married Eli Morigeau and ranched in the Valley Creek area and raised 9 children of which I am the oldest.

It's curious that she didn't say which tribe, just Indian, though she was specific as to European ancestry. The 1900 census said her father's side was Flathead or Kootenai (Kutenai) and her mother was Cree. The 1910 census said both sides were Kootenai.

Though Zelda explained how her father Eli Morigeau's family came to the Flathead Reservation, she gave no details about her mother. Zelda's son told me that Zelda's mother, Nancy Cameron, was kidnapped as a young girl in Canada and left at the boarding school at St. Ignatius to be raised by the sisters.

Then her grandson discovered more of the story. He found out that Jack Cameron was not Nancy's biological father. Her father was Bear Walker. Bear Walker was full-blooded Indian; his mother was Chippewa, or some say Blackfeet. Nancy's mother, Justine Bouneau (or Boneau or Bonneau or Boucher) was born in Manitoba and was Cree and French. I don't know what became of Bear Walker nor how this Scotsman Jack Cameron came into the picture. Justine's daughter Nancy and another daughter lived on a nearby ranch, the name I know but will omit. Word got back to Justine that the girls were being ill treated; they were working as chore girls, and the rancher beat them. The man was a scoundrel, so Justine snatched her daughters back. Justine took Nancy to the boarding school for Indian girls in St. Ignatius in northwestern Montana. There she was educated by the Sisters of Providence. Justine told the sisters that Nancy was twelve years old and was Metis Cree. This was in August of 1891.

Nancy finished school on April 28, 1896. The next year she married Eli Morigeau. The year after that, their first child, Zelda, was born.

Zelda was a member of what today is called the Confederated Salish and Kootenai Tribes of the Flathead Reservation. Indians have lived in that part of western Montana for nine thousand years. The Salish migrated there around 1700. Early trappers called them Flathead Indians because their language sounded like that of a coastal tribe that used to flatten the heads of babies. The tribes at Flathead didn't do that, but the name stuck.

In the early nineteenth century, Iroquois arrived with French trappers. The Iroquois told the Flathead/Salish Indians about the Black Robes who taught them about the God who promises eternal life. This hearkened memory of the prophet who foretold of the Black Robes, fair-skinned men who did not marry and would teach them the truth and a new way of praying. The Salish were determined to find such a Black Robe and off they went. The first delegation made it to St. Louis. Protestants sent a missionary who took a wrong turn in the wilderness. The Salish sent another delegation in 1835. The Catholic bishop in St. Louis said he would send a priest but no one arrived. The Salish sent another delegation in 1837 but they were killed by the Sioux. The Salish were not ones to give up. They sent yet another delegation in 1839 who happened to stop in Iowa where they happened to meet Father DeSmet, a thirty-eight-year-old Flemish

Jesuit priest in poor health who nonetheless said, yes, I'll go. He survived the arduous journey and built St. Mary's Mission. Father DeSmet planted the first wheat in what we now call Montana.

More Jesuits joined Father DeSmet, and they built many missions including one south of Flathead Lake called St. Ignatius, named for the founder of the Jesuits.

It was to St. Ignatius that Elias and Nancy Morigeau brought their baby Mary Azelda to be baptized in 1898.

The treaty of 1855 between the United States and the Kootenai, Pend d'Oreille, and Salish Indians created the Flathead Indian Reservation and promised teachers as well as blacksmith and carpentry tools for the Indians. The government looked to the Jesuits to educate Indian children. The Jesuits taught the boys. Nuns were needed to teach the girls. In 1864, four Sisters of Providence left their convent in Montreal and sailed through the St. Lawrence Seaway, down the eastern seaboard and across the Gulf of Mexico to Panama. They took the train across the yellow-fever-bearing-mosquito-infested jungle that covered the Isthmus, this at a time when a nun's formidable habit covered her from head to toe with only her face and hands exposed. Quite warm. At the other end of the Isthmus they boarded another ship and sailed up the Pacific coast to the Columbia River and up the river as far as they could, and then traveled overland by pack train to St. Ignatius. They were the first white women to cross the Rocky Mountains. One of the sisters wrote, "At night we enjoyed a rest sweetened by prayer, the singing of hymns and the best meal that

St. Ignatius Mission, Mission Mountains in the background, November 16, 1895.
Montana Historical Society 950-722, D.M. Ingalls, photographer

anyone could wish for. . . . Alone in our tent, we four chatted freely . . . reminding one another of and laughing at the few amusing things that had occurred during the day."

The sisters opened a school at St. Ignatius. This was the school Zelda's mother, Nancy Cameron, attended.

The Ursuline Sisters arrived in the 1890s and opened a pre-school, which they called a kindergarten. This was the first school Zelda attended. Then she attended Sacred Heart Academy, a boarding school in Missoula.

Though the federal government had promised to fund schools to teach the Indian children, by the time Zelda was born

Mary Azelda Morigeau.

the money had been cut off, chiefly because of the influence of the American Protective Association, which today we know as the Ku Klux Klan. They would rather have no school than a Catholic school for Indian children. Wealthy benefactors in the East made up the deficit, and the schools on the reservation remained open. The main benefactor was the Drexel family of Philadelphia.

Zelda's father, Eli Morigeau, taught her to fly fish on the creek in the mountains north of their ranch. Eli fashioned holding ponds in the creek out of stones. When he caught a trout, he put it in there, still alive, until he was done fishing for the day. He taught young Zelda how to gut the fish, which they did outside, and threw the entrails to the dogs and pigs.

When Zelda's grandmother Justine came to visit, she brought her teepee and slept in it. Justine would live out her final years in the Rocky Boy hill country east of Flathead.

Around age twelve, Zelda left Montana to attend the Indian boarding school in Lawrence, Kansas, the Haskell Institute. After she returned home, she worked as postmistress at Sloan's Ferry on the reservation. A good-looking, personable, athletic young man delivered the mail to Sloan's

Ferry. His name was Steve Lozar. And that is how Annie's brother, Steve, met the pretty postmistress Zelda. He was smitten.

Steve and Zelda married before a justice of the peace in Kalispell in 1921. He was twenty-four; she was twenty-three. Two years later they married before Father Diomedi at St. Ignatius.

Annie called Steve Squaw Man. She was always quick with a retort. However, it didn't take long for Zelda to win over Annie and the rest of

Steve and Zelda Lozar.

Zelda wearing a cradle board.

the Lozars. When Steve took Zelda to meet his parents, Zelda noticed that Steve's shirt cuffs were frayed. She told him to give her the shirt, which he did; she took off the cuffs, turned them around so the fray disappeared into the seam and quickly sewed the cuffs back on. Then and there, Zelda won over her father-in-law, Joe Lozar. This was not long before Joe died.

I suspect Caroline was delighted that Zelda was Catholic, even if she wasn't Slovenian.

Zelda was perpetually cheerful and efficient, practical and pretty, no nonsense, never one to whine. She simply rolled up her sleeves and got to work.

Steve had found a girl just like Ma.

Their first child was a daughter, Gladys, called Jo. Their second, a boy,

Steve and Zelda with children Jo and Buddy.

they named Stephen Aloysius and called him Buddy. He was born in 1925 in St. Ignatius.

Steve and Zelda settled in Arlee, a tiny hamlet of one hundred and fifty people on the reservation. Steve worked as the mechanic and bookkeeper for a garage. Around 1931, they moved to Butte, and Steve worked for Tony painting cars. They moved back to Flathead and lived in Dixon where Steve worked as acting postmaster. Then he went to work for the Flathead Agency (the federal Indian agency). He did well in that job. In 1936, he made $1,440. In 1942, he made $1,860. He saved up his money, left the agency, and bought the mercantile in Dixon. Now he was a merchant and his own boss, just as his father had been.

Steve and Zelda and the children lived in the back of the store.

They were a godsend to Tony and Annie when they arrived with that carload of groceries during the war.

Annie and Tony sent Teddy to spend the summer with his uncle Steve and aunt Zelda up in Dixon. Teddy put swimming trunks in his suitcase. Annie took them out.

Lozar Mercantile in Dixon, Montana, 1948.

Lozar Mercantile in Dixon, Montana, 1948.
Steve Lozar is behind the counter on the far left.

"Ma was always concerned about water, about kids drowning," Ted said. "If I went on a trip somewhere and took a bathing suit, Ma would take it out. When I was a little kid and took a bath, she'd put about that much water in the tub," motioning an inch.

Teddy helped Uncle Steve around the store. Steve called him Big Little Guy.

Teddy grew very attached to their dog. When the dog died, he was heart broken. He told me decades later that was why he never wanted a dog. He didn't want to feel that hurt and loss again.

IT IS LATE AFTERNOON. Zelda leaves the store and walks across the street to the Jocko River. Teddy goes with her. She attaches a fly to her fishing line and starts casting. Every trout she catches she tosses to Teddy. This will be dinner. She guts the fish, cuts off the heads, leaves the tails on, doesn't scale them. Back at the house, she drops a spoonful of lard into a hot cast-iron skillet and fries the trout. The tails get hard and crispy. Zelda calls them "fish tail potato chips." While the trout cook, she peels potatoes and cuts them in rounds about the size of a silver dollar. When the fish are done, she takes them out and throws in the potatoes.

She fished from a boat on Flathead Lake. She caught sockeye salmon, which she boiled and canned for winter. She also caught large lake trout and whitefish. She scaled the whitefish.

Teddy; Annie Leskovar; the child on Annie's lap is Steve and Zelda's grandson;
Caroline Lozar; Steve and Zelda's daughter, Jo Fouty; Zelda Lozar; Zelda's
niece and son; Steve Lozar and granddaughter, 1948, Flathead Lake.

35

RACINE

Teddy's brother Joe dropped out of high school and went to work at Gamer's making candy. He ate a lot of chocolate. He was so tall, he kept bumping his head on the hood of the stove. In the summer of '45 he worked at the Columbia Gardens taking tickets for the merry-go-round and biplanes.

One night Joe was out with friends and came home late, and, as a peace offering, he brought two quarts of beer for his mother, which he put in the washing machine.

"Why did you put the beer in the washing machine?" I asked.

"I don't know."

Another time, Annie caught Joe smoking. She said, "You want to smoke?" and she scurried off and found the dried-up stub of one of Tony's cigars. She gave it to Joe, lit it, and gave him a glass of red wine. She sat back and waited. He threw up, which was exactly what she knew would happen—red wine and a cigar with no food. He never smoked again, which was exactly her intention. Annie was dead set against smoking. She didn't care if it was in vogue. She detested smoking. I can't help but wonder if it was because Tony smoked.

Joe was out with friends one day, driving a Model T. A boy in the backseat complained about his driving, so Joe took off the steering wheel and handed it to him and said, "Here, you steer."

"Some guys said, 'Let's go to Anaconda and pick up some girls,'" Joe said. "Must have been four or five girls and three guys. I sat in the backseat. I was big enough, I could go into the liquor store. We took up a collection. I bought some wine, passed it around. One of the girls said, 'Joe, I bet you can't drink the rest of this bottle,' and I said, 'Oh yeah?' Pretty soon I was out cold. They dropped me on the sidewalk. And they saw a policeman, and they picked me up and put me back in the car. We drove back to Butte. I had brand-new black shoes. By the time we got to Butte, I was still out. So they took me home. I was a big guy. They had a heck of a time picking me up and getting me on the porch. They knocked on the door and said, 'Joey's drunk.' I think my mother opened the door. And they got me in the house."

The next morning Tony said, "We're lucky they brought him home."

Annie was upset because they scuffed up his new shoes when they dragged him down the sidewalk, shoes she had painstakingly saved pennies and nickels to buy, trying to keep up with her fast-growing teenage son's feet.

Joe liked to hang out at the Marine recruiting office. He liked their dress blues. The war was still on and he figured he'd rather join the Marines than be drafted. He looked old enough, he was so tall, but he was only seventeen and needed parental permission. He asked Tony to sign the papers, so he could enlist.

"Are you crazy?" Tony said.

When he turned eighteen, he joined the Marines. Tony didn't say a word. The war had ended.

PFC Joe Leskovar, with the Marines in Hawaii.

The Marines sent Joe to the island of Oahu in Hawaii. The cleanest job was painting, which he knew how to do, so he volunteered for that. The first day he walked into the paint shop, the Marine there said, "I've been waiting for you for three months." He threw Joe the keys and walked out and Joe never saw him again. He painted Marine insignia on airplanes.

An officer walked in one day and asked Joe, "What are you doing?"

"What I'm supposed to do, sir."

"What's that?"

"Report here every day."

Joe weighed 179 pounds when he enlisted. After one month, he weighed 203 pounds. He was six feet six inches tall.

The Marines were worn out from the war. The officers didn't push the guys; at least that was Joe's experience. He thoroughly enjoyed himself. The U.S. Marines paid him to be in Hawaii and didn't expect much from him.

In one letter to his parents he said, "I'm on Agony Hill." That worried Tony so much that he called his son Eddy in Seattle. Eddy reassured him.

Agony Hill was followed by liberty in Honolulu.

Private Joe Leskovar.

Annie Leskovar wearing the orchids son Joe sent her while serving in the Marines in Hawaii, July 9, 1947.

In his copious free time Joe painted cars. He charged officers one hundred dollars. Back in Butte, Tony charged thirty-five dollars. Every time Joe was paid, he sent money home to his mother. He knew they were still on hard times. He meant it for his parents and Teddy. Annie put the money in a bank account for Joe.

It was a great gig for Joe, but he never did get his dress blues.

THINGS CONTINUED TO BE TOUGH for Annie and Tony even after the war. Tony couldn't find much paint work. They were scraping by on what he earned as a musician, which wasn't full time. In the 1945 city directory, he is listed only as a musician, not as a painter.

"[Earlier] Pops had the shop behind the Chrysler Plymouth store," Ted said. "That's where Pops was doing his paint work. Then Wilson came in and bought the place out from under him, so Pops didn't have any place to operate out of. I guess he was trying to find another shop and start over again. He was selling his car, he needed cash. He was selling his typewriter, he needed cash. He sold his cash register, he needed cash. He had an adding machine, he sold that. He kept selling everything to get some money. He worked as a guard on The Hill for awhile [at one of the mines]. I don't know how long that lasted. I remember Pops being broke. He'd open his wallet; he didn't have any money in it. Pops said he never wanted to be in that position again. He said he'd rather be dead than broke."

Tony was almost sixty years old and flat broke.

Babe and Tony went into a partnership and ran a gas station. Tony spent all the money. Babe and Tony argued a lot.

"Pops opened a gas station right in the middle between McQueen and East Butte," Ted said. "None of the neighbors would buy gas from us."

Pancakes for breakfast, pancakes for lunch, pancakes for dinner. Tony would not allow Annie to get a job. He would not be supported by his wife. When things were really tough, Annie worked in a laundry. It had to be bad for Tony to allow that.

Teddy: "Ma, I'm hungry."

Annie: "Drink water."

Teddy: "Ma, how did Grandpa die?"

Annie: "He ate too much and busted!"

Tony's brother, Joe, in Racine, Wisconsin, came to visit. He convinced Annie and Tony to let him take Teddy back with him to Racine. Teddy put his swimming trunks in his suitcase. Annie took them out.

Tony's brother, Joseph Leskovar, was born March 9, 1883. Joe began his compulsory military service for the Austrian army when he turned twenty-one. His last post was Graz. Perhaps emboldened by the example of his little brother, Tony, who left home so young, Joe did not go back to the farm. The farm belonged to his sister and her husband. He boarded the train to Paris and from there to LeHavre where he boarded *La Gascogne*. The mighty ship steamed out of Le Havre on September 15, 1906. Joe was twenty-three years old. His brother, Tony, was still studying music in Ljubljana.

Joe traveled in steerage. After paying for his ticket, he had forty dollars in his pocket. He arrived in New York on September 24. His destination was Kenosha, Wisconsin. A friend lived there.

He heard about an opportunity in Aurora, Illinois, working as a meat cutter in a butcher shop, and there he went. He found a room in a boardinghouse. The couple from whom Joe rented a room were newly married. The husband was a carpenter and spoke only German. His wife spoke English. There were four other boarders besides Joe; three spoke Slovenian, one spoke German. Joe was the only boarder who spoke English. Many of the neighbors were German. Joe worked for the butcher in Aurora for several years, learning that trade. Tony joined him there when he first arrived.

Joe married Anna Horvat in Kenosha on November 15, 1911. Anna was also Slovenian from the Old Country. The midwife who delivered the Leskovar babies in Ptujska gora was Maria Horvat. A coincidence, perhaps, but I wonder if Joe knew Anna in the Old Country.

Now ready to branch out on their own, Joe and Anna moved to Racine, Wisconsin, and opened their own butcher shop. Joe butchered the meat. Anna waited on customers. This was around 1916 or 1917. There they would stay for the rest of their lives. One of their ads said, "KLOBASE with fine garlic taste, every one loves us, we already have hundreds of satisfied customers. I send to all the places of America, not less than 10 pounds. Price is 35¢ for pound without postage. You can send money in advance or pay by post delivery."

Decades later, I was living in Rockville, Maryland. A woman at my parish learned I had Slovenian heritage, as did her husband. That made her Slovenian by marriage. She was active in the Slovenian Women's Club. She invited me to their home for Easter dinner. As soon as I walked through the door she introduced me to her mother-in-law, who was sitting on the floor playing with the grandchildren. On hearing my name, she said, "I knew a Leskovar. The butcher. In Racine, Wisconsin. His wife, Anna, did the flowers for my wedding."

Now we pick up the part of the story where Joe brought Teddy to Racine. Teddy was twelve, almost thirteen. He helped his uncle Joe in the butcher shop and helped deliver klobase to the bars in Racine. Joe still did this the old way,

Tony's brother Joe Leskovar in Racine, Wisconsin, June 10, 1923.

Brothers Joe and Tony Leskovar, 1940.

Joe's wife Anna. She wrote on the back:
"This is the remains of last years snow. July 24, 1936."

the way he always had, with a horse-drawn wagon. Joe stayed at each bar long enough to drink a beer and catch up on the gossip. He also gave the horse beer at each bar. The horse wouldn't budge until he drank his beer.

"This was right after the war," Ted said. "All Germans around there. At every bar, they'd be singing 'Lili Marlene.'"

July 18 — 46

Dear Ted,

I received your letter yesterday. Your writing is improving quite a bit.

Well Ted I'm glad to hear that you passed. It's to bad Bobby didn't make it. Well the main thing Ted is to do your best in school, and when you go to high school, don't get mixed up with the guy who wants to miss classes. This may be a little early to tell you this but keep it in mind.

I go to work 7:30 in the morning start work at 8, get an hour off for lunch and we're finished four. Then I change clothes, go eat chow, then I write, read or wash my clothes at 7:30 we usually go to Barbers Point to see the movies. Then we get back at 9:30, and go to sleep at ten. It's getting monotonous going to sleep at ten, but after ten I can hardly keep my eyes open.

Well Ted write back right away. So long for now.

Your brother,

Joe

August 10. He didn't date his letters. The date is from the postmark.

Dear Mom & Dad,

I was down the Lake today boy it sure is rough the Lake is 4 blocks from the store it sure is hot day. It was a nice trip to Chicago. We took the Steamship from Chicago to Racine. Uncle Joe got a nice De Soto.

Ted

August 11
Saturday

Dear Mom and Dad,

I got your letter today. It takes four days to get here. Don't worry about be going to shows the nearest show is 10 blocks from the store. I hate to walk that far and I see the picture in Butte. Yesterday I watch them make winger [sausage] and I haven't had a stomach ache. Most of the time I sat in the car and read comic books most of the time some time all day. And at home I play with there dog Brown. When I sit in a chair and pet Brown I stop petting Brown a second he jump in my lap & sits at my bed every morning. That all for now. Write soon.

Ted

August 11

Dear Mom & Dad,

We are going out Sunday last night we there in the store till 9:00 o'clock fill in orders for Saturday. I am in the store all the time. And Chicago buildings are black from the factory. When we go in the hills you look down and see the big vally. Write soon.

Ted

August 13

Dear Mom & Dad,

I was up north Sunday with Uncle Joe. Wisconsin is a nice State but no mountain. I got a pass for the bus it cost me a dollar. You can ride the bus for a week as many times as you like to ride so I see the city on the bus.

Ted

Aug 13, 1946

Dear Teddy,

Your letter and card received, it certainly is good to hear from you. And I hope you have received all my cards & letter. I do hope you like that part of the country.

Tell Uncle Joe—Auntie Ann—that, John and Frances came in yesterday at 10:30a.m. and they left here 11:00a.m. They will try to make Spokane and if it will be too hot they will stay in Missoula we showed them Butte, and they enjoyed themself—have received card from my sister Mary saying Stephie sent Joey some cookies.

Joey is Private first class— so— when you write a letter to Joey — this is the way you write to him -

P.F.C. Joseph Leskovar 596762

Marine Transport Squd. 352

c/o Fleet Post Office

San Francisco California

I have sent you a birthday and a cute little card and a $1.00 bill and Best Regards, Mommy

Hello Teddy! I am glad to hear that you and uncle Joe got there allright and I hope that you like it over there will take you some time to get acquainted within the City of Racine.

Last Sunday Aug 11—I was selling gas from 8:00 oclock till 9 oclock p.m. I sold 200 gal, so I was quite busy and missed you to help checking tires. So when you come back from your nice vacation then you will help me again.

And I wish you happy birthday. I am enclosing a little gift.

Your Dad

I never thought to ask how Tony learned to speak, read, and write English. It's one thing to pick up a language audibly when one has an aptitude for language, which he did. It's quite another to learn the spelling and grammar.

> Wed
> Aug 14 — 1946
>
> Dear Teddy —
> It is so good to hear from you. How do you like the big City — Teddy how about writing me a long letter. John and Frances Pezdir left yesterday and they say they want to see you before you come back.
> The weather is getting colder. Bobby's Aunt, uncle cousins are here from Seattle, John & Frances Pezdir are going to visit Eddy. I do hope they will find the place where they live.
> Did you write to Joey yet — will close now with Best Regards and to your Uncle and Aunt—
> Mother

> Butte Montana
> Aug 15, 1946
>
> Dear Teddy —
> Today is your birthday and I am hoping you are having a good time, you did not mention in your letter how you like that part of the country. Teddy try and write your letter more plain. It seems to me that you are nervous so take your time and write nice, so you are having fun with Brownie.
> Teddy don't read the funnies while the auto is moving, if you do it is bad on the eyes.
> Bobby asked me if I hear from you. Tony is painting a car, that is the second one.
> The weather is getting colder and I am wearing my winter coat.
> Will close now with Best Regards and to your Uncle & Aunt —
> Mother

> Butte Mont.
> Aug. 17 — 1946
>
> Dear Teddy —
> By the cards you have sent, that town must be nicer than Butte I guess. Butte is for the tourist to see the town and get disappointed and go out fast. Well Teddy, you did not write, how you like the town.
> The weather is getting colder. It seems I got to have the fire going in the kitchen stove, won't be long now. School opening and snow on the ground.

Bobbie has asked me today if I hear from you. I do hope you are having a wonderful time.

Did you hear from Joey? I suppose when you will be home, then you will receive the letter.

The Butchers are still on strike, they are still fighting for $12.00 a day. The Butcher that sits in the garage during his lunch hour saying they are going to fight for that wage. It seems, they are not going to get it. The butchers are getting stubborn.

I just wrote Joey a letter and to you. And of course am expecting from both of you.

Will close now with

Best regards and to your Uncle and Aunt,

Mother

Postmark August 18, 1946

Dear Mom & Dad,

Gee thanks for the Tshirt and 3 dollars. I am saving my money and Eddy give me 1 dollar and Uncle Joe gave me 2 dollars. I have $5.00 save up and 1 dollar to buy things. I got a very nice watch from Uncle Joe & Aunt Ann and from Cris. Cris is the man that works in the back room he makes weiners. I got shoes from Uncle Joe and Aunt Ann. I help on the order. I can get eggs, butter, beans, fruit, can goods and weiners. I help a lot at the store today. We work tell 9:00 getting order for Saturday.

Aunt Ann want you to come with Bob if Bob can come that all for now.

From Teddy in Racine. I have the envelope. He forgot to sign his name.

Teddy, his aunt Anna and uncle Joe Leskovar, Racine, Wisconsin, July 1946.
I don't know who the two people on the right are.

> Butte Montana
> Aug 20, 1946
>
> Dear Teddy,
>
> No letters from you Monday or Tuesday — you must be terribly busy — well keep your self busy and you don't get in mischief so be a good boy.
>
> Nothing to write about only last night Babe is a member of the East Butte fire department & they will have a picnic Sunday and Babe is to help.
>
> The weather is warm and windy. It might rain, and we certainly do need it as it is very dry. I just got a letter from Joey saying he & Holmes were taking care of kid you know baby sitters — eating sandwich drinking beer, gosh Joey got all kinds of jobs - painting planes, painting offices, tending Bar at the enlisted men's club — being on guard duty, and Baby sitter. Next he will learn how to ride a mule or a donkey. The Marines learn everything.
>
> Well Teddy, there is nothing to write. Here at home is same as always.
>
> Will close with Best regards and to you Uncle and Aunt.
>
> Mother

> Butte Montana
> Aug 22, 1946
>
> Dear Teddy,
>
> How is my little business man getting along — do you know you are just like Joey in hand writing you even forget to put the date on or even sign your name.
>
> Doreen's mother and I are making a collection for Father Pirnat, he has an operation on his eyes. McQueen and East Butte are trying to make a collection of $600.00, last night we collected $23.00 in East Butte district. We got part of Racetrack and Gardens to collect yet, then we are through other women have part of Parrot Flat, Meaderville and McQueen.
>
> It is very hot today — there is nothing much of anything to write. Butte is same old way — as it was always.
>
> Will close now as I will get ready and go with Fena to race track to make more collection. So Best Regards to all.
>
> Mother

THE FATHER MICHAEL PIRNAT SHE MENTIONED was pastor of their parish, Holy Savior. He was Slovenian from the Old Country, a small, slight, self-effacing man. He was born in Ljubljana, where Tony studied music. He had three brothers who became priests. In 1908, the bishop sent him to Holy Savior in Butte and five years later named him pastor. Father Pirnat's sister Joanna immigrated after the First World War; she was his housekeeper at the rectory. He was pastor at Holy Savior for decades.

Late one night during the Second World War, he was at the hospital to administer last rites to a dying patient. He brought communion and was prepared to hear the patient's confession and administer the holy oils. As he made his way through the corridor to the patient's room, one of the nuns walked in front of him ringing a bell. Anyone hearing the bell stepped to the side and genuflected and crossed themselves, not to Father Pirnat but to the Blessed Sacrament they knew he was carrying for the dying patient.

On his way back to the priest's room at the hospital, he walked past the emergency room and heard a woman scream. He rushed in and saw a lunatic wielding a knife at the student nurse on duty. Father Pirnat quickly stepped in front of the student nurse and said to the man, "You'll have to kill me first." The man ran off.

JOE AND ANNA WERE SORRY to see Teddy go. They doted on him. They hadn't been blessed with children. They wanted him to stay for good. When Joe put him on the train back to Butte, he tipped the porter to keep an eye on him. Teddy never saw the porter again.

Letter from Joe's wife, Anna, in Racine to Tony's wife, Annie, in East Butte:

> Racine Wis
> Nov 19 — 1946
>
> Dear Ann,
> Well here I am writing to you again. I sure am a lazy one to write and when I do write a letter I forget to mail it I found one I wrote to you in one of my pocket books. I thought I mailed it and it's still here, well now I write a new one as that one had nothing but raving in it. I am still busy in store all day and so tired at night, I do a lot of packing at night and Sundays, up to now I haven't send nothing to Joe's people, I just don't have enough stuff there are too many men in the family. I send quite a bit to my sisters as they are much poorer they were all robbed and plundered by the Russians, they took all their bedding and clothes and what ever was loose, thats in Austria, and one sister is in Jugoslavia, I send her 50.00 dol last February, and up to now I have not heard if she got it or not. Joe's sister got her's. The receipt didn't come back yet either from my sister I wrote to her and she should inquire about it, but since that I don't hear from her. I hope Tito didn't put her in concentration camp for that. Well how is Teddy? I hope he is well and growing he should write some time even if its only a few lines.
> Business has slowed up a little everything is too high, but we have still too much work. I sure am getting fed up on it, I don't have no rest, my feet are like wood and they feel like the veins were going to bust thats from too much on the feet. The men they don't give a darn if a person dies, then they look for a another right away. We women are fools that

work so hard. The only thing is I got a little of my own money to spend that way. I don't think I could stand and beg for every penny. But there sure is always enough to spend in Tavern and to show off.

We miss little Teddy a lot, he sure was nice company, you tell him Peck's are gone to England, they are over there already. They sure thought a lot of him too.

By the way his ring is still here somewhere and I will send it to him as soon as I get to it, otherwise he will get it when he comes here. Tell Kay [Babe's wife] I am sorry I haven't answered her letter yet. If I get time I will write tonight yet, and I owe Joey one too, and my nephew too he is in San Francisco in Navy, I wish you were here you could be my Secretary. We read in papers you have lot of cold weather, we had a wonderful fall up to now was nice and warm.

Last Sunday started to get colder today was again nice and warm. Joe was away two days for Turkeys while he was away one of the men didn't come to work either, that's men for you. While Joe was out there by you, one was rigging up his own business two blocks away from ours but he is out already, so you see I had a hard Summer, Joe isn't a bit nice to me. I feel terrible disgusted I think some of these days I am going to give up People tell em a lot of times in Store that if I didn't take care of business as good as I am he couldn't go as much as he does.

Well we all have our troubles and I lay most of it to drinking. Where there is no drinking people live better.

Joey wrote to us too, and I also owe him a letter.

Well so long for this time wish you a happy thanksgiving wish you were here then I would roast a nice big Turkey for dinner so I don't think I bother.

Love Ann

SOMETIMES SHE WAS IN SUCH A BAD MOOD she forgot to sign her letters. I only knew it was Joe's wife, Anna, from the return address on the envelope.

I transcribed these letters as they were written. I didn't make corrections. Tony and his sister-in-law, Anna, grew up as peasants in Austria. They learned English only after they arrived.

36

⁓

ON THE RAMPAGE WITH
THAT SQUIRREL WHISKEY

August 21, 1947

Dear Mom & Dad & Ted,

Today is Sunday so I decided to get a letter off while I had time.

Our football team is in pretty good shape we were supposed to hold a scrimmage with some of the local boys this morning, but they cancelled it for some reason, . . . from what we heard the local team heard we were in good condition and had a fairly strong team, so they backed out. Well our first league game starts Saturday Sept 6, with a Navy team . . .

Since I've been out for football time has passed very fast, so it won't be very long before I'll be home.

I haven't been able to do much to the car. We start with football 1:30 in the afternoon and get finished about 5:30. So we kept very busy.

Well what the dope are we really moving out of Butte in a way it would be nice for the rest of you to get a change of scenery of course I have had a little change in scenery so I would like to kick around Butte a little before we moved out. Well I better close now, got a polish job to do on my shoes.

As always,

Joe

WHAT WAS THIS ABOUT MOVING out of Butte?

"We were down and out and some orchestra in Virginia offered Pops a job. He didn't take it," Ted said.

TEDDY WAS NOW IN SEVENTH GRADE at the Harrison School. The eighth graders played football against the seventh graders. They played on dirt. Teddy didn't like the idea of being hit by the bigger eighth graders, but one day he

Tony, Teddy, Joe, May 5, 1946.

thought he'd try it. Out he went and tackled Pinky, fellow East Butte Owl Pete Marinovich. Flattened him. All the eighth graders walked off the field.

One of Teddy's favorite pranks was putting garlic on the radiator.

There were five boys in his class when Teddy reached eighth grade. He would be the only one to finish high school. One joined the Air Force. One worked in the mines. The other two went to prison.

During recess one day, the future miner and future convict started yelling at each other. The future convict came charging at the future miner, who held out his fist and the other boy ran right into it.

"When we had fights in grade school, nobody paid any attention," Ted said.

When a child misbehaved, the teacher sent him to the cloak room.

SUMMER WAS PUNCTUATED with Butte Mines Band concerts. Tony performed in all of them. Annie took Teddy to every concert, as she had his brothers Eddy, Babe, and Joe. Annie yelled, "Play 'God Bless America,'" at every concert, and they did.

"Pops always played at the rodeo," Ted said. "If the rodeo was three days, we went for three days. When a rider fell off his horse, the drummer hit the bass drum. We always went to the band concerts. They'd play at bandstands around town, in different neighborhoods. Ma would bring a picnic. Pops played in the band in the parades. We went to all the parades. He played for Miners' Union Day at the Columbia Gardens. For a couple who didn't get along too good . . ."

When the band performed in a park, some people sat on the grass, some listened from their cars. Those listening from their cars honked in applause.

ONE DAY TEDDY WROTE "Kilroy was here" in chalk on an old shed in the neighborhood. He had heard that expression from men who came back from the Second World War. The owner of the shed caught him and slapped him, and then slapped him again. Later in the day, Teddy walked into another neighbor's house and the shed owner was there and he slapped him again.

It was just chalk. It would wash off.

Did you tell your mother?

"No," he said. "She probably would have thought I had it coming. They didn't make a fuss over stuff like that. You didn't go running home to your mother."

When Teddy was into mischief and Annie didn't like it, she'd say, "I'm gonna fix your little red wagon!"

The neighbor who slapped Teddy for writing on the shed got into a fight with Bluebird. The fight moved back and forth, in and out of the garage. Annie Bluebird tried to break it up.

In April of 1946, the miners went on strike. Salaried employees crossed the picket lines to maintain the pumps. If the pumps stopped, the mines would flood and be destroyed, and there would be no mining jobs. Even those manning the pumps were deemed the enemy and were called scabs. Mobs destroyed the homes and property of the strikebreakers. The Carpenters' Union forbade repairs. The mob threw the piano out the window of one house. They threw all the furniture out of several houses. In the melee, a little boy was shot in the eye. His name was Ray. His family happened to be driving by when the mob attacked a woman's house. She came out with a .22 and fired it to keep them from ransacking her house. The bullet took Ray's eye out. The woman got a phone call saying, You don't say anything, you don't complain, you don't say nothing.

The Company hired armed guards.

As a little boy, Teddy heard all this, saw a lot of it. It was a lot to take in.

"People from Butte wouldn't join the National Guard," Ted said. They saw them as strikebreakers.

EVERYTHING WAS A RITUAL FOR TONY, including shaving. He was methodical and believed anything worth doing was worth doing well. He shaved with a straight razor; he sharpened it on a strip of leather.

As Ted remembered it, "I was a little kid. They came and saw Pops at the house. They came in and said they were going to close him up because they caught him cleaning his spray gun after four thirty. He was shaving. Pops kicked them out.

Teddy Leskovar, 1946.

I was kind of scared. All it was was to close a competitor."

Joe said, "Four or five union guys showed up at the house. Pops was shaving. He walked out and waved his razor at them and said, 'If you ever come to my home again, you'll regret it.'"

They left.

The Swiss opera singer who helped Tony escape from France during the First World War was called Madame America, so we were told by Annie. Given Annie's propensity for assigning nicknames, who knows whether that was the opera singer's stage name or a name Annie made up. Annie firmly believed that one of her wifely duties was to torment Tony every chance she got. She was good at it. She worked at it. She would throw Madame America in his face, as if he had cheated on her before he met her with a woman who lived a continent and an ocean away in Switzerland.

Annie would light an old cigar stub and leave it smoldering in an ashtray so Tony would think she'd had a man over.

Tony would come home, smell something cooking, hungrily walk into the kitchen, see a large pot simmering away on the stove; he'd lift the lid and discover wood chips.

One morning Teddy saw his mother in the kitchen doorway and his father in the bathroom doorway. Tony was shaving. Tony poked his head out the door, said something in Slovenian, and Annie hurled a soup can at him. He ducked back into the bathroom. He poked his head out and said something, and she hurled another can at him, probably cussing her teeth loose while she was at it.

"There was always drama," Joe said. "My mother did all the talking. She was the loud one."

As adults Ted and Joe joked about it. As a child, it wasn't funny. It was terrifying. One time Tony took off after Annie with a knife. He chased her outside; they were running around the house, for all the neighbors to see, and young Teddy. He was petrified. Annie stopped, out of breath, turned toward Tony, held up her hand and said, "Wait a minute." Tony stopped and waited for her to catch her breath; both recognized the absurdity and cracked up laughing.

They had a weird marriage.

When Teddy was in bed and heard a chair push back sharply, it struck terror in his young heart. He wasn't afraid of what they might do to him; they never harmed him. He was afraid what they might do to each other.

Annie had enough. She took Teddy and left for Seattle.

This was around 1944, during the war. Teddy saw camouflage that looked like houses draped over bombers being built by Boeing. Annie and Teddy stayed with Eddy and his family. Annie worked at the Black Bear factory making jackets. She complained a lot. Tony kept calling, asking her to come back and bring Teddy. He went to Seattle to try to convince her. She wouldn't budge. She stayed through the summer and then took Teddy back to Butte. A few years later, she filed for divorce. That was all she did. She didn't go through with it. She and Tony stayed together.

"They'd rather fight than switch," Ted said.

"They couldn't live together, and they couldn't live apart," said Ted's cousin Buddy.

When Tony was on the rampage, Annie would say, "He's been drinking that squirrel whiskey again." This was when they were on hard times, and he couldn't afford Hennessy.

They argued in Slovenian. There was constant turmoil in the house.

The cupboards in the kitchen had glass in the doorframes. During one of Annie and Tony's fights, they broke all the glass. So Tony took off the doors. That's why there were no doors on the cupboards.

Ted said, "If that was marriage, I was going to stay single for the rest of my life."

37

A Quietly Spoken Mystery

When Annie's sister Mary left East Helena all those years ago during the First World War, she went to Great Falls where she lived in a little apartment and worked as a clerk at the Bee Hive. Later she sold cigars at the Rainbow Hotel. She lived in the Woodworth Apartments at 120 North Third Street. The other residents in her building were a newspaper editor who was a widower from Iowa, a woman whose parents were from the Irish Free State, a newspaper reporter from Illinois, a tailor, a teacher, a salesman at a dry goods store, a sales lady at a ready-to-wear store, a café owner, waitresses, an electrician, and the manager of a dry cleaners. All were American born except four Canadians, one Scot, and one Swede, quite a contrast from East Butte.

Mary lived in Butte for a little while around 1925. She rented her own room uptown and worked in a cigar shop. She went back to Great Falls and worked as a telephone operator at the Park Hotel until Stephie and Francie convinced her to join them in San Francisco. Since they were telephone operators, and she was a telephone operator, they could surely find her a job, and they did. By 1934, Mother Caroline and Annie's four sisters, Mary, Caroline, Stephie, and Francie, were living in a small flat on Russian Hill in San Francisco. Bobby lived with them too. He was Young Caroline's son, raised by Mother Caroline. He was all grown up now. Soon after Mary arrived, Francie married Ray Waters and left the nest.

On May 24, 1937, Mary married George Pelletier. She was forty-two and he was thirty-seven. It was the first marriage for both of them. He was the janitor at an apartment building at 775 Post Street; they lived there. Later he became the houseman.

Young Caroline was the first to move to San Francisco and the only one to leave. I don't know what became of her husband, John Davis, whether he died or they divorced. He vanished some time between 1930 and 1934. She continued to live with Mother Caroline and Stephie and work as forewoman at the MJB Coffee plant. On May 27, 1935, she ran off to Carson City, Nevada, to marry George Bronner. They moved to San Jose and then to Camarillo in southern California where they worked at the State Mental Hospital. This was in the 1940s. She worked as an attendant, he as a painter. He became a wheel in the painters' union. They lived in the nurses' living quarters.

While in Camarillo, something stirred in Young Caroline's heart. That bell called her home, home to the Catholic church. Father Ward at St. John Seminary sought her church records, so their marriage could be blessed (convalidated) by the church.

MEANWHILE BACK IN SAN FRANCISCO, Stephie and Mother Caroline moved to a flat at 1658 Sacramento Street, just up from Polk. Their rent was $33.50 in 1940. Their half flat was on the top floor, a fourth-floor walk-up, no elevator. Caroline was the only Viennese Slovenian around. The neighbors were American born. Mother Caroline spoke to Stephie in Slovenian, and Stephie answered in English. Caroline was always busy in the kitchen, going ninety miles an hour; she rarely sat. She cooked pot roast in beer. She loved to dress up and go out. She took pride in her appearance. She loved to travel. She loved having visitors. She loved to visit. She was good natured and tiny. She was an elderly, city-wise woman, comfortable with the hustle and bustle of city life, hearkening back to her early life in Vienna.

She walked to their parish church, St. Brigid's, for Mass. It was an easy (mostly flat) walk. She also attended Mass at St. Mary of the Assumption Cathedral on Van Ness, which was in the other direction. She was a Third Order Franciscan, meaning a lay member of the Franciscan order, the Catholic religious order started by St. Francis of Assisi, who by the way was a layperson, not a priest. Mother Caroline went to Mass every day. She loved that.

ONE DAY SHE BOARDS THE TRAIN or plane by herself to visit her children, grandchildren, and great-grandchildren in Montana. She is ever cheerful, lively, smiling, still a bundle of energy in her eighties, still with a heavy accent. She greets the children with a kiss on the head. "How are you doing, Grandma?" asks a grandson. "Pretty good, tanks," she says, never quite able to master that t-h sound. Up at Flathead, she sits on a cloth on the lawn in the sun and prays the rosary. Her granddaughter-in-law is expecting. She prays for a healthy baby and safe delivery.

Back home in San Francisco, she is always early for Mass. She makes two visits to St. Brigid's or the cathedral every day, once for Mass and again to say private prayers. I think it's safe to say that Mother Caroline was in her element living in San Francisco.

THE PASTOR AT ST. HELENA'S CATHEDRAL in Helena, Montana, Father Tougas, sat down at his desk and opened his mail. One item was a request for a certificate of baptism for a woman baptized in East Helena but now living in San Francisco. That woman was Stephanie Lozar. The request came from the pastor at St. Brigid's Catholic Church in San Francisco. It was a routine request for someone wishing to marry in the Catholic Church.

Father Tougas sent it on October 18, 1941.

Stephie didn't get married. Not then. Why not? She was thirty-six. Who was he? What happened?

A few weeks later, Francie sat down and wrote in her diary:

Sunday, December 7, 1941
Japan bombed Honolulu at 8am. Received word about 12:30pm

Monday, December 8
Ruth and Bill came to dinner. We experienced our 1st air raid [drill]. We went to the hospital to se Audrey. We drove in the blackout. It was awful.

Tuesday, December 9
Stayed home. Went to bed early. Couldn't sleep. Had an air raid [drill] at 3am. Ray gave me $5.

Wednesday, December 10
Stayed home again. Doctored my cold and had a good nites sleep. No air raid [drill].

Thursday, December 11
Saw Eleanor Roosevelt. She spoke at the board of Supervisors.

Friday, December 12
Margaret & Walter came over with a goose Margaret got from Kansas for X-mas. They invited us to dinner Sunday. Jimmy came over later

about 7pm. A 2½ hr black out started. We heard the planes very clearly. Were supposed to be Jap planes dropping red flares. Ray did very well serving drinks in the dark.

Sunday, December 13
Went up to Ma's at 10:30am & had breakfast. Ray, George, the Dickman's & Barbara picked me up about 2:30 & we went up to George's had a short blackout Saturday nite but we didn't know it, had a terrible rain storm Sat nite & had a good time. Got to bed at 2:30am.

Tuesday, December 16
Was told there was to be air raid [drill]. False alarm. Ray gave me $30.

Friday, December 19
Went up to the house and addressed Ma's Xmas cards. Betty and Bud brought me home and I addressed ours till after 11pm. Ray went to a dinner. He got home about 1am.

Saturday, December 20
Stayed home. Lillian & Bruce came over and we played cards. I found a pair of black gloves in Ray's car. In the afternoon Marion and Geo Deckman came over. Walter was here and Ray's bar arrived. Ray gave me $60.00.

LIFE WENT ON FOR FRANCIE AND RAY with no more mention of air raid drills but lots of socializing. "Party, party, party," said Stephie about Francie and Ray with a tsk, tsk, tsk of disapproval. Francie and Ray loved to throw parties and go to parties.

After the attack on Pearl Harbor, people were afraid that San Francisco could be next. Real estate near the ocean became undesirable. There was a nice affordable housing development in the Sunset District, south of Golden Gate Park on the flat leading to the ocean. Though others saw this as undesirable because of proximity to the ocean, this did not dissuade Frances Lozar Waters. Francie loved to dress well but she always bought on sale. What she saw was not an undesirable neighborhood but a bargain. She came home one day and told Ray, "I bought a house," which I imagine was followed by laughter because that would be Francie—bossy and happy. Tony called her *El Capitan*.

That is how the story was passed down to us. I love that story. But now here on my desk I have Francie's diaries, which tell a different story:

    Friday, May 2, 1941
    Carfare   19 cents
    Groceries   2.48
    Nuts   .25
Went up to Geo's office. Had a few drinks. Then went bowling with Geo & Jim. Got home at 11pm. Also had Italian dinner not very good.

    Saturday, May 3
    Cold cream   2.00
    Hair dresser   .75
    Carfare   .19
    Rent   30.00
Had dinner at B&G & went to see Charlie Chaplin . . . Borrowed $270 for the house.

    Sunday May 4
    House   200.00
    Geo   45.00
    Ray   5.00
Went out & bought the house. Geo came over for Breakfast & after buying the house went to Margaret Settman's. Had dinner with Margaret & Walter. Got home at 10PM.

I'VE NO DOUBT SHE CAME HOME and announced to Ray, "I bought a house," so casual about it, as if she just bought lamb chops. However, as you can see from the dates, she bought it several months before we were in the war. I try to corroborate everything I'm told for my books. I had not yet gone to San Francisco to find the date Francie and Ray bought the house. It was more fun to discover this by accident in her diaries. I have only four of Francie's tiny diaries covering a few months in 1936, 1941, 1950, and 1957. In those few I found several gems, help from beyond the grave it would seem.

Francie and Ray's house was right next to the houses on either side; all the houses together looked like one block-long building. Their house was two stories. After walking through the small interior courtyard the visitor walked up the stairs to the front door, which was on the second floor. This was the main floor of the house with the kitchen, front room, dining room, and two bedrooms. All the rooms were small. It was a small house. The bathroom had an anteroom with a skylight and a built-in vanity and vanity chair with soft flattering light. The front of the house faced west, so the living and dining rooms were sunny when there was sun. The rumpus room with a bar was on the ground floor next to the garage. Their guest room would become the place where Francie's siblings and nephews and nieces stayed when they came to visit. So patient was Ray with this steady stream of in-laws. I think he liked us.

As their ninth anniversary approached, Ray asked her, "For our anniversary do you want a fur coat or to be married in the Church?" Francie had always gone to Mass, but she didn't receive communion since she wasn't married sacramentally through the Catholic Church. She told Ray she wanted to be married in the Church, and so they were. Their marriage was convalidated before a Catholic priest. Mother Caroline was delighted. Ray bought Francie the fur coat anyway.

Francie used to say about money, "I'd rather wear it than eat it." She always dressed beautifully. She shopped the sales at I. Magnin. One of her great-nieces thought she was so elegant that San Francisco was named after her.

One day she came home from a wedding and declared, "Well, if I don't say so myself, I looked better than the bride."

Francie always prepared a yellow or orange vegetable and a green vegetable to accompany the meat she prepared for dinner. She insisted on serving hot food on a warm plate, never a cold plate. When Ray walked in the door from work, he unwound with his favorite cocktail, an Old Fashioned, before dinner. Francie never cooked klobase. "I'm not eating that old Bohunk food," she said. She wouldn't even admit to her mother's being Slovenian. "She's Viennese," she said.

Every Friday night, Francie and Ray and her sister Mary and Mary's husband, George, went to dinner at Mother Caroline and Stephie's flat on Sacramento Street.

Francie's diary, 1950:

> Friday, January 27
> Had dinner at Ma's. Went to basket ball game with Sue and Ray.

> Saturday, January 28
> Dinner at Ruth's. Played poker—broke even.

> Sunday, January 29
> Went to Church with Margaret. Played Bridge with Billie & Bob. Won $3.80

> Monday, February 6
> Took Ma to the show.

SHE PLAYED CANASTA. Played bridge. Took a friend to the doctor. Took Ma to the hairdresser. Had dinner at Mary's. Went to friends' for dinner. Had friends over for dinner. Often the friend who came for dinner stayed the night. Francie had plans almost every day. I have pictures of dinner parties in their house. The men are wearing tuxedos, the women are wearing off-the-shoulders evening gowns. The menu for one of those dinners was tomato shrimp aspic, lemony asparagus, and leg of lamb with mint jelly.

Ray used to go out to Alcatraz to watch the fights. I can't remember who sponsored these events. It might have been Pacific Gas and Electric. Ray

Mother Caroline Lozar and Francie Lozar Waters, San Francisco, 1942.

sold valve packing for Garlock, so PG&E would have been a customer. They had dinner, and then watched the prisoners box. "Only two dollars," he said.

> Tuesday, February 14
> Went to Church. Had dinner with Pauline & stayed all nite.

> Sunday, February 19
> Sue and Ray came over, worked in yard & stayed for dinner.

> Friday, February 24-March 4
> Week at Riga's. Lake Co.
> Played bridge
> Played canasta
> Polly & I washed the kitchen

> Wednesday, March 1
> Hung over.

> Friday, March 10
> Had dinner at Ma's. Went over to Mary's with Sue & Ray [Ryan]. Ray [Waters] picked me up at 9:30 went to see Hodge's new home.

Dinner party at the Waterses home in the Sunset District of San Francisco.
Francie is at the front on the left side of the table. Ray is at the back
by the window on the right side of the table.

Sunday, March 12
Went over to Mary's [her sister]. Traded suits.

Monday, March 13
Helped Ma. Had dinner at Mary's.

Friday, March 24
Ma's for dinner.
Gave Mary a permanent. Took Ma to Minstrel Show. Took Billie
to Church. Ray went to Lodge. I went over to Bogarts. Lost $3.38 in
Canasta. Took a swimming lesson. Worked on Ray's books. Another
swimming lesson. Gave Billie a permanent. Family for dinner. Bob took
us to the St. Francis for dinner at the Tonga Room. Over to Mary's for

dinner. Ray made Fizzes all afternoon. Went swimming and had dinner at Al's. Came home from the Lake at 11:30pm. Ray made Fizzs. We were all hung over. Charlo made super breakfast. All were very low. Low all day. Worst all day. Full of pep. Washed. Cleaned basement. Washed my hair. Wrote letter. No stopping me. Cooked a turkey. Real good. Played golf. Ray broke 90. Took Ma, Susie, Ray for a ride. Gave Sue & Ma a permanent. Took Ma to a movie. Hung over. Stayed in Bed all day. Did Mary's hair. Had dinner there. Home at 8pm. Ray worked on the stairs.

> Sunday, May 21
> Had the family for dinner—Ann, Steve, Zelda, Ma, Mary, George. Hamills.

APPARENTLY ANNIE AND STEVE AND ZELDA came to visit. There is no mention of Tony. This is still 1950.

> Monday, May 22
> Went to the races. Won $3.25

> Tuesday, May 23
> Showed the gang the city. Dinner at Mary's.

> Wednesday, May 24
> Hamills left. Took Ann & Zelda to town — bought Ann a complete outfit.

> Thursday, May 25
> Steve, Ann & Zelda left. Cleaned house all day.

SEVERAL TIMES FRANCIE MENTIONED Sue and Ray. Sue is Stephie. Why Francie called Stephie Susie, I don't know. Annie, who was generous with nicknames, always called her Stephie. I think Stephanie is a beautiful name. Even as a child, I wondered if Francie thought it sounded too Bohunk.

Ray was Ray Ryan, Stephie's husband. What, you say, I don't remember anything about Stephie getting married. When did she get married? That, dear reader, is the quietly spoken mystery I must tell you about. The real mystery is why the mystery at all. Perhaps you'll have theories.

Decades later, when Francie and Ray celebrated their fiftieth wedding anniversary, Mom asked Stephie, "Your anniversary must be coming up. When is it?" Stephie wouldn't answer. That shouldn't be a hard question.

Aunt Stephie reminded me of the little old ladies in *Arsenic and Old Lace*, not that she was doing in elderly men with poisoned elderberry wine, but I always had the sense there was something she wasn't telling us.

Francie Lozar Waters, Annie Lozar Leskovar,
Zelda Morigeau Lozar, San Francisco, 1950.

When Stephie and Ray came to Butte to visit, she said they couldn't stay with Annie and Tony. They had to stay at the Finlen Hotel because Ray was on a "secret mission." In Butte?

After Stephie and Ray returned from a trip to the Old Country (Yugoslavia), Ted asked whether she learned anything about the family. "There are some things it's better off not knowing," she said. And that was all she said.

As I set out to write this book, I wanted to find all the knowable facts,

Steve and Zelda Lozar, San Francisco.

all the data. I wanted birth records, marriage records, everything. I began looking for Stephie and Ray Ryan's marriage certificate. Who could have imagined that would be difficult.

The first place I found Stephie identified as Mrs. Ray Ryan was on her sister Mary's death certificate in 1956, so they must have been married by then.

I searched San Francisco marriage indices. I covered a broad swath of time. I couldn't find Stephanie Lozar in the indices by bride's name, so I looked for Ray Ryan by groom's name. I spent hours poring through those records. No Stephanie Lozar. No Ray Ryan. I thought, well, did they run off to Reno to get married, as did Francie and Ray Waters? Stephie and Ray were quiet and reserved and were both Catholics. It seemed quite in character for flighty Francie and non-Catholic Ray Waters to run off to Reno to get married. It didn't sound like Stephie or Ray Ryan at all, quite out of character, but I looked anyway. No, they didn't get married in Reno.

I had been told that Mother Caroline attended Mass at the cathedral. That was the one on Van Ness that burned down. I figured the new cathedral had the records, so I called. Stephie and Ray were not married at the cathedral.

I asked family members: when did Stephie and Ray get married? No one knew. One of my cousins, who lived down the peninsula from San Francisco, said they visited Aunt Stephie and Great-Grandma Caroline often; sometimes Ray Ryan was there, and sometimes he was not. Then one day they were told to call him Uncle Ray, and Aunt Stephie was Stephanie Ryan. No talk of a wedding. These cousins were teenagers, old enough to attend a wedding had there been one.

By this time, I was wondering, were they actually married? I went on to something else. Then I had an epiphany—Ray worked for the government at Mare Island. I'll request his personnel file. The government keeps copious records. Maybe I'll find a clue there. I ordered the records from the National Archives. His retirement paperwork listed Stephie as his wife and said they were married in Las Vegas, California. There is no Las Vegas, California. I live in Las Vegas, Nevada. I called the courthouse. Yep. Stephanie Lozar and Ray Ryan, two of the most sedate, reserved people I've known, ran off to Las Vegas to get married in 1949 and kept their marriage a secret for years. She was forty-five; he was fifty-two. She continued to live with her mother on Sacramento Street. Ray Ryan lived across the Bay in Vallejo during the week, near Mare Island where he worked. On the weekends, he lived with his mother and sister, Gertrude, at 1750 Washington Street in San Francisco.

Why keep their marriage a secret? Why run off to Las Vegas? People do that now, but for San Franciscans in the 1930s and 1940s, Reno was much easier, and Las Vegas was tiny back then. Being a telephone operator, Stephie knew the operators listened in on phone calls. Perhaps Stephie thought Reno was too close. But why the clandestine marriage? They were both Catholics, neither had been married before, there was no reason to run off to Las Vegas, no reason not to marry sacramentally in the Church.

Ted was told, by whom I neglected to ask, that they kept their marriage a secret from Ray's mother because there was a lot of money, and Ray wouldn't get it if he married. Was that true? To find out, we'll have to learn more about Ray Ryan.

"Ray Ryan had a briefcase locked to his wrist. He worked for the foreign service," a cousin told me. I listened politely, wrote it down, but didn't believe it. Later I thought, I need to have an open mind. I need to follow every possible thread. I asked other relatives, "Did you ever see Uncle Ray Ryan with a briefcase handcuffed to his wrist?"

"No."

"No."

"No."

"No."

Ray Ryan, secret agent man? My dear uncle Ray Ryan, so kind, so mild mannered, such a gentleman, the last person on earth about whom one would make up James Bond-esque stories. I never believed it, but I had to ask. He lived in Vallejo, California. He was a Marine at Mare Island during the war. After the war, he did the same job as a civilian. Was he with the Office of Strategic Services (the Second World War precursor to the CIA)? I doubted it, but I looked into it anyway. I looked at all the Ryans in the personnel files for the Office of Strategic Services, which are at the National Archives and conveniently online. No Ray Ryan. Considering all the secrecy during the war, had Ray's job in the Marines required him to be a courier? If so, the bit about the briefcase handcuffed to his wrist could be true. But I don't think Stephie knew Ray during the war, so none of my relatives would have known Ray Ryan during the war. Cold war secrecy perhaps?

How do these stories get started? And of all people, why such stories about my mild-mannered, gentle uncle Ray Ryan, a homebody like Stephie? Who was he?

Ray Ryan was born to Irish Catholic parents on June 24, 1897, in San Francisco. He was baptized at St. Brigid's. His father was an immigrant from Ireland and was forty-eight years old the year Ray was born. Ray's mother was a Bresnan; her parents had emigrated from Ireland. It was the Feast of St. John the Baptist the day Ray was born, hence he was baptized Raymond John Ryan. For some reason Ray grew up thinking his name was Raymond Joseph. The Navy straightened that out for him years later.

Ray's family lived at 2218 Greenwich, west of Fillmore. Their neighbors were Irish, the Cronins and the Sullivans. Ray's dad was a day laborer.

Seven-year-old Ray Ryan awoke with a jolt on April 18, 1906. Twenty seconds later, violent shaking began and went on for one very, very, very long minute, shaking felt from Oregon to Los Angeles, shaking that might well have thrown young Ray right out of bed. Later when he walked through the neighborhood, he saw cable car tracks twisted like spaghetti and the cobblestone streets reduced to loose stones.

Gas lines broke. The ensuing fire engulfed the Financial District. Water lines broke, no water to fight the fires. The army came in and dynamited mansions to create a fire break at Van Ness to stop the fire from moving even farther west and destroying the rest of The City. Ray's family lived west of Van Ness. They were okay.

Nearby Lobos Square became a refugee camp full of tents.

Ray Ryan's life would be bookended by disaster.

WE JUMP AHEAD SEVERAL DECADES, and Ray has joined the Marines. It is two years into the Second World War. He works as a supply officer at the Mare Island shipyard. After the war, he is discharged from the Marines and continues in the same job as a civilian.

He lived in Vallejo while working at the shipyard. On the weekends, he lived with his mother, Margaret Ryan, and his sister Gertrude Dwyer at their apartment on Washington Street, two blocks from Stephie and Caroline. Ray's mother and sister were widows. His sister married young and was widowed young. Her husband died of tuberculosis and chronic alcoholism. Ray listed his mother and his sister as dependents even though his sister Gertrude worked.

I like to see where the people in my books lived. While in San Francisco, I looked at the apartment buildings and houses where Mother Caroline and Stephie and Francie lived. I saw St. Brigid's and how close it was and realized it was their parish church. I couldn't remember whether I had checked the marriage records at St. Brigid's. When I returned home, I looked in my notes and found where I wrote, "Call St. Brigid's about Stephie's marriage records." I hadn't called yet. I called and was referred to the parish that keeps those old records.

On April 22, 1956, Stephie and Ray quietly had their marriage con-validated at St. Brigid's Church. They lived with Mother Caroline in the apartment on Sacramento Street. The nieces and nephews were told to call him Uncle Ray.

Ray's mother passed away three years later. She was ninety-six.

Why the secrecy? There was no Ryan family money. Ray supported his widowed mother. Was Ray's mother like Maureen O'Hara in the movie *Only the Lonely,* who didn't want her son to marry and tried to sabotage his romance because she was afraid he'd abandon her?

Though Ray's family didn't have money, as it turns out, Stephie did. Stephie worked for Pacific Bell. I'm told (but couldn't confirm) that during the Depression there were times when the phone company didn't have the

Mother Caroline, Ray Ryan, and Stephie, after the baptism of probably one of Bobby Lozar's children. Since Stephie is holding the baby in all the pictures I have, I'm guessing she is the godmother. Bobby was Young Caroline's son, who was raised by Mother Caroline.

cash to pay the employees and paid them in stock. By the time she retired, Stephie had amassed a substantial portfolio of telephone company stocks. Most of her stocks paid dividends. Very frugal, they were, Stephie and Ray. They lived simply, always in a small apartment. They both lived to a ripe old age and were pretty healthy up until the end.

IT'S TIME WE GET BACK TO BUTTE, but before we do, let's see what our social butterfly Francie has been up to. She and Ray bought a second home down the coast in Carmel.

Francie's diary, 1957:

Thursday, March 7
Irene Pitts called & asked if I would be Vera Miles double in a movie.
I said yes. Played golf.

Friday, March 8
Didn't get the job but registered as extra. Played bridge.

Took Ma to church. Bought her a dress. Ma to doctor. Golf. Lunch.
Bridge. Ray played Pebble Beach. Ma and Susie and Ray came over after
church.

Friday, March 22
Played bridge at Riga's. Ray won. Big earthquake.
[The biggest since 1906.]

Wednesday, May 22
Went down with Irene Pitts & joined the Screen Extras Guild.

Tuesday, June 4
Worked in the "Line Up." My 1st attempt at acting!

Sunday, October 6
Worked on Hitchcock picture with J. Stewart & Kim Novak [Vertigo].
Dinner with Ma.

Thursday, October 24
Shopped for the party.

Saturday, October 26
Big party finally here! A huge success—cops broke it up at 3:15am.

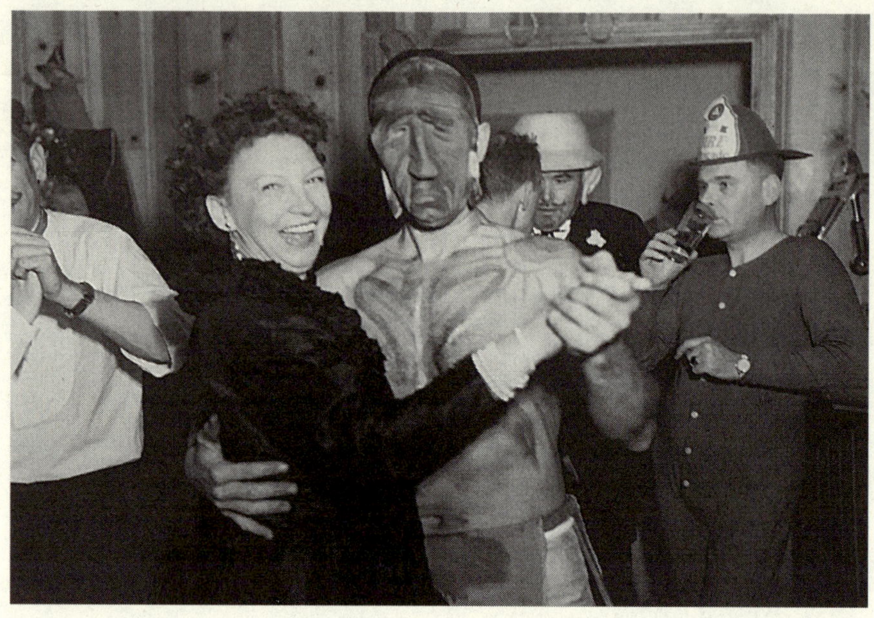

I'm guessing that sorry-looking sap dancing with Francie is Ray. This was taken during their wild Halloween party in the rumpus room of their house in the Sunset District, San Francisco, October 1957.

38

STRANGE BOHUNK LOGIC

"I worked for Joe Wilson [the Chrysler Plymouth dealer] when I was fifteen," Ted said. He worked as the lot boy, washing cars, sweeping the floors. It was his first job not working for his father.

Wilson flew his own plane. He took Teddy with him to fly to another part of the state to pick up a car. He got lost. In Montana, the first digit of a car license plate denotes the county. Silver Bow County is number one, so all Butte license plates begin with one. Wilson started buzzing farms to try to read license plates to try to figure out which county they were flying over. He regained his bearings and headed off in the right direction. Teddy drove the car back to Butte.

"Then I worked at the Craven Garage seven days a week. It was a gas station on South Main Street. There were always fights going on. You know where Pork Chop John's was at? It was right around the corner. I was a kid, and they'd say, 'Okay, Sweeney is buying the hamburgers.' So they'd give me the money, and I'd run over and buy the hamburgers. I told them, I said, 'You know one of these days when Sweeney comes in, I'm gonna have to thank him for buying all these hamburgers.' They said, 'No, no.' Sweeney didn't know he was buying hamburgers. Somebody would come in and pay cash for a tire repair or something like that, and they wouldn't ring it up and take the money and go buy hamburgers."

The girls who worked The Line in the cribs on Mercury Street parked their cars at the Craven Garage.

I can't remember what prompted this conversation:

"She was married to the fellow where you used to work."

"I thought his wife worked The Line."

"Maybe that was his first wife."

323

"This wife worked The Line."

The Line (the Red Light District) was along East Galena and East Mercury. As Teddy walked down that part of the street, he could hear the women in the cribs tapping their fingernails against the window. It makes me profoundly sad to think of that.

Teddy saw quite a parade of all manner of people from his vantage point at the Craven Garage. One day he saw a woman stumble out of the bar across the street with a man. She threw her coat over the guy's head and started walloping him with her high heel. She heard the sirens, put on her shoe, and walked away as if nothing happened.

A drunk used to sleep on the bench out front. Teddy would see him wake with a start and frantically brush off invisible bugs then fall back to sleep.

On treks uptown, Teddy passed the guy with the peg leg with the wheelchair with the dog with the pipe. The dog sat in the wheelchair, the dog had a pipe, the guy with the peg leg pushed the dog in the wheelchair.

Sometimes he saw Crazy Mary. She was a big woman who walked the streets uptown, always carrying a suitcase and wearing heavy red rouge. She had been jilted at the altar, at least that was the story. She was Butte's Miss Haversham. Teddy would see her buying lunch at the seedy Chili King.

Mom said when she heard the song "Delta Dawn," she immediately thought of Crazy Mary. *"Delta Dawn, what's that flower you have on? Could it be a faded rose from days gone by? . . . All the folks around Brownsville* [Butte] *say she's crazy 'cause she walks downtown with a suitcase in her hand . . ."*

Teddy saved his money and bought an NSU motorcycle. The Craven Garage was one of two gas stations in Butte that was open twenty-four hours a day. Late one very cold night, well below zero, Teddy was riding his motorcycle home from work through the deserted streets of Uptown Butte. He was going fast, very fast, sixty miles an hour; it was cold and he wanted to get home. The cops stopped him. They confiscated his bike, threw him in the dungeon (the jail), and then dropped him at the corner of Park and Main in the freezing cold. "I found an open bar and called Pops." Tony drove uptown, bawled out the cops for leaving Teddy out on the street in the freezing cold, and took Teddy home.

Another time when it was not cold, the engine was getting hot, so Teddy drove around the block fast to cool it off. He heard the siren. He zipped into the Craven Garage, parked his bike inside, and went outside to join the bystanders wondering whom the cop was chasing.

Teddy started high school in 1948, the same year he started working for someone other than his dad. The football team at Butte High played on a dirt field, no grass. The ground was frozen much of the season.

School didn't interest Teddy except history; in that, he did well. He was still a prankster. A teacher at Butte High was scolding Teddy for his mischief and got right in his face to do so. Teddy yawned a really big yawn, which made her angrier. "Students like you make me want to jump out the window!" she said.

Annie Bluebird would walk into their house at 210 Cherry and say, "Where's the old lady?" Growing up hearing this, Teddy and his buddies referred to their mothers as "the old lady." It drove the teachers at Butte High crazy to hear that. They thought it was disrespectful.

Speaking of the neighborhood, "I was only seventeen years old, not very big," Teddy said. "This big miner was looking for a fight and, of course, I wasn't interested in fighting anybody. The next-door neighbor came up and said, 'You could've took him. By the time he got tired out beating the hell out of ya, you could've took him.' I didn't think that was a good idea."

"Was he joking?"

"No."

Strange Bohunk logic.

By this time, Annie's cousin Mary had died of Addison's disease. Annie's aunt Anna Lozar Kogar Ulsher signed over her home to her step-grandson. She signed with a very shaky hand.

"Anna Kogar moved in with us for a while, and she was always demanding all these special meals. Ma cooked whatever she asked for. That didn't last very long."

When Joe came home from the Marines, he received forty weeks pay as part of the GI Bill. His brother Babe was the assistant service department manager at Wilson's, the Chrysler Plymouth dealer. He asked Joe if he wanted to work there in the paint shop.

"I had to join the union to work for Wilson," Joe said. "Oscar Gay, he worked for my father for years, I told him I wanted to join the union, thought maybe I could get into journeyman, otherwise I'd be an apprentice, less money. Oscar got up [at the union meeting] and said, 'I've known the family for years, he just finished serving his country in the Marines, I think we should make him a journeyman,' and they did."

When Joe drove home in a red Chrysler, Annie clucked her tongue and said, "That's some class in the alley!"

Painting insignia on all those airplanes in the Marines sparked Joe's interest in flying. He'd take Teddy up with him. One time they were flying against such a stiff headwind that cars were passing them. Joe gave up getting back to Butte and landed the plane on an abandoned airfield outside of Deer Lodge. They went inside the tiny building.

"There was an old crank telephone. It actually worked," Ted said. "We called Pops and he came out and picked us up."

Another time, Joe had to hurry up and land because he was out of fuel. The man at the airfield ran out and said, "What's wrong?"

"I ran out of fuel," Joe said.

"There's an auxiliary tank."

"Oh."

Another time they decided to fly up to Flathead to visit the Lozars. Steve and Zelda's family brought out their lawn chairs and sat along the runway waiting for them to land. It was very exciting in the 1950s to have relatives arrive by plane.

THE AMERICAN LEGION WAS THE NEXUS for socializing for veterans in Butte. There was a dance at the American Legion Hall every Saturday night. It was

Big Joe with some class in the alley.

Tony wrote: "Joey repairing 40 Chev cam shaft.
Annie gave instructions from repair manual. 1949."

*Babe and Kay Leskovar, Helen and Joe Leskovar on
Joe and Helen's wedding day, July 22, 1950.*

at one such dance that Joe met Helen, the vivacious redhead who turned his head, and he never looked back. He was completely tongue tied. He didn't know what to say to her. So he bought a joke book. He practiced the jokes, memorized them, and told her the jokes, and she laughed and laughed.

The day they were to marry, Joe went to the barber for a haircut and shave. The barber was drunk.

Helen wasn't Slovenian, and she wasn't Catholic, and Annie didn't like that, even though Annie and Tony never went to Mass.

Joe and Helen married on July 22, 1950. Joe was twenty-two. Helen was seventeen, though the marriage license said she was eighteen. They were married by Pastor Bracken from the Methodist Church.

The other painter at Wilson's, a fellow called Speed, would be off drinking at the Terminal Bar for two hours at a time. He was a senior painter and senior drunk. The boss thought Joe was the one slacking off and fired him.

Wilson later figured out that Speed was the problem, not Joe. He fired Speed and hired Joe back as a journeyman painter.

A few years earlier, Tony worked for Wilson as a journeyman painter. As soon as he could, Tony once again opened his own paint shop. He rented two stalls for thirty-five dollars a month. This was around 1949. As he built up business he needed help. He didn't have enough business for full-time help, so he hired Speed.

"Speed was a drunk," Ted said. "Unreliable. Pops didn't need anyone full time anyway."

Speed didn't show up half the time, which was fine because Tony needed only part-time help. He paid Speed for the work he did. The union fined Tony because he didn't have a journeyman working for him (even though he had been one himself).

"Pops worked as a journeyman," Ted said. "Then he opened his own shop at the tannery. He had all these creamery trucks all ready to paint, and they said, because he worked as a journeyman for two weeks, he lost his contracting card. A contracting card allowed you to open up your own paint shop. The creamery pulled their trucks out because they had teamster drivers, and they didn't want any trouble with the union. So they just pulled them all out. All Pops had to do was paint them." Tony had already done all the prepping and masking, which was the lion's share of the work. The painting was the easy part. Since the job was taken away, Tony wasn't paid.

Tony's competitors were using union rules to tamp down competition. Economists call this "rent seeking," using regulations, be they government or union, to keep down competition. It's the attitude of *I've got mine, and I'm not letting anyone else in. Rather than improve and compete, I'd rather use influence to manipulate the rules in my favor.* This worked against Tony.

Butte has been called the Gibraltar of Unionism. Just about everybody was organized. I found a letter from Sister Mary Donata of Girls Central High School to the musicians' union requesting permission for the school orchestra to perform at a fundraiser to raise money to help pay tuition for several girls whose families couldn't afford it. The letter was written in February of 1933, during the Great Depression.

The pastor at St. Ann's had to request permission from the musicians' union for parishioners who were union members to donate their time to perform with the choir for Christmas Mass.

Joe was at the painters' union meeting when one of the fellows said, "We're going to have to close up Tony Leskovar. He doesn't have a journeyman painter." Joe stood up and said, "Yes, he does." He walked into Tony's shop and said, "Pops, I'm your new painter." It was a big risk for Joe; he was married with a baby. Tony didn't have enough business to hire anyone full time.

"The other paint shops were using union rules to get rid of competitors," Ted said. "So they said they are going to close Pops up because he didn't have a journeyman painter there full time. You couldn't be a contracting painter unless you hired a journeyman. Joe was working for Wilson at the time and didn't know if Pops could afford to hire Joe full time because he had a wife and kid to support. So during the union meeting, Joe says, 'Naw, you aren't going to close him up. He's got a journeyman painter. It's me.' We were at the house, and Pops says, 'We'll make it somehow.' I was working for Pops after school part time."

It was rough for a while. Sometimes Tony didn't pay Joe and Ted.

IT WAS AROUND THIS TIME that Tony and several other musicians organized the Butte Civic Orchestra. Tony was the assistant director and later the director (conductor). It was also called the Butte Symphony. He was a member of the board of trustees.

"Those were his glory days," Annie said.

"When Pops was conducting, he didn't have much to do with the paint shop," Ted said.

Under Tony's direction, the orchestra performed Franz Schubert's *Unfinished Symphony in B Minor*, "Swedish Rhapsody" by Charles Wildman, the waltz from *Sleeping Beauty* by Tchaikovsky, the *Surprise Symphony* by Haydn, the "Chit-Chat Polka" by Johann Strauss, and more.

The Butte Mines Band had dissolved by this time. When a reporter asked Tony if the band might come back, he said, "The band will be reorganized some day. During the [Second World] War the organization lost many of its younger members to the service, and immediately following the war, it was difficult to present a band at full strength. This was discouraging, but the organization is far from defunct, and one day will again appear in full strength."

With Joe and Ted working with him, Tony grew steadier on his financial feet; he could give Annie ample money for groceries, so she could cook more than pancakes and polenta.

Annie was a good cook. She didn't own a cookbook. She learned from her mother. She cooked without a thermometer, without a timer; recipes were taught not read.

Her first stove burned wood. The only way to know when the oven was hot enough was to put your arm in it.

This day she is making noodles for her chicken noodle soup. She scoops flour into a bowl. She makes a well in the middle with her fingers. Into the well she cracks an egg and adds cooking oil and water. She mixes it with her fingers and kneads it. She lets the dough rest a while. She rolls out the dough, lets it sit and dry, then she rolls it up and slices the noodles with a sharp knife. She spreads them out on a tea towel and lets them dry for several hours. She cuts the noodles small enough to fit on a soup spoon. No sloppy slurping. She is Slovenian after all.

She fried chicken in peanut oil and butter. She skinned the chicken, dipped it in egg and then flour, and then fried it. You might ask, why take the skin off? Good question.

She sliced cucumbers paper thin, squeezed out the water with a towel, then dressed the cucumbers with vinegar and oil. I remember this as a child. It was delicious. I'm guessing she used apple cider vinegar since that was the vinegar her mother and Tony's kin used in the Old Country.

She served salad or cucumbers and bread with dinner.

She made pork roast with applesauce.

She shopped at an import grocery store. Patrons would stand around the butcher block eating salami.

For a special family dinner or picnic, Annie cooked a beef roast.

There was always a quart of ice cream in the icebox.

She made coffee the way her mother taught her, the way they made it in the Old Country, Turkish coffee. She boiled the water in a pot on the stove, added the coffee grounds and brought it back to the boil. It's bitter that way, so it's common to add sugar at the beginning, before boiling the water and adding the coffee. I don't know whether Annie added sugar.

"Ma, who's coming over for dinner?" Teddy asked.

"Mr. Dam, Mrs. Dam, and the whole Dam family."

STEVE AND ZELDA CAME TO VISIT in the summer and brought a crate of cherries from Flathead. What they didn't eat right away, Annie brandied. Liquor and honey were her preservatives.

When Tony and Annie went to visit Steve and Zelda up at Flathead, Tony brought a case of whiskey and sherry. As soon as Steve and Zelda's grandsons heard the car pull up, they would race to be the one to carry the case of liquor into the house. Tony would tip the lucky boy a silver dollar.

Tony always drove too fast for Steve's liking. Steve said, "A fast driver was a hearse looking for business."

Annie made delicious mashed potatoes for Thanksgiving and Christmas. She put them in a bowl, partially covered, over simmering water to keep them hot and moist until dinner. Tony supervised the gravy making. He wanted to be sure there were no lumps.

The rest of the year, Annie served boiled potatoes.

*Roadside picnic. Francie Lozar Waters, Teddy Leskovar, Tony Leskovar,
1947. Caroline Lozar is behind Francie.*

*Annie, Teddy, Francie, Joey at Blue Bay at Flathead Lake, circa 1949.
The little girl on the right in the background is one of Zelda's nieces.*

At dinner one night, Teddy asked, "Ma, why don't we ever have mashed potatoes?"

Annie took a fork and reached over to Teddy's plate . . . mash, mash, mash.

"There. They're mashed."

Teddy sat down at the kitchen table for breakfast. The table was next to the stove. Annie plunked a box of cereal in front of him.

"Ma, why don't we ever have a hot breakfast?"

She took his bowl of cornflakes, put it in the oven, gave it back to him, and said, "There's your hot breakfast!"

He quit asking about the food.

This brings to mind some Annie-isms:

"Better get going while your shoes are still good."

"Dawgonit!"

"The old lady, she died. That knocked them both to pieces."

"Don't sit on that cold step!"

"You're acting like a ragged-ass millionaire!" she said to Joe. I'm not sure why.

"Well if you don't look like the ___ ____ Blue Men of Morocco!" she said to her nephew who was playing in a pond that turned his skin blue.

"Drink out of the bottle, not the glass!" She was talking about beer. She worried the glass might not be clean, best to drink out of the bottle.

TEDDY CAME HOME ONE VERY HOT DAY and found Annie on the floor.

"Get the bucket! Get the bucket!" she said.

He ran to fetch the empty lard bucket and came back and saw the empty whiskey bottle on the floor next to her.

"Ma, why'd you drink all that?"

"I was thirsty!"

"Why didn't you drink water?"

"I'm not going to drink that stuff!"

39

∞

SNOOKIE'S

"You had a bar here and a bar here; this was a grocery store and it turned into a bar, and then here was Snookie's." That was Ted describing his neighborhood.

Snookie had a cure for everything. If you were sick, you asked Snookie. Stomachache? Blackberry brandy. Sore throat? Whiskey.

"You didn't ask Ma. She had the cure for everything too, but it was scary."

Snookie owned the corner bar. His real name was George Gergurich.

Ted had been going to Snookie's since he was a little boy, fetching beer in a lard bucket for Mrs. Cash and buying beer and a Hershey bar for Ma, which she shared with him.

"When I was in high school, you could buy drinks for the house at Snookie's for a dollar. A beer cost ten cents. People bought drinks on credit; Snookie ran a tab."

This wasn't a tab for the night. A customer ran a tab for a month or so. There was a law in Montana that prohibited selling drinks on credit, apparently ignored at Snookie's, just like the laws against underage drinking and gambling.

"Snookie had slot machines in the back with a cover where he could close it down. They were illegal. Nickel machines."

"We were sitting at the bar. It was me and Matt Casick and Orlich, Leechin and Squeaks Marsinich. And Wiener Shea comes up to Squeaks and asks to borrow ten dollars. And Squeaks says, 'I'm not gonna lend you ten dollars,' and Wiener says, 'Well I just wanted to know what you'd say,' and Leechin says, 'That's a heck of a thing to say to somebody,' and hit him."

"I asked Ma, what does Leechin mean? 'Bully.' Joe (Ted's brother) and Leechin sparred around a bit, and Joe held his own. This was at Snookie's."

334

Then somebody walked in and played the cordeen.

"They have these little whistles that you hook up to the spark plugs, and they'd whistle and blow and smoke, and Stevie and I go out to Orlich's car and hook up these whistles and so when he starts up the car it's whistling and smoking. He's jumping out of his car."

About another fellow I asked, "Did he live in East Butte?"

"I don't know where he lived. I think he was the class drunk," Ted said.

"Squeaks Marsinich, did he live in East Butte?"

"I don't know where he lived. All I know is he and Leechin were friends. . . . I started hanging out at Snookie's when I was seventeen."

"Was there a drinking age?"

"Yes, twenty-one. Sometimes the liquor guys would come around and tell everybody to stay away [everybody under age]. We'd go away for one day is all."

"What did you have for identification?"

"Nothing."

Joe didn't get a driver's license until he was thirty years old even though he'd been driving since he was a kid.

One night Ted and his buddies went to Luigi's, and for some reason the doorman asked for identification. Lubick said, "I have a picture of myself, will that do?"

Luigi was a one-man band. To get to the restroom, you had to cross the dance floor. Luigi would stop the music and wait until the person came out and then resume playing.

A couple lived in the apartment behind Snookie's. The husband would come home late, and the wife wouldn't let him in. He'd slip money under the door. She still wouldn't let him in. He slipped more money under the door, kept doing it until she let him in.

Another fellow passed out in the alley walking home from Snookie's. It was winter. He froze to death.

"Well, I guess they must be fighting by now," Ted said as he left the house to walk down to Snookie's. The wife of the couple he was talking about had fallen off a bar stool and broke her leg. As Ted walked in, he saw her throw her crutch at her husband. Another time, the wife and husband were sitting at the bar, and she moved his reading glasses. He said, "I didn't mind when she shacked up with the Indian, but when she started fooling with my cheaters . . ." and he took his glass and hit her. She fell on the floor, blood all over. The next morning someone found her in a snowbank at the Columbia Gardens. She was all right.

Whenever a wife called looking for her husband, Snookie said, "He just left." Every time she called back, "He just left."

If a fellow said, "I'll buy you a beer," the other fellow might say, "I'll have it coming." That meant I'll have it next time. The fellow would pay for the beer, and Snookie would mark it down for the next time.

When Ted heard about a fellow having a black eye, he asked, "Did he get in a beef in the joint?"

If something was a mess, he said, "It was all balled up."

After graduating from Butte High on May 27, 1952, Ted enrolled in the Montana School of Mines. Butte is over a mile high in the Rockies. Uptown Butte is on the side of the mountain going up from the Flat. The School of Mines is farther up the mountain from that. It's a steep climb to drive or walk up there. Butte had some of the worst weather in Montana. The roads were covered with snow much of the time. Somebody came up with the idea to put a traffic light on Park Street at the bottom of the hill below the school. Before the light was installed, drivers could get a running start to make it up the hill. Now they couldn't. As for going down the hill, cars slipped and slid down the hill in an effort to stop at the red light. One of Ted's friends, Johnny Richards, was a brilliant mining engineering student at the School of Mines. He didn't like the light being there, so he took his 22 and shot it. Very proud of what he'd done, he drove Ted and other friends over there in his dad's car. He parked right under the light, right in the middle of the intersection. They all piled out of the car and stood there staring up at the shot-out light. It was winter. Snow everywhere. Then came a car slipping and sliding down the snowy hill, trying to stop, trying to stop, couldn't stop, and BOOM, slammed right into Johnny's dad's new car.

Johnny's dad had been gassed in the First World War and had a constant tremor because of it and couldn't work. Johnny's sisters worked and gave the money to their mother. Johnny went on to become

Ted Leskovar, high school graduation portrait, 1952.
Zubick, photographer

a successful mining engineer. The School of Mines was very difficult; most of the students studied engineering or metallurgy.

"If the football team had a winning season, they fired the coach," Ted said. The focus was supposed to be on academics.

"Guys from the School of Mines worked in the mines on the weekends. They'd take dynamite and go up to Helena and blow up the C on the side of the hill [the C for Carroll College]. Rumor was one year the Carroll guys were going to blow up the Big M in Butte [M on the mountain above the school]. But those Carroll guys didn't know how to use dynamite, which the Butte guys did, but not all of them did. One year a School of Mines guy brought the dynamite into the dorm. 'What's that stuff leaking out?' he wanted to know. 'It's the nitroglycerin.'

"I think Butte, for a rough town, it had more character and more class. When we went uptown, we dressed up, coat, suit and tie. One night, Brutich [not his real name] squares off against the biggest guy in the joint, gets in a fight, blood everywhere, all from the other guy, and when it's over, Brutich says, 'You have to come home with me, you have to help me explain this to my mother.' We didn't want to, but we did. His mother bawled us out, 'If you're out after two o'clock in the morning you're looking for trouble!'

"It was said in McQueen [also a Bohunk neighborhood], if a kid got in a fight and lost, his father would slap him around for losing."

Another time, Ted and his buddies were at the It Club. Brutich swaggered up to a group of women. He stretched out his arm to lean against the coat rack and missed and fell down on the floor. He got up and saw some nasty-looking fellow staring at him and squared off against the guy, ready to take a swing at him, until he realized it was himself in the mirror on one of the pillars on the dance floor.

At the Arrow Club below the Rialto Theater, Ted was holding a bunch of coats while his friends danced and for no reason some guy hauled off and punched him. Pinky (Pete Marinovich) hit the guy who hit Ted. Other guys picked a fight with Pinky and threw him into the jukebox. His head went right through the cover. He could see the records going round and round.

Another time, as Ted walked down the stairs, he saw Brutich coming up the stairs dragging some guy and punching everyone he passed. "If you looked at him cross ways, he was gunning for a fight," Ted said.

Then there was the Stockman Bar and Dirty Mouth Jean. She could have been called Scary Dirty Mouth Jean. Jean Sorenson. She was notorious and scary. Ted and a friend were at the Stockman one day, and Ted's friend had the hiccups. Dirty Mouth Jean walked over and demanded, "Where's my #$%@ purse?!" This scared the two of them half to death. The hiccups stopped. "Cured your hiccups," she said and walked away.

She was arrested for murder for shooting a man in her house who was wearing nothing but underwear and wielding a knife. The jury decided it was self-defense. Later she went to prison for shooting and killing a man in her bar. She was sentenced to twenty-four years and was paroled after serving four.

"It seemed in East Butte, when the old man was old enough to collect social security, he died," Ted said. East Butte was becoming a neighborhood of widows. It wasn't only due to working in the mines. Two neighbors beat another neighbor to death. He was the father of one of Ted's friends. Nothing happened to them. I don't know why they did it. They said they danced on his grave.

When Bluebird died, Annie Bluebird came over to tell Annie. "Open the door, I can't catch my breath," she said.

Old Lady Cash had been a widow as long as Ted could remember. Back when he was a little boy fetching beer for her, she was already a widow. When she died, her daughter came over to tell Annie. Annie said, "Almost first of the year, somebody has to kick the bucket." The daughter ran out of the house crying.

"Ma had a network better than the FBI. She knew what I was doing before I did. I wouldn't say much, but she'd know. Where's Teddy? She'd say, 'I know where Teddy is at, he's at the bar.'"

"The East Butte guys were pretty close with a buck," Ted said. "Brutich made a hundred dollars a week. He lived at home and saved eighty from that hundred. He allowed himself twenty dollars spending money, and he saved out of that."

When Ted and Stevie went to Las Vegas, Stevie winced as he watched Ted put coins in a slot machine. A frugal, hardworking bunch they were, the guys Ted hung out with in East Butte.

Stevie and Chuck always paid cash for a car. Chuck took meticulous care of everything. Slovenian to the core, he was. Ted said, "If he had a bicycle, it was like new. When he had a new car, he'd park several blocks away to avoid a dent."

It was a Butte tradition to go out into the forest and cut down a Christmas tree. The idea was to cut down a tall tree, and then cut off the top six feet or so that would fit in the house. Ted and his fellow grown-up Owls took turns sawing and sawing. They sawed halfway through the trunk and pushed on it, but it wouldn't tip over. They took turns sawing and sawing. The tree still wouldn't tip over. They sawed all the way through the trunk and the tree still stood. They pushed it off and it fell off and stood upright next to the stump.

During good weather, Ted and his buddies went fishing in creeks outside of Butte. They smoked cigars to keep the mosquitos at bay.

Ted went to get a haircut. After the barber cut his hair, the barber looked at Ted and cracked up laughing. The barber had been celebrating the opening of a new shopping center. He was drunk.

"WHAT DID YOUR PARENTS SAY when you decided to go to college?"

"They said it was a good idea," Ted said. "Pops wanted me to stay in Butte. The trouble was when I was going to school there [at the School of Mines, living at home with his parents], Stevie or somebody was always coming around, I was going out all the time. I go to Missoula, everybody was staying home studying. So I went to the business school and I said, what is the toughest course in the business school. Accounting. I said, I'll start there and work my way down, I guess."

Ted enrolled in the University of Montana in Missoula. At first, he lived in the dorm. His roommate was a big guy, an athlete from Butte. We'll call him Big Athlete.

Ted: "What classes are you taking?"

Big Athlete: "Coaching baseball, coaching football, coaching basketball…"

Ted noticed that Big Athlete received letters frequently.

Ted: "Who are the letters from?"

Big Athlete: "My girlfriend."

Ted: "Is she in Butte?"

Big Athlete: "No, Deer Lodge."

Ted: "When is she coming to visit?"

Blank stare.

Ted: "How did you meet her?"

Blank stare.

He hadn't met her. He hadn't met her because she didn't exist. Ted soon found out that another guy in the dorm was writing letters to Big Athlete; he'd send the letters to his sister in Deer Lodge, and she would re-write them and mail them to Big Athlete.

Later Ted moved out of the dorm and rented a room in the basement at 610 Eddy.

He went home every weekend and did the books for Tony's paint shop. In the summer, he worked there full time, painting cars and doing the books.

"I remember standing out in front at Snookie's and seeing one shovel up there, picking away at the hill," Ted said. That was in 1954, the beginning of the Berkeley Pit, open-pit mining, which marked the beginning of the end of underground hard-rock mining in Butte.

While attending the University of Montana, Ted started smoking a pipe. It was the Joe College thing to do. Tony saw Ted with the pipe and cracked up laughing. That was the end of smoking a pipe.

One day while driving uptown, Tony accidentally bumped into the sheriff's car. The sheriff jumped out and asked, "Are you alright, Tony?"

EDDY AND LOUISE AND THE CHILDREN came to visit every few years. Butte's mineral-rich water upset the children's tummies, very different from Seattle water. Annie had a home cure for that too. She boiled water, dropped in a chicken bouillon cube, dissolved it, poured in a beaten egg, stirred it, and gave that to them. It did the trick. That was one of her not-scary cures.

THE BUTTE PAPER of May 22, 1955, reported on a performance by the Butte Civic Orchestra, Anton Leskovar conducting. Among the selections were the "Chit Chat Polka" by Johann Strauss, a waltz by Richard Strauss, and a piece by Schubert.

East Butte and the Berkeley Pit, 1956.
BUTTE-SILVER BOW PUBLIC ARCHIVES 11_213_03, SMITHERS, PHOTOGRAPHER

Mary Lozar Pellitier and her husband, George, in Francie and Ray's backyard, San Francisco.

On November 30, 1955, Anton Leskovar conducted the Butte Civic Orchestra at the Bow Theater. They performed the *Surprise Symphony* by Hayden, an orchestral version of the "Polonaise Militaire" by Chopin, the waltz from *Sleeping Beauty* by Tchaikovsky, the overture from *Rosamunde* by Schubert, and other pieces.

IN THE VACUUM created by the chaos of the Second World War, Yugoslavia became a communist country, though not aligned with the Soviet Union. In the communists versus fascists part of that horrible war, the communists won, and the lives of Eastern Europeans went from horrible to more horrible.

Annie and Tony sent money to Tony's niece in the Old Country, now communist Yugoslavia. His sister Terezija died May 7, 1956. She had still been plowing the fields into her eighties on the farm at Stogovci 8 near Ptujska gora.

Two months later, Annie's sister Mary died of cancer. She was sixty-one. She died on Annie's birthday, July 2, as had their father, Joe Lozar.

Effort to send supplies to impoverished families back in Yugoslavia.
Annie is in the second row, far right. Tony is in the middle of that row.
Butte-Silver Bow Public Archives PH316-005 No. 3. Zubick, photographer

40

❦

THE ROAD TO 39 EAST GALENA

"PAY THE BILLS FIRST," Tony told Ted. "Work for yourself, and you always have a job."

Tony taught Ted and Joe how to paint cars. He taught them to paint feather edge. Tony was meticulous. You didn't touch anything twice. You did it right the first time.

After Ted and Joe washed a car, Tony examined the windows right to the edges to be sure there were no streaks. To Tony, any job you did, you did to the best of your ability. It makes me think of the stonemason who put as much care into carving the gargoyles destined to sit high atop the cathedral as he did the statues destined to be placed at eye level. He carved for the eye of God. Tony instilled that work ethic in his sons. He told Ted, back home when they hired someone to work on the farm, "We work the hardest to set the pace." He taught Ted and Joe to be the pacesetters for the employees. For a time, there was only one place in town anyone dared have a luxury car painted, and that was Tony Leskovar's.

After painting a car, they saved all the paper they had used to mask the windows to reuse on the next car. They never threw out anything that could be reused. When there was a little bit of paint left over, not enough for a car, they mixed it with other little bits of paint and painted a used car with it. One day a woman came in with a purple purse and said she wanted her car painted to match her purse. They mixed paint to create the color. She was delighted.

"We did two completes a day," Ted said. Each cost thirty-five dollars. Tony paid Joe and Ted each one hundred dollars a week. They worked from nine in the morning to four thirty in the afternoon, Monday through Friday. Those were the hours dictated by the painters' union.

343

At lunchtime, Ted would run out and buy hamburgers at Greasy Gus' and bring them back—four hamburgers, two for him and two for Joe. Tony dined at a restaurant up the street. After a big lunch, he was sleepy.

"Pops would be taking a nap in one of the cars," Ted said. "Somebody would come in looking for him, and we'd find him sleeping, and we wouldn't bother him."

Back around 1949 or 1950, Ted Wellman, the Dodge dealer, told Tony that he could use the upstairs of his building at 39 East Galena to start a paint shop. He could have it rent free for the first six months. Of course, Tony took the offer. The Dodge dealership was on the ground floor. Wellman owned the building. This was uptown, near The Line (the Red Light District). There were cribs up the block across the street.

The paint shop was on the second floor. Ted or Joe or Tony would drive the car up the ramp and make a sharp turn at the top. They had to be skillful drivers not to scrape the cars.

Wellman operated his body shop on the second floor, so to be precise, Tony leased all of the second floor except the body shop. In 1955, Tony

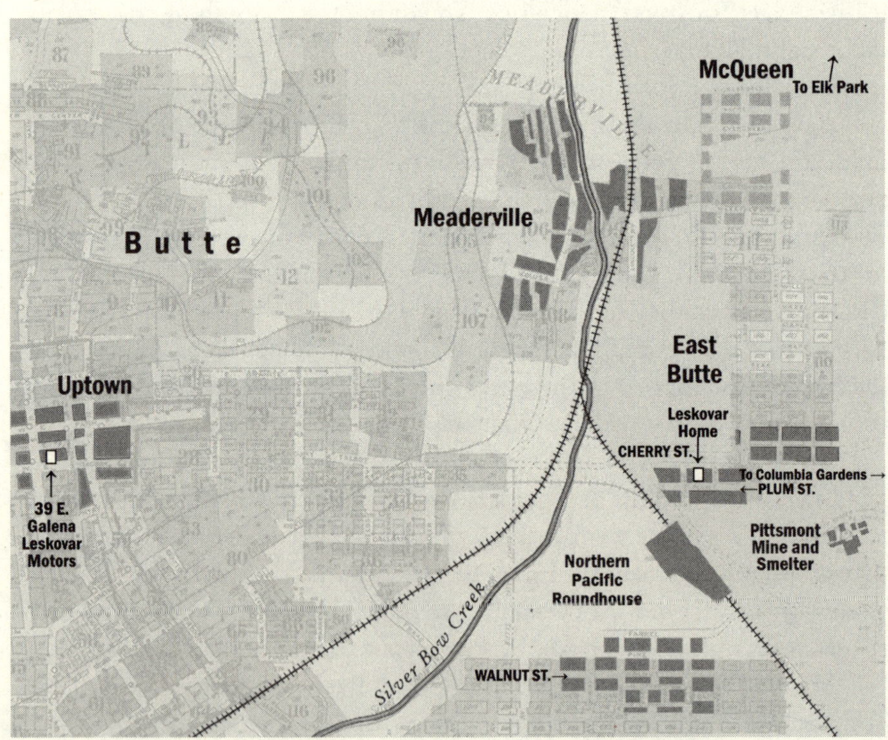

Partial map of Butte, Montana, and East Butte.
Derived from Sanborn map with additional details added.

signed a three-year lease with Wellman for the upstairs paint shop for $175 a month. When Wellman quit the body shop business, the Leskovars took that over. Now they operated a paint and body shop.

They had a contract with the post office to do body work. They'd repair the vehicle by the next day. They also had a contract to pull out mail trucks that were stuck in the snow.

"How did you do it?"

"We had a pickup," Ted said. "We hooked up a chain and took a run at it. Just a two-wheel-drive pickup."

Around 1956, Babe left Wilson's to work for Tony. Tony and Babe had a difficult father-son relationship, and it didn't improve by working together. Ted and Joe had different temperaments; they were able to roll with Tony's capricious ways. Music would always come first for Tony. He was first and foremost a musician. Gifted artists can be difficult. Tony was gifted and difficult. Ted and Joe understood that. And he was their father. When there was any slack from any direction, Ted and Joe picked it up. They took to heart the work ethic Tony instilled in them. They worked as owners, not as employees.

Letter from Annie to son Eddy and daughter-in-law Louise in Seattle:

> Butte Mont
> Jan 8 — 1957
>
> Dear Louise & Ed,
>
> Will write a quick letter, as I don't know what to write about — rushing to the shop. Making out the estimates or rather copy them, to be taken to the insurance co.
>
> Jobs are coming in fast and Joe does most of the painting it is impossible to get a good painter and also - being sober — have now 3 body men working on wrecked car. Tony is planning taking the down[stairs] also. I guess the rent will be about $500.00 and speaking of Tony he is all right. I guess the mean was coming out of him. Babe & Joe would like to see Tony away from the shop he is too darn bossy.
>
> But still he can help. What gets me, he sure rushes the paint job, and Joe has to keep on spraying. If Joe gets sick, I do wonder some times whose is going to do the work. Since Joe has been or is doing the painting we get lot of compliments also we do have lot of competition.
>
> The weather during xmas and New Years was surprisingly warm as you would call it banana weather. Now it is getting colder & very cold.
>
> Louise, how long did you have to stay in the hospital — hoping everything will come to a happy day.

I do want to thank Carol & Mary Lou for their nice note. I presume Johnny is studying hard in Hi school. How is he making out in the music or in the band.

At Xmas we had turkey dinner at Babe's — Helen's mother & family called from Chicago while we were having our dinner it was at 6pm Butte time. We all had tears in our eyes and it did kind of spoiled our dinner, for me it was good or I would have kept on for a third helping.

New Year's day had dinner at Joe's. Baked Ham this time believe me I had gained quite a bit.

Sunday Ted went back to school — he was disappointed of his report card. He got C's & C+. He did expect to get B's in his accounting. — it means he will have to study harder. He moved out of the Craig Hall and moved to a private home. They have rooms for students and if you want to write to him his address 610 Eddy St.

This is all for now. Will get ready & go up the shop.

So Happy New Year to you all.

Ann

TED DID STUDY HARDER AND BUMPED UP those accounting grades to A's. In 1957, the Army notified Ted that he was going to be drafted. He'd rather be a pilot, so he applied for the Air Force. Though he had perfect vision, he couldn't pass the vision test. His eyes had become muscle bound from studying. The doctor told him he needed to look away periodically when reading to allow his eyes to adjust. Even so, the doctor wouldn't clear him for flight school.

Ted opted for the Army Reserves. He put college on hold and off he went to Fort Ord, California, for basic training. He was part of a test group that did all physical training double time. He learned to be a marksman and trained for the Signal Corps, climbing up telephone poles to string phone lines.

TONY'S LANDLORD, WELLMAN, MOVED the Dodge dealership to Montana Street. That left the ground floor showroom and parts and service departments at 39 East Galena empty. Tony was afraid Wellman would sell the building out from under him, and he'd have to relocate, so he rented the whole place even though he didn't need it. It was a stretch to afford it. This was the summer of '57.

Wellman asked Joe if they would be willing to buy the building for twenty-five thousand dollars.

Wellman: "The payments would be twenty-five hundred a month."

Joe: "Can't afford it."

Private Ted Leskovar, Fort Ord, California, 1957.

Wellman: "How about fifteen hundred a month."
Joe: "Can't afford it."
Wellman: "One thousand."
Joe: "Can't afford it."
Wellman: "Two-fifty."
Joe: "We can do that." An attorney wrote it up. It was less than what they'd been paying in rent.

Soon after, a man from the Ford Motor Company came to town and offered the Edsel franchise to Wellman. He declined. "Talk to Leskovars," he said. "They have an empty showroom."

Tony had no money with which to buy the franchise. The Edsel people went to Metals Bank and looked at the financial statement. Joe and Ted and Babe put everything they could into Tony's assets to bump up the balance sheet. They had no working capital.

Letter from Annie, not dated:

Sunday
Dear Louise & Ed & all,
Am using Ted's writing material—I should have written before but have been very busy. Monday the fellows from Ford Co from Spokane & Seattle came in and I had to rush with the financial report for the bank and for the Ford Co. in Dearborn Mich.

The truth of all this deal we didn't care if we got it we were not going to be enthusiastic about the deal or about the metals bank giving the money for the floor plan (the floor plan is money for the cars to be sold of which will be about six cars).

So what happens — Bank approves the loan for 6 cars—about $2500.00 and a loan of $5000.00 extra working capital — gosh. I didn't know what to say. I guess it made Tony happy to think he has credit with the bank. They have asked Tony if he wanted $50,000.00. Tony said No — the smaller is the loan — the quicker it would be paid. The business & painting and body shop has slackened down a little — July the production of Building the Edsel cars and will be delivered to the Dealers in August. Now Tony is waiting to hear from the Ford Co. in Dearborn if he gets the Dealership! — Glad to hear the little Darling Ronald is doing fine. You didn't mention about his cold. Did he get over it?

You know, we have enjoyed ourselves very much with you all. Am sure Steve & Zelda did also. Also with your folks. It was really enjoying — two or three or four grandma & grandpas got together and Tony had some one to talk to and I hope next year if everything goes well that all meet together. Your Mother & Dad & us & Steve & Zelda.

Nothing much of news. It is all quiet on the Western Front — excepting the blasting that shakes the house from the open pit. It is raining the weather has been cold since we came home.

About molds [for ceramics] — they came in good shape. Have been very busy lately no time for ceramics.

If Tony gets the dealership the whole shop must be cleaned up & painted. Joe was saying something about visiting you people. So I don't know what his plans are. He doesn't know himself what he is going to do. I think he should stay home & finish up the house and move in. I guess this all for now.
Best regards to all
Ann

About Johnny [Eddy and Louise's eldest son] coming over here to work in the shop. What do you think about it. Do you think he is too young yet?
Will close now. Best regards to all.
Ann

39 East Galena, Butte, Montana, around 1957.

*Tony and Joe in front of the shop at 39 East Galena,
Butte, Montana, around 1957.*

"I'M PLEASED TO HAVE THE OPPORTUNITY of selling the most remarkable car in the country today — the Edsel," Tony said in an ad in the *Montana Standard*. "There never has been a car like the Edsel." Prices started as low as $2,642.50 for the two-door Ranger sedan.

The business was now called Leskovar Motors Sales & Service. They continued to operate the paint and body shop. Old habits are hard to break and some don't need to be broken. We would always refer to it as "the shop," since it began as a paint shop.

In the fall of 1957, Tony traveled to Helena to perform with the symphony orchestra. Now he's up in Helena again, and again, and again. Whenever the conductor needed a bassoonist, he hired Tony. Tony was a dedicated, disciplined, conscientious musician. He never passed up a gig. Until the day he died, he never stopped practicing; the consummate professional, he. Even when Tony and Annie visited Eddy and Louise and the children in Seattle, Tony brought his bassoon and practiced in the basement.

Ted returned from basic training at the end of December 1957. He lived at home with his parents and resumed doing the books at the shop. They were a mess. It would take some time for him to get them in shape. Finishing college would have to wait.

In July of 1958, Leskovars won the Edsel sales contest. The prize was an all-expense-paid trip for Tony and Annie to San Francisco. They sold more Edsels than any other dealer in Washington, Oregon, Idaho, and Montana. Tony never sold cars himself. He left the running of the shop and the tasks of selling cars and painting cars in the able hands of his sons. Annie worked in the office. When a customer came into the showroom, she rang a bell that rang upstairs where Ted and Joe were painting a car; one of them would take off his coveralls, underneath of which he wore slacks, a dress shirt, and tie, and he'd hurry down to wait on the customer.

41

∽

Hot Beer and Cold Women No More

Ted used to say hot beer and cold women were the story of his life . . . and then he met Patricia Thompson.

When there was talk of Butte annexing East Butte, Annie was dead set against it. "I don't want those Micks coming around here," she said.

When her nephew was headed uptown for a game, she warned him, "Watch out for those Micks!"

Annie and Tony wanted their sons to marry Slovenian girls. "That's the way it was supposed to be," Ted said. They were the offspring of Slovenian peasants, and they wanted their sons to marry within the tribe.

The first did. The second did. The third did not. When the fourth son, Ted, told his parents that he was going to marry Patricia Thompson and brought her over to meet them, they learned that not only was she not Slovenian, she was half Irish. But she was a schoolteacher. That was her saving grace. That made her acceptable in the eyes of Annie, more than acceptable—superb. Being a schoolteacher was the ultimate. It more than wiped away any shortcoming such as not being Slovenian, and even worse, being part Irish.

Back when the University of Vienna was founded in 1365, twenty percent of the students were Slovenian. The next year that number doubled, this out of a tiny Slovenian population. In time, many department heads and deans were Slovenians. It seems respect for education is also in the Slovenian DNA.

"That was the only thing that overcame that Irish stigma," Ted said, "being a schoolteacher."

Ted asked his parents to watch their language around Pat.

351

Tony and Annie were not unusual in wanting their children to marry within the tribe. This was common among immigrants, the understanding, whether consciously or subconsciously, that marriage is fraught with challenges, and the more the couple have in common, the easier it is to weather the storms of life. My other grandmother, Grandma T, advised her children, "Marry someone from your own religion and culture."

Though Annie and Tony did not attend Mass, being Catholic was part of their culture, and they raised their children in that culture. They wanted to retain that culture.

Pat Thompson was Catholic.

Those of you who read my first book, *One Night in a Bad Inn*, know all about Pat's (Patsy Ann's) notorious grandmother, Sarah Hughes. Sarah's bawdy boardinghouse was on Parrot Flat. Friends of Annie and Tony lived on Parrot Flat. Annie and Tony visited them often.

"I'm quite sure Ma knew the whole history of the Hugheses," Ted said. "There wasn't much going on that Ma didn't know about. They all gossiped. Ma and Pops had friends there on Parrot Flat. Govednick's father was over there, and he was a clarinet player, and they'd go over there, and they'd play together. They all gossiped. I'm sure she knew. Ma was second only to the FBI for information gathering. I'm quite sure she knew all about the Hugheses."

If Annie knew about Pat's notorious grandmother, she didn't say anything. Pat was a schoolteacher. That more than made up for any deficiency, including having grandparents who did time.

As for how Ted and Pat met, Pat was teaching at the junior high with Don Orlich and his wife, Patty. The Orliches organized a ski trip and invited Pat and several other teachers. Don invited two of his East Butte Owl buddies, Teddy and Stevie. Ted was just back from basic training at Fort Ord.

Don: "Do you want to come to West Yellowstone with us to go skiing?"
Ted: "I don't ski."
Don: "You can sit in the bar and drink."
Ted: "I can do that."
They all met in the Orlich's kitchen for the drive to West Yellowstone.

Pat's friend Rita Thomas came along too. She always brought a thermos of warm red wine. Her family was Lebanese.

"All the girls liked Ted," Pat said.
On Sunday, Pat told Ted she was going to Mass. He came along.

Back in Butte, one of the teachers who went skiing with them, a lady named Sarah, was in the hospital. Pat went to see her. While she and Sarah were visiting, in walked Ted. As they left, Ted asked Pat if she'd like to see a movie. She said yes.

Ted called to ask Pat out again, but she already had a date. This happened several times. He said, "I guess you just want someone to take you skiing." The next time she said yes and canceled her other plans. She stopped accepting dates from other men. She went out only with Ted. "I knew he was special," she said.

Pat grew up hearing the term Bohunk used as a derogatory slur. Now she was dating a fellow who called himself one.

They'd only been dating a couple months when Ted asked her, "What do you think about marriage?"

They met in January and married in September.

In marrying Pat, Ted rescued her from the troublesome students she was trying to teach at the junior high. Most of the students were well behaved. The few chronic misbehavers happened to be from the East Side.

As you know, Ted was from east of the East Side.

Patricia Ann Thompson was born in Helena, Montana, during the Great Depression. She was the fourth child born to Peter and Aila (A-*I*-la) Thompson. She was named Patricia after her aunt Patsy and called Patsy Ann. She actually did begin life in a log cabin, a dreary decrepit one. Her mother was pregnant when they lived there. She was a toddler when they moved back to Butte. She grew up on Walnut Street, which is in the area of Butte called The Flat.

She was four years old when her father, Peter Thompson, died.

When she asked about Santa Claus, her mother, Aila Thompson, said, "It's the spirit of love, dear." That tells you volumes about the woman who raised Patsy Ann.

After she turned six, Patsy Ann attended St. Ann's School, which was run by the Sisters of Charity of the Blessed Virgin Mary. In her class pictures, the parish priest is in the picture with the children, but not the nuns. Back then, some nuns would not be photographed, didn't go to parties, and didn't go out to dinner, not even to a parishioner's home.

There was a barn in their backyard. They didn't have livestock, so it was empty. Patsy Ann and the neighborhood children would drag discarded

Christmas trees over to the barn and pile them up. Then they'd climb up the ladder to the hayloft and jump out onto the pile of Christmas trees. I imagine excessive giggling every time one of them landed. They were so bundled up against the bitter cold—which could be forty below—that there was no worry of being scratched by pine needles.

Every summer, from all that playing outside in mile-high Butte, Patsy Ann got so sunburned that her mother had to call the doctor. He came to the house.

One day Patsy Ann asked her brother, Sammy, to turn on the radio. It was already on. Her mother sent her to an ear, nose, and throat doctor. By this time her mother was a widow and worked full time, so she sent Patsy Ann to the doctor by herself. She was eleven years old. The doctor put her on a board, reclined it back, and poured saline solution down her nose. It didn't work. He did this several times over several visits but she still couldn't hear. He discovered an abscess in her ear. He lanced it—no anesthesia. Her entire body jumped off the table in pain. But it worked. She could hear again.

A special treat for Patsy Ann and Sammy was to take the bus uptown, see a movie at the Park Theater, and then go to Greasy Gus' for hamburgers. A hamburger cost a nickel. Little hamburgers.

After St. Ann's, she attended Girls Central High School. It was run by a different order of Catholic nuns, the Sisters of Charity of Leavenworth, the same nuns who ran St. James Hospital.

At Girls Central she started calling herself Pat and studied Latin, history, algebra, biology, chemistry, physics, and religion. The nun who taught advanced algebra was transferred, so she wasn't able to take it. She excelled in everything, especially chemistry, for which she earned an A+ on her report card.

Her first job was cleaning a beauty shop on Saturdays and answering the phone. The owner was a friend of her mother's. The beauty shop was closed on Saturdays. With not much to do, she was bored. She asked her mother if it was okay to quit. She said yes.

When Pat was fifteen, she worked part time at the Park Theater. She sold tickets, and snacks at the concession stand, and she worked as an usherette, which meant she got to wear a snazzy uniform. People didn't know what time the movies started. Movies played continuously with no times posted. People went to the movie, if it was in the middle, they watched it again until the part they'd already seen, turn to each other, and say, "This is where we came in," and leave. There were always two movies, a double feature, and newsreels. People didn't have televisions. There were no television stations in Montana. (The first was KXLF in 1953.)

Since the movies played continuously, the theater was always dark. Pat's job as an usherette was to lead moviegoers to seats with her flashlight. She stood at the back until someone came in. She saw all the movies many times.

New movies were shown at the Rialto for three days and then left town. The movie reels were kept in big canisters and were taken to the next town by train. A year or so later, maybe two years, the movie came back, this time to the American Theater, stayed three days, and left town. A few years after that, the movie came back again, this time to the Park Theater. Movies shown at the Park were considered old movies. That's where Pat worked. At each successive theater, the price of admission was lower.

For this job, Pat had to join the Women's Protective Union. Attendance at union meetings was mandatory, even though it meant she had to skip class.

She worked as hostess at the restaurant in the Finlen Hotel. One day she started clearing tables, and a co-worker told her to stop. If the union inspector came in, she would be fined.

Her senior year of high school, Pat worked in the lab at St. James Hospital. She cleaned the needles. This was before everything was disposable. She had to run a wire through each needle then put them in the autoclave. A pathologist owned and ran the lab. He was a PhD, not a medical doctor. Pat quit when she became too busy being a senior in high school. Academics came easily to Pat, but she was involved in many extracurricular activities. She went to Girls State. She was elected class president. The summer after she graduated, Sister Seraphine found her a job working in the pharmacy at St. James Hospital. A little old nun was the pharmacist. She made salves in a huge vat. One of Pat's tasks was to stir the salve with a huge paddle.

When her co-workers in the lab saw her in the pharmacy, they asked why she didn't come back to work in the lab. She didn't think to ask. She didn't think they'd want her back since she quit.

One of the nuns at Girls Central insisted that all the seniors write essays for the American Legion essay contest. Pat's essay was an open letter to Stalin. She won statewide. The scholarship was enough money for more than a year's tuition of college.

"What did your mother say when you said you wanted to go to college?"

"She wanted me to go to college always," Pat said.

Off she went, far away from Butte, to Seattle University. It was a

Catholic school run by Jesuit priests. It began as an all men school but had been coed for quite a while. Pat lived in a residence hall for women students on Harvard Avenue, a few blocks from campus. She worked her way through college, as she had high school. She worked on a pie line, yes, like on *I Love Lucy*. She picked up each pie from a moving belt and put it in a small bag and then in a box. The first thing her house-mates asked when she walked in the door after work was, "Did you bring us anything to eat?" meaning what damaged dessert did you get to take home? Pat's house-mates loved her having that job.

At the end of her freshman year, her younger sister Mary got married. Pat decided to return to Montana. She enrolled at Carroll College in Helena, which is also a Catholic school, run by the Diocese of Helena. She told the president of the college, Father Kavanagh, that she would need to work to be able to afford the tuition. Father Kavanagh said, "We'll find you a job." He decided she could work for him as his secretary.

Pat was one of only seven women students besides those enrolled in the nursing program. She lived in Siena House, a residence hall run by Dominican nuns for young working women. It was in a beautiful mansion a short walk from campus.

She took the bus back to Butte every weekend. One time she decided to fly. She'd never been on an airplane and wanted to know what it was like.

In addition to taking a full load of demanding classes, she worked long hours for Father Kavanagh. She was burning the candle at both ends. One day she heard about a blood drive and went to give blood, which she had done before, but this time the man looked at her quizzically and said, "You need to see your doctor." She had become very anemic. She ended up spending so much money on doctor visits that she ran out of money for tuition. She dropped out of school. Her mother was so disappointed. She would have found a way to give Pat the money to continue school, but Pat didn't ask.

Pat returned to Butte and lived with her mother. She found a job with the Texas Oil Company working as the assistant mail room manager. The head of the mail room missed a lot of work, so Pat ended up running it. She was doing two jobs while being paid for one. She didn't hesitate when another opportunity came along.

She read in the newspaper about a new airline and wrote to them and said, "I'd like to work for you." They hired her. She gave her two-weeks notice at the Texas Oil Company, and the airline waited for her.

Pat's mother worried that she wouldn't go back and finish college.

The man who started Treasure State Airline saw an opportunity to ferry oil company employees to the oil fields in eastern Montana and North Dakota. The airline hired Pat to be the stewardess. She rented a room in Billings in a house across from St. Vincent's Hospital. They flew from Billings to Glendive to Sidney to Bismark to Sidney to Glendive to Billings. On a flight out of Glendive, the pilot had to make an emergency landing. The plane bumped along on uneven pasture until it came to a stop nose down/tail up in the middle of a farm. One of the passengers jumped out and ran away from the plane. Pat and the rest of the passengers climbed out through the cockpit window. No one was hurt, but that was the end of the airline and Pat's job.

Pat decided to stay in Billings and found a job as a dance instructor for Arthur Murray. She went through the training period, which consisted of a few hours of dance lessons every evening, and then they went out dancing to practice what they had learned, four of them, two women and two men. Halfway through the training she learned she would have to sign a contract and find her own students. That wouldn't do. She was new to Billings and didn't know many people. She needed a job with regular pay.

When she had saved enough money, she resumed her studies at Carroll College and graduated with a degree in social sciences (economics, political science, and history) and a minor in philosophy.

She wanted to be an FBI agent, but they didn't hire women as agents.

She found a job teaching high school in Lima, Montana, a ranching town a couple hours south of Butte. Some of the children rode forty miles on the bus to get to school. The superintendent of schools arranged for Pat to rent a room from a woman who was diabetic. The woman wanted Pat to give her insulin shots. Pat couldn't bring herself to do that. The superintendent then arranged for Pat to live with the head of the school board's family, Ralph and Thelma Stosich and their young children. That worked out splendidly. She would remain close to them for the rest of their lives.

One day a highway patrolman stopped Thelma and said, "I clocked you doing a hundred."

"A hundred?" she said. "I go faster than that backwards."

Once a week, other families invited Pat over for dinner after she taught catechism to the Catholic children and trained the altar boys.

It was a very small high school, so she taught many courses. When she taught Shakespeare, Pat had the students read the parts aloud, and then she

Pat Thompson's graduation from Carroll College, 1955.

led a discussion about what it meant. The students loved it. She taught the U.S. Constitution in depth. She didn't just have them read it; she explained what it meant. She taught French.

This was the first time Pat had ever been in a public school. She wasn't that much older than the students, and she was very pretty. She couldn't understand why some of the students were so mean. One of the other teachers explained why: the boys had crushes on her, so they acted up; the girls were jealous, so they acted up.

A student told her she was the best teacher she ever had.

Pat went home to Butte on the bus every weekend and returned on the train. Every Sunday she cried the whole way back to Lima. The porter on the train would ask, "What's wrong?" She cried and cried.

When the school year ended in the spring, she spent the summer in Yellowstone Park working as a "savage" at the soda fountain. That was the summer of 1956.

She decided to stick it out in Lima for another year, thinking having two years experience would help her find a teaching job in Butte.

Her perseverance paid off. She was hired to teach at the new junior high school in Butte. But before she started that job, she embarked on a grand adventure.

Pat's father died when she was four years old. To say that Pat's mother had a hardscrabble life is to put it lightly—widowed during the Great Depression with five children to support and an alcoholic mother to look after. Pat never wanted for anything growing up, but she grew up in humble circumstances. For a young woman at that time who grew up on Walnut Street in Butte, Montana, to decide to embark on a grand tour of Europe was remarkable. And that is what Pat decided to do.

Travel to Europe was not as common in the 1950s as it is today. She saved enough money; she could afford it, so she thought. At the last minute, she realized she was one hundred dollars short. A friend loaned her the money.

In June of 1957, Pat and her friend Joan boarded the train in Butte, their destination—Quebec City.

They originally booked a six-week tour of Europe with American Express. Not enough people signed up for the tour, so it was cancelled. The travel agent said he could book the same trip for them through American Express with all the same stops. Their first stop was supposed to be Quebec City. A man from American Express met them at the depot in Montreal and told them apologetically that the train didn't go to Quebec City that day, but not to worry, he booked them rooms at the YWCA and would give them a tour of Montreal, an added bonus. The next day they took the train to Quebec City, and after several days touring that charming city and visiting St. Anne de Beaupres, they boarded an ocean liner that took them through the St. Lawrence Seaway and across the Atlantic Ocean.

It was a very old ship with very few passengers. Pat and Joan traveled second class. The cruise director was the only one staying in a first-class cabin. The crew treated everyone as if they were first-class passengers. The journey took thirteen days. They had a wonderful time on the ship.

The ship docked at Liverpool. Though it wasn't part of the original tour, Pat wanted to visit her grandfather and aunts and uncles and cousins in Belfast, Northern Ireland, so that was their first destination. Then on to Dublin, then London, then across the Channel to the continent to visit Paris, Rome, Florence, San Remo and the Italian Riviera, Nice and the French Riviera, Lourdes, a bullfight in Madrid, Fatima, and Lisbon. While in Rome, Pat felt someone tap on her shoulder. She turned around and there was Jack Sladich, one of her friends from Carroll College. He was studying to be a priest and was in Rome on vacation.

As they took in the sights across Europe, every once in a while they'd run into someone they'd met on the ship. It was like seeing an old friend.

While in Paris, Pat and Joan went on a nightclub tour. When they returned to their hotel, it was gone. It makes me think of the movie *So Long at the Fair* in which a man and his hotel room vanish. But for Pat and Joan, it was the entire hotel. When the door was closed for the night, it became a wall. The porter heard their frantic voices outside and opened the door in the wall to let them in.

At each city, a representative from American Express met them at the train or ship and took them to their hotel and arranged tours for them.

After six weeks, their last stop was Lisbon. There they boarded another ocean liner, this one the newest in the fleet, and sailed to New York. This voyage took only six days. As they entered the harbor and saw the Statue of Liberty for the first time, Pat and Joan exclaimed in unison, "It's green!"

On the train trip home, they stopped in St. Louis, Cincinnati, and Denver to visit friends. The entire trip took two months.

In September, Pat began teaching at the new junior high school in Butte. Two of her fellow teachers were Don and Patty Orlich, the Don Orlich who was Ted's neighbor and fellow East Butte Owl.

When Ted and Pat decided to get married, they told their parents, and then they went to see Pat's pastor at St. Ann's, Father Plummer. He told them, "Marriage is like jumping off a cliff. Once you go, there's no turning back."

Anyone marrying in the Catholic Church has to go to confession before the wedding. When told this, Ted said, "I better bring my lunch."

Francie told Ted, "I won't come to your wedding if you don't get married in the Church." (Matrimony is a sacrament in the Catholic Church.) They did, they got married at St. Ann's Catholic Church, which was Pat's parish. Francie didn't come anyway, but Ted's grandmother Caroline did. Caroline flew up, all by herself, at a time when air travel was still a luxury, beyond the reach of many people. She was eighty-eight years old, still energetic, still adventurous. The little lady who thought nothing of boarding an ocean liner to go to a new country, thought nothing of boarding an airplane all by herself. She didn't want to miss her youngest grandson's wedding.

In all the wedding excitement, no one thought to introduce Pat to Ted's grandmother Caroline. Pat had to introduce herself.

Ted and Pat met in January and married seven months later on a beautiful Saturday morning in September. Catholic weddings were in the morning because Mass was part of the wedding, and in those days, people had to fast from midnight before receiving communion. Pat's mother, Aila, put on the reception at a hall. She prepared some of the food and had the rest catered.

Don Orlich and the other East Butte Owls kidnapped Ted from the

Pat and her mother,
Aila Thompson, 1958.

*Tony, Ted, Pat, Ted's grandmother Caroline, and Annie in front
of St. Ann's Church, Butte, Montana, 1958.*

Pat, Ted, Annie, Tony at the reception, 1958.

East Butte Owls' tradition of kidnapping the groom. Yes, there was plenty to drink at the reception but the Owls took Ted to a bar. Best man Chuck Flanik, Don Orlich, I don't know who the fellow is drinking the shot, Stevie Casick, next fellow unknown, then Ted, Butte, Montana, 1958.

reception and took him to a bar. There was plenty to drink at the reception, no need to leave. This was a zany East Butte Owl tradition that began when Don married. When they kidnapped Don from his reception, Don's wife, Patty, found out where they had taken him, called the bar, told one of the kidnapper Owls who owned an expensive camera, which he had left at the reception, "I am holding your camera, and if you don't bring Don back right now, I will drop it on the floor!"

Ted and Pat drove off on their honeymoon in an Edsel. They stopped in Las Vegas on their way to the Grand Canyon.

Their marriage fared much better than the Edsel.

*Ted's best man Chuck Flanik, Ted, Don Orlich,
Stevie Casick, I think that might be Pinky Marinovich,
next fellow unknown, Butte, 1958.*

*Don Orlich; best man Chuck Flanik; matron of honor Mary Lowney,
Pat's sister; Pat; Ted; Stevie Casick; 1958.*

42

∽

Madame Paumie
and Lincoln-Mercury

WE NOW GO BACK TO FRANCE, to Paris, long before Tony lived there, to the year 1888. Camille Paumie and his wife, Marie, pack up their belongings and take their two young children off to America, to New York, and soon after, I have no idea why, they go to Butte, Montana, a mining camp growing into a city which they believe is in need of a dying and dry cleaning establishment. It's a bold move. They are the first. Does a town full of rough and tumble copper miners actually need dying and dry cleaning? Apparently, they do. The Paumies do so well that first year that they build an entire block, the Paumie Block, on West Galena. It includes the Paumie Parisian Dye House and a twelve-room hotel.

Parisian Dye House, Butte, Montana.
BUTTE-SILVER BOW PUBLIC ARCHIVES PH148_07

Camille dies in 1899. Marie runs the business successfully. Her daughter Yvonne marries a Frenchman, Charles Lussy. Charles runs the hotel. They have a child they name Charles. He is called Charlie.

Time marches on. Madame Paumie sells the business to her employees. When her grandson, Charlie Lussy grows up, Marie helps him buy the Lincoln-Mercury dealership.

"Some guys out of California had the Lincoln-Mercury dealership in Butte," Ted said. "They were writing lots of bad loans, nonrecourse financing. Lussy bought the corporation, with all the liabilities. A bunch of these loans defaulted, and he lost the business. You never buy the corporation, just the property. There was no Lincoln-Mercury dealership for a while, then Lincoln-Mercury asked Pops if he'd be the dealer, since he had Edsel."

Marie Paumie.

That is how Leskovars came to be the Lincoln-Mercury dealer in Butte, Montana. It was a godsend. Who could have known that the Edsel would be discontinued one year later. Joe and Ted sold every Edsel they bought. Other dealers around the country didn't fare so well. Ford discontinued the short-lived Edsel.

The new name of the business was Leskovar Motors.

This was happening while Ted finished college. Both Ted and Pat worked their way through college. Whereas Pat worked while she was taking classes, Ted did not. When he ran out of money, he quit to save up, and then resumed his studies. Also, his education was interrupted while he did his basic training in the Army Reserves. As a result, he hadn't yet finished college when he and Pat married. After the honeymoon, they moved to Missoula, so Ted could finish his accounting degree at the University of Montana.

They lived in a mobile home they bought in Butte and towed to Missoula. They parked it in a trailer park. It was twenty-five feet long and eight feet wide.

"When I got up, I was already across the room," Pat said.

Pat worked as secretary for the philosophy department at the University of Montana. The department received a grant that required surveys. She assembled the materials for the surveyors. After the surveyors were on their way each morning, she didn't have much to do. She asked the head of the department, "Don't you have anything else for me to do?" He said no, she could read a book if she wanted. She did. And she entered contests, all kinds of contests. In twenty-five words or less she wrote about the wonders of the Hotpoint freezer and won one.

Pat: "We didn't have much of an income."

Ted: "Hotdogs and beans."

Pat: " Oh no. We ate well. I'd come home from work, and Ted would expect me to make dinner for him."

Ted: "I was too busy watching soap operas."

Pat: "I'd come home and he'd tell me about the soap operas. I never had sense enough to say, well, why don't you start dinner."

"The guys in East Butte would have been horrified," said Ted with a mischievous grin.

They drove back to Butte every weekend, so Ted could do the books for the shop. They stayed with Annie and Tony.

While in Butte for Christmas, the manager at the trailer park called to say ice was forming under and around the door of the trailer. They jumped into the car and drove back to Missoula. Joe went with them. The inside of the trailer was solid ice—at least three inches of ice. Ted and Joe went at it with pickaxes. Pat watched from outside. She could hear the crunch, crunch of Ted and Joe hitting the ice with the pickaxes and every so often a big hunk of ice would come flying out the door.

They stayed in Missoula through the summer. It got so hot in the trailer that their thermometer burst. It was like living in a hot tin can.

Ted finished his accounting degree after which he did his summer camp duty for the Army Reserves at the Yakima Firing Range. To get there, he and Pat drove through the barren desert of dusty sagebrush that is much of eastern Washington. Pat stayed with her friend Marie in Selah, and then with her cousin in Seattle.

They drove through eastern Washington another time to pick up a car in Oregon. Pat said, "Who would ever want to live in this godforsaken place?"

Who indeed.

43

THE HOUSE THAT TED BUILT

AFTER SUMMER CAMP, they returned to Butte and moved into a rickety, run-down apartment on Montana Street at Platinum. It was one of four apartments in a two-story house, a broken down wreck of a place on insecure ground, probably sinking into a mine labyrinth. Their apartment was on the second floor. Ted and Pat couldn't have a washing machine because the landlady was afraid the agitation might shake the whole place down.

They couldn't sit in the front room in the winter because the wind whipped through. It was bitter cold.

The landlady charged them higher rent than the other tenants, but when she raised the rent of the other tenants, she didn't raise Ted and Pat's rent.

That first August the place really shook. All of Butte shook in the huge 1959 earthquake. It was the largest earthquake to hit Montana—7.3 on the Richter scale. It killed twenty-eight people, cracked the federal building in Butte, created new geysers in Yellowstone Park, and caused a tremendous avalanche of rocks and timber and dirt that dammed the Madison River and created Quake Lake. It is called the day the mountain fell down. The shaking threw Pat's seven-year-old niece right out of bed.

Ted said, "Pops told Ma to quit walking around so heavy. She was shaking the house."

Even the earthquake was her fault.

I was born a few weeks later. That rickety apartment was my first home. I learned to walk on a kitchen floor with a six-inch slope. That's quite an incline for a one-year-old.

The first time Mom and Dad had Grandma and Grandpa [Annie and Tony] over for dinner, Mom cooked a beef roast. She didn't know how to cook until she got married. Her mother, who was an excellent cook, gave

Dad's graduation from the University of Montana. Since he finished college in the summer, he had to wait until the following spring to go through graduation. He wasn't going to and then changed his mind. It meant a lot to his parents. I was there too. Mom made her dress. Missoula, Montana, 1960.

Aunt Zelda and Uncle Steve came down for the graduation.

her a crash course. As Dad started to carve the roast, he gasped. Mom had cooked the beef roast to perfection, a perfect medium. Annie and Tony with their Old Country ways always ate meat well done, worried it was unsafe otherwise. Dad didn't say anything. Grandma and Grandpa didn't say anything. All enjoyed the delicious beef roast.

Mom [Pat]: "When we got engaged, Dad [Ted] and I were making the same annual salary—fifty-two hundred dollars a year. Grandpa [Tony] paid him one hundred dollars a week. I made the same annual salary, but I worked nine months. He worked twelve. I was teaching when we got engaged. I didn't teach after we got married."

She stayed home and took care of me. Dad worked at the shop selling and painting cars and doing the books.

When I was born, they had nothing for me. Grandma [Annie] went to the store with Dad and bought a bassinet.

They started saving for a house.

The miners had been on strike for seven weeks when I was born. There was no end in sight. It was bad for everyone. Bad for business. Very bad. The strike lasted until February of 1960, a six-month strike.

Mom: "We didn't do anything. We didn't go anywhere. We didn't ski or anything. We saved and saved and saved. We didn't have much of an income. We didn't buy anything that wasn't absolutely necessary."

A neighbor living behind them froze to death in his house when the fire went out during the night.

Mom withdrew her teacher retirement money, and she and Dad used it to buy an empty lot on Princeton Street down on The Flat, between the hospital and Whittier Grade School. The lot cost one thousand dollars.

"Why the lot on Princeton?"

Mom: "It was a good buy. It had a little view of the East Ridge. It was the only empty lot on the block."

They bought a kit home from CAP Homes. Dad would build the house himself with help from his brother Joe and friends, and he hired craftsmen. Back then, at least in Butte, when you built your own house, you just built it. You didn't have to get permission from anybody, you didn't have to tell anybody, you just built it.

The CAP home cost ten thousand dollars. Mom and Dad put twenty percent down; CAP Homes financed the remaining eight thousand. Mom and Dad took out another loan for materials not included with the CAP home.

Now they had to save up to have the basement dug and concrete poured.

Dad: "Pouring the basement wasn't part of the CAP home. We didn't borrow money for that. We didn't do anything. Just saved our money."

Once the basement was dug and the concrete poured, the people from CAP came in and framed the house. It took around eight hours.

Dad: "With a CAP home, you got everything, you built it. CAP Homes delivered everything on a big semi. So we had to unload it. Was it just me and Joe?"

Mom: "And Tiny West [her brother-in-law] and the two Holmes [friends of Joe]."

Dad: "Was Stevie there?"

Mom: "There were six of you. Yes, Stevie was there, because you said you were going to buy half a keg, and Stevie said, 'Oh don't be cheap,' and you bought the whole keg. I brought ham sandwiches and coleslaw, and you had the beer."

Dad: "When we got done unloading it, everybody was bombed. We were hauling the windows in. Big glass windows. Nothing was broken."

One of the men drove home and passed out in the bathtub.

After the CAP people framed it, the house was a skeleton. Dad had to do the rest—the walls, the floors, the molding, the windows, the roof. He wired it and plumbed it himself. He spent all his free time building the house.

Dad: "The molding was oak. Hardwood floors. Hard to take care of. It was all good quality stuff. All oak."

He hired craftsmen to put in the floors and finish the walls. "Those walls were perfect," he said. "Your mother wanted me to put a picture on it. I couldn't bring myself to put a nail in it."

Mom: "Dad came home and asked me what colors I'd like the rooms to be. And so I thought and I stewed, and I thought this would be nice, and we talked it over, and we decided on all these colors, and then I had nightmares about what I'd like and stuff like that. What if I picked the wrong colors? It was horrible, horrible. Dad spent about a week masking the windows and oak trim and covering the floors, so he wouldn't get paint on them. He worked in the evening and Saturday afternoons."

Then Dad and Uncle Joe donned white coveralls and masks and with the spray guns they used to paint cars, they painted the entire inside of the house white.

Me: "After you picked all those colors, and stewed and worried about it, they painted everything white?"

Mom: "[Laughing] I was perfectly happy. Why did he put me through that agony?"

Dad: "I thought if she was involved. . . . It took less time to paint the house than to mask everything."

Mom: "I went down to take them lunch and the two of them had these masks on. They looked like something from outer space. Their coveralls totally covered. It was very exciting."

It took six months to build the house.

Dad: "They [the CAP people] said once you move in you aren't going to do any work on it, and they were right."

Mom: "Something in the laundry room needed some finishing touches, paint or something, and it took Dad [another] six months to do that."

They had a rough time making ends meet while building the house. They had to heat both the apartment and the house, so they had two utility bills.

Dad: "Then we had to buy furniture because we were living in a furnished apartment. We had nothing."

Me: "Where did you buy the furniture?"

Dad: "Rosenberg or something on Montana Street. I was in there haggling and haggling. We finally got a price. I said okay, I don't want to pay for sixty days. The sixty days were up, so I borrowed the money. I said I don't want my payments to start for sixty days. We were talking about fifty dollars a month. It was a lot of money. I was making a hundred dollars a week. This was through the bank, so in the end we got four months before I started making any payments."

Me: "That was everything, our beds, kitchen table, chairs, . . .?"

Dad: "Fifteen hundred dollars. The appliances were separate from that —stove, washer and dryer, refrigerator."

They had to save up to buy all that too.

Dad: "We never ate out, did we?"

Mom: "No."

They pored through their expenses and couldn't find anything they could cut.

Dad: "We weren't big spenders. But just necessities were costing us a hundred and fifteen dollars a week, and Pops paid us a hundred dollars a week. I had to go and insist we needed more than we were being paid. I wound up getting more money [for him and Joe]. Pops at times wouldn't sign our checks. Not a happy time. He'd take an ornery turn, and he wouldn't sign our checks. How not to treat people . . ."

Dad insisted that his father pay him and Uncle Joe an additional fifteen dollars a week. Dad did the books. He knew Grandpa could afford it. Grandpa acquiesced.

Uncle Joe: "Pops would put off giving us our checks if he didn't think we worked hard enough."

Our house on Princeton had a front room, kitchen, laundry room, three bedrooms, and one bathroom all on one floor connected by halls. The houses that my parents grew up in did not have halls.

The full basement was unfinished but plumbed for another bathroom.

My earliest memory of being in the house, perhaps my earliest memory of anything, we had just moved in. I stepped onto the side porch still holding the screen door, which didn't have a catch yet. A gust of wind blew the door back against the house and took me with it. I flew off the porch and landed in gravel. The cement for the sidewalk had not yet been poured. I remember flying off the porch but not landing. I was fine. My parents weren't. But they recovered.

It was to be a redbrick house, but it took another year to save up for the bricks. In the meantime, Dad said with a grin, "We lived in a tar paper shack." Mom and Dad splurged one evening and went to see *Doctor Zhivago*. It was winter and snowing. When they returned home, the house looked like Varinko, completely white, the tar paper acting like flypaper catching snowflakes.

When they saved enough for the bricks, Dad hired bricklayers to do that. In the end, we had a beautiful redbrick house.

For the lawn, Dad bought sod, which was the only way to have a lawn in that cold climate.

One day Dad saw workmen tearing down Blonde Edna's Brothel, which was about a block from the shop. He stopped the car, pointed at the bushes and asked, "What are you going to do with those?"

"Throw them out."

"Could you throw them in my truck instead?"

"Sure."

Dad returned to the shop and came back with a truck; the workmen threw the bushes into the truck. Those were the bushes in our front yard.

As for the first house that Uncle Joe built, Joe said, "We weren't making much money. I'd go buy a wreck and work on it and sell it. When Helen and I first got married, I always thought I wouldn't have any money, so if I wanted a house, I'd have to build it. I had my pilot's license. I'd usually fly every weekend to build up my hours. It dawned on me, I shouldn't be doing this, I have a family. By chance I looked in the newspaper. Those lots were on sale for four hundred dollars. I asked my mother if she had the four hundred dollars, and she said yeah, and she gave it to me. [Joe considered it a loan.] And then a guy across the street came over, his name was Dave Jenson, he said, 'What are you doing?' and I said, 'I'm building a house,' and he said, 'Go see Bourke MacDonald at Largey Lumber.' I said, 'What do I do when I see him?' He said, 'Don't worry about it, just go ahead and tell him what you want to do.' I told him I've got the land. Bourke said to me, 'How much money you got, kid?' I had three hundred dollars in my pocket. I said, 'I've got a hundred dollars.' I gave him the money, and he said, 'Go to it, kid.' What I did is, I paid him maybe ten or fifteen dollars a month as I was buying the materials. I had no plan of what I was doing.

"The next guy that come up said, 'What are you doing?' I said, 'I'm gonna build a house. Why don't you go ahead and help me with it?' He said, 'Joe, if I help you with this . . . I'll tell you what I'm going to do. I'll come over here every evening after work and tell you what to do. I can't work on it. I'll tell you what you have to do. I'm going to charge you two dollars an hour.' I said that's fine. That's how I learned to do the carpentry work. He'd say, 'You cut the wood this way, and tomorrow I'll tell you what to do.' So I got a crash course."

In the end, Joe paid him two hundred dollars.

"I was taking Helen to church one day. I saw one of my friends, we used to ride motorcycles. I saw him digging a hole. I said, 'What are you doing?' He said he's building a basement so he can live there while he's building the house. It dawned on me, that's a good idea. I built a garage to begin with and then built the house."

Joe built the garage such that he could paint a car in it, just in case things took a bad turn. They lived in the garage while he built the house.

"Yeah. It's really strange how it all turned out," Joe said. "For my mother to give me the four hundred dollars, which was probably the only four hundred she had. It worked out really well. My in-laws paid for the concrete. That was nice. That was remarkable. Just luck again, as I call it. Got that house built. We got the Edsel dealership around the same time I finished building the house.

"When I got the wood work done, I had to start plumbing. I had to learn how to plumb. I bought one of those books, electrical and plumbing. Then I went down to the place where all the warehouses are. I don't know how

I run across these guys, they had a shed, they were selling all the plumbing stuff I needed. I said, 'I'm building a house. I need plumbing and electricity items. I can pay you ten dollars a week for that.' I had a loan to pay for it at four percent. Even my father gave me two thousand dollars. I went to pay him back, he said, 'What's that?' 'That's the money you loaned me.'"

Joe mortgaged the house and used the money to pay back his parents.

"Those were the only people I had to pay out of that loan. It was about the same time we got the Edsel. I felt pretty lucky in all that stuff. Starting out from scratch, without that help, I don't know where I would have gotten the money from. So that worked out all right."

After finishing their homes, Dad and Uncle Joe offered to build a new house for their parents. Grandpa said, "No, this house is fine. House in Old Country had a dirt floor. This house is fine."

When Grandma and Grandpa's house needed a new roof, Dad and Uncle Joe shingled it. They replaced the wood stove in the kitchen with an electric stove, which made life easier for Grandma. But when Grandpa came home and saw it, he was not happy. "How would you feel if I came in and did this in your house?" he said. It was a nice gesture, but as Joe said, "We should have asked first."

The "tar paper shack" as Dad called it, 1962. When he and Mom saved up enough money, they hired bricklayers to cover it with red bricks.

*Grandpa with three of his four sons, Dad, Uncle Babe, and Uncle Joe,
in the front room of our house on Princeton.*

SOMETIME IN BETWEEN FINISHING COLLEGE and having me, Dad taught
Mom to drive. She'd never had a car. She got around town on the bus or
walked. When she was a teenager and worked at the funeral home, sometimes the boss gave her a ride home in the hearse. "What will the neighbors
think," her mother said.

WE MOVED INTO OUR HOUSE on Princeton in January of 1962. My brother,
Jeff, was born in March. Mom was afraid to pick him up because he was
so thin; he weighed only five pounds. Back then mothers stayed in the
hospital for several days after delivering babies. The babies were kept in
the nursery. Snookie's daughter had a baby born premature while Mom
was in the hospital with Jeff.

"I went back to the nursery," Mom said. "He [Snookie's grandchild]
was two pounds or something. I was looking through the window and
here's this tiny baby, about this big, scooting with his heel up the bed. I
don't know how he could do that. I couldn't believe it. He was little but
he was tough. He survived just fine."

I was two years old when we moved from the dilapidated apartment
on Montana Street to our lovely new house on Princeton. I had slept in

the crib in the apartment. Dad took me by the hand (I don't remember this, Mom told me) and asked, "Do you want to sleep in this bed (pointing to the big bed) or this one (pointing to the crib)?" I picked the big bed.

As I learned to talk, Dad recognized that pronouncing Leskovar was difficult for a little one. He came up with the idea that we call our grandparents Grandma L (for Leskovar) and Grandma T (for Thompson). I had only one grandpa, Grandpa L, since Mom's father died when she was little. I called him Grandpa. When Jeff was little he called him Pom Pom.

My memories of life on Princeton are idyllic. There were twenty-seven children on our block. Dad called it Fertile Valley.

Every December Dad pulled us on the sled into the forest with Mom walking alongside. He'd cut down a tree for Christmas.

To be a child in my family meant to be cared for and loved, to be protected, to feel safe and secure. My only worry was of that big black dog chasing me, or I feared would chase me, or chased me in a dream, whose fierceness was probably more imaginary than real. It was a safe, peaceful existence. Our well-being was paramount. People came before things, and among people, family came first.

When I started losing baby teeth and the tooth was loose but still attached, I'd scurry across the street to the Burt's, and Peggy, the neighborhood nurse, would pull it out.

One day I was playing outside in the dirt and walked into the kitchen and announced to Mom that I had put pebbles up my nose. Mom called her sister who was a nurse.

"What do I do?" Mom said.

"I'll be right over," Aunt Aila said. She fished the pebbles out of my nose with tweezers.

I was four when I started kindergarten. Mom walked with me the first few times to be sure I knew the way, and then she let me walk by myself. Dad couldn't believe a child that small could walk the few blocks to school by herself. He followed me in the car. I only learned that a few years ago.

The next year I attended St. Ann's School, where Mom had gone. There were one hundred first graders split into two classes. Sister Mary Alvin taught all fifty of us to read. She divided us into three groups based on reading level. I was in the middle group until Mom and Dad took me out of school for a week to go skiing at Sun Valley. Mom tutored me during that week. Right after that, I came home from school and told Mom, "Sister said I'm a Cookie." Sister Mary Alvin had moved me to the Cookie group, the most advanced readers.

Tony Leskovar with his favorite instrument, the bassoon.

As for second grade and up, St. Ann's practiced the ungraded primary for reading. All the children took reading at the same time and went to the room based on their reading level. Precocious children weren't bored; children who struggled received the instruction they needed.

We carpooled to and from school with the neighbor kids and went home for lunch. Sometimes Mr. Mazzolini picked us up in the cement truck. We'd pile into the cab of the truck. It seemed normal to ride home in a cement truck.

It also seemed normal to visit the neighborhood taxidermist.

Mom joined the AAUW (the American Association of University Women). She was in the great books reading group. They read and discussed the classics. One of the women asked, "Are you Teddy's wife?" Mom said yes. The woman said she taught Teddy at the Harrison School. Having heard all those stories about Dad's antics in school, Mom said, "He turned out to be a very nice man!"

Often we went for a Sunday drive, sometimes along Harding Way to the cheese place in Whitehall. I can still taste the Gouda. We listened to *Monitor* on the radio on the way home.

Grandpa went to the shop every day. On Sundays, when they were closed, he practiced his bassoon in the showroom. When Uncle Joe asked why he practiced there, he said, "Very good acoustics. It helps me hear the notes really well."

I bet the best part of the acoustics was that Grandma wasn't yelling at him.

One Sunday Dad stopped at the shop to put gas in the car. They had their own gas pump. Some guy walked up and told Dad he couldn't do that on a Sunday. Dad was furious. It was his own gas pump. Grandpa was practicing his bassoon in the showroom and saw what was going on and walked out and calmed Dad down.

Gas stations couldn't open on Sundays unless they were open twenty-four hours a day. There were only two such gas stations in Butte; one was in a seedy part of town.

When they had a pump replaced at the shop, a teamster drove the plumber to the shop. When it was lunch time, another teamster came and drove the plumber to where he ate lunch. He couldn't eat his lunch at the job. Then another teamster took the plumber back to finish the job.

Union rules dictated that the shop close by four thirty on weekdays, except sales, which could stay open until six. They could sell cars on Saturdays but only until one o'clock. They were closed on Sundays. Dad moonlighted selling *World Book* encyclopedias. He rose to be the area manager.

One evening Dad went to a radio station party after work, a thank you for the advertisers. Dad was a beer drinker, but they were serving double martinis. The party went late into the evening. Dad drove home and staggered from the car to the house. He went straight to the bathroom. Mom found him hugging the toilet. "I'm so ashamed. I'm so ashamed," he said. "What if the children see me." We were in bed.

The next day, Mom had a hair appointment and had hired a sitter. Dad decided to stay home and nurse his hangover. He told Mom, since he was home, no need for a sitter. When the refrigerator repairman came to the door, my brother, Jeff, who was a toddler, answered the door and said, "I'm babysitting my dad." Then one of the people he was training to sell *World Book* came to the door. Seeing what bad shape Dad was in, he said he'd come back another day.

Dad swore off doubles.

People thought it was fun to get their guests roaring drunk, knowing they'd be driving home. It was a different time.

"He was so pathetic," Mom said laughing as she told me the story. "That's the only time that happened." Had it been a recurring event, it wouldn't have been funny.

Dad kept a bottle of Hennessy cognac in the house for Grandpa. Mom and Dad hired an elderly lady to babysit me and my brother when they went out. She was always very quiet when she arrived, but when Mom and Dad came home, she talked and talked and talked. One evening when Grandma and Grandpa were over for dinner, Dad poured a glass of Hennessy for Grandpa and noticed the very expensive bottle was short. "What happened?" he asked Mom after they left. She said, "I'm not drinking it [she didn't drink]. The children aren't drinking it." He marked the bottle. He marked all the bottles. The next time the quiet then talkative babysitter babysat, he checked the bottles. Sure enough. She'd been tippling quite a bit while she was supposed to be watching us. She didn't drink the cheap stuff. She drank the Hennessy. Needless to say, they never had her babysit again.

Dad: "When we went over for dinner, Pops might be there, he might not. He wanted everybody there, whether he showed up or not. When they came to our house for dinner, if Pops was ready to go and Ma wasn't, he'd leave, and I'd end up taking Ma home."

Dad, that might be Mom sitting at the table, the two Butte granddaughters, Uncle Joe, Grandpa wearing a suit, June 11, 1961.

Grandma L still loved to watch the opera on the radio, "The Voice of Firestone," which featured performances from the Metropolitan Opera. She watched *The Lawrence Welk Show* on TV. She whistled through her teeth and tapped her leg in time to the music. She watched the *Fight of the Week*. Her young grandson Joey would sit and watch with her as she shadowboxed during the fight. They ate Hershey bars and drank beer. She gave Joey a pony (a tiny beer).

She'd say, "We're going to the market," and once there, "go get the buggy." And she took her pocketbook; she didn't call it a purse.

She knitted and crocheted. It seems she was always busy. She liked to read fashion magazines. Grandma was captivated by all things European, except Grandpa.

Despite their fights and bickering, one thing Grandma L and Grandpa could agree on was to go on a picnic.

Grandma would call Uncle Joe and Dad and say, "We're going on a picnic."

For the picnic, she cooked a beef roast with carrots, onions, green peppers, and potatoes. She put the lid on the roasting pan and wrapped it with layers of kitchen towels to keep it warm. They'd also bring salami and Swiss cheese and French bread and red wine and beer.

We'd drive up to Elk Park and look for a good spot in the forest. If we saw anyone, we moved. Too crowded. The first time Dad went on a picnic in a park in Seattle with his brother Eddy's family, there were people sitting right next to them. He was horrified.

Grandpa would find some shade, stretch out on a lawn chair, and take a nap, content in the knowledge that his family was around him.

There is an old saying—well if there isn't there should be—don't let Grandma brush your hair when she's mad at Grandpa. It seemed Grandma was always mad at Grandpa. I don't remember her ever saying a civil word to him. He muttered in reply. When we came back from Elk Park, she'd usher me into the bathroom. I'd lean my head over the bathtub, and she would brush my hair with such vigor I thought she'd scalp me. She was trying to dislodge any ticks that might have dropped into my hair during our picnic in the forest. That is one of the most vivid memories of my childhood—not the picnics, but Grandma vigorously brushing my hair over the bathtub. I don't remember ever seeing a tick. Dad remembers her finding ticks in his hair when he was a boy. She'd drop them on the stove, and they'd sizzle.

44

FROM PAINTING TO SELLING

DAD: "DR. HALL CALLS UP JOE in the middle of the night. He just had an accident. Joe went out and rescued him and took him back to the shop. 'I'll take that one,' he said. It was a new Lincoln. Joe thought he just wanted a loaner, that was a pretty fancy loaner, but it was Dr. Hall, so Joe let him take it. He drove it for two or three weeks, and then he called up and said, 'What do I owe you for this car?'"

Dr. Hall was the doctor for grown-ups. He didn't take appointments. His office would be packed with people. The nurse would come around and take your name and find out why you were there. You might have to wait for hours.

It was a completely different situation with our pediatrician, Dr. Clapp. He took appointments. Mom would take us, and it would be as if we were his only patients because no one else except his nurse was there, even though he had a very large practice. The office was dimly lit and very quiet. There was always a cookie jar full of gingersnap cookies. Always gingersnaps. Now I know why; ginger helps settle the stomach. Children are always getting tummy aches. The dim lighting helps calm babies and small children. Dr. Clapp would gently press on my tummy and say, there's the egg, and the bacon, and the toast. And of course that was exactly what I had for breakfast. When we were sick, he told Mom to call at a particular time the next day to tell him how we were. One time when my brother was sick, he was sitting in the highchair while Mom was on the phone giving Dr. Clapp an update, and Jeff climbed out of the highchair. Mom said, "Well, I guess he's okay. He just climbed out of the highchair."

Later Dr. Clapp sold his practice and joined the Peace Corps.

Dad in the showroom of Leskovar Motors,
39 East Galena, Butte, Montana.

Dad: "Les Sheridan would buy a new Lincoln every year. He'd buy one for his wife, he'd buy one for his superintendent, and one for himself. Lincolns. Every year." He owned a construction company.

Les Sheridan would pull out his checkbook and write a check for all three Lincolns. One time as he was walking out of the showroom, he turned to Dad and said, "How much do you want for that station wagon?" Dad told him. He took out his checkbook and wrote a check and handed it to Dad and said, "Deliver it to the Sisters up at Immaculate Conception."

Dad and Uncle Joe had twelve customers who bought new Lincolns every year. All of them paid cash. In Butte it was unheard of to finance a luxury car.

A friend of Grandpa's, Teddy Traparish, bought a new luxury car every year, but he'd been buying Cadillacs long before Grandpa became the Lincoln-Mercury dealer, and he didn't want to change.

Teddy Traparish was the same age as Grandpa and was also from the former Austro-Hungarian Empire. Teddy was Croatian. His real name was Gabriel. He lived at the elegant Finlen Hotel. He had owned the

Rocky Mountain Café, a classic Butte supper club in Meaderville with dark wood booths and delicious steaks. Meaderville was the Italian hamlet next to Butte. It seemed old even for Butte, a rickety hodgepodge of streets, the houses faced every which way, full of nightclubs and supper clubs. *Collier's* magazine called the Rocky Mountain Café one of the best places to eat west of the Mississippi. As the Anaconda Company expanded open-pit mining, it gobbled up Meaderville, and with it, the Rocky Mountain. The Company bought out the homeowners and businesses as the pit encroached on them. Many moved to much nicer homes but were still unhappy about it. People don't like to be told to leave their homes. Teddy Traparish chose not to reopen the Rocky Mountain at another location. The restaurant closed in 1961.

Grandpa's friend Tino Grosso had owned the Aro Café, another Meaderville supper club. One specialty of the Aro was fried celery. Uncle Joe used to go to the Aro Café and buy a coffee can full of spaghetti to go for fifty cents. When Grandpa went there or anywhere for dinner, he told the waiter exactly how he wanted the food prepared.

Lydia's was a popular supper club on the south end of Butte. You drive south on Harrison Avenue, you think you missed it, you keep driving, and there it is. I guess Lydia figured she'd put her restaurant as far as possible from the Pit, so she wouldn't have to move. Lydia Micheletti emigrated from Italy with her mother and siblings back in 1920. Her father was already here. They settled in Meaderville. She cooked seven days a week at many of those supper clubs, including the Rocky Mountain Café. Teddy Traparish was the first boss to give Lydia a day off. She became a partner at another Meaderville establishment. As the story goes, her partners were the gambler who ran the casino (yes, still illegal) and the bartender. The gambler took care of the money. Scuttlebutt was, after the army drafted him, Lydia's take jumped sevenfold.

In 1946, she opened Lydia's at the south end of town. It was not unusual for people to arrive at midnight for dinner.

Dad would go to the backdoor at Lydia's and order one dinner to go. The entree choices were steak, prawns, half a fried chicken, and lobster tail. With the dinner came antipasto of beets and salami and cheese and green onions, iceberg lettuce salad with a choice of dressing, sweet potato salad, beef ravioli with red sauce, spaghetti with red meat sauce, French fries, and bread sticks. That one meal fed us for several days. The cook put the spaghetti and ravioli in big tomato cans for Dad's to-go bag.

Grandpa and Grandma L, Aunt Helen and Uncle Joe, Mom and Dad at the annual Metals Bank party for the car dealers, Finlen Hotel, Butte, 1964.

One time when we were all there for dinner, the waitress asked Grandma L, "Do you want a half fried chicken?" Grandma said, "No. I want mine cooked all the way."

A PHARMACIST WALKED INTO THE SHOWROOM at Leskovar Motors, looked at the sticker on a car, and paid full price. When anything went wrong, Dad and Uncle Joe fixed it for free.

Dad: "There was gambling called Pan at the M&M. The guy who ran the M&M, he made a lot of money on that. He'd come in and buy a new Continental. He owned the M&M. He'd come in, all cash, buy a new Lincoln, say, 'I don't need a receipt, you don't have to receipt it.' Some railroad guy was suing him because he lost twenty thousand dollars at the M&M. Still gambling in the 1960s behind closed doors. A card shark."

A customer wanted to buy a truck but he was short on cash. He said if his employer paid him his back pay, he'd have enough. Dad asked where he worked. A ski shop. Dad went to the owner of the ski shop and said, "Your employee wants to buy this truck, but he needs the money you owe him to pay for it." Dad worked out a deal where we got ski equipment equal to the amount the owner owed Dad's customer. The ski shop employee got the truck, the owner of the ski shop and the employee were square, and Dad made the deal, and we had new skis. Everybody was happy. I'm still confused.

Another customer, a beer distributor, was so delighted with his deal and his car and how he was treated and got to talking to Dad, and soon we started getting regular beer deliveries to the house. Dad paid for the beer—Lucky Lager—but the delivery was on the house, shall we say. We had beer and milk delivered to the front door. Everybody had milk delivered, but not beer.

Dad always test drove a car before delivering it. One time, the steering wheel fell off. Another time, there was a rattle in the door. The mechanic took it apart and discovered that the space behind the door panel was full of nuts and bolts. It came that way from the factory. Meanwhile in Japan, no nuts and bolts rattling around in the doors . . .

As Dad started to fill out a credit application for a customer, he realized he had to ask the most awkward of awkward questions to a man he'd known for years: "What is your name?" He owned Pork Chop John's. Dad started to write John Porkchop and realized, that wouldn't do for the bank. But then in Butte, maybe it would.

And there was Johnny Red Wrecker and Bicycle Charlie.

Grandpa went out to lunch every day; he'd go to one of the "knife and fork" clubs to which he belonged or the Finlen Hotel. After lunch, he was sleepy. He'd stretch out on the couch in the office at the back of the showroom. It was the only sales office, so Dad and Uncle Joe had to write car deals standing up, using the hood of a car as a table. They didn't want to take customers to the office and see the family patriarch asleep on the couch.

One day Grandpa pulled up to the shop after lunch, turned off the car, and didn't get out. Later Dad and Uncle Joe saw him in the car. Joe said, "Is he dead?" No, just asleep.

Dad to a customer: "You like the car?"

Customer: "Yes."

Dad: "You like the deal on your trade?"

Customer: "Yes."

Dad: "All you need is your wife's okay?"

Customer: "Yes."

Dad: "She's having lunch in Anaconda?"

Customer: "Yes."

Dad: "I'll follow you there."

Once he got there and saw they were both happy with the car, Dad didn't say a word. He simply wrote up the deal. People are often happy to have others help them make big decisions.

Dad worked at being the best salesman he could. He had a lifelong love of learning. He took a course in college on selling. He learned about all the cars, the products he sold as well as the competition. He learned the entire market. At that time, it was not unusual for the engine to die when driving a car. When the engine died on a General Motors car, the power brakes didn't work. Not so with a Ford; Lincoln-Mercury was part of Ford. Dad took a customer for a test drive in a Mercury, turned off the car while in motion, and pressed the brake with his finger to demonstrate how easy it was to stop the car.

A customer who bought a new Lincoln every year told the head geologist at the Anaconda Company, "If you don't buy your car from Leskovar's, they won't service it." This was not unique to Leskovars. Knowing this, he went all the way to the factory in Detroit to buy a new Lincoln. Summer came. It was hot. The air conditioning broke. He brought it to Leskovar Motors.

Joe: "You'll have to take it back to where you bought it to get it fixed."

Geologist: "That's in Detroit."

Joe: "Well, I guess you'll have to sweat it out."

Uncle Joe was showing a customer an old car with lots of miles on it. Joe said, "I'd sell this car to my mother." His mother didn't drive. He felt guilty when the woman bought the car. Any time there was a problem with it, Joe fixed it for free.

A madam came in to buy a car. She handed Dad a paper bag full of money. She was a regular customer.

One day the mechanic was syphoning gas out of a car back in the service department. There was a gas-heated hot water heater nearby with an open flame. The fumes caught fire.

Uncle Joe: "We had a fire, we just lost ninety thousand dollars."

Dad: "What happened?"

Joe: "They put it out."

Joe called the customer, who happened to be their insurance agent.

Joe: "I have good news and bad news."

Insurance agent: "What's the bad news?"

Joe: "We had a fire."

Insurance agent: "What's the good news?

Joe: "It was your car."

With his sons running the shop, Grandpa lived the life of Riley. He still went to the shop every day, and left at the same time every day, and walked through the front door of the Finlen Hotel at exactly four thirty every afternoon and headed straight to the bar. He enjoyed chatting with visiting musicians who stayed there.

Then he might drive to the Pacific Bar and have a drink and visit with Old Man Stajcar. Stajcar kept a bottle of Three Star Hennessy cognac for Grandpa; he was the only one who drank it. The backdoor of the bar was always locked, so when Stajcar's daughter, Ann, was young and came home from school, she had to walk through the bar to get to where the family lived in the back.

Grandpa's other regular haunts were the 156 and Evatz's Place on Parrot Flat. There was no such thing as a quick drink with Grandpa. He was deliberate, methodical, never in haste. He went to these places because the owners were his friends. He liked to visit. Eventually he'd go home and ball out Grandma because his dinner was dried out.

Mom asked Grandma, "Isn't it about time to celebrate yours and Tony's fiftieth wedding anniversary?"

"Who wants to celebrate fifty years of hell!" she snapped.

Grandpa would drive into the mountains to fill jugs with spring water at the roadside fountains.

"He'd have a coffee royale with Hennessy," Dad said.

"Did he have it for breakfast?" I asked.

"Oh yeah, for an eye opener."

His morning coffee royale was strong coffee, Hennessy cognac, and a layer of cream on top to keep the alcohol from evaporating.

Every evening he made a hot toddy of tea, Hennessy, and honey. I remember that so well as a small child, standing between the stove and the table in their tiny kitchen, looking up at Grandpa, watching him make it. Everything with Grandpa was a ritual, an elegant one. Whenever I smell cognac, it takes me back to that moment.

While he waited for the water to boil for his tea, he showed us the clarinet.

They lived in a humble little one bedroom home in East Butte, and he drank top-of-the-line Hennessy. "It's quality, not quantity," he said.

He kept his Three Star Hennessy locked in the trunk of his car.

Grandpa drank Hennessy, red wine, or beer—Heineken.

Grandma L drank beer or wine, usually beer.

When friends came to visit, they often sipped sherry.

Yes, Grandpa began and ended his day with Hennessy. No, he was not an alcoholic. He was, however, very relaxed when he was old, when I knew him.

"My father was the continental man," Uncle Joe said.

While Grandpa frequented the elegant bar at the Finlen Hotel uptown, his neighbors congregated at one of the bars in East Butte.

Grandpa and Grandma sent money to Grandpa's family in the Old Country, which was now Yugoslavia. Two world wars and now communism; they were impoverished. Grandpa's niece Pavlina wrote in thanks. She wrote in Slovenian. One of my cousins translated it for me:

> "Beloved Uncle and Aunt! I was excited by your gift . . . I wish that the dear Lord (on the other side, meaning in Heaven) will repay you. When I was at my sister's we discussed how you left the home of your birthplace and your nearest and dearest and went across the world to search for fortune and bread. And it seems you have found it and we wish you much more in the future. And yes I remember every word of my dearest mother in Heaven, who so many times told us about you. And of Uncle Joseph . . . and Aunt Anna, wife of Joseph who visited us when I was nine years old."

Grandma L loved to travel, loved to socialize, loved to visit. She and Grandpa were all set to take a trip to the Caribbean, a Lincoln-Mercury sales contest trip that Dad and Uncle Joe won, but at the last minute, Grandpa decided he didn't want to go. They were all set to visit the Old Country—Yugoslavia and Switzerland—and at the last minute, Grandpa decided he didn't want to go. Both times, Grandma was heartbroken.

I asked Uncle Joe why Grandpa cancelled the trips. "I think he wasn't feeling too good," he said.

Grandpa called Uncle Joe one day in considerable pain. Joe took him to see Dr. Kroeze. It was ten o'clock in the morning.

Joe: "Dr. Kroeze said you need an operation."

Grandpa: "No one puts the knife to me."

Joe: "Dr. Kroeze said if he doesn't operate right away, you're going to die—at four o'clock."

"Okay."

Grandpa handed his wallet to Joe for safekeeping. It was stuffed with eight thousand dollars.

An ulcer had burned a hole in Grandpa's stomach. He was bleeding internally. He was in good hands. By all accounts, Dr. Kroeze was an excellent doctor and formidable. If he said the patient must get the medication at 6:15pm, that did not mean 6:14pm or 6:16pm, it meant 6:15pm. He made sure the nurses did as told.

Grandpa expected Dad or Uncle Joe to be with him at the hospital all the time, even though they had families and a business to run. They couldn't be at the hospital all the time. Patients stayed in the hospital after surgery longer than they do today. It had been several days since the surgery. Grandpa wanted to go home but had no clothes. He called the Toggery and ordered a complete suit of clothes and shoes to be delivered to the hospital, so he could get dressed and leave.

The doctor put him on a strict diet, which Grandpa ignored. He smoked and ate and drank whatever he wanted. Grandma L followed the nutrition advice of the time, wrong though it was. She ate margarine instead of butter. Grandpa would live to be almost eighty-three, Grandma, eighty-one.

Apparently Grandpa thought he'd live forever. "Pops wouldn't make any arrangements [no will]," Dad said. "Pops was seventy-seven years old. I said, 'You've got to make plans. The franchise is in your name. I think you ought to provide some protection for us.' When something happened, we didn't know what Ford was going to do when the franchise was up for grabs. They could have thrown on impossible demands. I needed some protection for us. Maybe nothing would have happened, but who knows. We don't know what they would have done. They might have decided we no longer want an independent Lincoln-Mercury store here. We want to combine it with the Ford franchise. Or they might have said we want you to do this, or we want you to fix up the building or you don't get the franchise, or we'll put you on a contingency for a year. I wanted to get things settled. I said, 'Pops, what's the harm making plans for an orderly transition of the business?'"

Dad and Uncle Joe were running the business as partners. Dad wanted the franchise to be in their names to protect their families. Grandpa said no. So Dad left.

His friend Chuck Flanik was working for the Internal Revenue Service in San Francisco. He took that job right out of college. He lived at the YMCA until he found an apartment on Nob Hill with a fellow from work. Other friends lived at a residence club down by Market Street. It catered to young men and women. They could rent a room; breakfast and dinner were included and served in a common dining room. It was a great way for young people new to The City to meet others like themselves.

Through those friends Chuck met a young Canadian nurse named Norma. They married a year later.

Dad called Chuck and said he sent a job application to the Internal Revenue Service. Chuck put in a good word with his bosses. Dad was hired and went to work in the Oakland office. He lived with Aunt Francie and Uncle Ray. We went down for Christmas, and Mom and Dad started house hunting. Grandpa called and asked Dad to come back. Grandpa said 75-25. Dad said 50-50. Grandpa said okay. Dad and Uncle Joe bought out Grandpa and their brother Babe in April of 1967. Dad and Uncle Joe were the dealers, their names were now on the franchise, and they agreed to pay Grandpa a monthly salary. They agreed to take care of their parents for the rest of their lives.

In July, the miners went on strike again.

Soon it became apparent that Grandpa was dipping into the till. He took whatever he wanted. Grandma did too. She wrote "me" on the receipts. "With Ma it was only nickel and dime stuff," Dad said. Grandpa took out a lot. When Dad saw how much Grandpa was taking, he said to Uncle Joe, "Pops is taking out more than he's supposed to." Joe shrugged. They let it go. In only three years it amounted to twenty-five thousand dollars. That would be one hundred and sixty thousand dollars today.

BUTTE GREW INTO A CITY during the nineteenth century. Uptown there was the street, a sidewalk, and then the buildings. Leskovar Motors was uptown at 39 East Galena. There was no car lot. The showroom was barely big enough for two cars. Dad and Uncle Joe put additional cars upstairs in the paint and body shop. There wasn't a lot of room. They would park the cars as close together as possible and climb out the window. Dad decided to open a used car lot to showcase more cars to increase sales. This is commonplace today, but it wasn't back then. Grandpa was dead set against it, but Dad did it anyway. He worked the used car lot and did the books and wrote the ads. Uncle Joe painted cars and managed the body shop and sold cars.

Some kids stole a car off the lot. Even though the cops caught them red handed, the judge threw out the charges. He said it was Dad and Uncle Joe's fault for leaving cars out on the lot to tempt kids into becoming juvenile delinquents. This was the same judge who threw out the fraud charge against a rodeo star who boasted in a magazine article about all the miles he drove. This was a car he had leased from Dad

Leskovar Motors used car lot, Butte, Montana.

and Joe. When he brought the car back, it had way fewer miles than all the traveling he boasted about. This was in the old days when it was possible to "spin the odometer," fraudulently increasing the value of the car by showing fewer miles.

Uptown Butte is on the side of the mountain. The hills are steep and much of the year the streets are snowy and slippery. A lot of their body shop work came from people sliding into the parking meter while parallel parking. People didn't use chains while driving in town. The advent of snow tires put a dent in their body shop business. Snow tires prevented a lot of sliding and crashing.

THE MINERS' UNION CONTRACT used to come up every year. Every year the threat of a strike loomed. On August 23, 1954, the International Union of Mine, Mill and Smelter Workers went on strike against the Anaconda Copper Mining Company. The Company put a notice in the paper that striking employees could pay the employee "share of the group insurance premium and monthly hospital contribution of $1," so their insurance wouldn't lapse. They were out until October 15, seven weeks out of work.

Beginning in 1956, the contract would be renegotiated every three years.

Many customers borrowed money to buy their cars. Leskovar Motors guaranteed those loans with the bank. Butte was a one-shop town, so when the miners went on strike, commerce collapsed. With no ore being mined, there was no ore to process—the smelter in Anaconda shut down. When miners weren't drawing a paycheck, they weren't spending money. This dominoed onto other businesses that didn't have enough customers and were forced to cut back on employees or reduce their hours. Some small business owners had no choice but to close. It was a downward economic vortex pulling all down, down, down.

On August 19, 1959, the International Union of Mine, Mill and Smelter Workers went on strike again against the Anaconda Company (the name of the company changed in 1955). The miners in Butte and the smeltermen in Anaconda and East Helena and Great Falls were out of work, as well as men whose jobs were affected by the strike. It dragged on for six months.

Now in July of 1967, they went on strike again. This one dragged on for almost nine months. Needless to say, the miners weren't making car payments during the strikes. Strike relief was a pittance. Since the union called the strike, the miners couldn't apply for unemployment. Dad and Uncle Joe gave the striking miners extension after extension on their car loans, so the miners wouldn't lose their cars. Once the strike was over and they were back to work, they paid up. All but one made good on his missed car payments. It was rough on those miners and smeltermen and those out of work because the mines and smelters were idle.

Successful homesteaders knew that the good years had to carry them through the bad. Rain and snow didn't always come in sufficient amounts.

There would be drought years. Families had to save and not spend too much or they wouldn't make it. It was the same for the people of Butte, though they didn't ranch or farm. Instead of drought, it was a strike. A strike would come along. Many striking miners left town to find work until the strike ended.

Merchants such as Grandpa and Uncle Joe and Dad, and doctors and dentists, and restaurant owners couldn't pick up and leave to find work elsewhere and come back when the strike was over. If they left, they left for good. They either held on with a tremendous drop in business or they left. Thus began the great Butte diaspora.

The miners suffered, their families suffered, the merchants suffered, the doctors, the dentists, the restaurant owners suffered during those prolonged strikes.

The Sword of Damocles hung over the town every time the union contract came up for negotiation. The norm for a car loan other places was forty-eight months. In Butte it was thirty-six months. Every three years the contract came up for negotiation, and there could be a strike.

Now it is 1967. The miners are on strike. It is summer. Weeks go by, months go by, the miners are still on strike, another month, another month, now it is 1968 . . .

Lincoln-Mercury called.

45

KENNEWICK AND THE LADY BANKER

Lincoln-Mercury: "We have a place in Kennewick."

Dad: "I'll go."

He went home and asked Mom, "Do you want to move to Kennewick?"

Mom: "Sure. Where is Kennewick?"

Dad: "Remember that godforsaken place we passed on the way to pick up that car in Oregon?"

When Mom told her sister Mary that we were moving, Mary said, "But you'll leave your beautiful house."

Mom: "We'll have a nice house there too."

Me: "What did Grandma and Grandpa say when you said you were moving to Kennewick?"

Dad: "I don't remember. What could you do in Butte when you just got through with a strike? Butte was heading downhill. Constant strikes. Six-month strike, nine-month strike. They said next time you guys go on strike, it will be a year. All I know is it was not a good business climate, and I should get out of Butte. They called us, Lincoln-Mercury, and asked if we could come over and look at Kennewick. It was just the opposite. It was growing, Butte was shrinking."

Mom called Dr. Hall's office to find out how much she owed, so she could pay the bill before we left. If Dr. Hall didn't think you could afford it, he didn't send a bill. He never sent a bill.

Compelling geological evidence tells us that long ago the polar icecap extended all the way through what we call Canada and into the Pacific Northwest. Over many millennia the ice receded. There was a giant lake over present-day western Montana. Periodically the ice dam would break, sending tremendous floods through what is now eastern Washington. With the gushing waters came granite boulders and lots of dirt. The pattern repeated every ten thousand years or so. Geologists can see the markings on the basalt. The result is that today, southeastern Washington, a barren desert between the Cascades and the Rockies, is covered with rich, fertile soil. That and the climate and access to water make it perfect for growing winter wheat, asparagus, cherries, potatoes, and more, and yes, apples, all fed by irrigation water drawn from the mighty Columbia, Snake, and Yakima Rivers. It is also a land of exceptional *terroir* for wine grapes, a perfect place to make wine.

During the Second World War, the federal government decided it was the perfect place to make plutonium, part of the Manhattan Project.

Kennewick, Pasco, and Richland make up the Tri-Cities. The Manhattan Project work producing plutonium was outside of Richland, which is across the Yakima River from Kennewick. Pasco began as a railroad town and is across the Columbia River from Kennewick.

It couldn't have been more different from Butte. Kennewick is an Indian word meaning winter paradise. It is an unusually low place between two mountain ranges, only three hundred feet above sea level. Lewis and Clark passed by on their search for the Northwest Passage.

Mom and Dad quickly grew to love it there. They were both thirty-five when we moved.

But before we could move, they needed money. Sure Lincoln-Mercury was offering the franchise, and the Kennewick store was bankrupt, but Dad and Uncle Joe still needed money to buy the business. They planned to continue as partners: Uncle Joe would run the Butte store; Dad would run the Kennewick store. They needed sixty thousand dollars to buy the Kennewick store. Neither had anything close to that kind of money. They borrowed thirty thousand dollars from Ford Motor Credit. They needed another thirty thousand. They went to Metals Bank in Butte; they'd been customers of the bank for years. Metals Bank said they'd have to go through FHA. Even though they'd been doing business in Butte for a long time and knew the local bankers, no bank in Butte would loan them the money without going through FHA, which would take too long. If they didn't get the money fast, another buyer might step in to buy the Kennewick store.

Joe called his friend Ruth Opie out in Whitehall.

Whitehall is a little no-stoplight town across the Continental Divide east of Butte. It is a ranching town. Ruth Robert was born there on December

31, 1916. She went to work at her father's Whitehall State Bank right out of high school in 1934. She worked there during the summers while she went to college. She did the posting ledger and daily statements and checked the signatures on checks they cashed from other banks. She earned twenty-five dollars a month. She paid her mother five dollars for room and board and spent the other twenty on clothes and movies. After she finished business school, she married Bo Opie, a miner at the gold mine outside of Whitehall. By the time we entered the Second World War, Ruth and Bo had two children. She was a full-time housewife and mother, but whenever her father needed help at the bank, Ruth found a babysitter and went to help him. Bo left mining and went to work at the electrical substation for the Milwaukee Road, which took them out of Whitehall. Even so, when Ruth's father needed help at the bank, she'd get on the train and go back to Whitehall to help him. It could be for a week or two at a time. By 1948, Ruth and Bo had four children. In 1955, Ruth went to work at Security Bank (now Glacier Bank) in Butte, which one of her brothers was running. In 1960, Ruth and Bo moved back to Whitehall. In time she owned the Whitehall State Bank and the Bank of Sheridan, both of which her father started and she inherited, and she founded the Three Forks Security Bank.

Ruth's husband bought Lincolns from Uncle Joe. Uncle Joe and Aunt Helen socialized with Ruth and Bo; they'd go out to Whitehall for parties. Joe called Ruth and explained that he needed fifteen thousand dollars to buy the Lincoln-Mercury store in Kennewick, Washington. She said, "Sure, I'll loan you the money. Send me your financial statement." Then she added, "You have such a good rate on the mortgage on your house, let's leave that alone." She made this a second loan.

Uncle Joe suggested Dad call Ruth. He did and told Ruth he needed fifteen thousand to buy the business and five thousand more to move. Ruth said she'd loan him the money and to send her his financial statement. Before they hung up, she said, "You are going to pay me back, aren't you?"

Dad and Uncle Joe put their homes as collateral for the loan from Ford Motor Credit. They risked everything.

"It was scary," Dad said.

If it didn't work out, both families could lose everything.

Mom and Dad had almost paid off the house when we left Butte. They owed two thousand dollars on it. They'd had the house seven years.

Before we moved, Dad hired a bookkeeper and trained her to do the books for the Butte store.

Car dealers need a lot of working capital. New car dealerships are franchises. They buy the cars from the factory, in this case, the Ford Motor Company. Car dealers borrow money to buy the cars. Rather than a loan for each car, car dealers have a line of credit with a bank or with the automobile manufacturer. This is called flooring. It is the means of putting cars on the showroom floor. In Dad's case, the flooring was with Ford Motor Credit. This was in addition to the money Dad and Uncle Joe borrowed to buy the business.

Five months after we moved to Kennewick, Mom and Dad sold the house in Butte and paid off $18,227 on the $20,000 loan with Ruth Opie's bank.

The previous Lincoln-Mercury dealer in Kennewick had been losing fifty thousand dollars a year. Dad turned it around in one year. He was breaking even. The next month, he made five thousand dollars. This was in 1970.

Things were looking good.

Then came a bully throwing sand in the gears.

What shall we call this guy? We could call him Mr. Shameless. Or Mr. Mooch. How about Mr. Shameless Mooch. Yes, I like that one.

Mr. Shameless Mooch was the head of Ford Motor Credit in Spokane. Before Dad and Uncle Joe entered the picture, he wanted to buy the Kennewick store but lost his nerve when he saw what a financial disaster the store was. Once he saw Dad turn it around, he decided this was his chance. He'd walk in and pluck it away. He refused to renew Dad and Uncle Joe's note with Ford Motor Credit, thereby sabotaging the business. He had the power to pull the rug right out from under them.

Dad told Uncle Joe that Mooch was refusing to renew their note. "Joe called a friend at Ford, a wheel in Detroit," Dad said. "He was a countryman from Anaconda named Blaskovich. Blaskovich said, 'We're going to renew your loan for thirty thousand and loan you another ten thousand.'" Dad said he didn't need the extra ten thousand. Blaskovich said, "You're getting it anyway."

The loan kept him in business, and he quickly paid it off.

Dad was shocked that customers in Kennewick actually borrowed money to buy a Lincoln.

The business was not unionized in Kennewick, so the sales hours were longer. Dad worked "bell to bell" as he said. If there was a customer interested in buying a car, he stayed late. Mom always waited until he was home to serve dinner, so we could eat as a family. When we were little, if it was late, she'd give us a snack to tide us over. We ate breakfast as a family too: soft boiled eggs, bacon, and toast.

Dad normally had a beer when he came home from work. I knew it was a rough day when he had a boilermaker (a shot of whiskey with a beer chaser).

One day Dad sat down with a new customer and started to fill out the credit application.

Dad: "Where do you live?"

What Dad heard the customer say: "I own Oregon."

Dad: "You do?"

What the customer actually said: "Ione, Oregon."

Dad sweeping the lot on Avenue C, Kennewick, Washington, 1969.

Dealership Dad built on Clearwater Avenue in Kennewick.

Another customer came in demanding five hundred dollars over invoice.
Customer: "Will you match that price?!"
Salesman: "Our price is less than that."
Customer: "But will you match that price?"
Salesman: "Okay."

THE KENNEWICK STORE was in a small, old, dilapidated building on Avenue C. Very soon, Dad looked to expand and build. He researched the area and decided that Clearwater Avenue near I-395 was the place to build. It was empty desert on both sides of the street, nothing there, but it was close to the highway, and it was on the way to the new shopping mall, Columbia Center. He saw it as a perfect spot for growth. He and two other car dealers bought contiguous properties. He took out loans to build a much larger dealership and a house at the same time. Annie advised him to wait. He didn't. He marched ahead and it proved the right thing to do.

BACK IN BUTTE, the Anaconda Company used enormous trucks to haul the ore out of the pit. The Company bought parts for the trucks from the Ford dealer. Shortly before we left, Dad offered to give the Company a discount if they would buy parts from Leskovar's. He was ahead of his time, thinking they'd make the money in quantity even though the price per part was less. Again, this is commonplace now but wasn't at the time. The Company said no. Large, old companies are often reluctant to change, even when it is in their best interest. Dad wouldn't give up. He pursued the Company to get the parts business. They kept saying no. He persisted and persisted until the manager said he'd give Leskovar Motors a try. The Company stayed with Leskovar's. It was a steady stream of money, selling parts for those enormous trucks hauling ore out of the Berkeley Pit.

Every afternoon Grandpa walked through the front door of the Finlen Hotel at exactly four thirty. The bartender, Charlie Gallagher, could set his watch to Grandpa's entry. Grandpa would have a drink at the bar and visit. Then he might stop at another favorite haunt for another drink and more visiting. Then he'd go home and complain to Grandma that dinner was cold.

Every Sunday, he went up to the shop and practiced his bassoon in the showroom.

On Friday, May 8, 1970, Grandpa had a drink at the 156 with Old Man Mihelich.

Grandma called Uncle Joe early the next morning.

"Tony's dead," she said.

"Naw, he isn't," Joe said. He went over to the house and looked around. He didn't see Grandpa. "Ma, he must have gone up to the shop."

"Look over there next to the stove," she said.

There he was on the floor between the stove and the cupboard. The bottle of Hennessy was on the counter. He had made his last hot toddy.

His routine ended only in death.

A friend of Grandpa's, the man who took care of the flowers at the Columbia Gardens, walked into the shop later that morning and asked Joe, "Where's Tony?"

"He died."

"Did he die fast?"

"Yes."

"Good." And he turned and walked out.

Uncle Joe made the rounds to tell the bartenders. "I knew something was wrong when your father did not walk through that door at four thirty," said Charlie Gallagher at the Finlen.

Grandma wrote to Grandpa's cousin Cecilia in Yugoslavia. Grandma kept a copy of the letter. I found it among her papers. Thank you, Grandma.

> Butte Montana
> May 13th-1970
>
> Dear Cecilia,
> It is with sadness that I wrote to you to let you know our Anton died of a heart attack Saturday May 9th ~ 2:30AM . . . He has been ill for a number of years although he was very determined that he could overcome any illness that came his way. He got up about 2:00AM Sat. morning complaining of a terrific stomachache and thought if he could have a glass of hot water with lemon juice and whiskey in it that it would ease the pain. I was half asleep when I heard a thump on the kitchen floor and thinking it was only a dish that fell I went back to sleep. When I awoke in the morning I didn't see him in bed and thought he was having coffee. I went in to join him and found him on the floor between the kitchen sink and stove. He died instantly which was a blessing.
> We had the funeral Monday May 11th had Rosary and Requiem Mass. He had a very nice wake and funeral, so many of his friends came and those who couldn't come to the funeral send flowers and cards to our home.
> Thought we might have to bury Tony in a snow storm, the night of the wake Butte had quite a storm. There was about 4 inches of snow on the ground the next morning. But thank goodness the weather cleared and had a few moments of sunshine during service in Church and cemetery.

*Grandma L and Grandpa in the front room of
their home, 210 Cherry, East Butte.*

I only wish Tony and I were able to visit the old country as he always
wanted to go back home and see you folks. He had planned to answer
your letters, but his eyes were failing him and each day kept putting it
off hoping his eyes would get better.

Don't know what my plans are for the future, but will have to move from
here as the mines are going to take all this property in this area for their use.

Hope all is well with you and everyone.

My very best to all of you.

Ann Leskovar

GRANDPA'S OBITUARY WAS ON THE FRONT PAGE of the Sunday paper on
May 10, 1970. Grandma cried and cried at the funeral. I remember her
walking up the aisle at Holy Savior Church, Dad on one arm, Uncle Joe
on the other, her halting, limping steps. With Tony gone, the fight went out
of her, the life went out of her. Never again would he walk into the house
after having been to the Finlen and complain that his dinner was cold, and
she would miss him dearly. She missed the fight. Her contender was gone.
Living with Tony had been impossible. Living without him was worse.

46

REMINISCENCES AND LOOSE ENDS

"I'M NOT CRAZY. I've just been in a bad mood for the past fifty years!" When I heard that in *Steel Magnolias*, I thought of Grandma L, her temperament toward Grandpa though not toward us. I remember her as a kind, no-nonsense grandma; the only exception was when she thought I'd been playing with matches, which I hadn't. Maybe it was her way of making sure I never did.

I remember Grandpa L holding Jeff. I remember Grandpa holding me on the piano bench. He was kind and gentle. I remember watching in awe as he made his evening toddy and showed us the clarinet.

We have home movies of Grandpa holding me in one arm, a cigarette dangling from his other hand. He used to put me on his lap and give me a cigarette, and I coughed and coughed. We have no pictures of Grandma holding either of us, and I have no memory of Grandma holding Jeff or putting me on her lap. This is no doubt because Grandma commandeered the camera, and she was always bustling about putting food on the table. The only thing I remember Grandma sitting and holding was a can of beer.

Grandpa played classical music records on the stereo in the showroom really loud. When I was learning to play the flute, he'd take me over to the stereo and say, "Hear the flute?"

I remember Grandma L bustling about, making dinner, sewing, crocheting, making ceramics, spreading a cloth on the dining room table to make potica, though I didn't understand at the time that was what she was doing.

She made porcelain clocks and wall figurines. She painted them. It was very intricate work. She was tough as nails with beautiful penmanship and an eye for color and beauty.

She and Aunt Zelda made me a pink cape for Easter. At least I thought they made it together.

*Grandpa holding me and Grandma L in the front room of their house
at 210 Cherry, Butte, Montana, 1960.*

Grandma L said to me when I was around seven, "You're going to be a
schoolteacher!" I said, "No, Grandma, I'm going to grow up and become
a mechanical engineer and work on nuclear power plants and then quit my
job to write a book about you." Not really. I didn't say that. I didn't think
that. Declarative statements were Grandma L's favorite way of conversing
and always in an exclamatory tone. "You're a liar about the car!" she barked
at her cantankerous nephew Bobby.

One time we were visiting from Kennewick and stayed at Grandma
and Grandpa's. I slept on the couch and was awoken by Grandma yelling
at Grandpa, "SHUT UP OR YOU'LL WAKE UP THE KIDS!"

My two grandmas could not have been more different: Grandma T,
sweetness and light, sipping tea; Grandma L with all the subtlety of a Mack
truck, shadowboxing while watching the *Fight of the Week* and drinking
a beer. They were both so good to me. I loved them both.

Grandma L with me and my brother in the front room at 210 Cherry.

We'd arrive at their front door and before we even walked through it, Grandma L would say, "Go get a Hershey bar!" and my brother and I would dash to the kitchen to that bottom drawer and grab one. She never said a chocolate bar, always a Hershey bar.

I asked my brother and cousins, "What do you remember about Grandma and Grandpa L?"

"When I pulled the sheet over my head, Grandma said, 'Pull that down or you'll suffocate!'" my brother, Jeff, said.

My cousins said:

"He was very continental. I was in awe of him."

"I think she was a frustrated creative person. She loved Grandpa, we could see that after he died. She almost shrank physically. Here was this woman who grew up as a barmaid basically. It was sad to see. Even though they might have fought, they both got life from it. It's kind of a different culture then and now. We put people under a microscope now. They didn't do that back then. We are looking at them through our glasses. Grandpa was continental, gracious, not warm and cuddly but not standoffish. Grandpa was polished and straight. Grandma was frumpy."

"Grandpa was European. His carriage was European."

"Our grandfather was a very mellow guy. He seemed to like simple things. I remember going out to the front yard of his house and his having a cigarette and talking about how beautiful the mountains are in Butte. I remember he was very quiet, and he didn't mind me playing in the cars at the dealership. And Grandma, she was really fun, we always played Michigan rummy when she came to the house; she loved to gamble. She'd tap on her coins as she was waiting. She'd say, 'Do you have your money?' We'd play Michigan rummy from sunup to sundown and beyond. She loved to watch soap operas. When I was talking back to Mom, Grandma said, 'You're getting too big for your britches!'"

She liked to bet on the ponies at the racetrack. She played the slot machines and keno in Las Vegas. When she was losing while playing Michigan rummy, she said, "*Und alle weg*," which is German for "that's the way it goes."

One of my cousins from Seattle said he loved visiting Grandma and Grandpa when he was a boy. When I asked why, he said one reason was hearing the dynamite explode in the pit. I grew up hearing that, so I thought it was normal. I guess it isn't normal. "They are blasting in the mine," we'd say. "You could set your watch to it," Mom said.

Another cousin said, "You never go to Grandma's house and tell her you have a tummy ache—she'd think you need an enema. Grandpa would take me to Stajcar's bar. He'd have Hennessy. I'd have root beer and a Hershey bar."

"When Grandma babysat me, she'd give me a hot bath, and then we listened to the opera."

When I was a child, they had a lovely lawn. Their yard was impeccable.

"Grandpa had me mow the lawn, which made Grandpa thirsty, so he took me to the 156. Grandpa had a glass of beer and a hard-boiled egg. He gave me a nickel to play pinball."

One of their nephews said, "There was always action around Aunt Annie. I called her my outrageous aunt. It was really secure to be a kid around the Lozars and Leskovars. Walt Disney reminded me of Uncle Tony."

A neighbor said, "Somebody was always yelling."

When Grandma wanted to say something to Dad, she'd say rapid fire, "Eddy, Babe, Joe, Ted!" When she addressed Mom, she'd say, "Louise, Kay, Helen, Pat!" She went through the list in order of birth, oldest to youngest, every time.

I was ten when Grandpa died. After that, Grandma came to visit us in Kennewick. She had a bad hip. I was talking to her in the bedroom one day when suddenly, down she went, a slow, graceful fall, straight down on the floor. She cracked up laughing. She'd sit in the wheelchair in the living room, and I'd bring her a beer. One time she was dozing and woke to see a very large woman leaning over her. "My God you're fat!" she said. Never one for subtleties. She was no tiny thing herself. She was round through the middle, shaped like a Slavic peasant woman working the fields in her *babushka*, but I never saw Grandma L wear a *babushka*. She wore hats.

I never saw Grandma L in anything but a dress or skirt. I don't think she owned a pair of slacks. Of course Aunt Francie wore slacks. She was the modern one. I never saw Aunt Stephie in slacks, always a dress or skirt. Aunt Zelda wore slacks. She and Francie were golfers.

I never saw Grandpa in anything but a suit. Around the house, he took off the jacket. He wore his suit without the jacket under his coveralls when he painted a car. When we went to Canyon Ferry, he wore a suit. When we went to Elk Park for a picnic in the forest, he wore a suit. He'd take off the jacket, but still a suit. He wore suspenders. He wore a vest, his gold watch tucked into his vest pocket. He would take out the watch and wind it, slowly, methodically. Everything was a ritual for Grandpa L, making his evening toddy, preparing his cigarette. He'd take a cigarette out of his pack of Lucky Strikes, which had no filter, roll it between his hands to loosen the tobacco, tap it on the table so the tobacco would fall to one end, put the other end in his mouth, strike a match and light it. He had a continental way of holding his cigarette between his thumb and first two fingers. He held his cigarette such that if any ashes dropped, they would fall into the palm of his hand, not on the floor, not on his clothes. Everything about him was methodical and purposeful. I remember his raspy cigarette whiskey voice, his heavy accent, and Grandma yelling at him.

Grandpa was attentive to us and seemed delighted by his grandchildren.

As for Annie's siblings, Young Caroline and her husband, George, moved back to the Bay Area. While driving home after dinner at Mother Caroline's, Young Caroline collapsed. George drove straight to the hospital, but she was already gone. The autopsy showed a ruptured aneurysm. She was sixty-three. That was April 21, 1962. A few months later, on December 18, Mother Caroline died. She was ninety-three.

Aunt Zelda became a tribal judge. She and Uncle Steve lived out the rest of their years in Polson on Flathead Lake. We visited Aunt Zelda shortly after Uncle Steve died at age eighty-two. All she talked about was Steve. She followed him into that good night four years later.

On Saturday, November 29, 1980, the San Francisco papers reported a fire at Polk and Sacramento Streets. It had started at four o'clock in the morning in a four-story wooden apartment building. The firemen smelled something flammable and suspected arson. One man leapt to his death before firemen could save him. A woman, unable to get out, crawled into her bathtub and died. "The five alarm fire was also marked by the extraordinary

Francie Lozar Waters, Caroline Lozar, George Bronner, and
Caroline Lozar Bronner at the Bronner's home.

*Grandma L (Annie Lozar Leskovar) at Stephie and Ray Ryan's
apartment in San Francisco, 1962. This was the year Grandma's
sister Caroline and mother, Caroline, passed away.
This trip to San Francisco was to attend one of those funerals.*

heroism of a young couple and an 83 year old man, who among them saved
six people from the burning building," said the paper.

That eighty-three-year-old man was our Ray Ryan.

Uncle Ray led Aunt Stephie and their neighbors up to the roof and onto
the roof of the next building. Stephie had phlebitis; she needed a lot of help.

San Francisco Fire Chief Casper offered to buy Ray a double shot of
bourbon for his heroism.

The previous Monday there had been fires at 1429 Polk and 1600 California. Those fires started nine minutes apart. Earlier in the month, there

Grandpa (Tony), Uncle Ray Waters, Grandma L (Annie), Uncle Ray Ryan,
Aunt Francie Lozar Waters, San Francisco Airport, 1962.

had been a fire at Polk and Bush. It was arson. The fire at Aunt Stephie
and Uncle Ray's building was the fourth in the neighborhood that month.

Stephie and Ray escaped but left everything behind, including their teeth
and glasses. Only four years earlier, in 1976, I wrote to Aunt Stephie asking
about the family. This was for an American Literature assignment to write my
family history. Aunt Stephie wrote the wonderful letter I quoted throughout
this book. She also sent many of the pictures. Thank God, she did.

They lived several more years. Ray Ryan was eighty-nine when he
passed away; Stephie was eighty-seven.

WHEN MY BROTHER AND I WERE LITTLE and we visited Aunt Francie and
Uncle Ray Waters at their house in the Sunset District of San Francisco,
we'd all be in the front room, the grown-ups visiting, and then Aunt Francie would say, "Why don't you kids go play the slot machine," and she'd
give us a roll of nickels. We'd go downstairs to the little half bath tucked

Grandma L, Aunt Stephie, Aunt Francie, San Francisco Airport, 1962.

under the stairs. We'd put the toilet seat cover down and sit on it facing the secret cupboard to the side. We'd open the cupboard, and there was the slot machine. It had been in the rumpus room until someone told on Uncle Ray. Yes, it was illegal to have it.

Once when Grandma L and Aunt Francie and Uncle Ray were visiting us in Kennewick, Mom was driving. Grandma was in the front seat. Aunt Francie and I were in the backseat. Grandma said she wanted Kentucky Fried Chicken for dinner. She requested this every time she visited and insisted on paying. Mom figured she did it to give Mom a break from cooking. Francie ignored what Grandma said and leaned forward and asked Grandma, what do you want for dinner, Annie, do you want this, do you want that, . . .? "Shut up, Francie!" Grandma said.

Aunt Francie brought a jar of whiskey balls she'd made. She gave the jar to Grandma and said, "Don't let the kids have any of those. There's whiskey in them." As soon as Francie left the room, Grandma held out the jar to me and said, "Do you want one?" I was around twelve.

Aunt Francie looked straight at you when she talked, which is polite, but she did this even when she was driving, and she never stopped talking, even when she drove up Twin Peaks. It was terrifying. Occasionally she glanced at the road.

One year when she and Ray went up to Santa Rosa to celebrate New Year's Eve with friends, while playing golf, Ray collapsed. The ambulance took him to the hospital. One of the men called Francie. She was already dressed for the New Year's Eve party and rushed to the hospital. The doctor was still with Ray; she couldn't see him. She paced up and down the waiting area in her black velvet cocktail dress and pearls saying, "I need to call the funeral home. I need to reserve the hall. I need to call the caterer . . ." and out walked the doctor. No, Ray wasn't dead. Too much booze and too much golf. But the doctor wanted to keep him overnight for observation anyway. Ray was mad as a hornet at Francie, because he was going to miss the football games on television. Somehow this was all her fault.

Francie never did plan Ray's funeral. He outlived her. She passed away at age eighty-five; Ray died five years later at age ninety.

After we moved to Kennewick, Dad needed someone he trusted to do the books at the shop. That person was Mom. She worked while we were at school. She was home while we were home. One time when Grandma L was visiting, Mom said, "I'm going to work, and Grandma is going to teach you to make potica." I was around eleven years old. It was Grandma's idea, and Mom was all for it. Grandma sat in her wheelchair and told me what to do. First the dough: hot roll mix, yeast, egg, and oil. "What should I use to mix it with?" I asked. "Your hands," she said. I used a wooden spoon. I had never mixed ingredients with my hands. It seemed messy.

Every time she came to visit, we made potica, and every time she remembered another ingredient—brown sugar, honey—and I added it to the recipe I'd written down. My cousin Mary Lou told of the time Grandma L and her grandma Lousen were visiting and taught her to make potica. They cooked the filling. Grandma L didn't teach me to cook the filling. Mary Lou said one of them tasted the pot of filling on the stove and said, "It needs more brandy." She poured in some brandy, and then went off to do something else. Then the other would walk up, give it a stir, taste it and say, "It needs more brandy." Perhaps brandy would have been the next ingredient she remembered had there been another visit.

Passing on her potica recipe feels akin to passing on a precious gold ring. It is a treasure. I included it at the end of the book.

This was the walnut potica made with a yeast dough. The first time Grandma L taught me to make cheese potica, which is without yeast, she sent me to the refrigerator to get the cottage cheese. Remember I was a kid, around eleven years old. I saw the cottage cheese container. I took it out of the refrigerator and gave it to Grandma. She opened it. "It looks pretty dry," she said. I said, "It says cottage cheese." Mom was at work. We proceeded to mix it with two eggs, spread it on the paper-thin dough, sprinkle generously with cinnamon and sugar, and pour vegetable oil on top, then roll it up strudel fashion and wind it into a snail shape in the round pan, and bake it. We ate it hot from the oven for dessert. It was okay, not very good. Grandma knew something was wrong with the cottage cheese, but she didn't say anything. The next day Mom looked for the leftover mashed potatoes that she had put in a cottage cheese container. All she could find was cottage cheese.

Grandma L visited us several times in Kennewick after Grandpa died. Then she broke her hip and was too infirm to travel. Dad called her regularly. She didn't say anything. We'd talk anyway. Cousin Joey would go see her at the rest home and say, "Grandma, if you aren't gonna talk to me, I'm leaving!" And he'd start to leave, and she'd say, "Wait." She passed away five years after Grandpa.

As I come to a close finishing this book, I see my grandparents in a different light, as people apart from being my grandparents. I hadn't thought about it until now—what a ride it was for Grandpa, for Tony Leskovar, from his family farm in the hinterlands of Austria to the Paris opera house to delivering groceries in a Montana smelter town to painting cars and conducting the symphony in Butte, to being down on his luck with hardly a penny to his name, then Edsel dealer, then Lincoln-Mercury dealer with the next generations growing up around him. A wild ride indeed.

Uncle Ed and Aunt Louise recorded Grandpa talking about this life. I had those old reel-to-reel tapes converted to compact disks. I listened to them over and over and transcribed them. That's how I was able to quote Grandpa so much. It brought back memories hearing his heavily accented raspy voice.

My dear, wonderful dad passed away while I was writing this. At the end of his life, the cadence of his speech sounded much like Grandpa's. It hadn't before.

Afterword

A Few Tidbits About How I Found All This

It all goes back to Chopin and Churchill.

When I read Volume I of *The Last Lion*, the biography of Winston Churchill by William Manchester, one of my favorite parts was when Manchester described what life was like in London at the time Churchill was born. His description put me in London. I wanted to do that for you for Paris and Vienna. But how?

While at a sale at the library, I picked up an audiobook of a biography of Chopin, one of my favorite composers to play and listen to. It included letters Chopin wrote; some of them described one of the revolutions that plagued France in the nineteenth century. Chopin described a birds-eye view of what was happening in the streets. I thought, I'll look for luminaries who lived in Paris and Vienna during the period of my book in hopes they wrote letters or diaries or memoirs. While looking for something else, I stumbled into learning that Edith Wharton lived in Paris at the same time as Grandpa (Tony). I asked friend and history professor Brigit Farley about Austrian writers. She told me about Stefan Zweig's memoir, *The World of Yesterday*. It turned out he lived in Vienna and Paris and Switzerland during the time of my book. His memoir became an incredible source. He even named the café near the Paris opera house that Grandpa's countrymen frequented.

Mitch Yockelson at the National Archives was a tremendous help when I was researching the First World War part of *One Night in a Bad Inn*. I asked if he had any ideas about how I could find out what was happening in Paris when the First World War started. I wanted to know what was happening around Grandpa. Mitch suggested that I read the diplomatic cables at the time the war started. Great idea. That was my plan, but it was a big trip to go back to Maryland. (A large part of the National Archives collection is in the Maryland suburbs of Washington, D.C.) I put it on the back burner in case another reason to make a trip back East came up. Then I thought, I'll look online. I googled American ambassador Paris 1914 and up popped an as-told-to book, a biographical autobiography, the American ambassador's own words and his cables about what was happening in Paris when the war began, and he was in the thick of it. There was only one copy of the book for sale online, and it was in London. I bought it. It's the most expensive book I ever bought and well worth it. It added so much to that part of the story and answered my question as to why people couldn't get their own money out of the bank when the war started. Thank you, Mitch. Thank you, Ambassador Herrick.

A friend observed that I had relatives on both sides of the First World War. I said, "You are right. I hadn't thought about it."

I like to read novelists of the time and places I'm researching, not for factual research, but to help steep myself in the time about which I am writing. One such author was Mark Twain. Of course I had read *Tom Sawyer* and *Huckleberry Finn* long ago. Now I read some of his lesser-known works, which were great, such as *The Gilded Age: A Tale of Today*. While reading a book of his sketches I discovered that he lived in Vienna around the same time as my great-grandmother Caroline—an added bonus and the stories were hilarious.

I sought out Austrian novelists of the late nineteenth and early twentieth centuries. Brigit told me about Stefan Zweig. I asked the librarians in Vienna while doing research there; blank stares all around. Later in the day one of the librarians gave me a list of Austrian writers. I was looking for the Austrian Dickens. After a lot of searching, I discovered: he doesn't exist. Austria has no great literary tradition. Two Austrian historians I read said as much. Even so, I read, or rather I tried to read Robert Musil's *The Man Without Qualities*. I could do a play on words with the title, but I won't. I found it depressing and strange. Stefan Zweig's memoir, *The World of Yesterday,* was a wonderful, fascinating, helpful book. As for his fiction, I found it despondent, hopeless, and pessimistic, pointlessly so.

One historian posited the reason for Austria's woeful lack of a great literary tradition as stemming from state censorship of plays and books that began around 1800. The emperor at the time, Franz I, worried that the bloodbath created by the Reign of Terror in France could pour over into Austria. Subversive ideas that could lead to such must not infect his empire. He didn't want his subjects absorbing bad ideas. Paid informers listened in on conversations in the coffeehouses. Books and plays were censored. This endured until the 1848 revolution. No doubt residual effects lingered. At least that was one historian's take on it.

Austria's great contribution to western civilization was not in letters but in notes—music.

During that trip to Vienna, we stayed at a tiny hotel in the center of the old city. One afternoon I went downstairs to where they served afternoon tea, and there above the tea table on the wall was a large sign that said *Anna Stangl*. Caroline's last name. It seemed a God wink. The man at the front desk said it was an old sign from an old store.

The article I found in the *Wall Street Journal* about the impact of President Roosevelt's decision to cease civilian manufacture of automobiles during the Second World War was dated May 17, Grandpa's birthday.

Long after my grandparents passed away, Dad was going through their things and found letters written in Slovenian. He made a copy of the return address and pasted it onto an envelope and sent a letter. A letter came back inviting us to visit, and we did. Our cousins took us to the old thatched-roof house where Grandpa L grew up. Family members were living in it. They were in the process of building a new brick house on the same property. When the cousin who lived in the house saw us, she became very animated, and ran inside and came back out with pictures—of us.

That visit was in 1987, when it was still communist Yugoslavia. People in the shops seemed skittish, even fearful, about talking to us. When we went back in 2008, after Slovenia declared independence from communist Yugoslavia, it was completely different. People were happy and welcoming and helpful and eager to talk. No fear. What a change from the heavy hand of communism to liberty.

WHILE HUNTING AROUND ONLINE FOR CLUES, I found a 1920 census record on Ancestry.com for a coal miner in Wyoming who could be a Leskovar (handwriting is difficult to decipher). It said he was Slovenian from Slovakland. This was a case of the census taker improvising. It is confusing. Today there is Slovenia, which is south of Austria, and there's Slovakia, which is east of Austria; and there's Slavonia, which is part of Croatia. Back when that man in the census was born, it was all part of the Austro-Hungarian Empire.

WE FLEW THROUGH LONDON on our way to Slovenia. On the outbound transatlantic flight, I chatted with a man from Boeing; it turned out his father and grandfather had lived in Butte. On the return flight, I chatted with a woman whose grandmother lived in Butte.

Poring through the old church books at the Archdiocese Archives in Ljubljana, looking for Great-grandma Caroline, I could have been reading the Butte or Helena city directories from the early twentieth century. So many names were familiar: Plut, Majerle, Sustarsic. Many entries were written in Gothic German. For that, I needed help from the staff. A man from Vienna saw us puzzling over one of the books and translated the Gothic German for us.

As we drove through the Slovenian countryside, again and again I saw a beautiful historic church atop a hill surrounded by a broad valley. It looked like something out of a fairy tale. Every time we passed a grove of trees, we saw the church atop the hill, like a beacon, seen for miles around. I would learn that was our destination. That was my grandfather's church in Ptujska gora.

After a morning with the archivist in Novo mesto and a lovely lunch at a castle, we returned to our hotel in Ljubljana. It was nap time for Dad, and he quickly fell asleep. Mom and I heard church bells. It was Mom's birthday, a weekday. We followed the sound of the bells to the Franciscan Church on the main square just around the corner from our hotel. We went in. It was packed. We found a spot in one of the last pews. Soon it was standing room only. We were by far the oldest people in the church. They were all college age. The choir sang music unlike any I'd ever heard. The voices of the choir were unlike any I'd ever heard—beautiful, magical, mystical. Took my breath away.

On another trip, which was in September, while driving through the Slovenian countryside, we saw people in a field sitting together seeding pumpkins, then a little farther on we saw fields covered with pumpkin carcasses. Driving down from Vienna, we saw pumpkin patches not yet harvested.

The farms were neat and tidy. No junk lying about.

At the castle in Ptuj we saw a group of schoolchildren in Slovenian folk costumes. One of my cousins remarked that one sees more folk costumes in Austria than in Slovenia. The communists had tried to erase history and culture. The Slovenians were still getting it back.

To understand this part of the world, to put the story in historical context, I had go back to the fall of Rome in 432 AD to be sure I understood the context and used the correct terminology.

Bᴀᴄᴋ ɪɴ ᴛʜᴇ USA, remember John Neill, my great-grandfather Joe Lozar's nemesis in the claim jumping lawsuit? I like to see the places I'm writing about and the homes of the people, so on one of my trips to Helena, I looked up John Neill's house in the city directory and drove over to see it. I was stunned. It was a huge mansion. Beautiful.

Then one morning I awoke with the thought: wait a minute — how did the man who ran the newspaper in Helena, Montana, afford such a huge house? Where did he get the money? Was that the original house? Had it been smaller and added onto? I needed to find out.

The next day I played golf, my usual Saturday morning routine. We played on a small par three course near my home in Las Vegas. It usually isn't busy, but this day it was. The starter asked us to join the couple in front of us, which we were happy to do. It had never happened before, and it hasn't since. They were from out of town. They said their son was a coach on the U.S. Ski Team. I asked if they knew the Wilsons, nephews of a friend of mine who is from Butte. The husband said, "Butte?"

"Yes. I'm from Butte too," I said.

"I'm from Helena."

"I've been researching John Neill."

"John Neill!" said he and started talking about the house. He'd been in the house, yes it was the original house, he'd insured the house.

I had not mentioned the house.

That's how I found out it was the original house.

Oɴ ᴍʏ ɴᴇxᴛ ᴛʀɪᴘ ᴛᴏ Mᴏɴᴛᴀɴᴀ, I wanted to see the scene of the dastardly crime of fence mending. I drove through the area on my way from Boulder back to Helena. The ranch might not have been anywhere near the road, but I stuck to the road. I saw hilly, rugged terrain, difficult to access except on horseback. The road I traveled in 2016 was dirt, much of it washboard. It was one lane most of the way. I honked at blind curves.

I ʜᴜɴᴛᴇᴅ ꜰᴏʀ Jᴏᴇ ᴀɴᴅ Cᴀʀᴏʟɪɴᴇ's marriage license, hoping it would shed more light on Caroline's parents. I called the courthouse in Helena—nothing. I called the Montana Historical Society—nothing. I tried Butte—nothing. Oh, well. I thought, on a future trip to Helena, I'll ask if I can search the actual marriage licenses, rather than just the index. I asked Ellen Rae Thiel in Boulder. She said the marriage licenses are at the library in Helena, and she'd ask someone to look for me. I went on to something else. Then lo and behold, the marriage license arrived mysteriously in the mail. The cover letter from Brian Shovers at the Montana Historical Society said a patron had dropped this off and asked if these could be my relatives. The spelling was odd, but there was enough corroborating data to be sure, yes, it was the marriage license and certificate for my great-grandparents Joe and Caroline Lozar. Thank you, Ellen Rae Thiel and Pat Jenks and Brian.

As for when Great-grandma Caroline arrived in this country, I never found her on a passenger list. She arrived before Ellis Island opened in 1892. Before that, passengers who arrived at New York processed through the Castle Garden Immigration Depot. I couldn't find her there. She could have arrived at any number of ports. As for finding Grandpa L, it was difficult because his name was misspelled on the passenger list—Antoine Leskover instead of Anton Leskovar. I knew it was he because of corroborating information.

ELLIS ISLAND HAS TAKEN ON SUCH A MYTHIC romantic aura that I thought all immigrants passed through Ellis Island. They didn't. Only steerage passengers and those deemed suspicious arriving in New York passed through Ellis Island. Not all immigrants traveled in steerage. Not all immigrants arrived at New York. My Irish grandfather and his aunts traveled second class. They did not have to go through Ellis Island.

This confusion is perpetuated by the fact that all the passenger lists for the years Ellis Island was in operation are at www.ellisislandrecords.org, including those who did not pass through Ellis Island.

I WAS MESMERIZED BY DAD'S STORIES. I took notes. I recorded him. Sometimes it wasn't possible to do either at the time. I didn't want to interrupt his train of thought while I fetched my notebook or recorder. I tried to write down what he said as soon as I could. I remember his telling funny stories about their antics going to Virginia City, but I can't remember the details.

Once when Dad was talking about the East Butte Owls and their shed, the old abandoned boxcar, I mentioned a fellow from Livingston I met on a flight out of Billings who said he put an old caboose on an empty lot and made it his house. Mom said the principal of the school where she taught in Lima put a boxcar next to his house and planned to make it an addition. That seems odd but practical. People made do with what they had, what they could find, what they could afford.

Uncle Joe told me about finding Grandpa after he died. "There was the Hennessy. It looked like middle of the night. He's got the drink there, and then said goodbye more or less. 'Here's to ya.'"

Hennessy being so much a part of Grandpa, even though I'm not much of a drinker, I thought I should give it a try. I bought a bottle of Hennessy that was closest to the Three Star Grandpa used to drink. Toward the end of finishing this book, I was having trouble sleeping and thought I'd try a hot toddy with Hennessy. I made a small one. I slept great and awoke with my mind swimming with things I'd forgotten to include in the book. I jumped up and wrote them down before I forgot.

I was intrigued to learn about the lady banker who was instrumental in my family's fortune—loaning us the money to buy the Kennewick Lincoln-Mercury store. I tracked down Ruth Opie and interviewed her over the phone. I said I'd be in Butte the next summer and would like to meet her and chat more. She said, "If I'm still here." She died that December.

While taking a water aerobics class at my neighborhood pool here in Las Vegas, I mentioned I was going to Butte. Our instructor was a nurse who ran care homes for elderly people. She said one of her patients mentioned Butte. Turns out he was Ruth's brother, Paris. I interviewed him, too.

While at the Butte Archives, one of the staff members approached me and said she hadn't read my books, but she recently found something she was sure would be of help. I was getting ready to leave but she was insistent. I followed her down into the bowels of the Archives. She said the records she found were conditional bills of sale. A person would agree to pay a specified amount by a certain date for a large item that was not a house or land. These agreements were recorded at the courthouse. She said, "I'll show you an example." She pulled a random book off a random shelf and opened to a random page. I said, "Oh, the H's," and read the page. There was Aila Hughes, my maternal grandmother, Grandma T. 1916. She was a teenager. Her mother must have sent her. I can't remember if it was a sofa or the piano they were buying. The day I saw it was August 21, 2012. August 21 was Grandma T's birthday.

One afternoon Uncle Joe and my cousin Nancy took me to Holy Cross Cemetery in Butte, so I could visit my paternal grandparents' and great-grandfather's graves. Uncle Joe drove us to the back of the cemetery, where the paupers' graves were marked by little crosses somewhat askew.

Gazing out the window, Nancy said, "It looks like something from the old Wild West." I said, "It is the old Wild West."

HOW EASY IT IS TO MAKE A FACTUAL ERROR. Under "Strikes" in a state report, I read that the newsboys in Butte rioted in 1914. It didn't say it was a wildcat strike, so I thought they were organized. I was about to use that as an example of how strongly unionized Butte was, then I thought I better look into it; perhaps they were organized everywhere. Well, they weren't. They rioted, but it wasn't a strike, not even a wildcat strike. Grownups sowing discord incited them to riot. They beat one miner almost unconscious. They broke a boy's ribs. Once the police arrived, they ran off. Maybe they weren't even newsboys, just hoodlums pretending to be.

I didn't have as much luck finding records in Helena as I had in Butte. Some of the old county records in Helena were stored in the old coal bunker at the trolley barn at the fairgrounds. I spent several hours in that coal bunker, poring through the old county books. That was one of the more unusual spots along my treasure hunt into family history.

What is history but a collection of family stories and individual stories strung together. It all goes back to oral history. Even if it's in a diary or letter or memoir, that's someone writing down oral history, what he or she remembers, which can vary from person to person. Military history is based on the cumulative oral histories of the participants, and the letters and messages they sent. Other than a stenographer taking down what people said verbatim, most history goes back to oral history. I tried to corroborate all I was told. That wasn't always possible. The next step was to ascertain whether the person was reliable.

It's one thing to find the story, it's another to write it. I talked about my approach to writing in my second book, *Finding the Bad Inn: Discovering My Family's Hidden Past*. To that I will add something I heard recently: to be a good writer, be good and write naturally. I would add: seek truth. Writing that sounds contrived rings of falsehood. I don't like that. If something sounds false or pretentious, I quit reading. Since I write nonfiction, and there is a wealth of material from which to choose, in deciding what to include, I ask myself: does it develop a character, does it set the stage, does it advance the story, and is it true—true in the factual sense, true in the philosophical sense.

That is good advice for any writer.

Be good, seek truth, and write naturally.

A Family Recipe

Annie Lozar Leskovar's Walnut Potica

Even the grandchildren of her Croatian neighbor said Grandma L's potica (po-tee-za) was better than their grandmother's. It is better known in Butte as po-vi-tee-za, which, as I understand, is the Croatian pronunciation. There were more Croatians than Slovenians in Butte. I make it the way Grandma taught me with one change: I toast the walnuts. Also, she did not give me quantities for the brown sugar and honey. The amounts in the recipe were developed over many poticas.

I am so glad Grandma taught me to make potica.

It is very different from how potica is made in Slovenia today, which is more of a marbled sweet bread. The way Grandma taught me is much richer, and the dough is paper thin. Perhaps the recipe changed because of austerity after the wars and more austerity due to communism. Who could afford all those walnuts?

The walnut potica is made with yeast dough. Grandma took help where the result was just as good, and as such, she used Pillsbury Hot Roll mix for the dough which she embellished so the dough would stretch.

Once when I was making it (this was after Grandma had passed away), the dough wouldn't pull. I tried another batch. It still wouldn't pull. Mom looked at the box and looked at another box she had bought earlier and realized the quantity had changed. She called Pillsbury at the phone number on the box and explained the situation. The woman at Pillsbury asked for our dough recipe and said she'd call back. Very shortly she did, with new quantities for the oil and water. The dough rose and pulled just fine. Those quantities are in this recipe.

From the extensive research I did regarding potica making, I have concluded that Grandma's is the richest potica around. How close it was to how her mother made it, whether it was exactly the same or Grandma embellished it, I never thought to ask.

A woman I met in Butte told me when she got married, her husband told her she had to learn how to make potica and introduced her to a woman who would show her how.

While on a flight out of southern California, I was chatting with the man seated next to me. It turned out he was from Butte and knew my cousin Joey. Somehow the subject of potica came up. When I said I made it, his face lit up.

I just made it again to kitchen-test the recipe. Normally I use Aunt Sue's Raw Wild Honey but bought another one because it came in a one-pound bottle. It made a big difference. It was not nearly as good as usual. It is much better with Aunt Sue's. The kind of walnuts you use and the honey and the brown sugar all make a big difference.

It is delicious. It is a lot of work, but it feeds a lot of people, it keeps well because of the honey, and it freezes well. It's good with breakfast as a coffee cake, and it's good for dessert. It isn't any more work than making pies or cookies or cakes for that many people. Be brave. Give it a try. Watch the video on my YouTube channel showing how to stretch the dough. It will help.

HERE IS THE RECIPE

From start until the potica is in the pan takes 2½ hours. Resting and cooking takes another 2½ hours. Cooling takes a few hours. Yield is about 48 pieces of potica.

Lightly toast **2 pounds of Diamond walnuts**: put the walnuts in a shallow rimmed pan (a jelly roll or half sheet pan), toast on the top rack of a 350°F preheated oven, 10-12 minutes until lightly toasted. As soon as you smell the walnuts, take them out of the oven, even if before the timer goes off. Better they be under-toasted than over-toasted. Do this first, so the walnuts have time to cool. We taste-tested other grocery store brands. We liked Diamond walnuts the best. Set the walnuts aside for now.

Prepare the pan. I use an old, heavy Club Aluminum oval turkey roaster. It is a 15×11-inch pan with high sides, about 8 inches high. The sides of the pan must be at least 3 inches high. Spray the pan with **cooking spray**. Line it with **parchment**, such that the parchment goes up the sides. Spray the parchment with cooking spray and sprinkle the bottom with a little **corn meal**.

Then make the **dough**:
2 boxes Pillsbury Hot Roll Mix
1¼ teaspoons sugar
2 eggs
⅝ cup (5oz) corn oil
1⅞ cup (15oz) hot tap water (this yeast requires HOT tap water, let it run until good and hot)

Mix the hot roll mix, yeast from the boxes, and the sugar in a large bowl. Make a well in the center. Add the eggs, then oil, then the HOT water to the well, stir until the dough forms into a ball, then dump the dough onto a floured board and knead for 5 minutes. Continue to add flour to the board as needed to keep the dough from sticking. Knead until the dough is smooth and bounces back when tapped lightly.

Put the dough back into the bowl, cover with a kitchen towel, let rise until double in bulk, around 30 minutes. I usually let it rise in the oven—a cold oven turned on for one minute, then turn it off, and then put the dough in to rise.

While the dough is rising, make the **filling**:
Grind the toasted walnuts with a **meat grinder**. I use the finest blade with the meat grinder attachment to my Kitchen Aid stand mixer and grind it into the large bowl that comes with the mixer. The meat grinder at the finest setting is essential. The nuts must be smashed to release the oils. A food processor or blender cannot do this. I tried.

Put the bowl full of ground walnuts on the mixer with the paddle attachment. Add the following one at a time, stir on low speed:

⅓ cup of sugar
2 tablespoons cinnamon
4 eggs
1 can Bordens Sweetened Condensed Milk
1 stick of butter, melted
The sugar and cinnamon don't have to be exact, rounded up is fine.

With the mixer on low speed, add **1½ cups whole milk**, a little at a time, until the filling is thin enough to spread easily over the dough with your fingers. It will thicken on sitting.

Put a **tablecloth or a sheet** over a large table, big enough to seat six. Generously flour the tablecloth and rub it into the cloth with your hands.

Once you start stretching the dough, you can't stop until the potica is in the pan, otherwise the dough will dry and crack.

When the dough is ready, dump it onto the floured tablecloth, roll up your sleeves (literally), remove all rings and watches, and begin stretching it. Fingernails must be short to prevent poking holes in the dough as you stretch it. The more humid the air, the easier it is to pull. Stretch the dough until it covers the entire tablecloth and is paper thin, thin as parchment. Keep stretching the dough as it drops down the sides of the table. While stretching, if the dough breaks, patch it. When you finish stretching the dough, use kitchen shears or a sharp paring knife to trim the thick edges along the perimeter of the dough. Save this and make dinner rolls out of it.

Gently spread the filling over the dough with your fingers. I drop it in big spoonfuls all over the dough. You need to work quickly but gently. The thinner the dough, the more quickly it dries and breaks. If it does break, don't worry about it. Flip any dough hanging down the side of the table onto the filling and put more filling on that.

Once all the filling is on the dough, and any dough hanging down is on the filling, drizzle and sprinkle over the top:

16 ounces Aunt Sue's Raw Wild Honey
1 pound brown sugar
1 stick melted butter

With arms outstretched, pick up a long side of the tablecloth and roll up the potica. Then put it in the pan in a snail shape. Cover with the tablecloth and let rest ½ hour. You can let it rest as long as 1½ hours. When ready to bake, break an **egg** into a small bowl and mix with a fork. Using your fingers, gently spread this all over the top of the potica to give it a nice glaze. Be careful not to poke the dough.

Bake in a pre-heated 325°F oven on the bottom shelf for 1 hour and 25 minutes.

When done, the potica will be a deep walnut color. Take it out of the oven, put the pan on a wire rack, and let it cool in the pan for 30 minutes. Then put the wire rack on top, say a prayer, maybe two, flip it over (it's heavy), and lift off the pan. Then remove the parchment and put it aside for later. Let the potica cool completely before cutting. This will take several hours. Slide it to another spot on the counter every now and then as it cools. It heats up the counter, which creates condensation and slows cooling.

When it is completely cool, put the parchment paper back on the bottom of the potica. Tear off a piece of extra-wide aluminum foil long enough to wrap the potica. Put the foil on the parchment paper. Say another prayer and flip the whole thing over. (The parchment paper will keep the gooey bottom of the potica from sticking to the foil.) Then seal the foil. When ready to eat, using a long serrated bread knife, I cut slices about an inch thick and cut each slice into three or four pieces. I cut only what we will eat at that meal, then cover the cut with plastic wrap and reseal the foil. I like it with butter.

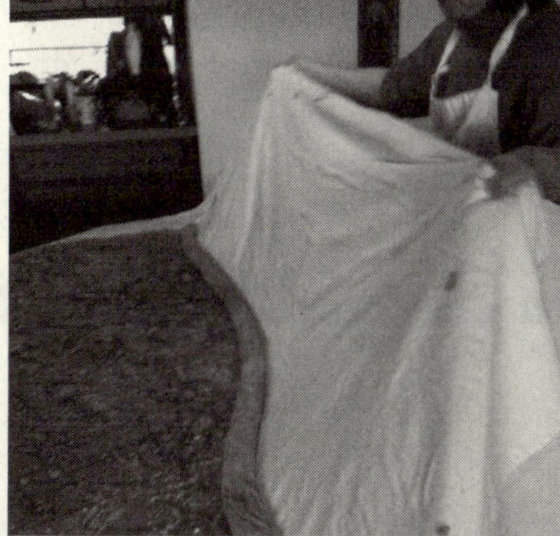
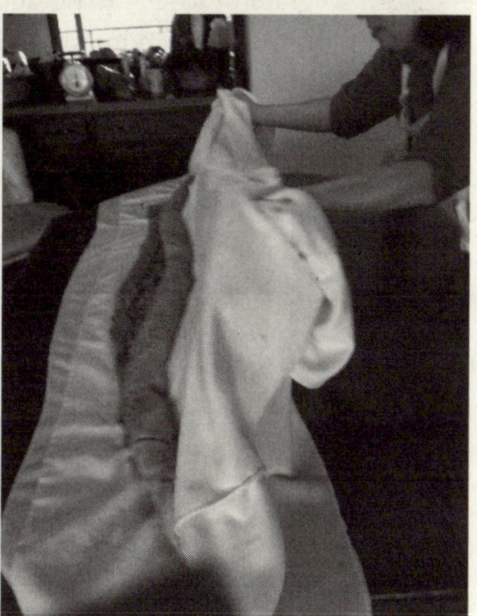

Acknowledgments

First and foremost I thank my family. My parents have been a tremendous help since I announced my decision to step away from my engineering career to write a book about their parents, which morphed into three books. Dad was forever patient with my questions and generous in telling me his stories. My brother, Jeff, is one of the best readers/reviewers I could have. Mom's attention to detail was invaluable. She picks up things easily missed by others. I am so grateful to Uncle Ed and Aunt Louise for recording Grandpa and Grandma about Grandpa's life. They and Uncle Joe, cousins and their spouses, patiently answered my questions and provided pictures and letters. I must single out my cousin Tatjana and her parents, Kristina and Marjan, in Slovenia, without whose help I never could have brought to life Grandpa's (Tony's) life in Ptuska gora. Tatjana translated family letters from Slovenian to English and answered my many questions about life in Slovenia.

I must also single out Dad's neighbor and fellow East Butte Owl, Don Orlich, for answering my many questions over the years I took to write this. My brother and I are eternally grateful to Don and his wife for introducing our parents. And I thank that other Owl, Chuck Flanik, Dad's best man, for his hilarious rundown on all the Anns and Marys who populated the neighborhood and telling me his memories of East Butte.

And thanks to dear Ron for taking me to the places where my great-aunts and uncles and great-grandmother lived in San Francisco, and for his excellent ideas about enhancing the cover art.

Cousin Steve Lozar was a big help with the part about his grandparents Steve and Zelda, and he provided pictures.

Heartfelt thanks also go to:

Ellen Crain, Nikole Evankovich, Irene Scheidecker, Kim Kohn and the rest of the staff at the Butte-Silver Bow Public Archives. Doing research there is a delight and the resources vast. Sam Treloar's Butte Mines Band papers surfaced while I was researching this book. How fortuitous. Irene helped Ann Simonich write her book about the Slovenian and Croatian communities in Butte and as such was a great help to me, as was Ann.

Brian Shovers, Roberta Gebhardt, Zoe Ann Stoltz and the rest of the helpful staff at the Montana Historical Society.

Majda Vucko who tapped into the Canadian Slovenian community for me.

Sister Dolores at the Diocese of Helena Archives for providing sacrament records and translating them from Latin, and for providing the picture of Father Pirnat and answering my many questions.

Marjan Penca at the archives in Novo mesto, Slovenia, who dug up sources I didn't know to ask for.

Felix Gundracker in Vienna for answering my many questions about genealogy sources from Austria-Hungary.

Julijana Visočnik from the Archdiocese of Ljubljana Archives for help with the church books and translating entries written in Gothic German and answering my many questions.

The staff at the Slovenian State Archives for help finding pictures of Ljubljana at the time Grandpa lived there.

The librarians at the Wienbibliothek im Rathaus in Vienna. I even have a library card.

Pat Jenks of the Lewis and Clark Genealogy Society for taking it upon herself to find Joe and Caroline's marriage license and certificate. Also Mary Pitch for her help.

Rita Gibson at the State Law Library of Montana has helped now with two of my books, providing transcripts of Montana Supreme Court cases.

Iris Maness of East Helena for answering my many questions about life in East Helena. Aunt Francie was her mother's maid of honor.

Bill Borznick went to grade school with my aunt Mary and worked for the smelter company. He was very helpful in answering my technical questions. I wanted to be sure my terminology was correct.

Dad's golf buddy Jack Monrean for answering my union questions.

Catherine Carlisle and Kimberley Dowdle with the Bureau of Land Management in Billings for finding even more of my great-grandfather's land ventures.

Ruth Opie for telling me her story. I found the whole idea fascinating of the lady banker from little Whitehall saving the day, so my family could buy the Kennewick store.

Jeremiah Mason, the archivist at Keweenaw National Historical Park, for helping with the Michigan part of the story.

Carol Rascon, who I met by chance at the Butte airport after the An Ri Ra (the Irish festival), sent me helpful articles that corrected the modern myth about names being changed at Ellis Island.

Washington State University history professor Dr. Brigit Farley for her recommended reading list. She introduced me to Stefan Zweig.

Branka Lapjne's book about Slovenian life was a great help, and she was so kind to answer my questions.

Peter Hawlina for answering my questions about Slovenian genealogy.

Ruth Setterquist of the Solano County Genealogical Society found Uncle Ray's whereabouts for me in their city directories.

Charliann Becker at the National Archives in Seattle for digging up the case of the government against my great-grandfather (fence mending) and against my grandfather (mining).

Sherrie Stewart at Butte High for digging up my Lozar aunts' transcripts from a hundred years ago. She said it might take a while. I think it took ten minutes.

Patty Dean for answering questions about the Montana Club and John Neill's home.

Terry at St. Vincent de Paul Parish in San Francisco. She found Stephie and Ray's convalidation in the St. Brigid books. It took her all of one minute. It was on the first page she opened to in the first book she picked up.

Bradley Hansen at Carroll College for finding Steve Lozar's school records.

Marilyn Craft, the Jefferson County Clerk of Court.

The staffs at the Silver Bow County Clerk and Recorder and the Clerk of Court, and at the Lewis and Clark County Clerk and Recorder and the Clerk of Court, and San Francisco County Clerk.

The librarians at the Seattle Public Library who helped with my research into the Coliseum.

Elizabeth Russell, associate archivist with the Sisters of Providence Archives, who provided the records for Zelda's mother.

Professor Marc Bernadot of University of Le Havre, France, whom I found as a source in a Wikipedia article about internment camps in France, and then I contacted him through www.academia.edu. He recommended several sources about the treatment of enemy alien civilians during the First World War, some of which were in English. Yes, I speak French, but reading an academic article in French would have been a struggle.

Ellen Suess for reading and commenting on the manuscript. Jami Carpenter for editing. Ann Seifert for proofreading. Kathy Springmeyer for help in bringing this to publication. Thanks to Susan Wolfe for her advice about the cover.

This is my third book with Arrow Graphics; they have been great to work with.

Notes

The following notes provide sources for quotes where not cited in the text. Unless noted otherwise, quotes by relatives were recorded on tape or in letters or diaries or spoken to me.

CHAPTER 1
"One can make up later for neglecting to exercise the muscles, but the mind can be trained only in those crucial years of development . . .": Zweig, *The World of Yesterday*, p. 80.

CHAPTER 2
"one of the fastest-growing economies in Europe": Clark, *The Sleepwalkers: How Europe Went to War in 1914*, p. 70.
"Free markets and competition across the empire's vast customs union stimulated technical progress and the introduction of new products": Ibid, p. 69.
"Tell him we only drink Hennessy": Roth, *The Radetzky March*.
"the heart of modern civilization": Quoted in Auclair et al., "Verdi, Wagner and the Paris Opera."

CHAPTER 3
"full of confidence in the present and the future": Somary, *The Raven of Zurich: The Memoirs of Felix Somary*, p. 68.

CHAPTER 4
"Haven't you heard? The Archduke Ferdinand assassinated . . . at Sarajevo": Wharton, *A Backward Glance*, p. 336.
"What happens now?" "Why should anything happen?": Quoted in Pitzer, "Enemy Aliens: The life of Austrian painter Paul Cohen-Portheim and the forgotten history of World War I internment camps," *Laphams Quarterly*.

Kaiser is the German word for emperor. I wrote Kaiser Wilhelm of Germany and Emperor Franz Josef of Austria-Hungary even though I could have referred to both as kaiser or emperor.

"The political consequences of this act are being greatly exaggerated.": Quoted in de Waal, *The Hare with the Amber Eyes: A Family's Century of Art and Loss*, p. 178. This was written in the Vienna newspaper the Thursday after the archduke was shot.

"Our placid student life was blown to bits . . .": Stein, *Life in a Jewish Family 1891-1916*, p. 293.

"if we march on Serbia, Russia will march on us": Quoted in Morton, *Thunder at Twilight: Vienna 1913/1914*, p. 38.

"duty of government to preserve peace": Quoted in Clark, *The Sleepwalkers: How Europe Went to War in 1914*, p. 117.

"seized with the darkest of forebodings": Quoted in Mott, *Myron T. Herrick Friend of France: An Autobiographical Biography*, p. 118.

"CONFIDENTIAL— To be communicated to the President . . .": Ibid.

"Is there in your opinion any likelihood that the good offices of the United States . . .": Ibid.

"militarism run stark mad" "an awful cataclysm": Quoted in Morton, *Thunder at Twilight*, p. 210.

"It would be an irony of fate if my administration had to deal chiefly with foreign affairs": Quoted in Johnson, *Modern Times: The World from the Twenties to the Eighties*, p. 22.

"The [German] Foreign Ministry are behaving as if they intend to repudiate our treaties.": Quoted in Somary, *The Raven of Zurich: The Memoirs of Felix Somary*, p. 74.

"Germany does not desire war": Quoted in Neiberg, *Dance of the Furies: Europe and the Outbreak of World War I*, p. 90.

"was intoxicated by war fever": Somary, *The Raven of Zurich: The Memoirs of Felix Somary*, p. 80.

"The irrepressible Viennese gaiety": Ibid.

"resignation without hope": Ibid.

"What nonsense! It can't be war": Wharton, *A Backward Glance*, p. 338.

"Thrilling Scenes in Paris with Cries 'On to Berlin'": *Helena Independent*, August 2, 1914, p. 1.

"One thing was certain . . . beat them back": Stein, *Life in a Jewish Family 1891–1916*, p. 297.

"World war. World ruin.": Quoted in de Waal, *The Hare with the Amber Eyes: A Family's Century of Art and Loss*, p. 181.

"The lamps are going out all over Europe . . .": Quoted in "Timeline: Jul-1914: The July Crisis. The Month of Plotters." *Trenches on the Web*.

"The Chancellor expects that a war, whatever its outcome . . .": Quoted in Johnson, *Modern Times: The World from the Twenties to the Eighties*, p. 12.

"France was paralyzed with horror": Wharton, *A Backward Glance*, p. 339.

CHAPTER 5

"We are at war . . .": Quoted in Mott, *Myron T. Herrick Friend of France: An Autobiographical Biography*, p. 125.

"This would never be done . . . It is better that the capital be laid in ashes than that France surrender": Ibid, p. 125.

"You will defend Paris to the last ditch": Ibid, p. 164.

CHAPTER 8

"Making music, dancing, . . .": Zweig, *The World of Yesterday*, loc 520 of ebook.

"I lay myself at the gracious lady's feet" : Morton, *A Nervous Splendor: Vienna 1888/1889*, p. 42.

"*The party whom I have the honor . . .*": Ibid, p. 43.

"Messenger boys were quite enough . . . :" Day, *Life with Father*, p. 133.

"belonged to the same family . . .": Twain, *Essays and Sketches of Mark Twain*, p. 8.

"Strenuous merrymaking": Solmssen, *Alexander's Feast*.

"would have entrusted his daughter . . .": Zweig, *The World of Yesterday*, p. 103.

"deep-seated veneration": Hayes, *Contemporary Europe Since 1870*, p. 158.

"It was simply assumed that the Habsburg Empire . . .": Johnston, *Vienna Vienna: The Golden Age 1815–1914*, p. 9.

"a date that ought to be among the most famous in all of history": Belloc, *The Great Heresies*, p. 85.

"would produce with irresistible force an edifying . . .": Schorske, *Fin de Siecle Vienna: Politics and Culture*, p. 39.

"Most English women have just about . . .": Sellers, "How to organize a people's kitchen in London," from Knowles, ed., *The Nineteeth Century: A Monthly Review*, January-June 1895, p. 413.

CHAPTER 9

"all dreamed of America . . .": Morton, *A Nervous Splendor: Vienna 1888/1889*, p. 50.

"how many possibilities this young country held . . .": Zweig, *The World of Yesterday*, p. 212.

CHAPTER 11

"caught the fever of speculation": Twain and Warner, *The Gilded Age: A Tale of Today*, p. 358.

CHAPTER 12

"certain to end in sunshine": Lewis, *It Can't Happen Here*, p. 105.

"The best part of this factory . . .": Quoted in the *Independent Record*, August 4, 1975, p. 1A.

"I couldn't afford to pay her . . . good money": Gorsich, OH453, Montana Historical Society.

"Business men are blue": *Kalispell Bee*, May 2, 1901.

"Merchants feel good in the old town.": *Kalispell Bee*, May 15, 1901.

"East Helena Smeltermen May Return to Work . . . To Renounce their Unionism": *Kalispell Bee*, July 8, 1902.

CHAPTER 13

"Hard rock mining is characterized by uncertainty . . .": Gerard, "The Mining Law of 1872: Digging a Little Deeper."

"Much of the ground in this district . . .": State of Montana, 6th Annual Agr, Labor, & Industry Report, November 30,1898, p. 31–32.

"pick up a fortune, simply pick it up": Twain and Warner, *The Gilded Age: A Tale of Today*, p. 99.

"greatest gold mine in Montana": Malone et al., *Montana: A History of Two Centuries*, p. 190.

"I saw almost four inches of nice looking ore" and "I had my full confidence that it was going to turn out better": Joseph Lozar testimony, Joseph Lozar vs John S. M. Neill and Henry Neill, Montana District Court, Lewis and Clark County.

CHAPTER 14

"Do not let this man have anything in future . . .": Note from JSM Neill to C.H. Fortman, Hay Grain, Coal, February 1, 1904, MC 248, Folder 9, Montana Historical Society.

"I never can make a considerable sum of money . . ." and "a man without means.": Quoted in Swibold, *Copper Chorus: Mining, Politics, and the Montana Press*, p. 88.

"No man in the state of Montana exerted a more potent influence . . .": Sanders, *A History of Montana, Volume II*.

"marked power in the manipulation of political agencies": *Progressive Men of Montana*, p. 1403

"he was looked to whenever aggressive action was necessary": Ibid.

"An organ of the Democrat Party": Sanders, *A History of Montana, Volume II*.

"False charges, vilification, assassination of character . . .": *Helena Tax Payer*, July 21, 1899.

"Persistent and relentless withdrawals . . .": Quoted in *Ravalli Republican*, February 17, 1897.

"You know my feelings in regard to Clark . . .": Letter from John Neill to W.G. Eggleston, May 10, 1900, MC 248, Box 2, Folder 1, Montana Historical Society.

"a prime mover in the management": Sanders, *A History of Montana, Volume II*.

"money flowed like water down a duck's back . . .": Siringo, *A Cowboy Detective*, ebook. Remark was made in a different context, not about the Clark senate campaign, but it fit.

"There were piles of political letters and receipts for votes . . .": Ibid.

"raged and tore around like a mad bull": *Kalispell Bee*, June 29, 1900, p. 4.

"and it was declared carried . . ." and rest of quotes to "Outrageous Rulings . . .": *Helena Independent*, June 21, 1900, p.1.

CHAPTER 15

"a dog's task": Quoted in Foor, "The Senatorial Aspirations of William A. Clark, 1898–1901: a Study in Montana Politics," p. 92.

"I presume the senatorial election cost . . .": Letter from John Neill to W.G. Eggleston, May 10, 1900, MC 248, Box 2, Folder 1, Montana Historical Society.

"a Self-Confessed Criminal": *Helena Independent*, January 12, 1899, quoted in *The Battle for Butte: Mining and Politics on the Northern Frontier, 1864–1906*, p. 116.

, "after paying all obligations . . ." : Letter from John Neill to G. Evans, August 26, 1902, MC 248, Box 2, Folder 1, Montana Historical Society.

"carefully laid trap . . .": Letter from E.C. Day to John Neill, MC 248, Box 1, Folder 3, Montana Historical Society.

"thousands of railroad passengers marooned": *Billings Gazette*, June 5, 1908, p. 1.

"I have always believed that there was mineral in those lodes . . .": Letter from Henry Neill to George Neill, February 27, 1926, MC 248, Box 4, Folder 8, Montana Historical Society.

"which gives to the monied might . . .": Dickens, *Bleak House*, p. 19.

CHAPTER 18

"An unofficial, but creditable report . . .": *Helena Independent*, August 2, 1914, p. 1.

"Rumored Emperor Josef is Assassinated . . .": *Helena Independent*, August 3, 1914, p. 1.

"All trade at least for the moment blocked": *Helena Independent*, August 4, 1914, p. 1.

"Worst slaughter . . .": *Helena Independent*, August 8, 1914, p. 1.

CHAPTER 20

"There are no gentry . . .": Letter from minister in Butte to his daughter Sarah in England, October 10, 1884.

"servant girl problem" and "adequate domestic help": State of Montana, 4th Biennial Report of the Department of Labor and Industry 1919 - 1920, p. 47.

"Housekeepers expect one girl . . .": Ibid.

"It is quite natural, inasmuch as any woman with a spark of ambition . . .": Ibid.

CHAPTER 21

"ringleaders in German plots, conspiracies and machinations": *Helena Daily Independent*, April 7, 1917, p. 1.

"Bail will be refused in each case . . . the entire group will be locked up": Ibid.

"For the first time in more than a century . . .": Ibid.

"They became part of the bone, blood, and sinew of the nation . . .": Ibid, p. 4.

"Though appearing in a satirical publication . . .": *Helena Daily Independent*, July 8, 1917, first page of part two.

"the most despised language in history": *Helena Daily Independent*, August 31, 1917, p. 4.

"Airship Seen Flying Above Helena . . ." *Helena Daily Independent*, September 1, 1917, p. 1.

"EXTRA! 2000 killed in German Air-Sea Raid . . .": *Helena Daily Independent*, September 2, 1917, p. 1.

"How soon will the Germans raid New York City from sea and sky?": Ibid, p. 4.

"Are Germans about to bomb the capital of Montana?": *Helena Daily Independent*, October 18, 1917, quoted in Malone et al., *Montana: A History of Two Centuries*, p. 270.

"It is, therefore, an effort in the interest of Germany . . .": Roosevelt, *Fear God and Take Your Own Part*, p. 19.

"is the most heinous act that a citizen of this country can commit": Quoted in Work, *Darkest Before Dawn: Sedition and Free Speech in the American West*, p. 182.

"YOUR NEIGHBOR, YOUR MAID, YOUR LAWYER, YOUR WAITER MAY BE A GERMAN SPY": Quoted in Swibold, *Copper Chorus: Mining, Politics, and the Montana Press*, p. 165.

CHAPTER 22

"Of all those expensive and uncertain projects which bring bankruptcy . . .": Smith, *The Wealth of Nations*, quoted in Gerard, "The Mining Law of 1872: Digging a Little Deeper."

"the torso of a Yale halfback": Quoted in Bruner and Carr, *The Panic of 1907: Lessons Learned from the Market's Perfect Storm*, p. 39.

"the irritant": Quoted in Bruner and Carr, *The Panic of 1907: Lessons Learned from the Market's Perfect Storm*, p. 24.

"there is a tremendous productive capacity in this country.." Ibid, p. 22.

"Money simply didn't exist . . .": Hilton, *Be My Guest*, p. 61.

"Just at the moment of recovery . . .": State of Montana, 11th Report of Agr, Labor and Industry 1907–1908, p. 185.

"The war . . . played havoc with the mercantile business . . .": Hilton, *Be My Guest*, p. 90.

CHAPTER 23

"the cradle of anarchy":" Siringo, *A Cowboy Detective*, ebook.

"the people are very kind but there will be frost and snow till June": Letter from minister in Butte to his daughter Sarah in England, October 10, 1884.

"At the outset of hostilities . . .": Marcosson, *Anaconda*, p. 160.

CHAPTER 26

"Letter received accept engagement will arrive Deer Lodge Thursday morning 10:30": MC738, Box 2 Folder 2, Butte Silver Bow Public Archives.

"voluntarily serenaded the Finlen . . .": Ibid.

"were appreciated, winning name and fame for Montana": Ibid.

"will give all Patrons of the Fair . . .": Ibid.

"Anton Leskovar bassoon player living at East Helena met the Milwaukee train . . .": MC738, Box 2, Folder 3, Butte Silver Bow Public Archives.

"A. Leskovar Bassoon player telephoned . . .": Ibid.

"Arranged for Mr. Leskovar bassoon player auto painter . . .": Ibid.

CHAPTER 27

"There is nothing so warm and moving as the sight of a symphony orchestra . . .": Chaplin, *My Autobiography*, p. 395.

CHAPTER 28

"the world's largest and finest photoplay palace": Flom, "Coliseum opens in Seattle on January 8, 1916."

"Mr. Anton Leskovar of Butte. Formerly bassoonist with a symphony orchestra in Austria . . .": Letter from Joseph Adam to members of the Montana State Symphony Orchestra, in Anton Leskovar's personal papers, undated.

"Please let me know at once your financial demands . . .": Letter from Joseph Adam to Anton Leskovar, April 7, 1927, Anton Leskovar's personal papers.

CHAPTER 30

"a person whom one didn't know . . .": Proust, *Swann's Way*, p. 60.

CHAPTER 31

"a place of recreation for the general public": The United States of America vs Anton Leskovar, February 16, 1938, National Archives and Records Administration.

"forest officials from using the area as a public camp ground": Ibid.

CHAPTER 32
"Woman of the House . . . American Beer": Quoted in Devlin, *Missoulian*, "History's got hops," Missoulian, September 14, 2007.

CHAPTER 33
"Each one hopes that if he feeds the crocodile enough, the crocodile will eat him last.": Churchill, BBC radio speech, January 20, 1940. https://quoteinvestigator.com/2016/04/18/crocodile/

"bloodshed and terror": *Montana Standard*, March 11, 1938.

"universal compulsory military training": Quoted in the *Montana Standard*, June 8, 1940.

"all real defense measures . . . dictatorial powers to the executive": Quoted in the *Montana Standard*, June 9, 1940.

"Too few allies . . .": Quoted in Paxton, *Vichy France*, p. 21.

"[B]igger businesses tended to do well, for they were the ones who became government partners": Shlaes, *The Forgotten Man*, ebook.

CHAPTER 34
"At night we enjoyed a rest sweetened by prayer . . .": Quoted in Schrems, *Uncommon Women, Unmarked Trails: The Courageous Journey of Catholic Missionary Sisters in Frontier Montana*, p. 11–12.

BIBLIOGRAPHY

Two of the biggest challenges in researching the historical backdrop for this book were language and obscurity. I do not speak or read Slovenian or German, nor do I read Gothic script. (Not to be confused with calligraphy, Gothic is an entirely different alphabet.) Sources in English at the level of detail I was seeking were few and far between. Sometimes I consulted a Wikipedia article to find source documents and then consulted those sources directly. I did this with books as well. As much as possible, I sought primary sources. Wikipedia was the only place I found the date for when the train extended to Novo mesto. The sources for these articles were in Slovenian, and as such, beyond my reach. In some cases, the Wikipedia articles were in Slovenian, but using Google Translate, I could at least glean the gist, knowing that auto-translate tools have limitations. I feel better about using a source when someone has taken responsibility by assigning his or her name to it, which is not the case with Wikipedia. Have I found errors in Wikipedia articles? I have. Have I found errors in nonfiction history books written by academics? I have, some quite glaring.

Though I used primary sources as much as possible, for some parts of my research, such as the Panic of 1907, biographical information about the Habsburgs, and *l'Affaire Redl*, I relied on the work of other historians; otherwise I never would have finished my book. I tried to consult more than one author in such cases and see which sources they used.

For a fast fact, I subscribed to *Encyclopedia Britannica* online.

I interviewed family and friends. I drew heavily from my grandparents' papers, letters, Aunt Francie Lozar Waters's diary, and recordings of my grandparents Annie and Tony Leskovar.

ARCHIVES
ARCHDIOCESE OF LJUBLJANA AND ARCHDIOCESE OF MARIBOR, SLOVENIA: Church
books which contain baptism, marriage, death records; status animarum

BUTTE SILVER BOW PUBLIC ARCHIVES:
City Directories
Chattel Mortgages
Cemetery index
Conditional Bills of Sale
LH006, American Federation of Musicians Local #241
Miners employment log books and cards
MC491, Tom Jovick Memoir
MC585, East Butte Slovenian Community
MC738, Sam Treloar Collection
Pauper application for aid
School census
SM004, Butte Musicians' Mutual Protective Union Local No. 241
SM075, John Keil Richards Collection
VF0178.1, East Butte: Vital Records
Ljubljana City Archives: pictures

MONTANA HISTORICAL SOCIETY:
Assessment Book City of Helena 1905
East Helena Vertical File
Helena City Directories
Helena College Catalog
LG84, Record of Communicable Diseases
MC37, Samuel Hauser
MC248, Neill Family Papers
Small Collections, 1900-1907, Assay Office
OH 453, Frank Gorsich Oral History

RS477, Box 30, Lewis and Clarke County, Business License fee receipt book
622.009, ASARCo
Vertical File Gen 929.2 C15, The Highlander

NATIONAL ARCHIVES AND RECORDS ADMINISTRATION:
Personnel records for Raymond Ryan, Mare Island.
Military pay records for Stephen Lozar. (The NARA could not find his service
records. Many First World War records were destroyed in a fire.)
Military records for Wilbur Fisk Sanders (Civil War)

Novo mesto, Slovenia, Archives
Slovenian State Archives: Pictures

BOOKS AND ARTICLES

Allen, Frederick. *A Decent, Orderly Lynching: The Montana Vigilantes*. Norman: University of Oklahoma Press, 2004.

Andrews, Evan. "9 Things You May Not Know about Ellis Island." *History*, November 12, 2014. http://www.history.com/news/9thingsyoumaynot-knowaboutellisisland (accessed August 10, 2015).

Auclair, Mathias; Christophe Ghristi and Pierre Vidal. "Verdi, Wagner and the Paris Opera." *Opera National de Paris*. http://www.operadeparis.fr/node/3621 (accessed July 17, 2015).

Austin, Michel; Monir Tayeb. "Berlioz: Pioneers and Champions." *Hector Berlioz Website*, March 15, 2012. http://www.hberlioz.com/champions/operas6914e.htm (accessed July 17, 2015).

Axelrod, Alan. *The International Encyclopedia of Secret Societies and Fraternal Orders*. New York: Facts On File, 1997.

Axline, Jon. "American Smelting & Refining Company (ASARCO) East Helena Smelter, Assistant Superintendent's House." Historic American Engineering Record, May 2010.

Axline, Jon; et al. *More from the Quarries of Last Chance Gulch*. Helena: Helena Independent Record, 1995.

Axline, Jon; et al. *More from the Quarries of Last Chance Gulch Volume II*. Helena: Helena Independent Record, 1996.

Bancroft Library. http://bancroft.berkeley.edu/collections/earthquakeandfire/interactivemap/region03.html (accessed March 31, 1918).

Baucus, Jean; Vivian Paladin. *Helena: An Illustrated History*. Helena: Montana Historical Society Press, 1983, 1996.

Baumler, Ellen. "A Cross in the Wilderness: St. Mary's Mission Celebrates 175 Years." *Montana the Magazine of Western History*, Spring 2016, Volume 66, Number 1.

Bell, Bethany. "Dancing over the edge: Vienna in 1914." *BBC News Magazine*, January 6, 1914. http://www.bbc.com/news/magazine25576645 (accessed April 11, 1915).

Belloc, Hilaire. *The Great Heresies*. Manassas, Virginia: Trinity Communications, 1938, 1987.

Bodissey, Baron. "The Other September 11th." Gates of Vienna Blog, September 11, 2006. http://gatesofvienna.blogspot.com/2006/09/otherseptember11th.html (accessed April 24, 2015).

Bossard, Floyd. "Unionism in Butte mines contributes to city's fascinating history." Montana Standard, May 1, 2015.

"Brief History of Gottschee." Gottscheer History and Genealogy Association. http://www.gottschee.org/history.html (accessed April 29, 2015).

Bruner, Robert F.; Sean D. Carr. *The Panic of 1907: Lessons Learned from the Market's Perfect Storm*. Hoboken, NJ: John Wiley & Sons, Inc., 2007.

Burlingame, Merrill G.; Toole, K. Ross. *A History of Montana*, Vol. 1. New York: Lewis Historical Publishing, 1957.

Butte Daily Bulletin, August 20, 1919.

Cannato, Vincent J. *American Passage: the History of Ellis Island*. New York: Harper Collins, 2009.

"Carnival-Vienna." Wiener Hofburg-Orchester. www.hofburgorchester.at (accessed April 11, 2015).

Carr, Jonathan. *Mahler: A Biography*. Woodstock and New York: The Overlook Press, 1997. Pages 30-31.

Chaplin, Charles. *My Autobiography*. New York: Simon & Schuster, 1964.

Cheney, Roberta Carkeek. *Names on the Face of Montana: The Story of Montana's Place Names*. Missoula: Mountain Press Publishing Company, 1984.

Ciglenečki, Marjeta. *Ptuj*. Maribor: Art Cabinet Primož Premzl, 1995.

Clark, Christopher. *The Sleepwalkers: How Europe Went to War in 1914*. New York: Harper Collins, 2013.

"Concentration Camps in France." *Wikipedia*. Source: Bernardot, Marc; *Camps d'etrangers* (in French). Paris: Terra, 2008, p. 142-143. https://en.wikipedia. org/wiki/Concentration_camps_in_France (accessed July 16, 2015).

Copper Curb and Mining Outlook. New York: August 26, 1914.

Čuješ, Rudolf; Vladimir V.B Mauko; edited by. *This is Slovenia: A Glance at the Land and its People*. Publication No. 1 of the Research Center for Slovenian Culture. Toronto: Slovenian National Federation of Canada, 1958.

Curie, Eve. *Madame Curie*. Translated by Vincent Sheean. New York: Da Capo Press, 1937.

Davison, Fern F. Pamphlet "East Helena's Diamond Jubilee: 1888-1963." Article about East Helena, 1933.

Day, Clarence. *Life with Father*. New York: Alfred A. Knopf, Inc., 1935. Reprint of complete text, Pleasantville, New York: The Readers Digest Association, Inc., 1993.

Day, David T, et al. *Mineral Resources of the United States*. Washington: Government Printing Office, for calendar years 1888-1917.

Devlin, Vince. "History's got hops. Polsen beer connoisseur's museum spins stories of state's spuds." *Missoulian*, September 14, 2007.

Dežman, Jože; et al. *The Making of Slovenia*. Edited by Štepec, Marko. Translated by Martin Cregeen. Ljubljana: National Museum of Contemporary History, 2006.

Dickens, Charles. *Bleak House*. New York: Barnes & Noble Classics, 2005 (originally serialized in 1852).

"Do You Remember? Earthquakes felt in Butte." *Montana Standard*, May 10, 2015.

East Helena Historical Society. *Prickly Pear Junction Vol I: East Helena's Heritage*. 2004.

Editors of Encyclopedia Britannica. "Balkan Wars." *Encyclopedia Britannica* (online edition accessed July 30, 2015).

Editors of Encyclopedia Britannica. "Serbo Turkish War" and "Russo Turkish War." *Encyclopedia Brittanica* (online edition accessed July 29, 2015).

Editors of Encyclopedia Britannica. "Trieste." *Encyclopedia Britannica* (online edition accessed May 9, 2015).

"Ellis Island" documentary. *History*, http://www.history.com/topics/ellisisland (accessed August 10, 2015).

Everett, George. "When Toil Meant Trouble: Butte's Labor Heritage." Downloaded March 20, 2018.

Flaherty, Cornelia M. *Go with Haste into the Mountains: A History of the Diocese of Helena*. Helena, Montana, 1984.

Flom, Eric L. "Coliseum opens in Seattle on January 8, 1916." http://www.historylink.org/File/2538

Foor, Forrest LeRoy. "The Senatorial Aspirations of William A. Clark, 1898-1901: a Study in Montana Politics." Dissertation, University of California, deposited in the University Library June 13, 1941.

Ford Motor Company. http://corporate.ford.com/company/history.html (accessed February 11, 2016).

Foreman, Amanda. "Historically Speaking: A Century of Russian-Run Traitors." *Wall Street Journal*, August 9, 1914, p. C12.

Foreman, Amanda. "Historically Speaking: On the Road with Walt and Ike." *Wall Street Journal*, July 16-17, 2016, p. C4.

General Mining Act of 1872, US Congress, 1872, http://www.usminer.com/thegeneralminingactof1872/ (accessed October 6, 2015).

"George I of Greece." New World Encyclopedia. http://www.newworld-encyclopedia.org/entry/George_I_of_Greece (accessed August 28, 2015).

Gerard, David. "The Mining Law of 1872: Digging a Little Deeper." *Property and Environment Research Center*. http://www.perc.org/articles/mininglaw18720 (accessed October 3, 2015).

Gordon, John Steele. *The Business of America*. New York: Walker & Company, 2001.

Grant, Ulysses S. *The Personal Memoirs of U. S. Grant*. Old Saybrook, Connecticut: Konecky & Konecky.

Hahn, Sylvia. "Nowhere at home: Female migrants in the 19th-century Habsburg Empire." From Sharpe, Pamela, ed. *Women, Gender, and Labour Migrations: Historical and Cultural Perspectives*, Chapter 6. London: Routledge, 2001.

Hansen, Jim. "Prickly Pear Junction's Role in the Establishment of East Helena, Montana." East Helena Vertical File, Montana Historical Society.

Harries, Meirion and Susie. *The Last Days of Innocence: America at War, 1917–1918*. New York: Random House, 1997.

Hayes, Carlton J. H. *Contemporary Europe Since 1870*. New York: The Macmillan Company, 1965.

Herman, Arthur. "Review of *Freedom's Forge*." *Wall Street Journal*, May 17, 2012, p. A13.

Hill, Jennifer J. "Going Public: Childbirth, the Board of Health, and Montana Women, 1860–1920." *Montana the Magazine of Western History*. Summer 2015

Hilton, Conrad N. *Be My Guest*. Englewood Cliffs, New Jersey: Prentice-Hall, 1957.

Howard, Joseph Kinsey. *Montana High, Wide and Handsome*. Lincoln and London: University of Nebraska Press, 1943.

Hülsmann, Jörg Guido. *Mises: The Last Knight of Liberalism*. Auburn, Alabama: The Ludwig von Mises Institute, 2007.

Ide, Arthur W.; W.D. Rumsey et al. *Helena Montana: Its Past, Present and Future*. Helena, Montana: Arthur W. Ide and W.D. Rumsey. [Not dated, but from context, it was published in 1891.]

Johnson, Paul. *Modern Times: The World from the Twenties to the Eighties*. New York: Harper & Row, 1983.

Johnston, William M. *Vienna Vienna: The Golden Age 1815-1914*. New York: Clarkson N. Otter, Inc. Publishers, 1980.

Keršič-Svetel, Marjeta. *Ljubljana*. Translated by Henrik Ciglič and Marjeta Keršič-Svetel. Ljubljana: Zaklad, 2007.

Kmecl, Matjaž. *A Short Cultural History of the Slovenians*. Translated from Slovenian by Maja Visenjak-Limon. Ljubljana: Slovenian PEN: 2005.

Knight, Kevin, edited by. "Krain." *Catholic Encyclopedia*. http://newadvent.org/cathen/08686a.htm (accessed June 23, 2014).

Knight, Kevin, edited by. "Styria." *Catholic Encyclopedia*. http://www.newadvent.org/cathen/14318a.htm (accessed April 4, 2014).

Kuret, Primož. *Slovenska Filharmonija Academia Philharmonicorum 1701-2001*. Translated by Primož Kuret and Maja Visenjak-Limon. Ljubliana: Kataložni zapis o publikaciji, Narodna in univerzitetna knjižnica, 2001.

Lampe, John R. "Serbia." *Encyclopedia Britannica* (online edition accessed July 29, 2015).

Lapajne, Branka. *Researching Your Slovenian Ancestors*. Willowdale Ontario: BML Publishing Co. Inc., 1996.

Lewis, R.W.B, and Lewis, Nancy, edited by. *The Letters of Edith Wharton*. New York: Collier Books, an imprint of Macmillan Publishing, 1988.

"Ljubljana." *Wikipedia*. http://en.wikipedia.org/wiki/Ljubljana (accessed April 2, 2014).

MacMillan, Margaret. *The War that Ended Peace: The Road to 1914*. New York: Random House, 2014.

Malone, Michael P. *The Battle for Butte: Mining and Politics on the Northern Frontier, 1864–1906*. Seattle and London: University of Washington Press, 1981.

Malone, Michael P., Roeder, Richard. B., Lang, William L. *Montana: A History of Two Centuries*. Seattle and London: University of Washington Press, 1976.

Marcosson, Isaac F. *Anaconda*. New York: Dodd, Mead & Company, 1957.

Mattox, Henry E. *Chronology of World Terrorism, 1901–2001*. Jefferson, North Carolina: McFarland & Co., Inc., 2004.

McCormick, Andrea. "A Taste for Butte: Lydia Micheletti." *Motherlode*, edited by Janet L. Finn and Ellen Crain, Clark City Press, 2005.

McDonnell, Anne. "The Catholic Indian Missions in Montana." Chapter V of *A History of Montana* by Merrill G. Burlingame, Vol. 1, K. Ross Toole, Lewis Historical Publishing Co, Inc, NY, 1957.

Miller, Joaquin. *Illustrated History of the State of Montana*. Chicago: The Lewis Publishing Company, 1894.

"Mineral Claim without Mineral Ruled Void." *Lima Ledger*, January 26, 1939.

Montana Wesleyan University Bulletin, May 1, 1911, Bulletin Vol 3, No. 1, Helena, Montana.

Morat, Daniel, edited by. *Sounds of Modern History: Auditory Cultures in 19th and 20th Century Europe*. Berghahn Books, 2014.

Morton, Frederic. *A Nervous Splendor: Vienna 1888/1889*. New York: Penguin Books, 1980.

Morton, Frederic. *Thunder at Twilight: Vienna 1913/1914*. Cambridge: Da Capo Press, 2001.

Mott, Col T. Bentley. *Myron T. Herrick Friend of France: An Autobiographical Biography*. Garden City, New York: Doubleday, 1929.

Neiberg, Michael S. *Dance of the Furies: Europe and the Outbreak of World War I*. Cambridge and London: The Belknap Press, 2011.

Oscarrson, Victoria. "From Feast to Fast: Fasching in Vienna." *The Vienna Review*, February 1, 2008. http://www.viennareview.net/onthetown/citylife/fromfeasttofast (accessed April 11, 1915).

Parish history for St. Cyril and Methodius, East Helena, Montana. February 2002.

Paxton, Robert O. *Vichy France*. New York: Columbia University Press, 1972.

Pickering, Paula. "Bosnia and Herzegovina." *Encyclopedia Britannica* (online edition accessed July 29, 2015).

Pitzer, Andrea. "Enemy Aliens: The life of Austrian painter Paul Cohen-Portheim and the forgotten history of World War I internment camps." *Laphams Quarterly*, http://www.laphamsquarterly.org/foreigners/enemyaliens (accessed July 15, 2015).

Powell, Margaret. *Below Stairs*. New York: St. Martin's Press, 1968.

Progressive Men of Montana. Chicago: A.W. Bowen & Co., 1902.

Puhek, Lenore McKelvey. "Thomas Cruse." *Montana Cowboy Hall of Fame*. http://www.montanacowboyfame.com/151001/180073.html (accessed September 26, 2015).

Rakić, Kosta. *Treasures of Yugoslavia: An Encyclopedic Touring Guide*. Translated by Madge Phillips-Tomašević and Karin Radovanović. Beograd: Yugoslaviapublic.

Rapport, Mike. *1848: Year of Revolution*. New York: Basic Books, 2008.

Rapoša, Kazimir, ed. *Discover Slovenia*. Translated by Martin Cregeen. Ljubljana: Cankarjeva založba,1995.

Reichman, Ruth. "Karneval — Fastnacht — Fasching" and "Fasching." http://www.mrshea.com/germusa/customs/karneval.htm (accessed April 11, 2015).

Reynolds, David. "A Brief Overview of the Musical Achievements of the Butte Mines Band," *Cadenza*, Volume 42, Number 3, April 1998. Montana Music Educators Association.

Reynolds, David. "The Beginning of a Legend: Samuel Treloar and the Butte Mines Band," *Cadenza*, Volume 42, No. 2, January 1998. Montana Music Educators Association.

Roosevelt, Theodore. *Fear God and Take Your Own Part*. New York: George H. Doran Company, 1916.

Sanders, Helen Fitzgerald. *A History of Montana, Volume II*. Chicago and New York: The Lewis Publishing Company, 1913.

Schofield, Hugh. "La Belle Epoque." *Magazine*, January 7, 2014. http://www.bbc.com/news/magazine25619822 (accessed July 18, 2015).

Schoon, Kenneth J. *Calumet Beginnings: Ancient Shorelines and Setttlements at the South Edge of Lake Michigan*. Bloomington: Indiana University Press, 2003.

Schorske, Carl E. *Fin de Siecle Vienna: Politics and Culture*. New York: Vintage Books, 1981.

Schrems, Suzanne H., Ph.D. *Uncommon Women, Unmarked Trails: The Courageous Journey of Catholic Missionary Sisters in Frontier Montana*. Norman, Oklahoma: Horse Creek Publications, Inc., 2003.

Sellers, Edith. "How to organize a people's kitchen in London." From James Knowles, ed. *The Nineteeth Century: A Monthly Review*, January-June 1895, Vol XXXVII. London: Sampson, Low, Marston & Company, Limited, 1895.

Shields, Jacqueline. "The Jewish Virtual World: Austria." *Jewish Virtual Library*. http://www.jewishvirtuallibrary.org/jsource/vjw/Austria.html (accessed April 16, 2015).

Shlaes, Amity. *The Forgotten Man: A New History of the Great Depression*. Harper Collins e-books, 2007.

Silber, William L. "What happened to liquidity when World War I shut the NYSE?" *Journal of Financial Economics*, 2001 (accessed February 24, 2016).

Simonich, Ann Stajcar. *Butte's Croatian Slovenian Americans*. Butte, Montana: 2012.

Siringo, Chas. A. *A Cowboy Detective*. Chicago: W.B. Conkey Company, 1912.

Sked, Alan. "A Patriot for Whom? Colonel Redl and a Question of Identity." *History Today*, Volume: 36, Issue: 7 (1986). http://www.historytoday.com/alansked/patriotwhomcolonelredlandquestionidentity

Smith, Marian L. "Women and Naturalization, ca. 1802-1940." *Prologue Magazine*, Summer 1998, Vol. 30, No. 2. http://www.archives.gov/publications/prologue/1998/summer/womenandnaturalization1.html

Sodac, David G. "Antonja: Growing Up in Gottschee." *Zarja* 85, No. 3 (May/June 2013): p. 12-16.

Solmssen, Arthur R.G. *Alexander's Feast*. Boston & Toronto: Little, Brown and Company, 2004. http://www.acamedia.info/literature/alexanders_feast/10.htm

Somary, Felix. *The Raven of Zurich: The Memoirs of Felix Somary*. Translated by A. J. Sherman. New York: St. Martin's Press, 1986 [first published in 1960].

Sorenson, Jean, obit. Dirty Mouth Jean obit, *Montana Standard*, July 31, 1986. Downloaded September 18, 2019.

State of Montana. Department of Agriculture, Labor and Industry and Department of Labor and Industry reports 1882-1920.

Stein, Edith. *Life in a Jewish Family 1891-1916*. Edited by L. Gelber and Romaeus Leuven, OCD. Translated by Josephine Koeppel, OCD. Washington, D.C.: ICS Publications, 1986.

Stibbe, Matthew. "The Internment of Civilians by Belligerent States during the First World War and the Response of the International Committee of the Red Cross." *Journal of Contemporary History*, Vol. 41, No. 1 (January 2006): p. 5–19. Sage Publications, Ltd. http://www.gvsd.org/cms/lib02/pa01001045/centricity/domain/610/internmentarticle.pdf.

Stout, Tom, edited by. *Montana: Its Story and Biography, Volume II*. Chicago and New York: The American Historical Society, 1921.

Straubing, Harold Elk, edited by. *The Last Magnificent War: Rare Journalistic and Eye Witness Accounts of World War I*. New York: Paragon House, 1989.

Swartout, Robert R, Jr. *Bold Minds & Blessed Hands: The First Century of Montana's Carroll College*. Helena: Carroll College, 2009.

Swibold, Dennis. *Copper Chorus: Mining, Politics, and the Montana Press*. Helena: Montana Historical Society Press, 2006.

Switzerland and the First World War. http://www.switzerland19141918.net/ (accessed July 31, 2015).

Taylor, Richard. *Images of America: Houghton County 1870-1920*. Charleston: Arcadia Publishing, 2006.

"This Day in History: The city of Helena, Montana, is founded after miners discover gold." http://www.history.com/thisdayinhistory/thecityofhelena-montanaisfoundedafterminersdiscovergold (accessed May 15, 2015).

"Timeline of Austria." *Timeline of History*. http://www.timelines.ws/countries/AUSTRIA.HTML (accessed May 13, 2014).

"Timeline: Jul-1914: The July Crisis: The Month of Plotters." *Trenches on the Web*. http://www.worldwar1.com/tlplot.htm (accessed July 23, 2015).

"The History." *Palais Garnier*. http://visitepalaisgarnier.fr (accessed June 7, 2015).

Toole, K. Ross. *Twentieth Century Montana: A State of Extremes*. Norman and London: University of Oklahoma Press, 1972.

Trapp, Maria Augusta. *The Story of the Trapp Family Singers*. New York: Scholastic Book Services, 1949, 1971.

Tuchman, Barbara W. *The Proud Tower: A Portrait of the World Before the War, 1890-1914*. New York: MacMillan Company, 1966.

Twain, Mark. *Autobiography of Mark Twain, Volume I*. Berkeley and Los Angeles: University of California Press, 2010.

Twain, Mark. Selected and with an introduction by Stuart Miller. *Essays and Sketches of Mark Twain*. New York: Barnes & Noble, 1995.

Twain, Mark, and Warner, Charles Dudly. *The Gilded Age: A Tale of Today*. New York: Penguin Books, 2001. (First published by The American Publishing Co, 1873.)

Twenty-fourth Annual Report, Employment Security in Montana, for the fiscal year ending June 30, 1960.

U.S. Department of Commerce and Labor. Bulletin of the Bureau of Labor No. 89, July 1910. *Child Labor Legislation in Europe*, by C.W.A. Veditz. Chapter on Austria. Washington: Government Printing Office, 1910.

Waal, Edmund de. *The Hare with the Amber Eyes: A Family's Century of Art and Loss*. New York: Farrar, Straus, Giroux, 2010.

Wachter, Daniel. "Switzerland from 1848 to the Present." *Encyclopedia Britannica* (online edition accessed August 1, 2015).

Wadlow, Flo. *Over a Hot Stove: A Kitchen Maid's Story*. London: Allison & Busby Limited, 2007.

"War: 1st August 1914, General Mobilization in France." *France-Pub*, August 1, 2014, http://www.francepub.com/forum/2014/08/01/mobilizationfrance/ (accessed July 23, 2015).

Waugh, Alexander. *The House of Wittgenstein: A Family at War*. New York: Anchor Books, 2008.

Wharton, Edith. *A Backward Glance*. Philadelphia: The Curtis Publishing Company, 1933. Reprint, New York: Touchstone, an imprint of Simon & Schuster, 1998.

Wolmar, Christian. *Blood, Iron and Gold: How the Railroads Transformed the World*. New York: Public Affairs, 2010.

Womack, Emmett. *Official Register of the United States, Containing a List of the Officers and Employees in the Civil, Military, and Naval Service on the First of July, 1895,* Volume I. Washington: Government Printing Office, 1895.

Work, Clemens P. *Darkest Before Dawn: Sedition and Free Speech in the American West*. Albuquerque: University of New Mexico Press, 2005.

World Book Encyclopedia. Chicago: World Book, Inc, 1988.

Zimmerman, Arthur. Speech, March 29, 1917, https://www.firstworldwar.com/source/zimmermann_speech.htm (accessed January 17, 2020).

Zweig, Stefan. *The World of Yesterday*. English translation by Anthea Bell. London: Pushkin Press, 2011.

COUNTY AND STATE

Andrew Ulsher vs Annie Ulsher, Montana District Court, County of Silver Bow, 1917–1918.

Andrew Ulsher vs Great Northern Railroad, Montana District Court, County of Silver Bow, 1911–1913.

Compiled Statues of Montana Enacted at the Regular Session of the Fifteenth Legislative Assembly of Montana, 1888.

Delinquent Taxes Lewis and Clark County, 1911–1922.

1895 Tax Assessment, Lewis & Clark County.

Annual and Biennial Reports of the Bureau of Agriculture, Labor and Industry of Montana, for the years 1893 to 1932.

Jefferson County, Montana, deed books, mining records.

Joseph Lozar vs. Annie Kristman, District Court of the First Judicial District, State of Montana, County of Lewis and Clark, 1903.

Joseph Lozar vs. Henry Rohde, District Court of the Fifth Judicial District of the State of Montana, County of Jefferson, 1904.

Joseph Lozar vs John S. M. Neill and Henry Neill, District Court of the First Judicial District, State of Montana, County of Lewis and Clark, 1908.

Joseph Lozar vs. J.S.M. Neill and Henry Neill, Supreme Court of the State of Montana, 1908.

Joseph Pirnauer vs Joseph Lozar, District Court of the First Judicial District, State of Montana, Country of Lewis and Clark, 1911.

Laws, Resolutions and Memorials of the State of Montana Passed at the Fifth Regular Session of the Legislative Assembly, 1897.

Lewis and Clark County, Montana; deed books, mortgage books, mining records, naturalization records, vital records, jail register.

Lozar, Joseph et al., Caroline Lozar et al., Debtor vs John Sasek, District Court of the First Judicial District, State of Montana, County of Lewis and Clark, 1918.

Reports of Cases Argued and Determined in the Supreme Court of the State of Montana, June 5, 1899, to February 9, 1900, Official Report, Volume XXIII.

Reports of Cases Argued and Determined in the Supreme Court of the State of Montana, March 5, 1908, to November 13, 1908, Official Report, Volume 37.

Reports of Cases Argued and Determined in the Supreme Court of the State of Montana, June 26, 1922 to November 4, 1922, Official Report, Volume 64.

San Francisco County, California, marriage and probate records.

Silver Bow County, Montana; deed books, mortgage books, plat books, vital records.

FEDERAL

Bureau of Land Management, Coal Declaratory Statement, Joe Lozar et al., Serial No. 7269, August 3, 1912, appeal lost May 17, 1914.

Bureau of Land Management, patent 503764, homestead granted to Caleb Gennette, same land as Joe Lozar coal declaratory statement.

The United States of America vs Anton Leskovar, 1938.

The United State of America vs. Joseph Lozar, District of Montana, 1904.

NEWSPAPERS

Anaconda Standard, Butte, Montana
Billings Gazette, Billings, Montana
Butte Inter Mountain, Butte, Montana
Butte Miner, Butte, Montana
Daily Independent, Helena, Montana
Daily Inter Mountain, Butte, Montana
East Helena Record, East Helena, Montana
Helena Tax-Payer, Helena, Montana
Helena Daily Independent,, Helena, Montana
Helena Daily Record, Helena, Montana
Helena Independent, Helena, Montana
Helena Independent Record, Helena, Montana
Montana Standard, Butte, Montana
Kalispell Bee, Kalispell, Montana
Missoulian, Missoula, Montana
Montana Post, Virginia City
Ravalli Republic, Ravalli, Montana

Republican, East Helena, Montana
The State, Helena, Montana
Wall Street Journal

WEBSITES
I used many websites throughout my research. I opted not to list all of them.

www.Ancestry.com: Census records, vital records, city directories, military,
   naturalization, and other resources that popped up. I also used MyHeritage
   and FamilySearch, but primarily Ancestry.
http://archiveswest.orbiscascade.org, Montana history
www.blm.gov, Bureau of Land Management
www.EllisIslandRecords.org, ship manifests
www.encyclopedia.com
www.firstworldwar.com
www.helenahistory.org
www.historycentral.com
www.historylink.org
www.mtmemory.org, Joe Lozar brand, #63904
www.newadvent.org, Catholic encyclopedia
www.ohiohistorycentral.org
www.presidency.ucsb.edu
www.slovenia.info
www.slovenia.si
www.visitljubljana.com

ALSO BY CHRISTY LESKOVAR

One Night in a Bad Inn tells the true story of two colorful families, one Welsh, one Irish, who overcome scandal, war, murder, and mayhem in the coal mining town of Wilkes-Barre, Pennsylvania, on a desolate Montana homestead, in the raucous copper metropolis of Butte, and on the bloody battlefields of the First World War. It was a 2007 High Plains Book Award finalist for nonfiction, a true story in which the reader learns intriguing history through the lives of intriguing people who happen to be the author's ancestors.

Imagine while at a quiet family gathering, your aunt happens to mention a fire and a dead body and that your great-grandmother was arrested for murdering your great-grandfather. After you pick your jaw up off the floor, what do you do? Of course, you abandon your engineering career and go traipsing across the globe from Butte to Belfast to Belgium to find out what happened and write a book about it. That is what Christy Leskovar did, and that is the true story told in *Finding the Bad Inn: Discovering My Family's Hidden Past.* In addition to being an entertaining read, it is also a helpful primer for anyone looking into his/her family's past.

The books are available in print, e-book, and digital audiobook. Pictures and maps are exclusive to the print editions. www.christyleskovar.com

UNITED STATES